Historical Collections Relating to
Gwynedd

A Township of
Montgomery County
Pennsylvania
Settled 1698, by Welsh Immigrants

WITH SOME DATA REFERRING TO THE ADJOINING
TOWNSHIP OF MONTGOMERY
ALSO A WELSH SETTLEMENT

Howard M. Jenkins

HERITAGE BOOKS
2008

HERITAGE BOOKS
AN IMPRINT OF HERITAGE BOOKS, INC.

Books, CDs, and more—Worldwide

For our listing of thousands of titles see our website at
www.HeritageBooks.com

A Facsimile Reprint
Published 2008 by
HERITAGE BOOKS, INC.
Publishing Division
100 Railroad Ave. #104
Westminster, Maryland 21157

Originally published
Philadelphia, Pennsylvania
1884

— Publisher's Notice —
In reprints such as this, it is often not possible to remove blemishes from the original. We feel the contents of this book warrant its reissue despite these blemishes and hope you will agree and read it with pleasure.

International Standard Book Number: 978-0-7884-1739-9

PREFACE.

THIS volume is by no means a History of Gwynedd. I have not attempted to make it that. I have simply gathered materials of a historical and biographical nature relating to Gwynedd, and have arranged them as nearly as practicable in the order of time. The careful reader who may observe that many things are not dealt with, which it would be the duty of a history to include, will find an explanation of the fact in the plan itself.

So far as the materials which the volume does contain may be considered, I believe them very trustworthy. My effort especially has been to achieve that degree of accuracy where the percentage of error does no harm. Of errors there are some, no doubt: no such collection of facts, made up largely of specific statements, with names and dates, has ever, with the extremest case of author and printer, been able to avoid some mistakes. Those which have been noticed as the work was passing through the press are stated below.

The size of the work has disappointed me. I have reached the limit assigned it without exhausting the materials I had collected for it, and many subjects which I had intended to treat fully have been of necessity treated briefly.

It should be explained that the dates used have respect always to "Old" and "New Style." In 1752, the English Parliament passed an act by which the new year subsequently began on January 1st, and January became, therefore, the "First Month," as now. Previously, March had been the "First Month." This fact should be carefully kept in mind. In all dates in the book, preceding 1753, the months' numbers correspond with the old rule: beginning with that year they correspond with our present system.

With respect to the spelling of names, both of families and of individuals, considerable variation will be remarked. The simple explanation of this is that in the documents and printed matter which furnish my authorities, these spellings vary continually. The same person is often differently called — *e.g.*, William John is sometimes William Jones; the female name Ellen is spelled also Ellin, and again Eleanor, — even when referring to one and the same individual. My plan has therefore been to use names as I found them, unless the spelling was plainly an error.

Acknowledgment should be especially made, here, for the assistance I have had in the collection of materials. To Rev. Geo. D. Foust, for his article on St. Peter's Church, to Mr. Wm. J. Buck, for aid and suggestions, to Mr. S. B. Helffenstein, for notes concerning his grandfather's family; my thanks are due. Mr. Charles Roberts, of Philadelphia, who is collecting the data for an elaborate and complete genealogical record of his family, has aided me with unwearied interest. Mrs. Wm. Parker Foulke, whose death, some months before the completion of the work, deprived me of a most valuable coadjutor, made an important contribution to it, by preparing a full record of her husband's branch of his family. And in conclusion it must be due to Mr. Edward Mathews to say that no one has made more faithful, patient, or valuable original research into the township's early history. His papers I have carefully consulted, and in certain parts of the book freely drawn upon.

ADDITIONS AND CORRECTIONS.

On page 1, 10th line from top, for "pass," read "passes." Same page, 4th line from bottom, for "villages," read "valleys."

On page 59, "where Silas White now lives," should be "where S. W. recently lived." He owns (1884) the old Robert Evans place, but does not live there. In connection, I remark that the house now standing was more likely built by George Roberts's father, Amos, than by George.

On page 65, "Tron Goch" should be "Fron (or Vron) Goch"—*i. e.* breast red, or red breasted. (I found this in one document "Fron-y-Goch," which is no sort of good Welsh.)

On page 69, Hugh Evans is said to have died in 1771: the correct date of his death was 1772. (See his family record, p. 152.)

On page 70, Robert Evans, the second, is said to have been "of Merion" in 1705. This was too early. See correct statement near the bottom of page 150.

On page 67, seventh line from the bottom, between "of" and "Philadelphia," insert "Bristol township."

Page 86, sixteenth line from bottom, "fifty-five" should be "forty-four."

Top of page 114, Elizabeth Roberts, who married Daniel Morgan, was the daughter, not of Robert Roberts, as would appear, but of Robert Cadwalader, the father of the four Roberts brothers.

Page 119, George *Morris* should be George *Maris*.

Page 150, *Sarah* Evans (No. 35), should be *Mary* Evans.

Page 162, fourth line from the top, the blank after "Hannah" should be filled with the surname Morris. (She was the daughter of Susanna Morris, a distinguished preacher among Friends.)

Page 167, it has been ascertained that Ruth Evans, the widow of Nathan, having returned to Gwynedd from Wilmington, subsequently m. Moses Peters, and they removed to Oxford, Philadelphia county, where Moses died, 1784. In his will he names his step-sons, Daniel, Lemuel, and Elijah Evans. On the same page, fifth line from the top, for *Samana*, read *Samaria*.

Page 160, nineteenth line from the top, for Dolgellan, read Dolgellau, (Dolgelly).

Page 190. It appears that Nicholas Roberts, in 1728, m. a second time Gainor Bowen, widow. As his first wife, Margaret, bore her last child, 1723, her death must have occurred between that and 1728.

Page 234. Caleb Foulke's purchase of the Owen Evans (Meredith), farm was probably 1776, not 1766.

Page 249, sixth line from top, insert "not" between "probably" and "in."

Page 361, third line from the top, for 1849 read 1862.

Page 367, seventh line from bottom, for *Josiah* read *Isaiah*.

Page 342, eighteenth line from top, for *Mary* read *Lydia*.

Page 374, eighteenth line from top, for *Philip*, read *Peter*.

Rev. H. E. Thomas, of Idlewood, Allegheny Co., Pa., has kindly furnished me with some Welsh spellings correcting those used in the book. Thus, it should be Berfeddlad (p. 45); Llwyn Gwril (p. 94); Llwyndu (p. 94); and Ynyscedwin (p. 208). Fron Goch(or Vron), mentioned on page 144, as "probably in Denbighshire," is in Merionethshire, about three miles from Bala.

Page 310. The raid of the British, mentioned by the *New Jersey Gazette*, is no doubt that alluded to by General Lacey, in his letter to the Provincial Council, Feb. 15, 1778. He says: "A party of Light Horse came up as far as Butler's tavern, on the Old York Road, about fourteen miles from Philadelphia, the night of the 13th inst., took Mr. Butler, and then struck across the country to Major Wright's tavern, near White Marsh,—took the Major, with some others, prisoners, and retired to the city."

In reference to Christian Dull, page 322, my dependence upon traditions as to his business "nearness" may do him injustice. Mr. W. J. Buck is of opinion that he was the son of Christian Dull, of Perkiomen (resident there, with seven children, in 1756), and that the latter's daughter, who married a Krauth, was the mother of the distinguished Lutheran scholar, the late Rev. Charles P. Krauth.

Page 262. The wife of Alexander Edwards, "Margaret, and her daughters Margaret and Martha, and sons Alexander and Thomas," reached Philadelphia in the ship *Vine*, William Preeson, master, 7th mo. 17th, 1784. (On the same ship came Robert and Jane Owen, and Reese John and his family.) Alexander Edwards, himself, appears to have come over before his family. It also appears that he married a second time, as his wife, mentioned in his will, was named Katharine.

LIST OF ILLUSTRATIONS.

PRESENT HOUSE ON THE SITE OF EDWARD FOULKE'S ORIGINAL DWELLING. ETCHING BY MISS BLANCHE DILLAYE, ... 32

PLAN, SHOWING LOCATION OF FIRST SETTLERS' TRACTS, ... 57

THE OLD HOUSE OF OWEN EVANS (LATER THE RESIDENCE OF CALEB FOULKE, AND DR. MEREDITH). ETCHING BY MISS BLANCHE DILLAYE, ... 71

THE MEADOW BANK AT ROBERT EVANS'S. ETCHING BY MISS BLANCHE DILLAYE, ... 75

FRIENDS' MEETING HOUSE AT GWYNEDD, BUILT 1823. PHOTOTYPE BY F. GUTEKUNST & CO., OF A SKETCH BY MISS E. F. BONSALL, ... 81

JOB ROBERTS. PHOTOTYPE BY F. GUTEKUNST & CO., FROM AN AMBROTYPE, ... 199

CHARLES ROBERTS, OF PHILADEPHIA. PHOTOTYPE BY F. GUTEKUNST & CO., FROM A PAINTING, ... 203

JOSEPH FOULKE. PHOTOTYPE BY F. GUTEKUNST & CO., FROM A PHOTOGRAPH, - 239

THE PRESENT FOULKE MILL AT PENLLYN. ETCHING BY MISS BLANCHE DILLAYE, ... 358

EVAN JONES. ETCHING, FOR THE AUTHOR (BY M. C. B.), FROM THE PHOTOGRAPH OF A PAINTING, ... 368

BENJAMIN F. HANCOCK. ENGRAVING BY WHITECHURCH,. 391

CHARLES F. JENKINS. PHOTOTYPE BY F. GUTEKUNST & CO., FROM A PHOTOGRAPH, ... 395

I.

The Place: The Scope of its History.

FROM Independence Hall, in Philadelphia, a line drawn west of north and extended eighteen miles will end in the Township of Gwynedd. Approaching the place on such a line, the surface of the country rises, and at last attains an elevation of four hundred feet above the sea, where it forms the water-shed that divides the drainages of the Delaware and the Schuylkill rivers. Upon the western slopes of this watershed the lands of the township chiefly lie, and the greater part of their rain-fall, feeding affluents of the Wissahickon, that rise in springs within the township, pass by them, or by the main stream,— which traverses Gwynedd from north to south, having risen just over the line, in Montgomery,— down to the Schuylkill. From the north-western part of the township, however, the drainage goes west by north through the Towamencin and other tributaries of the Skippack, into the Perkiomen, and thus reaches the Schuylkill far above the Wissahickon; while the rain-fall upon a few hundred acres in the extreme eastern corner of the township passes south and east to the Neshaminy, and through it to the Delaware.

The township is a parallelogram, containing nearly seventeen square miles, and occupied by over three thousand people. Fairly to be called a hill country, if compared with levels beside the sea, or villages along the great rivers, it yet is no more than a moderately elevated part of that remarkable agricultural region which, occupying all south-eastern Pennsylvania, reaches northward and westward to the Blue Mountains and the river Susquehanna. Covered with woods when the white settlers came, at the end of the seventeenth century, then cleared, and since continuously tilled, this is a township, simply, of farming land; its surface rolling, but not rough; its soil moderately fertile, but demanding patient and careful tillage. Natural wealth, except that of the soil, it has none; if minerals lie beneath the surface, they are at such a depth as would baffle the most zealous miner.

Such history as may be presented concerning this township and its people is necessarily limited in scope. Beginning less than two centuries ago, when its occupancy by European settlers began, we resign to the mists of the unknown all the life it may have had in the ages preceding. And even within the period of our knowledge, its movements and experiences have been void of extraordinary features. During two hundred years, the upland farmers, leveling their woods, plowing, planting, harvesting, threshing, seeking the markets of the city with their surplus, have typified the rural industry of their country. Neither sea nor river was at hand to disturb their occupations of tillage; the great highways of travel lay upon other routes; the coal, the iron, the oil, that elsewhere have attracted new people, changed ownerships, built towns and cities, and altered alike the face of the country and the composition of society, have been here unknown. The echoes of the Revolutionary cannon reached the place, but other than this all its knowledge of wars has been brought from far beyond its borders. No Indians molested the early settlers; wild beasts did not prey upon them; pestilence did not destroy, nor famine starve them.

What history, then, belongs to the place? Such only as a quiet community of plain people, sharing the general interests of their country, concerned for its welfare, agitated by its dangers, rejoiced by its successes, may have had; such as the condition of a simple and orderly existence may present;

such as comes from those features of human experience which are common to man everywhere, — his birth, his struggle for existence, his defeats and triumphs, despairs and rejoicings, sickness and health, death and burial; the character he presents in life, the name he leaves behind him. With such materials the present volume must be content chiefly to deal, making its pages justify themselves, if possible, by merits of sincerity and precision, — contributing thus to the great records of the time a leaf of small dimensions, but careful and trustworthy so far as it extends. To that historical method which begins by the patient accumulation of facts, and which draws no conclusion until the facts are faithfully studied, the highest respect is due, and it therefore is fair to suppose that the glimpse which we obtain of a people's life, by the study of the experiences of a single community, has a substantial value in history. To cut down through the strata at a single place may disclose the formation underlying a wide district.

Analyzing the township's history, it might be said that in a large way, and having reference partly to its exterior relations, it has had these five periods:

1. That of the Settlement: 1698 – 1720.
2. That of Growth: 1720 – 1775.
3. That of the Revolutionary War: 1775 – 1783.
4. That of the Changes, social, industrial, and political, which followed the Revolution: 1783 – 1820.
5. That of Development and Culture, since 1820.

But an outline, less general, and more distinctly drawn from the place, may be presented. The township's own experiences, it may be said, have been these:

I. That of the first settlement, its conditions new and strange to the Welsh husbandmen; the marked characteristics of the little colony; its distinctly Welsh features: the unity of nearly every member in a single family, by ties of blood or marriage, the friendly habit of mutual help, the simplicity of manners, the fervor of religious expression. In this time the Quaker element was predominant, the headship of Penn commanded an almost filial respect, and the movement of the community was centred in the Friends' meeting, whose spiritual and temporal affairs were the great objects of its attention.

II. Following this there came a time of removals and changes. Of the original company some were dead. There were departures to Richland, to Perkiomen, to Providence, to the Oley settlement on the upper Schuylkill. Thomas Evans, re-married in his old age, removed to Goshen, and Cadwallader Foulke, quitting farm life for city life, went to Philadelphia. Later, the tide of migration to Virginia and the Carolinas, which took the Boones, Hanks, Lincolns, and others, from Berks county, shook the settlement of Gwynedd and Montgomery, in which the departing pioneers had many kinsmen. But in this period, too, there were new comers. The German element began to appear. The Schwenkfeldters came in a body. The Welsh homogeneity began to break up, and the township became, as the Pennsylvania colony did, and as the State to-day is, one of varied population and characteristics.

III. To this succeeded the time when in this community, as in every one from Boston to Savannah, the earlier colonial influences declined, and the new springs of energy which in the wider field were to manifest themselves in the effort for Independence, began to show themselves. There were some changes in agriculture. The earlier methods had to be improved. Pasture and hay lands spread from the meadows into the upland fields, by the sowing of timothy seed, and later by the sowing of clover seed, and the use of land plaster. Grazing therefore increased, and a rotation of crops began to be followed; hedges were planted, tillage became more thorough, and presently the plow with the iron mould-board appeared.

This period included the time of the Revolution, but from

that great convulsion there sprang new conditions that must be separately mentioned.

IV. The struggle for Independence, its successful result, and the formation of the national constitution, profoundly agitating the country at large, stirred to the depths the life of each community, however remote and rural. These events brought hot political contention. Parties arose, and their lines were sharply drawn. The simple social conditions of the earlier time were modified, and while there were complaints of a decline in religious warmth, it was said, too, that morals were more lax, and intemperance more common. But there appeared then a development of a material nature. Turnpikes began to be made, the almost universal habit of riding on horseback was modified by the the appearance of "pleasure carriages," the streams were bridged, common roads increased and received more care in their construction. At the same time, stimulated by the party excitements, county newspapers began to be established, and the rise of a taste for reading caused the formation of the small, but yet useful, local libraries.

To this period may be assigned all the years from the close of the Revolution up to and including the War of 1812-15.

V. From the close of the second war with Great Britain, a period of twenty-five years, ending in 1840, was marked by many new and interesting features. The financial depression of 1817, following the collapse of the excessive and depreciated paper money of the war, tended strongly to develop and increase the removals to the Western country,—chiefly Ohio, Indiana, and Illinois,—which then continued for many years. Between 1820 and 1840 was the great period of the State's "internal improvements," the multiplication of turnpikes, the digging of canals, the beginning of railroads. This, it is true, had but a reflected influence in Gwynedd, yet it, like every other part of the State, felt the stimulus of the general activity and enterprise. In this period the public school system was definitely established in the township, and the general tendency toward more education and culture was strongly shown. The county newspapers had reached a position of enlarged importance, and political discussion, though it was now partially relieved of the bitterness and heat which had accompanied the earlier party contests, was conducted earnestly and vigorously during the campaigns in which first John Quincy Adams once, and then General Jackson twice, won the Presidency. The political activity of the people, and their movement by local leadership — indicating the wider distribution of intelligence and political interest — is quite observable during this time. In it, too, the postal service was increased, the mails were more frequently carried, and new post-offices were established; and it is notable that the influence of the proximity and growth of Philadelphia began to be more felt.

VI. Since 1840, one general and two special conditions have marked the life of the township. The one is that unexampled and wonderful advance toward greater luxury and culture which has been everywhere the experience of the American people, and in which this community shared. The others have been the revolution in agricultural operations effected by the invention of better implements and machines; and the changes in the township's population, order of life, occupations, and interests, which followed the construction of the railroad. All these were part of a large movement; they occurred within the same period; and it is not entirely practicable to distinguish the precise influences which each exerted; yet they may be to some degree separately described. The change in agriculture had already given some signs of its presence, in 1840, but it has chiefly been effected since. The flail gave way to the thresher, the sickle to the cradle, and it to the reaping machine, the scythe to the mower, the rude "fans" or "windmills" to improved and elaborate cleaners. The horse-rake has been two or three times developed, the hay tedder and manure spreader have come into occasional use, and while the grain drill has almost completely superseded the picturesque marching man who scattered his seeds broadcast, the self-binding machine has partly taken the place of the "hands" who entered the harvest field to rake and bind. In fine, the whole system of farming is changed; in the busiest season one man does at least the old work of three, and operations that were once necessarily tedious and small of proportion have risen to extensive methods and great possibilities.

The building of the railroad gave the township a new life. Enlarged knowledge of and communication with the outer world, the enormous increase of actual locomotion, the influx of new people, the rise in the price of lands, the building of villages and ultimately of considerable towns at the railroad stations, the creation of a new market system, the changes in the form of the produce sent to the city for sale, were in part the results of the new influence. But besides these, there came from the city many more visitors and boarders, many more purchasers of land. The social structure as it had existed was first dissolved and then made over, and it became greatly less homogeneous and unified. When the railway trains began to run, the old life of the township ended, and a new age was reached.

The general changes that have taken place in the country, and which are to be seen in Gwynedd, included, as I have already said, those which came directly from the railroad, and if it had not been constructed at all they would still have occurred, much the same in character, though not so marked in their extent. With the schools established, the county newspapers increased in influence, the little libraries slowly increasing, and all the great outer world thundering so near by, the township could not fail to rouse and stir. Mails that had come once or twice a week now came on every working day, and daily newspapers from the great cities were found a necessity to those who would keep abreast with the course of affairs. The movement in all ways became more quick. The pressure of occupation upon time became more urgent. Before this period the fast horse had been a runner to be ridden; now he became a trotter to be driven. From the interest in Lady Suffolk and Tacony and Flora Temple came their swift successors whose speed made "two-forty" seem slow. The old "gigs" and "chairs," with their round springs, disappeared, and the family, driving to church or meeting, or setting out on some distant visit, called for a comfortable carriage instead of the old and plain "dearborn" wagon. The harness began to have silver mountings, the driver covered his knees, not with a quilt or "coverlid" from the housewife's stock, but with a robe of buffalo-skin. The young man going out on errands of gallantry, had his "falling-top," the successor of the "tilbury," and no longer was content to own a horse and saddle. Dress grew more costly and elegant, the country tailors were crowded outside by the influx of "ready-made" clothing from the cities, and the country stores that had been able to satisfy their female customers with calico or delaine, saw them go to the great city bazaars for more costly and elegant fabrics. Organs and even pianos found their places in the farmers' houses,—an innovation and a step in luxury that a decade or two before would have been thought monstrous,—while the young women, as they glanced at their music-books, the farmer as he read his newspaper, or footed up his market account, the wife as she sewed, or mended, or darned, had the aid, not of the old candle, nor even of the later "camphene" and "fluid," but of "coal oil," warranted to stand the "fire test," and equaling in the quality of its light the best which could be commanded by luxurious dwellers in cities.

Altogether, these and the many other changes by which they were accompanied, amounted to a revolution of social conditions. The extent of the progress has been wonderful, but in no particular more so than by comparison. If we shall divide the history of Gwynedd since its settlement into one period of a century and a half, and another of less than half a century, and compare the changes of the two, we shall see the former appear a monotonous and stagnant level, while in the later and briefer one, Enterprise, Ingenuity, and Culture have gone forward by leaps rather than by steps.

Chronological Sketch.

1698, March, the Township purchased for the Welsh Company.
    April, the Welsh Company sail from Liverpool.
    July, they reach Philadelphia.
    November (?) the settlers occupy their lands.
1700, The first Meeting-House built.
1700-1701 (?), William Penn visits Gwynedd.
1701-1702, Re-surveys and commissioners' patents for the lands.
1712, The second Meeting-House built.
1714, The Friends' Monthly Meeting established.
    [1718, death of William Penn.]
1719, Montgomery Baptist Church organized.
1731, Baptist Church of stone, at Montgomery.
1734, Arrival of the Schwenkfeldters.
1740, Boehm's Church (German Reformed, Whitpain), built.
1745, Malignant and fatal epidemic.
1769, St. John's Church (Lutheran, Whitpain), organized (probably).
1772-76, St. Peter's Lutheran and Reformed Church established.
    [1775, Outbreak of the Revolution.]
    [1776, Declaration of Independence.]
1777, October, the American troops in the township; march to and retreat from Germantown.
    November, movement of the troops to Whitemarsh.
    December, their movement to Valley Forge.
1778, June, Movement of the army from Valley Forge to New Jersey.
    [1783, Independence acknowledged by Great Britain.]
1784, Montgomery County erected.

1796, The Library at Montgomery Square established.
  [1799, Sower's newspaper begun at Norristown.]
  [1800, Wilson's (later Winnard's) newspaper begun at Norristown.]
  [1804, Asher Miner's newspaper begun at Doylestown.]
1804-05, Chestnut Hill and Spring-House turnpike built.
  [1812-15, War with Great Britain.]
1813, Bethlehem Turnpike begun.
1823, Third (present) Friends' Meeting-House built.
1830, State Road laid out.
1840, Public School system adopted by the Township.
  [1846-47, War with Mexico.]
1847-48, Spring-House and Sumneytown Turnpike built.
1856, North Pennsylvania Railroad completed to Gwynedd.
1857, North Pennsylvania Railroad opened to the Lehigh river.
  [1861-65, War of the Rebellion.]
1869, Borough of North Wales incorporated.
1872, Borough of Lansdale incorporated.
1874, Stony Creek Railroad completed.

II.
Remarks upon the Geology of the Township.

GWYNEDD lies along the southern edge of, and just within, the extensive but simple and monotonous formation called by geologists the Mezozoic, or Red Sandstone, belt. The underlying rocks of the township vary in color, though they are mostly red, or reddish, and range from a tolerable sandstone to a decomposing shale; except that through the hill upon the Swedes-Ford road, tunneled at one point by the railroad, there passes a trap dyke of much harder rock, of an earlier formation than the Mezozoic.

The belt of Mezozoic, says Prof. Rogers, in his report of the Geological Survey of Pennsylvania, is very extensive. Beginning upon the right bank of the Hudson river, and extending along it from New York Bay to the base of the first ridges of the Highlands, it stretches south-west, traversing New Jersey, Pennsylvania, Maryland, and, in a more interrupted manner, Virginia and North Carolina, so that its total length is not less than five hundred miles. In Pennsylvania, it begins with a breadth of thirty miles, along the Delaware, its southern limit being a point about half way between Yardleyville and Morrisville, and thence, with a southern limit more or less sharply defined by streams and escarpments, it passes westward to the Schuylkill above Norristown. Its width there is less than on the Delaware, and for the remainder of its course through Berks, Lancaster, Dauphin, York, and Adams, it spreads over a section about ten miles wide between the Schuylkill and Susquehanna, and about fifteen between the latter river and the line of Maryland.[1]

The Mezozoic are those of the secondary formation, and containing evidences of plant and animal existence in what is regarded as the second age of life. These rocks are conglomerate sandstone, slate, and shale, their predominating color being red or rusty gray,—hence the alternative name given the belt which they characterize,—the New Red Sandstone.

Prof. J. P. Lesley, State Geologist of Pennsylvania,—chief, for many years, of the "Second Geological Survey of Pennsylvania,"—sends me these notes on the geology of Gwynedd:

"In Bucks and Montgomery counties, the geology of the southern belt has been well worked up. But the rest of both counties contains but one monotonous formation, that of the Mezozoic red sandstone and shale, the rocks all dipping one way, and containing no minerals of any value,—only building stone and trap dykes. Gwynedd township is situated in the lower part of this great formation. The geology is exceedingly simple; but a local geologist in any township might find a few fossils by long and laborious search.

"In Gwynedd, the most interesting point is a small trap dyke which was cut in the body of the hills through which the North Pennsylvania railroad tunnel was driven. The next most interesting point is the fact of the presence of a plant bed similar to that cut by the Phœnixville tunnel. No connection between them has yet been established, but they may very well be the same.

---

[1] It may be suggested that this is the region of the German farmers of Pennsylvania,—the "High Dutch" Palatinates,—Lutherans and German Reformed; and the explanation of the fact that they chiefly hold these red-rock lands would involve a curious study of the characteristics of the varied nationalities that have peopled south-eastern Pennsylvania. Broadly speaking, the German farmers have held this region, and gradually bought out other nationalities, because of their closer economy in agricultural methods, and their contentment with smaller returns.

GEOLOGY OF THE TOWNSHIP. 13

"Whether this trap be connected—underground—with the trap of Bowman's hill, south of Lambertville, on the Delaware; or whether it be in any way connected with the great fault of Barrville, Greenville, and Centre, east of Doylestown, is not known. This last fault brings up [in Bucks county] the limestone floor, on which the Mezozoic rocks repose; how deep this floor lies under Gwynedd township is a problem, but it must be at least one or two thousand feet.

"This is absolutely all the geology of Gwynedd that can be *generally* stated. No region can be more barren of general geological interest. But there are special problems of high scientific interest to be settled by special local work."

Prof. H. Carvill Lewis, of Philadelphia, who has made important studies in the geology of south-eastern Pennsylvania, has been particularly attracted by the plant bed opened in the tunnel referred to by Professor Lesley. In a letter, March 14th, 1884, he says: "I have recently obtained quite a number of fossils, both shells and plants, from the railroad cut at Gwynedd, and find some of them identical with those occurring in a certain plant bed on the Schuylkill above Phœnixville. There are three fossil horizons near Phœnixville—the bone bed in the old tunnel, the plant bed in some old quarries near the north end of the old tunnel, and the shell bed at the lower end of the tunnel. The latter lies probably one thousand feet below the others. I believe the plant bed to be identical with that at Gwynedd. Fossil foot-marks of turtles occur in this bed at Phœnixville; at Gwynedd there occur stems of calamites, seeds of a land plant, marine fucoids, foot-prints, minute shells of a species of Posidonia, etc., showing as at Phœnixville a commingling of fresh water and marine organisms. The theory that the Triassic deposit was made by a great north-east flowing river, which, in the neighborhood of Phœnixville, widened to become a marine estuary, emptying into the ocean near the mouth of the Hudson, is confirmed by my recent investigations.¹ Both sides of the deposit are bounded by a conglomerate, representing the pebbly beach."

In the lower end of the township the soil is more or less sandy; the clay loam lies above the line of the Spring-House. Southward from this place, on the low ridge along the road to Penllyn, and down the turnpike toward Philadelphia, there are banks of good building sand, from whose quarries supplies have been drawn for local use, during many years. But in contrast with this, the flat lands near North Wales (distant from these sand pits, say 3½ miles), have a bed of good clay from which bricks for building purposes have been and still are (1884) made; and even along the southern slope of the Treweryn, less than a mile from the Spring-House, enough clay was found, some twenty-five years ago, to warrant the erection of a kiln, and the burning of bricks.²

The building stone from the quarries of the township vary in quality. The best of them have been freely used in dwellings, bridges, and other structures. The fault of the red rocks usually is their soft and shaley nature, which will not withstand the influences of air and moisture; but care in selecting the hardest generally secures a satisfactory wall.

---

[1] This is a bold and striking theory. The "Triassic deposit" of which Prof. Lewis speaks is, in other words, the "belt" of Mezozoic or red rocks; and the explanation that they are simply the deposit of a gigantic river, rising probably in North Carolina, and flowing north-east to the great sea, above New York city, is a remarkable chapter in modern geological research. Assuming the truth of the theory, nearly the whole of Gwynedd lay in this great river, whose shore ran along the south-eastern border of the township.

[2] This kiln was built by Robert Scarlett, on his field near "Brushtown," by the road that leads southwest from the toll-gate.

III.
Traces of the Indians.

OF those inhabitants of Gwynedd, few or many, who were here before the Welsh settlers came, we know but little. They have left us but few evidences of their occupancy. That the place was not entirely a solitude is proved by the discovery, here and there, of some of the stone implements and weapons such as it is known the Indians used. These, however, are comparatively rare, and though I cannot claim to have made a thorough examination or inquiry concerning every part of the township, yet I feel safe in saying that the aboriginal remains in Gwynedd are only sufficient to show that the place was visited by the Indians, and may have been, at times, occupied by small numbers of them. This, indeed, might be predicated of the place from a knowledge of its situation and natural features. The Indians of south-eastern Pennsylvania were not a large body of people, and they did not make their homes in the high grounds, but in the lower, along the large streams, and where fertile, open spaces made it easy to plant their crops. But Gwynedd would have been a place resorted to by hunting parties, and occupied occasionally, or even permanently, by a band under some minor chief. The arrow-heads and other objects that have been found in certain places suggest the latter; they indicate by their number more than a passing chase, or even a brief stay at that point.

Of record evidence, concerning the Indians in Gwynedd, there is next to nothing. I have met with but one allusion in print which is worth attention. In the memorial of Gwynedd Monthly Meeting concerning Ellen Evans, wife of John (son of Cadwallader the immigrant), who died in 1765, it is recorded that she "delighted to converse with our uninstructed Indians about their sentiments of the Superior Being; and often said she 'discovered evident traces of divine goodness in their uncultivated minds.'"

Nor are the traditions concerning them very numerous. One of the most interesting is that of the Indian who brought coal to the smith's shop, where Mumbower's mill now stands, on the Wissahickon. The story is this: This mill property was owned from 1777 to 1794 by Samuel Wheeler, a blacksmith, and apparently something of a cutler and tool maker. (It is said that he made swords during the Revolutionary time.) To his shop there came, one day, some Indians, who wanted repairs made to a gun. Wheeler said he could not make them, as he had no coal, when an Indian, departing for a short time, returned, bringing with him enough coal for the purpose. This tradition is ascribed to a daughter of Wheeler, a Mrs. Johnson, of Germantown, who many years afterward used to occasionally visit Gwynedd. (The question with Wheeler was as to the place where the Indians got the coal, but it had doubtless been brought from a distance, probably the upper Schuylkill.)

Mrs. Sheive, the mother of Mrs. John B. Johnson, who died at a very advanced age, say thirty years ago, spoke of the time "when the Indians went away" from the neighborhood, and said that one of them, an old woman, stayed behind, and continued to live, by herself, in a hut or "wigwam," in what was known, in later times, as the "back woods" on Johnson's farm.

Mr. Mathews, in his articles on Gwynedd, says that in the eastern corner of Thomas Layman's farm, half a mile southwest of North Wales, there have been and may be found a great number of arrow-heads and other Indian relics. "Tradition relates that here was the scene of a battle between two hostile tribes of Indians, in which the missiles of destruction flew thick and fast."

The same idea of a battle has been formed concerning a locality on the Treweryn, near Ellen Evans's. David C. Land, who has made a collection of Indian relics, says he found many, including axes, spear-heads, and arrow-heads, at this place, and he thought the presence of so large a number indicated a hostile encounter. But it is natural that the stone relics should be found along or near the streams. There is where the Indians would fix their lodges, convenient for fishing, and also to utilize a sunny open space for their corn-field. And in such a place, after they had thus been encamped for a season or a longer time, their arrow- and spear-heads, etc., would naturally be discovered. John Bowman says that he found many arrow-heads and some other relics in the meadow along the run, east of his father's house; and on the Treweryn, Thomas Scarlett found an axe, "with a hole neatly drilled through it," the finest axe, I am told, discovered in the township.

Ellwood Roberts, now of Norristown, but for several years a resident on the State road, just up the hill westward from the Wissahickon, made quite a collection of arrow-heads, spear-heads, etc., picked up on the fields in the vicinity. He has kindly furnished me drawings and descriptions of several specimens. One is a hammer, which he thinks may have been used "in fashioning the flint implements, by pounding on a rude knife of bone or horn." His arrow-heads are mostly white flint; one spear-head is jasper.• Some articles that were found, he says, were unfortunately not preserved; "among the rest I remember a small fragment of stone hollowed out, no doubt part of a mortar used for pounding hominy in. I also have a dim recollection of a stone that had been used as the pestle." All these objects, Ellwood says, "were found on the upland, near the house in which I lived," and not along the creek in the meadows, but he adds: "I have always believed, from certain indications, that the right bank of the Wissahickon, just above the State road, where 'the old fulling-mill' formerly stood, is rich in such remains, but as it has not been plowed within my recollection, I have had no opportunity of verifying my conclusions."

Charles L. Preston has shown me some arrow-heads and other relics. They were to be found, he says, in plowing the fields of the Foulke estate (Dr. Antrim's), near the meeting-house. David C. Land gave an axe, found along the Treweryn, to the son of the author; and John Bowman gave me a curious implement, in form something like an axe, but with a point, rather than sharp edge, and one end ground off obliquely, and with perfect smoothness, near the grooved place where the handle had been fitted. John also had a round pestle, such as was used by the squaws for pounding corn in the mortar. Charles F. Jenkins, besides the axe given him, as stated, has a small collection of other objects, mostly arrow-heads. Some of these are very perfect. Usually they are flint, but one is a fine jasper, and one is of the softer bluish gray stone found in the township. Prof. Brunner,[1] of North Wales, describes to me two arrow-heads, found by Benjamin Bertolet, in 1880, in a field adjoining the Stony Creek Railroad, on the farm now owned by Seth Lukens (formerly the Pope farm). One of these is a white flint, and the other a flint of a greenish tinge.

It will be seen from the details I have given[2] that the Indian relics of the township are moderately numerous, and

---

[1] I wrote to Prof. Brunner concerning the collection of Indian relics at his academy (belonging to Dr. Slifer), but none of them were certainly known to have been found in Gwynedd.

[2] As it is more than likely that collections of relics found in the township have not come to my attention, I can only say that I printed communications in the newspapers at North Wales and Norristown, asking information concerning the subject, to which I received one reply,—that of Ellwood Roberts. But whatever else there may be doubtless is of the same general sort as those described, and therefore of no special importance as increasing our knowledge of the subject.

found in all parts of it, but more frequently along the streams; and that they are such as have been studied and classified by collectors in other parts of south-eastern Pennsylvania[1] — the general habitat of the tribes to whom such Indians as were hunters, or visitors, or dwellers in Gwynedd belonged. The list includes arrow-heads for the chase, or for war; the larger "spear-heads," which may have been used as weapons, or as knives for skinning animals, cutting up their flesh, etc.; the heavy flat axes, grooved around for the reception of the thong or strips of hide which attached it to the handle; the other axes, more round than flat, which may have been used to gouge out the charred interior of a tree, set on fire to cause its fall, or make it available as a boat,— and indeed for many other purposes; the mortars and pestles for pounding corn; and perhaps some others. I have seen no bone relics, nor any of pottery, found in the township.

I conclude my notes on the subject with some details furnished me by my friend Hugh Foulke, now of Swarthmore, concerning an interesting locality, associated with the Indians by tradition. In a letter, written in the autumn of 1883, he says: "More than fifty years ago, my father took me to Yocum's woods, and pointed out a clearing of perhaps half an acre, which he told me was called 'the Indian Garden.' I afterwards visited it several times. It then impressed me as something quite phenomenal, being entirely free from underbushes, or any other growth, save the monotonous furze grass which one sees on poor, worn-out land. As I remember, it was a perfect square of about half an acre, and was surrounded by dense woods. I think it is about half a mile from the

---

[1] A very intelligent and thorough study of the subject, with a great number of engravings showing the different forms of Indian relics, will be found in Prof. D. B. Brunner's work (Reading: 1881), "The Indians of Berks County." He substantially disposes of the subject, within reasonable limits, for all south-eastern Pennsylvania.

Spring-House, and in a direction a little west of north. From it the ground descends to the Treweryn, which is a few rods distant. It was not far from the lands of Jacob Danenhower (now George H.), Peter Lukens, and Wm. Buzby; but I think it belonged to Reuben Yocum."

IV.

The Arrival of the Welsh Settlers.

'TWO Welsh farmers, William John and Thomas ap Evan,[1] representatives of a company of friends and neighbors in Wales who had decided to emigrate to Pennsylvania, were in Philadelphia at the end of the year 1697.[2] Their presence there was due to a series of circumstances. Fourteen years before, the great "Welsh Tract" of forty thousand acres, on the west bank of the Schuylkill, embracing what is now the townships of Lower Merion, Haverford, and Radnor, had been bought and in time occupied[3] by Welsh people, many of them from the northern counties of Wales,—principally Merionethshire, Denbighshire, Montgomeryshire, and Flintshire. This large body of emigrants, containing many persons of character and quite a number of considerable means and cultivation, had prospered in the new colony. The "Welsh Tract," wisely located, including much fertile land, near to the markets

---

[1] See the Thomas Evans patent, which calls them "yeomen."

[2] In February, which was then ("Old Style") the last month of the year.

[3] "This intended barony had its origin in the desire of the Welsh purchasers of Pennsylvania lands to be seated together, and in a promise exacted from Penn before leaving Wales that this desire should be gratified."—*Smith's Hist. Del. Co.* Penn's warrant to Thomas Holmes, Surveyor General, directing him "to lay out ye s^d tract of land in as uniform a manner as conveniently may be, upon ye West side of Skoolkill river, running three miles upon ye same & two miles backward, & then extend y^t parallel with ye river six miles, and to run westwardly so far as till ye s^d quantity of land be Compleately surveyed to y^m," was dated at Pennsbury, 1st mo. 13th, 1684. David Powell, a Welshman, whom we shall meet in Gwynedd, was sent by Holmes to do the field work of the surveys, beginning in April of that year.

of Penn's quickly rising city on the Delaware, became in ten years after its purchase populous and attractive. The records of the Friends' meetings at Merion, Haverford, and Radnor show the extensive communication between the settlers on this Tract and their friends and kindred in the old country, between 1684 and 1698. Many new comers brought certificates from home, and several who were here went back on different errands. Undoubtedly, there was much said and thought, amongst the Welsh highlands, of the settlement on the Schuylkill. "Now I return," says Samuel Smith, in his *History of Pennsylvania,*

"to give some account of the Welsh settlers. Those that were already arrived were of the stock of the ancient Britons. They came chiefly from Merrioneth Shire, North Wales, in Great Britain, being mostly relations and neighbors in their own country, several of them being tenants and having great families. They had heard a good report of Pennsylvania, that lands were cheap, taxes light, clear from oppression as to Tythes and church rates, and most them were religious men, of good report in their own country. About this time, Hugh Roberts, a zealous minister among the Quakers, of whom we have seen some mention before, went from Pennsylvania to visit Wales, his native country, and had a successful visit to the end of his mission and greatly to the satisfaction of his country-folks, who held him in great esteem."

This visit of Hugh Roberts to his old home was in the year 1697, and to it we may ascribe, largely, the migration of the Welsh company who found their new homes in Gwynedd. Hugh Roberts commanded a large influence among the Welsh Friends. Joining them early, suffering persecution with them, he was a preacher of considerable power, and a man of activity and energy,[1] and he appears to have had more than an average share of wealth. Having come to Merion, with the first Welsh immigrants, in 1683,[2] he had bought several

---

[1] "He was a man of much enthusiasm,—'a live man,' as would be said in these days,—and his journals and letters abound with evidences of it."— Dr. James J. Levick's paper on the Merion Friends, in *Penna. Magazine*, No. 15.

ARRIVAL OF THE WELSH SETTLERS. 23

tracts of land, and had helped much to promote the contentedness and comfort of the people. He twice visited Wales, after his first removal, it being on his second visit that he gathered the Gwynedd company. Samuel Smith, in his *History*, already cited, further says :

"1698. Several settlers, as we have seen, have already arrived from Wales, to Pennsylvania. Hugh Roberts, whom we left on a visit there from hence, stayed from this year, when, being about to return, a number of the inhabitants of North Wales who had resolved to return with him, having settled their affairs for that purpose, they together in the spring sailed from Liverpool in a vessel belonging to Robert Haydock, Ralph Williams commander, and touching at Dublin, sailed from thence the first of the Third month."

To the success of the Merion colony, therefore, and to the active persuasions of Hugh Roberts, the emigration of the Gwynedd company is largely to be ascribed.

The two "yeomen," William John and Thomas ap Evan, were in advance of the main company. They had come to select a place, and from this circumstance, as from other evidences, we must regard them as the chiefs, so far as business inter-

---

[2] Hugh Roberts and family, of Llanvawr parish, Merionethshire, brought their certificate, dated 5th mo. 2d, 1683, from Penllyn monthly meeting, to Friends in Pennsylvania. On his return from his second visit home, he brought a certificate from the meeting at Llyn Braner, dated 1st mo. 16, 1697-8. In 1695 he and Joseph Kirkbride, of Bucks county, went on a religious visit to New England, they being the first from Pennsylvania who had preached there, except John Delavall and Jacob Tilner, in 1692. It was on another visit of the sort that he (H.R.) died, on Long Island, at the house of John Rodman, in the 6th mo. (August), 1702. His will, which is dated the 25th of the preceding month, shows his large ownership of property. He divided it amongst his three sons, Robert, Owen, and Edward, the last named receiving his home plantation, in Merion, 200 acres, "called Chestnut Hill." The will mentions other tracts—one of 1100 acres "at Goshen," and one of 400 acres, "that was Jos. Claypoole's." It was a part of his original purchase in Merion that, having passed from his son Edward, in 1721, to the George family, was in 1867 given to the City of Philadelphia by Jesse and Rebecca George, and is now the beautiful part of Fairmount Park known as "George's Hill." His son Robert removed to Maryland; Owen and Edward were prominent citizens, the latter a merchant in Philadelphia, and Mayor of that city.

ests are concerned, in the Gwynedd settlement. That they preceded the other immigrants, to choose land, was according to the habit of the Welsh. Speaking of Rowland Ellis, of Merion, Proud says, in his *History:*

"In 1682, he sent over Thomas Owen and his family to make a settlement. This was the custom of divers others of the Welsh, at first, to send persons over to take up land for them, and to prepare it against their coming afterward."

How much examination the two agents gave to the lands offered them before they made a selection is not known. There is no distinct evidence that they ever saw the Gwynedd tract, before purchasing it, but we may presume they did. That they rode up from Philadelphia for the purpose,— or, possibly, came across from Merion, with some friend and guide,— is a reasonable presumption. There is a tradition that they passed through Whitemarsh, but declined to buy there because the heavy timber on the limestone lands of that township would make the labor of clearing heavy.[1] But while it may easily be that they looked at Whitemarsh, this explanation of a choice elsewhere seems questionable; as a matter of fact, the Gwynedd lands were heavily timbered, as the descriptions by metes and bounds of the several tracts show. I can easily see strong reasons, entirely aside from this, why a purchase in Whitemarsh would not suit: in that township, prices of land had already risen and there remained no large undivided tract, such as the Welsh party required. They desired to settle together, and therefore would wish to buy an extensive and compact body of land.

The land at Gwynedd was owned by Robert Turner, of Philadelphia. How it happened to be his is fully recited in the confirmed titles which the settlers subsequently acquired by patents from William Penn, in 1702, and though it cum-

---

[1] See Wm. A. Yeakle's Historical Papers on Whitemarsh. The tradition was preserved by the late Benjamin Jones, son-in-law of John Wilson.

bers this chapter, and interrupts my narrative, I think it best to present at this point the full text of one of these confirmatory patents,—that to Thomas Evans. It is as follows :

WILLIAM PENN true and Absolute Proprietary and Governor in chief of the Proviance of Pennsylvania and Territories thereunto belonging,
To all to whom these presence shall come Greeting—
WHEREAS by my Indenture of Lease and Release bearing date the two and twentieth and three and twentieth days of March in the Year One thousand Six hundred and Eighty-one, for the consideration therein mentioned, I granted to Robert Turner his heirs and Assigns Five thousand Acres of land in this Proviance under the Yearly quitrent of One Shilling Sterling for Every hundred acres forever and by my Indenture bearing date the fifteenth day of August in the Year one thousand Six hundred and Eighty-two for the Consideration herein mentioned I released to the said Robert Turner his heirs and Assigns forty-five Shillings Sterling part of the said yearly Rent, to the End that five shillings only should remain and be paid Yearly for the said Five thousand Acres for Ever;
AND WHEREAS by Severall Like Indentures of Lease and Release bearing date therein mentioned I granted to John Gee of the Kingdom of Ireland his heirs and assigns Two thousand five hundred acres, to Joseph Fuller of the said Kingdom his heirs and Assigns Twelve hundred and fifty Acres, and to Jacob Fuller also of the said Kingdom Twelve hundred and fifty Acres, being in the whole Five thousand Acres under the Yearly quitrent of one Shilling Sterling for Every hundred Acres thereof forever, which said last recited severall parcells of Two thousand five hundred Acres, Twelve hundred and fifty Acres, and Twelve hundred and fifty acres the said John Gee, Joseph Fuller and Jacob Fuller by Several Indentures of Lease and Release duly Executed did grant and make over to the said Robert Turner his heirs and Assigns To hold to the said Robert his heirs and Assigns forever, By which said severall hereinbefore recited Indentures the said Robert became Invested with a right to Ten thousand Acres of Land in the said Province, part of which being laid out in severall parts thereof the remainder and full Compliment of the said quantity, being Seven thousand Eight hundred and twenty Acres,.was laid out by Virtue of several warrants from myself in one tract in the County of Philadelphia in the said Proviance ; AND WHEREAS the said Robert Turner by his Deed poll duly Executed bearing date the tenth day of the first Month March One thousand Six hundred and Ninety-Eight, for the Consideration

herein specified did grant and convey the whole Seven thousand Eight hundred and twenty Acres of land to William John and Thomas Evan both of the County of Philadelphia, Yeomen, to hold to them their heirs and assigns forever a certain part of which Seven thousand Eight hundred and twenty Acres of land Reputed to contain Seven hundred acres of land in the actual possession of the said Thomas Evan then being, was Resurveyed by Virtue of a general warrant from my now Commissioners of Property bearing date the Nine and twentieth day of September last past and found to be situate and bounded and Containing as follows viz.: Situate in the Township of Gwinned in the County of Philadelphia Beginning at a stake standing at the Corner of Edward ap Hughs land from thence running by a line of Marked trees South East two hundred perches to a corner, Marked hickery tree growing at the corner of the land of Cadwallder ap Evan, from thence running by a line of Marked trees by the said land of Cadwallder ap Evan and the Land of Robert ap Evan South forty-four degrees and a half West Nine hundred perches to a corner Marked hickery tree, from thence running North west one hundred and Seventy-six perches to a Marked tree growing at the corner of Robert Johns Land, from thence running by the said Land of Robert John and the said Edward ap Hughs land North forty-three degrees and a half East Nine hundred perches to the first Mentioned Corner Stake, being the place of beginning. Containing one thousand and forty-nine Acres, to Seven hundred acres whereof the said Thomas Evan having a right as aforesaid and seventy acres more being allowed in measure, and requesting to purchase of me the remaining two hundred and Seventy-nine acres and thereupon a confirmation of the whole One thousand and forty-nine acres of land at the Yearly quitrent of one English Silver Shilling for ever under my great Seal of the said Proviance.

Know Ye that as well in Consideration of the severall hereinbefore recited grants and conveyances as of the sum of Sixty-one pounds Eight pence three farthings Silver money of the said proviance to my use paid by the said Thomas Evan for the purchase of the Two hundred and Seventy-nine acres and for Redeming the quitrent as aforesaid, and in full of all arrears of quitrent for the said one thousand and forty-nine acres to the first day of this instant first Month called March the Receipt of which Sixty-one pounds Eight pence three farthings I doe hereby acknowledge and thereof and of every part and parcell thereof I doe acquitt, release and by these presents forever discharge the said Thomas Evan his heirs, Executors and Administrators, I have given granted released and Confirmed and by these presents for me my heirs and successors do give grant release and confirm unto the said Thomas Evan his heirs and assigns forever All that the said one thousand and forty-nine Acres of Land as the the same is now set forth bounded and limited as aforesaid with all Mines Minerals, quarries Meadows pastures Marshes Swamps Cripples Savannas Woods under-woods Timber and Trees, Ways passages Yards Houses Edifices Buildings Improvements, Waters, Water Courses Liberties Proffets Comodities Advantages Hereditaments and Appurtenances whatsoever to the said One thousand forty-nine acres of Land as to any part or parcell thereof belonging or in any wise appertaining and Lying within the bounds and limits aforesaid, and also all free leave right and Liberty to and for the said Thomas Evan his heirs and assigns to Hawk Hunt Fish and Fowle in and upon the hereby granted land and Premises or upon any part thereof (three full and cleer fifth parts of all Royal Mines free from deductions and Reprisalls for diging and refining the same only Excepted and hereby reserved);

To HAVE AND TO HOLD the said one thousand and forty-nine acres of Land and all and singular other the premises hereby granted with their and Every of their appurtenances (Except before excepted) to the said Thomas Evans his heirs and assigns to the only proper use and behoof of the said Thomas Evan his heirs and assigns forever. To be holden of me my heirs and Successory Proprietaries of Pennsylvania as of our Manor or reputed Manor of Springetsbury in the said County of Philadelphia in free and Common Succage by fealty only in Lieu of all other services, Yealding and paying therefor Yearly from the first day of this instant first Month called March to me my heirs and successors at or upon the first day of the first Month called March in Every Year forever thereafter at Philadelphia one English Silver Shilling or value thereof in Coyn Currant to such person or persons as shall be appointed from time to time to receive the same.

In Witness I have (by Virtue of My Commission to my Proprietary Deputies hereinafter named for the said Proviance and Territories bearing date the Eight and twentieth day of October which was in the Year of our Lord One thousand Seven hundred and one) Caused my great Seal of the Province to be be affixed hereunto.

Witness Edward Shippen Griffith Owen Thomas Story and James Logan my said Deputies or any three of them at Philadelphia the Eighth day of the first Month called March in the Second Year of the Reign of our Soverayn Queen Ann of England &c. and the three and twentieth of my Government Anno Domini one thousand seven hundred and two.

       EDWARD SHIPPEN GRIFFITH OWEN
       THOMAS STORY   JAMES LOGAN

[Recorded the 26th 1st Mo., 1703.]

It will be seen that Robert Turner had acquired his title to the lands which we are considering, as the net result of several purchases of rights to locate, and that he was presumed to have in the tract no more than 7820 acres. On Holmes's "Map of Original Surveys," the drafts of which were begun about 1681, but which were continued and added to, for some time afterward, the locality of Gwynedd is shown divided lengthwise about equally, the north-eastern half being marked "John Gee & Company," and the lower, or southwestern, "Robert Turner." At the time, therefore, when this part of the map was made, the transactions between Gee and Turner, by which, as recited in the patent, the latter acquired the entire title, had not been completed; and at what date their completion was effected is left uncertain. But it was before 1698; when the two Welshmen, in Philadelphia, were seeking for land, Turner's large and compact tract drew their attention, and he, doubtless, having waited a good while for a purchaser, cheerfully bargained with them.[1]

---

[1] Robert Turner was a prominent man in the early history of Pennsylvania. He came here about 1682, and died in 1701. Before coming he was a merchant in Dublin, and it was to him that Penn addressed the letter from London, in March, 1681, in which he announces the final granting of the patent for the Province:

"Thrive I have, and for my business here know that after many waitings, watchings, solicitings, and disputes in council, this day my country was confirmed to me under the great seal of England, with large powers and privileges, by the name of Pennsylvania,—a name the King would give it in honor of my father. I chose New Wales, being, as this, a pretty hilly country, but Penn being Welsh for a "head," as Penmanmoir, in Wales, and Penrith, in Cumberland, and Penn, in Buckinghamshire, the highest land in England, called this Pennsylvania, which is the high or head woodlands; for I proposed, when the Secretary, a Welshman, refused to have it New Wales, *Sylvania*, and they added *Penn* to it,—" etc.—See letter at length in Janney's *Life of Penn*.

Robert Turner was one of the Quaker company (which included Wm. Penn) that purchased East Jersey in 1681-82, from the estate of Sir George Carteret, and as the Pennsylvania undertaking was largely the outgrowth of that in New Jersey, he was, no doubt, one of Penn's intimate business friends. He was an active man in Philadelphia, and built, it is said, the first brick house

ARRIVAL OF THE WELSH SETTLERS. 29

The title of Turner was passed to John and Evans, as appears by the recital in the patent, on the 10th of First month [March], 1698. No doubt they entered immediately into possession, but as to this we have no certain knowledge. The most definite account we have of the time when the settlers actually entered upon their lands, is that given by Edward Foulke,— which I shall quote in full, later,— and he was one of the main company of immigrants, who did not reach Philadelphia until July. (On March 10th they had not set out from their homes in Wales. It was the 3d of the month following that Edward and his family left Coed-y-foel, to take the ship at Liverpool.)

But it is fair to presume that the two representatives lost no time in repairing to their purchase. It was a wooded upland. The timber was well grown,— oaks, hickories, chestnuts the most conspicuous and useful. Of Indians there were few, if any. Of neighbors there were some in the townships below, but none in those beyond Gwynedd. Horsham had been taken up soon after Penn's first visit, and Upper Dublin received some settlers a little later. In Whitpain, the family of that name had located as early as 1685, and other settlers in the interval. But Montgomery, Hatfield, and Towamencin were unoccupied, and the Welshmen, as they began to ply their axes, waked the echoes of the undisturbed wilderness. They were on the frontier of civilization, at this part of the line.

The main company of immigrants sailed from Liverpool on

---

in the city, at the south-western corner of Front and Mulberry streets. From 1687 to 1689 he was one of the Commissioners for Penn who carried on the government of the Province, and from 1686 to 1694, and again in 1700–1701, he was one of the Provincial Council. He was also a justice of the peace, and a commissioner of property. In the controversy between the Friends and George Keith, he, for a while, supported the latter. He left two daughters, from whom numerous Philadelphia families trace a line of descent — the Leamings, Rawles, Colemans, Pembertons, Fishers, and Hollingsworths.

the 18th of April. Their ship was the *Robert and Elizabeth*, its master Ralph Williams, its owner Robert Haydock, of Liverpool. They touched at Dublin, before proceeding on their voyage, and it was not until the 1st of May, that they finally spread the ship's sails for the new world. Precisely who were on board, besides Edward Foulke and his family, it is unsafe to say, but Hugh Roberts, returning from his visit, was with the company, and it is safe, undoubtedly, to regard the three brothers of Thomas Evans,— Robert, Owen, and Cadwallader,— Hugh Griffith, John Hugh, and John Humphrey, with their families, as of the number. As to the others, who are known to have been first settlers, we can only suppose them to have been aboard this particular ship because the company is commonly spoken of by all authorities as coming together; and I expressly reserve Robert John from the list, because I think it extremely probable that he was first a settler in Merion.[1]

Forty-five of the passengers,— a very large part, doubtless, of the whole number,— and three of the sailors, died of dysentery.[2] It was not until the 17th of July,[3] eleven weeks to a day after they had left Dublin, and fifteen after starting from their homes in Wales, that they reached port in Philadelphia, and set foot in the land of their adoption. Edward Foulke's narrative shows that they were received, as we should feel sure they would be, by the Welsh settlers who already were settled here; and the women and children found homes for several weeks among old friends or kinsfolk in Philadel-

---

[1] My reasons for this opinion, though they are not conclusive, will be stated farther on.

[2] Smith's *History of Pennsylvania* makes this statement; Edward Foulke does not mention the three sailors.

[3] Smith, who is followed by Proud, says the 7th of July; but Edward Foulke, mentioning the 17th, adds, "We were eleven weeks at sea," which fixes the latter date.

ARRIVAL OF THE WELSH SETTLERS.   31

phia, or at Merion, until the men had prepared shelter, and laid in some food for the winter.[1] It was "at the beginning of November," that Edward Foulke says he "settled" in his new home, "and divers others of our company who came over sea with us settled near us at the same time." This is explicit enough; the interval from the middle of July to the beginning of November had been occupied in the erection of houses, and probably the gathering of such crops as had been planted by William John and Thomas Evans, after getting possession in the spring. Something might have been done, indeed, by the settlers, after their arrival in July, to secure provisions for winter. They could have made a crop of buckwheat,[2] and they could have saved some forage for their cattle from the natural meadows along the streams. In August, the blackberries would be ripe, and later the chicken- and fox-grapes, the chestnuts, shellbarks, and walnuts. But their great dependence, naturally, was of two sorts: the crop of Indian corn, such as it might be, which William John and Thomas Evans had procured to be planted; and the supplies of food secured from the settlers in adjoining townships. Nor can we doubt that their old countrymen west of the Schuylkill gave them liberal aid, without money and without price. To have failed in this would have made them unworthy the name of Welshmen.

---

[1] Smith's account is this: "Shortly after they got to sea the bloody flux began among the passengers, and proved very mortal, forty-five of them and three sailors having died before their arrival at Philadelphia, which was not till the seventh of the Fifth month following. When arrived, they met with a kind reception, not only from their relations and acquaintance that were in the country before, but from others who were the more strangers to them in that they understood not their language, so that it then appeared to them that Christian love presided even among those of different speech and profession, for they were not now many of them of those called Quakers."

[2] The Swedish settlers, who preceded the Welsh, raised buckwheat here, and their habit was to sow it about the end of July. Early in August turnips could be sown, but they were not much raised, Acrelius says, even as late as 1750.

V.

Edward Foulke's Narrative of his Removal.

FOUR years after the arrival of the settlers, Edward Foulke wrote, in Welsh, an account of his removal. This, translated into English, many years later, by his grandson Samuel Foulke, of Richland,[1] is a unique document. It is the only account of this immigration, known to exist, written by one of the Gwynedd company, and it is more circumstantial and precise than almost any other referring to any of the Welsh settlers in Pennsylvania. Many copies of it are in existence, and it has been three or four times printed. No version of it within my knowledge differs materially from any other as to essential facts, but there are slight differences among different copies in the genealogical accounts which it presents. The copy here used is from that preserved by the late William Parker Foulke, of Philadelphia, as follows:

A brief Genealogy of Edward Foulke, with an account of his family and their removal from Great Britain to Pennsylvania, written by himself, originally in British.[2]

"I, Edward Foulke, was the son of Foulke, ap Thomas, ap Evan, ap Thomas, ap Robert, ap David Lloyd, ap David, ap Evan Vaughan (ap Evan), ap Griffith, ap Madoc, ap Jerwert, ap Madoc, ap Ririd Flaidd[3] Lord of Penllyn, who dwelt at Rhiwaedog.

---

[1] Who was a member of the Colonial Assembly, 1761-68. See data concerning him, in this volume.

[2] This introduction was added, no doubt, by Samuel Foulke, upon making the translation into English.

[3] This name, in nearly all the copies of the narrative that I have seen, is given as Ririd Blaidd, which is an error. Rhirid Flaidd was a well-known figure in Welsh history, and is strictly identified with the person meant by Edward Foulke, by the fact that he was "Lord of Penllyn." See *post*.

"My mother's name was Lowry, the daughter of Edward, ap David, ap Ellis, ap Robert, of the Parish of Llanvor in Merionethshire.

"I was born on the 13th of 5th month, 1651, and when arrived at mature age, I married Eleanor the daughter of Hugh, ap Cadwallader, ap Rhys, of the Parish of Spytu in Denbighshire; her mother's name was Gwen, the daughter of Ellis, ap William, ap Hugh, ap Thomas, ap David, ap Madoc, ap Evan, ap Cott, ap Evan, ap Griffith, ap Madoc, ap Einion, ap Meredith of Cai-Fadog; and (she) was born in the same parish and shire with her husband.

"I had, by my said wife, nine children, whose names are as follows: Thomas, Hugh, Cadwallader, and Evan; Grace, Gwen, Jane, Catherine, and Margaret. We lived at a place called Coed-y-foel, a beautiful farm, belonging to Roger Price, Esq., of Rhiwlas, Merionethshire, aforesaid. But in process of time, I had an inclination to remove with my family to the Province of Pennsylvania; and, in order thereto, we set out on the 3d day of the 2d month, A.D. 1698, and came in two days to Liverpool, where, with divers others who intended to go the voyage, we took shipping, the 17th of the same month, on board the *Robert and Elizabeth*, and the next day set sail for Ireland, where we arrived, and staid until the first of the 3d month, May, and then sailed again for Pennsylvania, and were about eleven weeks at sea. And the sore distemper of the bloodyflux broke out in the vessel, of which died five and forty persons in our passage; the distemper was so mortal that two or three corpses were cast overboard every day while it lasted. But through the favor and mercy of Divine Providence, I, with my wife and nine children, escaped that sore mortality, and arrived safe at Philadelphia, the 17th of the 5th month, July, where we were kindly received and hospitably entertained by our friends and old acquaintance.

"I soon purchased a fine tract of land of about seven hundred acres, sixteen miles from Philadelphia, on a part of which I settled, and divers others of our company who came over sea with us, settled near me at the same time. This was the beginning of November, 1698, aforesaid, and the township was called Gwynedd, or North Wales. This account was written the 14th of the 11th month (January) A.D. 1702, by Edward Foulke. Translated from British into English by Samuel Foulke."

Referring to the ancestry mentioned by Edward Foulke, it may be remarked that Rhirid Flaidd, "who dwelt at

Rhiwaedog," is frequently alluded to in the Welsh chronicles of the later half of the twelfth century. Details may be conveniently found concerning him and several families of North Wales who trace their descent from him, in the *Annals and Antiquities of the Counties and County Families of Wales*,[1] under the particular chapter devoted to Merionethshire. It says (p. 678):

"This distinguished man, Lord of Penllyn (a cantref containing five parishes north of the Bala Lake), Eifonydd, Pennant, Melangell, and Glyn, in Powis, and, as some say, of eleven towns or *trefs* in the hundred of Oswestry, has been occasionally described, but erroneously, as founder of one of the fifteen noble tribes of North Wales. At the same time his territories were larger and his influence much more extensive than those of several of the founders of noble tribes. He flourished at the time of Henry II., and his son, Richard I.[2] Paternally his descent was from Cynedda Wledig, but maternally it is alleged that his lineage was Norman, his mother being a descendant of Richard Earl of Avranches, by his son William, whose brother was Hugh Lupus, Earl of Chester. Whether Rhirid was called *Flaidd* (the wolf), from a cognomen of his maternal ancestors, or from the possession of a hungry and savage nature, it is not easy to say. His eldest son Madoc[3] had a son, Rhirid *Fychan* (the younger, or the little), who married into the family of Fychan (*Vaughan*), of Nannau, and from him were descended the subsequents Vaughans of Nannau and Rhug. From his son David Pothon, who married Cicely, daughter of Sir Alexander Myddelton, Lord of Myddelton, in Shropshire, the Myddeltons of Chirk Castle were descended, retaining the maternal name."

[P. 684.] "*Vaughan of Llanuwchllyn.*— This family of Vaughan, of the sept of Rhirid Flaidd, Lord of Penllyn, were long settled in the parish of Llanuwchllyn, probably at Glan-Llynn, on the margin of Bala Lake * * * * The head of this house in 1588 was Robert Vaughan, Esq. His arms according to *Dwnn*, were — *Vert, a chevron between three wolves' heads erased, arg.*— the insignia of Rhirid Flaidd.

---

[1] By Thomas Nicholas, M. A., Ph. D., F. G. S. London : 1872.

[2] This was late in the twelfth century. Henry II. reigned 1154 to 1189, and Richard 1189 to 1199.

[3] Edward Foulke, it will be observed, traces his line to Madoc.

"*Edwards of Prysg.*— John Edwards of Prysg, near Llanuwchllyn, living in 1588, was of the lineage of *Rhirid Flaidd*, Lord of Penllyn, in the same line * * * with the Vaughans of Llanuwchllyn, mentioned above. The arms of Edwards of Prysg were those of Rhirid Flaidd,— *Vert, a chevron between three wolves' heads erased, arg.*"

[P. 682.] "Rhiwaedog, near Bala, a spot of historic interest by reason of the great battle which tradition relates was fought here between the Welsh, under *Llywarch Hen*, the prince-bard, and the Saxons, when the aged bard lost Cynddelw, the last survivor of twenty-four sons, whose sanguinary character gave its name to the place (*rhiw*, a declivity; and *gwaedog*, bloody). It is situated in the narrow and long valley of Hirnant, nearly two miles from the Dee, and an equal distance from the mansion of *Aberhirnant*. Rhirid Flaidd is said by Yorke ('*Royal Tribes*'), to have dwelt at Rhiwaedog."

[P. 682.] "While *Meirionydd* was the central and most prominent district in these parts, and as such most frequently mentioned, the cantref of *Penllyn*, about the Bala Lake, now forming parts of Merionethshire, was also an important lordship, always or mostly under separate government * * * * . Penllyn was the patrimony of Rhirid Flaidd, *temp.* Henry II., and continued in his son Madoc and grandson Rhirid *Fychan* (corrupted 'Vaughan'), from whom several of the chief old families of Merionethshire bearing that name are traced."

[P. 705.] "*Lloyd, John, Esq., of Plas-issaf, Merionethshire.*[1] * * * * This family derives its descent from Rhirid Flaidd, of Rhiwaedog, Lord of Penllyn, from whom are descended the Lloyds of Rhiwaedog, * * * * etc."

Edward Foulke, whatever may have been the relative rank and influence of his ancestor Rhirid Flaidd, in the rude age when he figured as a local chieftain, was himself a plain Welsh farmer, occupying, as he says, the farm of Coed-y-foel, a part of the estate of Roger Price,[2] of Rhiwlas. This farm is still known by that name, and is owned (1883) by Richard J. Lloyd-Price, Esq., of Rhiwlas, a lineal descendant of Roger. Its name signifies "the wood of the bare hill,"—*i. e.* a wood

---

[1] His arms are those of Rhirid Flaidd, with a crest added,— a wolf's head erased.

[2] He was High Sheriff of Merionethshire, in 1710.

around the base of a hill whose crown is bare,—and this describes the place. It lies along the river Treweryn, in a charming valley, on the east side of the stream.[1] Rhiwlas is distant a mile, and the market-town of Bala about two miles. The Treweryn is a considerable stream, coming down from the mountains north-west of Bala, and flowing for several miles east and south through a narrow valley between the mountains called, on one side, Arenig Vawr (great), and Arenig Bach (little). The parish is Llanvor, from which many of the Welsh settlers in Eastern Pennsylvania came, and the region, picturesque and romantic, is fairly characteristic of Northern Wales. Many names near by will be recognized by students of the records of immigration that came from these parts,— Bala, the town and the lake; the river Dee, famous for its beauty; Rhiwaedog, celebrated in Welsh history; the swift and clear Treweryn; and numerous others mentioned in the old accounts.

His narrative of his removal indicates that Edward Foulke possessed some education, and it must have been superior to the average of his time. His "Exhortation," addressed to his children, late in life, is a good piece of composition. Some details concerning his life in Wales, previous to his removal, have come down by tradition, and are doubtless trustworthy. His purpose of immigration, it is said, was formed from his conviction of the hardships and injustice inflicted upon those subjects to a monarchical government. He had attended, the tradition says, at a military muster or drill, required by law, when a person in his company, a kinsman, engaged in exercise with a broad-sword or other weapon, had the cap of his knee struck off by his antagonist. The bystanders, with the one who had inflicted the injury, showed no regret at the oc-

---

[1] For assistance as to these details I am indebted to Howel W. Lloyd, Esq., M. A., London, a native of that part of Wales here described.

currence, but rather exulted over it, while Edward, distressed at the suffering of his kinsman, was shocked to consider that the barbarous occurrence was a natural outgrowth of the system under which they lived. His mind turned to Pennsylvania as a place of escape, but he felt extreme reluctance to undertake the difficulties and perils of the long voyage with his large family. He "opened" the matter, however, to his wife, and she, as the tradition says, regarded the impression that had been made upon his mind as having a Divine origin, and while he hesitated and argued the pecuniary disadvantage a removal might be, she earnestly declared to him that "He that revealed this to thee can bless a very little in America to us, and can blast a great deal in our native land."

Being accounted an excellent singer,[1] large companies were in the habit of collecting at their house on First-days to hear Edward sing. "But with this he became uneasy, as he found that his company was of no advantage to him, nor he to them, as their time was spent in vain and trifling amusements. On one occasion, expressing his uneasiness to his wife, he found that she shared the feeling, and was dissatisfied both with the singing and some of the singers. She urged that the way to spend First-day with profit would be to read the Scriptures, and said that then the undesirable part of the company would soon become weary and leave them, while their truest and most valuable friends would adhere to them more closely. The plan being adopted, it was found as his wife anticipated; when companies had collected, and Edward was tempted to undue levity, she would say, 'Put away, and get the Bible.' The light and unprofitable portion of their visitors soon fell away, while others more weighty and solid continued with them. Their meeting and Scripture reading continued for some time, and the gathering at their house in-

---

[1] This statement of facts is taken in substance from the MS. journal of Joseph Foulke, of Gwynedd.

creased. At length Eleanor reminded her husband of his exercise of mind on the subject of emigration, and said that as they had so evidently benefited by their following the path of duty in regard to the observance of First-day, it remained for them to proceed in the removal to Pennsylvania, which had also been indicated to them. And when they resolved upon the step, some who had attended their meeting came with them."

The insight we get by this narrative helps us to estimate very precisely the character of Edward Foulke and his family. But it must be distinctly observed that at the time of their coming they were not Friends. Like the Evanses, and all the other settlers except John Hugh and John Humphrey, they had been inclined to the Friends, but had not actually joined them.

VI.

The Origin of the Township's Name.

IT is curious enough that there should have been, ever, any speculation or doubt concerning the origin of the township's name. For Gwynedd was a geographical designation among the Welsh people, more than a thousand years old, when the arriving settlers applied it freshly to their little block of Pennsylvania land. The name was that which had long been applied to the northern part of Wales. By the English that region was called North Wales; but the people themselves for hundred of years had named it Gwynedd. Many of the most prominent and able of the Welsh leaders, from the sixth century to the thirteenth, are known as princes or so-called kings of Gwynedd, and for a time after the reign of Rhodry Mawr, or Roderick the Great, in the middle of the ninth century, Gwynedd claimed and to some extent possessed a political supremacy over the whole of Wales.

Gwynedd was in fact the stronghold of the Welsh. In it were the homes of a large part of the Kymry people, descendants of those Britons who faced Cæsar on the shores by Deal, when, half a century before Christ, he crossed from Gaul to invade their island. It is the wildest portion of "Wild Wales." Enclosed within the bent arm of the Dee, the fastnesses around the base of Snowdon were naturally, as they became historically, the last refuge of the Britons against the relentless pressure of invasion, first Angle, then Norman, which came upon them from their eastern border, and, fastening upon southern and central Wales, left them, at last, nothing but these rocky recesses in the north.¹ There, it may be said, was the seat of the most persistent British spirit. Not more intense, perhaps, than that which marked portions of southern Wales, it was better situated for resistance. In the halls of Aberffraw (in Anglesey), Gwynedd's last capital, the bards sang to the end praises of their heroes, and fanned with their tales of old prophecy the spark of national feeling which kindled into a flame—though but for an instant—so late as the days of Glendower.²

But, though the name of Gwynedd belongs so distinctly, for so long a time, to the northern part of Wales, there was, apparently, a greater Gwynedd than this before 600. In the vague chronicles of that time, for a half century or more, we hear of British chiefs — sometimes called kings, sometimes named by other titles — who, as they fought against Anglo-Saxon encroachment in the north of England, ruled over a Gwynedd that extended northward from the Dee's mouth across the Mersey and up into the lake and mountain region which is now Lancashire, Westmoreland, and Cumberland. For such a union of British power, including part or all of the present Wales, and that northwestern part of England just described, the city which we now call Chester, the "Caerlleon on Dee" of the Britons, was the natural capital.

---

¹ "It hath been," says Sir John Price, as edited by Humphrey Lloyd, speaking of Gwynedd, "a great while the chiefest seat of the last kings of Britain, because it was and is the strongest country within this isle, full of high mountains, craggy rocks, great woods, and deep valleys, strait and dangerous places, deep and swift rivers." Woodward, in his *History of Wales* (London, 1850–52), remarks that "the pride and the glory of the Kymry has been that last retreat of British independence, the principality of Gwynedd."

² In Gwynedd, in the fastnesses about Snowdon, Llewelyn (second of the name conspicuous in Welsh history, Llewelyn ap Griffith) made his last struggle with the overwhelming force of Edward I. Failing there, his death shortly after ended finally—except the episode of Glendower—the effort to maintain Welsh independence. The eldest son of the English king became then, in fact as in name, Prince of Wales.

ORIGIN OF THE NAME GWYNEDD.

To this larger district the king or prince known as Maelgwn Gwynedd, whose name stands out in the chronicles about the middle of the sixth century, appears attached. The theatre of his action seems to have been more in north-western England than in Wales. He was resisting that advance of the Angles which came across Yorkshire, from the place of their descent upon the coast, about the mouth of the Humber. The Britons in his time had been forced by the pressure of invasion into the three natural strongholds in the western side of their island. In the extreme south they had been driven into the long point of land—the counties now of Somerset, Devon, and Cornwall—which form the Cornwall peninsula, and, when, A. D. 577, the West Saxons under Ceawlin defeated them at the great and decisive battle of Deorham,[1] these Britons were cut off, by their enemies' hold upon the Severn, from connection with those who held the middle region north of that river. This region above the Severn—the Wales of our day—was then called by the Saxons North Wales, and so appears on the maps which represent that time, for the Cornwall region was known as West Wales. The third stronghold was that of north-western England, the "Lake Country" of our later time, and from it the Britons joined hands with allies still farther in the north, along and beyond the Clyde.

Confining ourselves to a view of the greater Gwynedd that included, as has been said, part or all of modern Wales, and most of the modern "Lake Country," it will easily be seen how this hinged upon Chester, and how, when the Saxons cut through to the sea's edge upon the west by the capture of that city (probably about A. D. 613, under Æthelfrith), they severed the Britons of the great central stronghold from those in the northern one, and so divided Gwynedd. Precisely who

---

[1] Deorham was a village northward of Bath, on hills overlooking the Severn.

had made the fight against the Saxons after Maelgwn's time is uncertain. But before the victory of Æthelfrith, Gwynedd had been boldly and fiercely defended. Its territory, says Green,[1] besides embracing the bulk of the present North Wales, pushed forward, by its outlying fastness of Elmet,[2] into the heart of southern Deira.[3] In Elmet the Britons long held their rude homes. By the Welsh chronicle, which, though it must be quoted with great caution, may be, after all, as trustworthy as that of Saxon or Angle, there followed Maelgwn Gwynedd, in direct succession, father and son, Run, Beli, Cadvan, Cadwallon, and Cadwallader. These were "Kings of Gwynedd," or, as Welsh authority says of the last three, "Kings of Britain;" they were at any rate chiefs who headed the British struggle. In A. D. 589, when the kingdom of Deira had been overrun by its Bernician neighbors, it was to the protection of a king of Gwynedd that the sons of Ælla, the Deiran king, then just dead, fled for protection.[4]

That the Britons did lose their hold at Chester in A. D. 613, by a victory of Æthelfrith, we accept on the authority of Green. The chronicle of the Welsh, known as that of Caradawg of Llangarvan avers that this (Chester) " chief city of Venedotia" was taken by Egbert the Saxon about A. D. 883, having "hitherto remained in the hands of the Welsh." It may be that the possession of Æthelfrith was not made permanent, and that, again falling for a while into British hands, the city was a second time taken in Egbert's day. But it does not seem that after the close of the sixth century

---

[1] *The Making of England*, p. 232 (New York, 1882).
[2] The wooded region north of "The Peak" of Derbyshire.
[3] The Saxon Deira was a large part of the present Yorkshire.
[4] History can never forget the kingdom of Ælla, for thence it was that there came to Rome as slaves those blue-eyed, fair haired youths whom Gregory saw and stopped to enquire about, as he passed through the marketplace of the Eternal City. "Angels, not Angles," he exclaimed as he viewed them, and departed to organize his work of Christianity in Britain.

ORIGIN OF THE NAME GWYNEDD.

there was anything of the kingdom or principality of Gwynedd northward from the mouth of the Dee, and this is what chiefly concerns the present inquiry. We may remark only how natural it was, so long as their passage from the one region to the other was kept open by the possession of Chester, that the Britons of Wales and those of northwestern England should have been bound together in some rude form of national unity. For the two regions are very similar natural fastnesses; the crags and glens southwest of the Dee find their counterpart in the wild scenery northward of the Mersey. While Cader-Idris and Snowdon rise in the one region, and through the deep clear waters of Bala the current of the Dee flows unchanged and unmingling,[1] in the other the Scawfells, Helvellyn, and Skiddaw lift their heads above the charming lakes of Cumberland. Two such regions, easily defensible, nearly adjoining, and inhabited by a kindred people, were natural allies at the least.

This Gwynedd is easily recognized by the name itself. For Gwyn-edd means *The White Land.* In the symbolism of patriotic association the white meant, doubtless, the pure, the beautiful, the untaken, the virgin land; but in the snows that crowned Snowdon and Helvellyn another reason might be found for the name. Gwen is a favorite Welsh name for a woman — corresponding to Blanche, as belonging to a light-haired, fair-skinned beauty. The white stones that inclosed "the place of session," in Welsh law, were the "meini *gwyn*ion." In the Lake of Bala a famous white fish is known as the *Gwyn*iad.[2] In fact, the word *gwyn* or *gwen* will be continu-

---

[1] Such is the old and familiar tradition.

[2] Oddly enough, and quoted as part of the proof that some part of the American Indians are of Welsh descent — probably come from Madoc's voyages in the twelfth century — there is a salmonoid fish (*Corogonus fera*) in the waters of British Columbia, with silvery scales, closely resembling that in Bala, and its name, as given by the natives, is the *Quinnat.*

ally met with in Welsh, and has always the same significance —to be white, pure, unsullied. Justice, patriotism, the beauty of fair women, the snowy heights of the unconquered mountains, the recesses of the unravaged home of the Kymry, all were represented in the adjective.

Taking *Gwyn*, then, as the root, the termination *edd* has simply the significance of a land, a region, a country. The pronunciation of it is not *edd*, as in English, but *eth*, the *th* soft, as in "with." *Gwen-eth* may therefore be assumed as the name spoken, and its significance, the white or fair land.[1]

Returning to that Gwynedd which was but the northern third of what we now know as Wales, it may be said that between A. D. 613, when Æthelfrith took Chester, and the time of Rhodry Mawr, about A. D. 843, little is known concerning it geographically, and nothing in the chronicle of its feuds and wars is of importance to this inquiry. But Rhodry Mawr, when he died in A. D. 877, divided all Wales amongst his three sons, and named definite boundaries for their territories. In the north he gave Gwynedd to his eldest son Anarawd, and he ordered that Merfyn, the Prince of Powys, the middle division, and Cadelh, of Deheubarth, the southern, should, with their heirs and successors, acknowledge the superior sovereignty of Anarawd. These divisions long continued to have a practical and actual existence; for four hundred years they were regarded; and they still have, as a basis of historical and descriptive method, a certain acknowledged importance.[2]

---

[1] It need hardly be said after this explanation, that while Gwynedd means the same thing as North Wales, in the sense that both names were long applied to the same region of country, they have no other relationship whatever, and no other similar meaning. What the Kymry called Gwynedd the English knew as North Wales, till geographically the designations became interchangeable.

[2] This division of the kingdom, tending to divide its strength in the face of the Saxon enemy, the Welsh chroniclers much lament; but it was according to the general tenor of the Welsh system, which required, as in the *gavel-kind* of the

ORIGIN OF THE NAME GWYNEDD. 45

In this division by Rhodry Mawr, "Gwynedd," says Sir John Price, "had upon the north side the sea, from the river Dee, at Basingwerke, to Aberdyfi, and upon the west and southwest the river Dyfi,[1] which divideth it from South Wales [Deheubarth, Prince Cadelh's possession], and in some places from Powys Land. And on the south and east it is divided from Powys, sometimes with mountains and sometimes with rivers, till it come to the river Dee again."

The same authority describes Gwynedd as "of old time" divided into four parts — the island of Mon (Anglesey), Arfon (Caernarvon), Merioneth, and Y Berfedwlad, which may be Englished the inland or middle country." Substantially these four divisions were Anglesey, the whole of Caernarvon, nearly all the present Merioneth, the greater part of Denbighshire, and all of Flintshire, except a small section. It would include rather less than a third of the area of modern Wales.

It is not germane to the present purpose to trace the history of the Gwynedd over which Anarawd was left the ruler. It figures, however, as has already been stated, in all the chronicles of subsequent Welsh struggle. In the twelfth century, Owain Gwynedd made himself a name equal to that of Rhodry and Maelgwn, though inferior, perhaps, to that of the two desperate and heroic Llewelyns. And it was Madoc, son of Owain Gwynedd, who, as Welsh authority claims, crossed the Atlantic to the American continent, more than three hundred years before the caravels of Columbus sailed out from Palos. It would be useless to enter the well-beaten

---

old English law, a distribution of the father's possessions among his children. ("The custom of gavel-kind," says Blackstone, "is undoubtedly of British origin.")

[1] By looking at the map these lines will be easily followed, and the description is inserted for that purpose, but the points of the compass given are misleading; the sea lay on the west, as well as on the north, and the Dyfi (Dovey) could only be fairly described as bounding on the south and in part on the south-east.

field wherein the claims of Madoc have been disputed, but it is enough to say that some of these claims are in modern time accepted as probably true. That Madoc was a real person, the son of Owain Gwynedd, that he sailed from Wales in one or two voyages about 1170–72, and that he bore away into the Atlantic westward "by a route leaving Ireland on the north," is conceded. But what land he reached, if any, and whether any descendants of himself and his company have ever been found, either in North or South America, are questions quite beyond settlement;[1] in the Welsh Triads themselves Madoc's second and final voyage is accounted one of "The Three Losses by Disappearance" sustained by "The Isle of Britain."

In the "Triads" we may find abundant allusions to Gwynedd. In those that are historical and geographical, as well as those that refer to "the social state" of the Welsh, the name frequently appears. "There are three courts of country and law—one in Powys, one at Caerleon-on-Usk, which is that of Glamorgan and Deheubarth, and one in Gwynedd." "The court of country and law in Gwynedd is constituted of the lord of the commot (unless the prince himself be present), the mayor, chancellor," etc. There were "three invading tribes that came into the Isle of Britain, and departed from it," one of these being "the hosts of Ganvel the Gwyddel [Irishman], who came to Gwynedd, and were there twenty-nine years, until they were driven out by Caswallon, the son of Beli." Of "the Three Primary Tribes of the Nation of the Cymry," the Gwyndydians, the men of Gwynedd and Powys, formed one. Rhun, who was the son of Maelgwn and the first of "Three Fair Princes of the Isle of Britain," reigned over Gwynedd, it is

---

[1] For an estimate of the importance now assigned to Madoc and his voyages, see Bryant's *History of the United States*. The various speculations have assigned his landing place, settlements, and descendants to nearly the whole east coast of the American continent from Canada to Patagonia.

said, from A. D. 560 to A. D. 586. Cadavael, the son of Cynvedw, in Gwynedd, is recorded as one of "the Three Plebeian Princes of the Isle of Britain," and he is handed down in disgrace by another Triad as having inflicted one of the "Three Heinous Hatchet Blows" that caused the death of Iago ap Beli, the sovereign of Gwynedd.

The poetry of the bards, much of it inspired amongst the hills of northern Wales, and relating to events that had occurred there, makes Gwynedd and those associated with the name repeatedly a theme. Owain Gwynedd is celebrated by numerous bards. Llywarch, of Powys, singing the bravery of a Powys prince (about A. D. 1160) calls him "Gwynedd's foe." Madoc, the voyager, was a favorite subject: the Prince Llewelyn is referred to in the verse of Llywarch, a bard, as

"The lion i' the breach, ruler of Gwynedd,"

and as the

"Nephew of Madog, whom we more and more
Lament that he is gone."

Meredydd ap Rhys (about A. D. 1440) says:—

"Madog the brave, of aspect fair,
Owain of Gwynedd's offspring true,
Would have no land — man of my soul!—
Nor any wealth except the seas."

Elidir Sais, who wrote in the thirteenth century, and was one of the earliest Welsh composers of religious verse, says:—

"The chieftains of Deheubarth and Gwynedd,[1]
Pillars of battle, throned have I seen."

And Einion ap Madog ap Rhawaid, in a eulogy upon Griffith, the unhappy son[2] of Llewelyn the Great, says:—

---

[1] The rhythm places the accent on the second syllable, as it should be.
[2] His brother Davydd treacherously took him prisoner, and Henry III. kept him in the Tower of London, in attempting to escape from which he was killed.

> "The eagle of Gwynedd, he is not nigh.
> Though placable, he will no insult bear;
> And though a youth, his daring horsemanship
> Fastening on him the strangers' wondering eyes."

And one more stanza, by an author whose name is not precisely given in the authority here quoted, runs thus:—

> "Gwynedd! for princes gen'rous famed — and songs,
> By Gruffydd's son[1] unshamed
> Thou art; he, hawk untamed,
> Is praised where'er thy glory is proclaimed."

---

[1] The second Llewelyn.

VII.

Number of the First Settlers: Growth of Population.

FROM the first the Gwynedd settlement had a certain distinction. It was talked of and written about. Contemporary accounts mention it, and these mentionings are conspicuous in the meagre annals which have been handed down to us. In 1705, Samuel Carpenter, of Philadelphia, offering for sale, in a letter to Jonathan Dickinson, a large tract of land in Bucks county, near the line, describes it as being " about four miles from North Wales."

The reason for this, obviously, was the fact that the settlement was strong from the beginning. The arrival of the settlers in a body, their purchase and immediate occupancy of a whole township, made up a notable proceeding. The adjoining townships filled up slowly; families came by ones and twos; their growth was almost unperceived; but the Welsh company, composed of a dozen families or more, and moving with a concerted and harmonious step, commanded attention.

To estimate with confidence the number who arrived in the first immigration, and who, as the snow fell in November, 1698, were at home in the township, is impossible. Yet I think it cannot have been far from one hundred persons, of all ages. In several families we know very exactly the number of sons and daughters born before 1698, and who therefore must have come with their parents in the immigration. Thus—

Edward Foulke expressly speaks of his wife and nine children, as being on the *Robert and Elizabeth*, and arriving safely.

Thomas Evans' family included his wife and at least eight sons and daughters, who all appear to have been born in Wales.

To Robert Evans are assigned, besides his wife, seven sons and daughters, all probably born in Wales.

Cadwallader Evans and his wife had one son and one daughter, both born in Wales.

To Owen Evans and his wife are assigned six children, born in Wales. (Two others, making up the eight named in our Genealogy of the family, were born in Gwynedd.)

William John's will (1712) names his wife and six children, and all of the six were probably born in Wales.

John Humphrey's will (1736) names one son, and three daughters, all of them married, and some of them having children (to whom he leaves legacies). The comparison of dates, etc., inclines me to the belief that all his children were born before 1698, and therefore were among the immigrants.

John Hugh's family was small; his son Ellis, who was married in 1713, must have been born before 1698, and his daughter Gainor, married in 1723, may have been,—there is some reason for thinking that she was.

Hugh Griffith's son Evan was married in 1705; his son Griffith [called Griffith Hugh] was married in 1718. The former certainly, the latter probably, may be counted as among the immigrants.

As to the other families I do not attempt anything. The Pughs [ap Hughs] included several men, but the time of their arrival may not have been before 1699. Robert John was married in 1706, and probably had no family when he came into the township. Of Evan Robert's and Ellis David's families I have no data to present.

NUMBER OF THE FIRST SETTLERS.

Summing up, however, what has been stated above, we have these figures:

Edward Foulke's family,	11 persons.
Thomas Evans' family,	10 persons.
Robert Evans' family,	9 persons.
Cadwallader Evans' family,	4 persons.
Owen Evans' family,	8 persons.
William John's family,	8 persons.
John Humphrey's family,	6 persons.
John Hugh's family (say)	5 persons.
Hugh Griffith's family (say)	5 persons.
Total,	66

To this, if we add thirty-four to cover all the others, including servants,—of whom I have no account,—ample allowance will no doubt be made. The number who came into Gwynedd the first year was probably under rather than over one hundred.

A petition presented to the Court of Quarter Sessions, in Philadelphia, in June, 1704 (asking for a road *via* Whitemarsh), and headed, "Petition of the Inhabitants of North Wales, in Philadelphia County," recites that "there are in said township above thirty families already settled." (I am inclined to think that those over the line, in what is now Montgomery, were included. I doubt whether Montgomery was then organized.)

In 1741, Gwynedd contained 93 taxables,[1] and Montgomery township 54. Gwynedd was then one of the largest in taxable population in Philadelphia county; it was exceeded only by six others in what is now Montgomery county, as follows: Salford, 174; Providence, 146; Moreland, 125; Manatawny, 111; Lower Merion, 101; Upper Hanover, 97. Salford, it must be noted, then included both the present townships of that

---

[1] See *Watson's Annals*, Vol. II., p. 403.

name,— Upper and Lower; and Providence included Upper and Lower Providence. In the same year (1741, as above), all the townships adjoining and near to Gwynedd had a less number of taxables. Their numbers were as follows: Horsham, 80; Perkiomen and Skippack, 73; Plymouth, 46; Towamencin, 55; Whitpain, 56; Worcester, 70; Upper Dublin, 77; Whitemarsh, 89.

In the table below I give figures from the censuses since 1800, as far as I have been able conveniently to obtain them. Of the census of 1830, I am able to give, however, some special details.[1] Under 5 years there were 228; between 60 and 70 years, 52; between 70 and 80 years, 30; between 80 and 90 years, 10; between 90 and 100 years, 1. Montgomery township had 911 population, 472 male, 439 female; 4 of the total colored. In the two townships collectively there were 7 aliens, not naturalized, none blind, none deaf and dumb.

Population of Gwynedd by several Censuses.

Year.	Total.	Male.	Female.	White.	Colored.	Native.	For'gn.
1800	906	470	427	897	9	. .	. .
1810	1078	. .	. .	. .	.	. .	. .
1820	1221	648	573	. .	.	. .	. .
1830	1402	701	701	1397	5	. .	. .
1840	. .	. .	. .	. .		. .	. .
1850	1571	807	764	1561	10	. .	. .
1860	1976	1018	958	1965	11	. .	. .
1870	2501	. .	. .	2477	24	2349	152
1880	3412	. .	. .	. .	.	. .	. .

[NOTES.— In the figures for 1800, the numbers by sex are of whites only; the 9 colored persons must be counted in to make up the total 906.

The figures for 1870 include North Wales borough, 407 (native, 385; foreign, 22).

---

[1] See *Hazard's Register*, Vol. VI., p. 31.

The figures for 1880 include North Wales borough, 673; and 500 of the population of the borough of Lansdale,— an estimate of that portion of the borough's total (798), which was on the Gwynedd side of the township line.

The census for 1790, the first taken by the United States, cannot be given, as an examination of the original records in the Census Office, at Washington (kindly made for me by Mr. Chas. H. Ingram, of the Internal Revenue Bureau), shows that the return of Gwynedd township was not made separately.

Figures for 1810 and 1840 are left blank, because the Census Office has no copy of the printed complete returns of either year; and it seemed unnecessary to search out and tabulate the original returns.

Details of the native and foreign born were not ascertained in the censuses prior to 1850, and were not published until 1870.]

VIII.

The First Settlers' Homes; Personal Details.

DEEDS were made to the other settlers by William John and Thomas Evan, within a few months after the settlement, when it had been decided how much land each should take.[1] The plots were marked off, however, upon the suppo-

---

[1] Ten of these deeds are dated 4th mo. (June) 5, 1699, and the others, also, appear to have been then executed; except Wm. John's conveyance to Thomas Evan, and the latter's conveyance to the former, which are dated 6th mo. (August) 30, of that year.

These deeds show that the township was actually divided up among the settlers. William John and Thomas Evan paid Robert Turner "508 pounds, current money of Pensilvania," for it; and in the distribution each colonist was charged at this rate,—6 pounds 10 shillings for each 100 acres. Thus, the conveyances from John and Evan were as follows:

	Acres.	£	s.
Robert Jones,	500	32	10
Cadwallader ap Evan,	500	32	10
Robert ap Evan,	500	32	10
John Hugh,	500	32	10
Thomas Evan,	700	45	10
Wm. John,	2150	139	15
Owen ap Evan,	400	26	0
Edward Ffoulk,	400	26	0
John Humphrey,	400	26	0
H. & E. Griffith,	300	19	10
Hugh David,	220	14	6
Evan Hugh,	100	6	10
Total,	6670	433	11

The list is not quite complete; the other conveyances (which I did not readily find on the records) will make up the 7,820 acres, and 509 pounds. (John Humphrey, above, is assigned 400 acres; the patent gives him, of first right, 450; also, Wm. John's two tracts, above, make 2,150 acres; but in the two patents he is allowed 1,900 and 150, making 2,050. Perhaps the Evan Robert tract, 100 acres, is included in the 2,150, above.)

sition that the township contained the area assigned to it in the purchase from Robert Turner, 7,820 acres, whereas its actual area was about fifty per cent. greater. Thus William John was presumed to have 1,900 acres in his large tract, but really had 2,866; Evan ap Hugh's title was for 700, whereas his plot contained 1,068; Cadwallader Evan had title for 500, and received 609; Edward Foulke for 400, and received 720; John Humphrey for 450, and received 574; and so on throughout the list. (The patent of Thomas Evan, already cited at length, shows that his purchase was 700 acres, and that his tract contained 1,049 acres.)

These facts were developed by a re-survey, made in pursuance of a general law, passed by the Provincial Assembly about 1701. There had been a re-survey of all recently patented lands. Penn, in leaving the colony for England, in November, 1701, had particularly urged the matter on the attention of James Logan.[1] To perform the work in Gwynedd, David Powell, the Welsh surveyor, who had run the lines in Merion, when that township was taken up, and who had since been an assistant to the Surveyor-General of the province, was assigned. He came over from Merion, and was engaged in Gwynedd at different times during the year 1702.[2] (The patent to Thomas Evans shows that a general warrant for the re-surveys was issued by Penn's Commissioners of Property, on September 29th, 1701, and the date of the patent is March 8th,

---

[1] Writing from the ship *Dolmahoy*, on his way down the Delaware, on November 3d, Penn adds a postscript: "Cause all the province and territories to be re-surveyed in the most frugal manner, with the assistance of my brother-in-law, Edward Penington, within the two years prescribed by the law, if possible." Logan replies to this, December 2d: "We intend to set about re-surveys with all expedition," and in a later letter he remarks that the overplus found by the surveyors is much greater than had been expected.

[2] David's plots, showing the several tracts, returned by him to the Land Office, are still to be seen in the Department of Internal Affairs, at Harrisburg. They are small, plain, and not elaborate.

1702. Between these dates, of course, David ran the lines. Other records show that the order for the survey of William John's tract was made 7th mo. 29th, 1702, and that he made his return to the "General Surveyor's Office," 10th mo. 2d, ensuing; in John Humphrey's tract he makes return of re-survey, 10th mo. 25th, 1702.)

The re-surveys being completed, the Commissioners issued patents to the holders of the several tracts in the township. These patents confirmed the title acquired through Turner,[1] and they also conveyed the overplus land in excess of the amount to which he had a right. The plan of doing this was not illiberal. Each settler was confirmed not only the amount he had bought, but ten per cent. additional, and for the remaining acres a moderate price was charged. Thomas Evan's patent shows that after confirming him his 700 acres, he was allowed 70 more, and for the remaining 279 was to pay 61 pounds, 8 shillings, 3 farthings.

---

[1] Robert Turner's deed to John and Evan for the colony should have been described more particularly at page 28 of this volume. He recites that he had received from Penn four warrants: one in 1683, for 1000 acres, another, same year, for 5600, another, in 1684, for 720, and the fourth, same year, for 500, and these were "laid out by yᵉ Surveyor General's order, in one tract," in Philadelphia county, "Beginning at a black oak tree marked for a corner, standing in yᵉ line of Wm. Harman's land, and on yᵉ east side of a small run of water, thence n. e. by the same and the land of Tryall Kolme, 780 p. to a post, then n. w. by the lands of Joseph Fisher and Wm. Stanley, John West & John Day, 1604 p. to a post for a corner; then s. w. by the land of James Peters, 780 p. to another corner post; then s. e. by yᵉ township laid out for Richard Whitpaine, Chas. Marshall, Thomas Cox, John Bassley, and others, 1604 p. to the place of beginning;" "the survey thereof completed on yᵉ 2d day of the 12th mo. 1694, as by return of yᵉ sd warrants in Surveyor General's office, 1st mo. 10th, 1698-99, will appear," etc., etc.

This shows that the surveys of the land were made especially for the purpose of the conveyance to John and Evan. The record also shows that Thomas Fairman made the survey,—though it must have been a very imperfect one, as the township's lines given above are but 1604 perches on the long sides, while Powell's re-survey showed them to be really over 2000. (It seems doubtful whether Fairman really went on the ground, at all.)

Towamencin Twp.

[Griffith Jones] [James Peters]

Wm. John.
2866 a.

Evan Ap. Hugh.
1068 a.

Robt. John.
720 a.

Robt.
Ap Hugh
232 a.

Thos. Ap. Evan.
1049 a.

Robt Ap Evan.
1034 a.

Cadw
Ap. Evan.
609 a.

Owen Ap Evan.
538 a.

E. Ap.
Hugh
116 a.

Edw.
Foulke.
712 a.

John.
Humphrey
574 a.

Wm. John.
322 a.

Ellis
David.
231 a.

Robt. Evan.
399 a.

E. Robert
110 a.

Hugh + Ev.
Griffith
376 a.

John Hugh
648 a. 132 p.

[Whitpaines Township]
Worcester Twp.
[Richard Whitpaine + Co.]
Whitpain Twp.
[Line of marked trees]
[Joseph Fisher]
Montgomery Twp.
Horsham Twp.
[Thos. Siddon]
Upper Dublin Twp.

THE FIRST SETTLERS' HOMES.

A statement of the amounts in the several tracts, as shown by the re-surveys, may be made as follows:

	First Purchase.	Area Patented.
Thomas Evan,	700	1049
William John,	1900	2866
Evan ap Hugh,	700	1068
Robert John,	500	720
Robert ap Hugh,	200	232
Robert Evan,	500	1034
Cadwallader Evan,	500	609
Owen Evan,	400	538
Edward Foulke,	400	712
Evan ap Hugh (lower tract),	100	110
John Humphrey,	450	574
William John (lower tract),	150	322
Robert Evan (lower tract),	200	250
Hugh and Evan Griffith,	300	376
Ellis David,	220	231
Evan Robert,	100	110
John Hugh,	500	648
Total acres,	7820	11,449

The location of the several tracts is shown by the skeleton map of the township given herewith. William John's large tract occupied the upper end, and extended downward to a point below Kneedler's tavern. The road leaving the turnpike at the toll-gate and running south-westward by West Point station, must have been very nearly his lower line.

The lower line of Thomas Evan's tract was very nearly, or exactly, the present Swedes' Ford road. The lower line of Edward Foulke's tract was along the present road from Spring-House to Penllyn, and the eastern corner of his property was almost precisely at the former place. John Humphrey's tract joined him, therefore, at or close by the Spring-House, and John's north corner, on the township line (Welsh road), must have been on the top of the hill, above John

Stong's old smith-shop, just about the point where is the corner-stone of Gwynedd, Horsham, and Montgomery townships. From this point extended south-westward across the township the lower line of Owen Evans, and it must have crossed the turnpike near the bridge over the Treweryn. Robert Evan's main tract, bounded on the upper side by the Swedes' Ford road, must have extended, down the turnpike, to about where the road to Gwynedd station now crosses, just above Ellen H. Evans's. Robert's line adjoining his brother Cadwallader's land passed a short distance north-east of the meeting-house. Going up the turnpike, from the Swedes' Ford road crossing, Thomas Evan's tract must have extended nearly to the top of the hill, about where the old St. Peter's burying-ground now is; and Robert John, adjoining above, took in most of the site of North Wales borough. Above him, and extending to William John's line, near Kneedler's, was Evan ap Hugh's tract.

Where the settlers lived is in part definitely known, and in part surmised. The residences of the four Evans brothers fall in the former category. There is preserved by their descendants a genealogical sketch of the family, several copies of which have come to my notice during my searches for the facts contained in this volume. This genealogical sketch, it is stated on one of the copies, was compiled from materials furnished in October, 1797, by John Evans, Sen. (son of John; grandson of Cadwallader), and his sister Elizabeth. John was then 67 years old, and his sister 71. The data were taken down by Cadwallader Evans, of Philadelphia (son of Rowland), and a memorandum on the copy now in the possession of Jonathan Evans, of Germantown, says that "some additions [have been] made since by Charles Evans, but no alterations."

On this old document, the statement is made of the residences of the four brothers. It is as follows:—

THE FIRST SETTLERS' HOMES.   59

"Thomas Evans lived where —— Heist now keeps tavern, by the run, half a mile above the meeting-house.

"Robert Evans lived where George Roberts now lives, half a mile west of George Maris's late residence.

"Owen Evans lived where his grandson Thomas Evans now lives, by the Great Road, one mile below the meeting-house.

"Cadwallader lived where his grandson John Evans lately lived and died, and where his son Cadwallader now lives, near the meeting-house."

The localities here mentioned are all easily identified. Thomas's house, where Heist kept tavern ninety years ago, is on the turnpike just above Evans' Run,—the house occupied within my recollection by George Wagner, John Preston, Silas H. Land, William Rowland, and others, and now owned by Fritz Hartman. Robert's house was where Silas White now lives, lately William J. Linnard's place, and long before his ownership belonging to George Roberts. (The present house, though antiquated enough, I do not suppose was Robert Evan's, or any part of it; more likely it was built by George Roberts.) Owen Evan's place was that now occupied by Ellen H. Evans; his house probably stood between her present house and the turnpike, where there used to be marks of an old well and of a building.

(It may be remarked, here, that the Ellen H. Evans farm has come down to herself and children directly through the inheritance of her husband, Cadwallader, from his ancestor, Owen, and has never been out of the family. I know of no other such instance in the township. No single acre of land in Gwynedd, I believe, except this, is now owned by any direct descendant of an original settler, with a family title straight down.)

Cadwallader's house, of course, was that which he and his descendants held for over a hundred years, which then passed (after a short ownership by Charles Willing Hare) into the possession of Evan Jones, and is now the residence of M. L.

Bellows. The mansion house — not the other and smaller dwelling — stands on the site where Cadwallader lived.

It was at Thomas Evan's house, according to the tradition preserved by his son Hugh, that William Penn stayed overnight when he visited Gwynedd. The story of this visit was first printed by Watson,[1] in his *Annals*, and he had it from Susan Nancarro, the granddaughter of Hugh Evans. His account is this:

"Mrs. Nancarro had often seen and conversed with her grandfather, Hugh Evans, who lived to be ninety years of age. When he was a boy of twelve he remembered that William Penn, with his daughter Letitia, and a servant (in the year 1699 or 1700), came out on horseback to visit his father, Thomas Evans. Their house was then superior, in that it was of *barked* logs, a refinement surpassing the common rank. The same place is now E. Jones's, near the Gwynedd meeting-house.[2] At that house William Penn ascended steps on the outside to go to his chamber; and the boy of twelve, being anxious to see all he could of so distinguished a man, went up afterwards to peep through the apertures at him; and there he well remembered to have seen him on his knees praying, and giving thanks to God for such peaceful and excellent shelter in the wilderness. * * * * I heard Mrs. D. L.[3] say that she had also heard the same fact from Hugh Evans.

"There was at this time a great preparation among the Indians near there for some public festival. Letitia Penn, then a lively young girl, greatly desired to be present, but her father would not give his consent, though she entreated much. The same informant says she ran out chagrined, and seeming to wish for something to dissipate her regret, snatched up a flail near some grain, at which she began to labour playfully, when she inadvertently brought the unwieldy instrument severely about her head and shoulders; and was thus quickly constrained to retreat into the house, with quite a new concern upon her mind. This fact made a last-

---

[1] See *Watson's Annals*, Vol. II., p. 79. It has been copied from Watson into Day's *Historical Collections of Pennsylvania*, and elsewhere.

[2] This error we must ascribe to Watson, or possibly to Mrs. Nancarro; Hugh Evans, of course, would have known that the Evan Jones place was his uncle Cadwallader's.

[3] Deborah Logan, no doubt.

THE FIRST SETTLERS' HOMES. 61

ing impression upon the memory of the lad aforesaid, who then was a witness."

The time of this visit Watson fixes as above, in 1699 or 1700. That it was in 1699 is possible, but very improbable, for it was not until the 1st of December, the former year, that Penn reached this country (on his second visit), and came ashore at Chester. The excursion to Gwynedd doubtless occurred in 1700 or 1701.

The allusion to the material of which Thomas Evans's house was built,— barked logs,— and the statement that this was superior to the houses of the other settlers, gives us sufficient light on the subject of their general character, fixing them as log cabins, with the bark unremoved. Such, no doubt, the first dwellings of the township were.

Besides the four Evans dwellings, we can fix with certainty the home of Edward Foulke. The house at Penllyn station, for many years Jesse Spencer's, lately the property of D. C. Wharton, and now occupied by members of his family, is on the site of Edward's house. Thomas Foulke, his eldest son, settled, when he married, in 1706, on a part of his father's lands, and the house which was long occupied by William Foulke, his great-great-grandson, afterward sold to D. C. Wharton, and lately part of his estate, was Thomas's residence. Joseph Foulke's book says: "A stone milk-house is yet standing (1846), in good repair, dated (*i.e.* Thomas and Gwen Foulke, 1728).

    F
T   G
1728

John Humphrey's house, one of the two places at which the Friends held their meetings, was near the Spring-House, at the place known in recent time as Reuben Yocum's, up the Bethlehem turnpike, north of the hotel,— such, at least, is the well-preserved tradition. John was a somewhat notable person. A brief memorial of him, by Gwynedd monthly meeting, is preserved in the John Smith manuscript collection, as follows:

"John Humphrey arrived here from Wales in the year 1698, was one of the first settlers of Gwynedd, and an elder several years. He departed this life 14th of 9th month, 1738, and was buried at Gwynedd, aged 70 years."

His will is on record in Philadelphia. It is dated 7th mo. 3, 1736, and was proved December (10th mo.) 2d, 1738. He appoints as "overseers" of the will "my cousin John Jones, and my friends John Jones, carpenter, and John Evans." The witnesses are Rowland Roberts, who signs his name with his mark, "R. R."; Thomas Evans (Owen's son, no doubt), who signs with a mark T. E., joined in a monogram; and Isaac Cook, who makes his initials only, "i. c." John Humphrey himself signs with his mark, "I. H," in rude letters. The contents of the will are of some interest. He leaves 30 pounds to his sister Elizabeth Thomas, 5 pounds to the children of Evan Griffith, 5 to his son-in-law Cadwallader Jones, 5 to his son-in-law Hugh Jones, 5 to his "daughter-in-law" Elizabeth Davies, 5 to his niece Gainor Jones, and 5 to his niece Catharine Lloyd. To Gwynedd preparative meeting he leaves 50 pounds, the interest to be applied to the relief of its poor and indigent members, but he expresses the hope that if any of his relations, members of the Society, though not of this meeting, should be in want, their claims will be considered. To his grandson, John Jones, he leaves 30 pounds, and his riding-horse,— to receive them when he is 15 years old. To his grandson Humphrey Jones he leaves 30 pounds, and to his granddaughter Jane Jones 25 pounds and a case of drawers, which she is to receive at the age of 18. To his granddaughter Sibill Jones he leaves 27 pounds, with a brass kettle, which she is to have at 15, and to his granddaughters Elizabeth and Gainor Jones 30 pounds apiece. But as to these legacies to his grandchildren, he particularly says that they are to receive nothing unless "by their good conduct they recommend themselves worthy and deserving." He gives a legacy to his daughter-in-law Katharine Jones, and to his

THE FIRST SETTLERS' HOMES. 63

son Humphrey Jones all his remaining estate, real and personal, appointing him executor.

The number of these legacies and their amounts indicate that John Humphrey was comparatively rich. Upon this point, however, we get more light from the inventory filed with his will. This exhibits him as an extensive money lender. He must have been the banker of the neighboring country. The total of the inventory (personal estate only) is 1,027 pounds 9 shillings, of which but 80 pounds 18 shillings is for household or other goods, the remainder being made up by a mortgage of Robert Hugh, 60 pounds, and by " obligations,"—which we may assume to mean bonds and notes,—numbering no less than *eighty-two*, altogether. The list of debtors who had given these obligations is a long one, and includes many of the second generation of the Gwynedd people, with others in Montgomery and elsewhere. Five of the notes are by Rowland Roberts, four by William Mellchor, three by John Clayton, two by William Williams, two by Hugh Foulke, two by Barnard Young, the others generally one each by different persons.

That his interest in his money-lending had been regarded as somewhat absorbing may be inferred from the very guarded memorial of the monthly meeting; but Joseph Foulke, in his Journal, records a statement as coming from his mother, Ann Foulke (born Roberts), which is still more distinct. She describes him as having been, at one time, a very exemplary Friend, meek and humble, enduring suffering and persecution, etc., and then she adds: "But when he became settled in Gwynedd, and was well rewarded for his industry and economy, he became rich, his bonds and mortgages increased, and as they did so the fine gold became dim, and his usefulness in the church declined apace." A Friend from Richland[1] attended the monthly meeting at Gwynedd, and in the afternoon rode

---
[1] Adds J. F., in his Journal.

to his home, twenty miles distant, under great exercise of mind concerning John Humphrey. He passed a restless night at home, and rode back to John Evans' (the son of Cadwallader), in the morning. Arriving there, he would not eat or drink until he had delivered his message, so, taking John Evans with him, they went to John Humphrey and told him " he had better burn all his bonds and mortgages than preserve them; that it would be much better for himself and his posterity, and this was the word of the Lord to him." The Friend then returned with John Evans, ate and drank, and rode home to Richland with a peaceful mind!

It will be observed that John Humphrey's son is called Humphrey Jones. This was following the ordinary Welsh usage of the time, keeping no family name, but changing it with each generation, by adopting as the surname the first name of the parent.[1] This custom existed among the Welsh immigrants, at the time of their arrival, and it was followed by them after coming, in a number of cases, though generally the English usage of preserving a family name was adopted. The five brothers Roberts (whose genealogy is elsewhere given in this volume), were the sons of Robert Cadwallader. John Griffith, of Merion (who married Edward Foulke's daughter Jane), and his brother, Evan Griffith, were the sons of Griffith John. The children of Evan Pugh of Gwynedd appear to have generally taken the name of Evan, and not Pugh; at any rate, the meeting records show the marriages of Jane Evan, daughter of Evan Pugh, in 1709; Hugh Evan, son of Evan Pugh (to Mary Robert, daughter of Robert John), in 1716; Catherine Evan, daughter of Evan Pugh, in 1717; and Cadwallader Evan, son of Evan Pugh, in 1722. The marriage lists

---

[1] Mr. Paxton Hood, in his Life of Cromwell, says Henry VIII., who, as a Tudor, might claim the right to advise, urged the Welsh strongly to abandon their custom, and adopt the family surname system of the English. But the Welsh were slow to give up national customs.

show several other instances: Edward Jones and Evan Jones, who both married daughters of Thomas Evans, of Gwynedd, were sons of John Evan, of Radnor; Robert Hugh, son of Hugh Griffith, is recorded as marrying, in 1717; Griffith Hugh, son of Hugh Griffith, in 1718; and John Roger, son of Roger Roberts (of Merion), in 1717.

A curious instance of the effect of this change of surname is seen in the case of the four brothers Evans, of Gwynedd, and the Owens, of Merion,—descendants of Robert and Jane. The father of the Evans brothers, and the father of Robert Owen, were brothers,—being the sons of Evan Robert Lewis, of Tron Goch, in Wales. They were named respectively Owen ap Evan, and Evan ap Evan, and the children of the former, having come to Pennsylvania, were known thereafter as Owens, while those of the latter were known as Evanses.

Humphrey Jones, John Humphrey's son, married, in 1719, Catharine, the daughter of William John. Her father was then deceased, having died in 1712. It seems likely that he was a man advanced in years, and older than his wife, Jane, for she survived until about 1740. The place of his residence is not certain, but Mr. Mathews thinks, and this is likely, that he lived at the place owned for many years by George W. Danehower, and occupied in recent times by Frank Myers, on the West Point road, just south-west of the toll-gate by Kneedler's. The house is old, and there are plain date marks upon it of the year 1712. It stands within the southern limit,—though very close to the line,—of William John's tract, and the probability is strong that it is William John's house; and though it will be noted that the year of its erection was the same year in which he died, yet as his will is dated in August, and proved in November, he may have been the man who built this house.[1]

---

[1] The date is cut in a stone near the peak of the western gable, and also in a stone close to the south door-way. The building is a two-story stone house with a wing kitchen. It has wide deep chimney-places, and one upper window,

Dwelling for a moment on William John and his family,—as they will not come into any of the genealogies hereafter to be given,— he was the richest man in the township, if we may judge by the size of his tract, which was nearly three times as large as any other. I cannot trace what relation he was, if any, to Robert John, or to Griffith John, of Merion,[1] but that they were related is indicated by the fact that in several instances they signed marriage certificates in a group,— a distinct evidence of relationship, as it was the usage for relatives of the marrying parties to sign by families, in the order of their nearness of connection.

William John had several children, including at least five daughters and one son, as follows:

1. Gwen, m., 1704, William Lewis, of Newtown, Chester county; d. before 1717-18, when her husband re-married.
2. Margaret, m., 1st, 1705, Robert Ellis, of Merion; and 2d, 1709, David Llewellyn, of Haverford, widower.
3. Gainor, m., 1714, Abraham Musgrave, "son of Thomas, late of Halifax, Yorkshire, Great Britain, yeoman, deceased."
4. Catharine, m., 1719, Humphrey Jones.
5. Ellin.
6. John, m. Margaret ———.

All these children were living at the time of William John's death, and they or their husbands are all named in his will. The son John, being appointed executor with the widow, Jane, may have been older than some of his sisters,— for instance, Gainor and Catharine, who were single then, and for some years after. To John was left 1400 acres of land with the dwelling,

---

in which the ancient sash have been allowed to remain, is filled with little panes of glass, six inches by two. There is some appearance that the wing kitchen was built earlier than the main dwelling, and tradition says that a log cabin, still earlier in date, stood a little distance to the southward, by a spring. A depression in the ground at this place is supposed to be the site of the cabin, which was no doubt the original home of William John and his family.

[1] John Humphrey's will indicates that he and William John were brothers-in-law.

plantation, etc., which the testator had made, life-right of one-half being reserved to the widow. To Gainor, Ellin, and Catharine was left the detached tract of 322 acres in the lower end of the township, adjoining Edward Foulke's, at Penllyn.

Next below William John's tract was that of Evan ap Hugh. His life in Gwynedd was brief. In May, 1703, he received the confirmatory patent for his land from Penn's commissioners, and on nearly the same date made his will.[1] His death occurred soon after. Of the 1068 acres which his tract proved to contain he had sold 454 (200 acres of it to Meredith David, and 150 to John Roberts), and by his will he divided the remaining 614 acres equally between his two sons, Hugh, the elder and "heir-at-law," and David, the younger. The will provided, however, that Hugh should have the end of the tract containing "the house and settlement" which the father had made. This house must have been just above North Wales, and on the eastern side of the turnpike, but the tract of Hugh, on which it stood, lay chiefly on the other side of the present road, extending for some distance, while the 307 acres that David got adjoined, and reached over to the line of Worcester townships. Both the brothers, in a few years, sold their tracts: Hugh his, in 1718, to Cadwallader Foulke (Edward's son), for 180 pounds; and David his to Humphrey Bate, who had married their mother, Ann, the widow of Evan ap Hugh.

The Bates, Humphrey and his wife, left the township, probably about 1720, and we find them recorded as of Philadelphia county; and in 1723 they, with David and Hugh Pugh, joined in a deed for David's tract to William Lewis, of Newtown, Chester county. This William was, no doubt, the one who married William John's daughter, Grace, as recorded above. She had, however, died before this purchase of 1723, and he had married, at Gwynedd meeting, in March, 1717-18, "Lowry

---

[1] The will is dated May 21, the patent May 22.

Jones, widow," whom I take to be Lowry, daughter of Thomas Evans, who in 1711 had married Evan Jones, son of John Evan, of Radnor.

Of Robert John, who owned the tract next below Evan ap Hugh, we know considerable, from the records. He was one of the richest of the first settlers, as is indicated by the character and extent of the inventory of his personal property at the time of his death, in 1732. My impression is that he had been in Merion, before 1698, and that he came from there to Gwynedd.[1] He was, it appears by his will, a nephew of Thomas Evans, and of Cadwallader Evans, for he appoints "my loving uncle Cadwallader Evans, [and] my cousins Evan Evans, Owen Evans [the sons of Thomas], John Jones, carpenter, and John Evans" [son of Cadwallader], to be overseers of his will. The relationships disclosed in this lead to the conjecture that Robert John was the son of Evan John, of Merion, who was brother to Reese John, and that Evan John's wife was the sister of the four Evans brothers. In this way Robert would be first cousin to John Jones, carpenter (son of Reese John), and to the sons of Thomas and Cadwallader Evans.

We know, further, that Robert John, of Gwynedd, married, in 1706, Gainor Lloyd, of Merion, widow, and that, at his death, in 1732, he left two children, John and Ellin. The records of Gwynedd meeting show:

1. John, b. 5th mo. 8th, 1707.
2. Ellin, b. 4th mo. 19th, 1709.

In his will, Robert John (now calling himself Jones) appoints his widow and his son John executors. He gives John "the plantation I now live on," containing 300 acres, and also

---

[1] A Robert John (but that it was the same I do not pretend to say) brought a certificate to Haverford meeting, 12th mo. 10, 1696, from Hendre Mawr meeting, in Merionethshire, Wales. At the same time Hugh Griffith, and children (who may have been, after all, the same that settled in Gwynedd in 1698), brought their certificate from the same place.

"all that part of the tract of land lately bought of Cadwallader Foulke, which lyeth the east side of the great road, containing by estimation about 185 acres," with its buildings and appurtenances.[1] To Ellin he leaves the remainder of the Cadwallader Foulke tract, "being divided from the other part by the great road, containing 150 acres." He also gives Ellin "one case and drawers, and the table belonging to the same, both standing in the new house[2] chamber."

Robert John, in the deed to him, by Cadwallader Foulke, is called "gentleman." He was a justice of the peace for many years, and was a member of the Provincial Assembly,—altogether a useful and excellent citizen.

Thomas Evan, whose house we have definitely located as on the site of the old Heist hotel (now Hartman's), had, besides daughters, who will be fully mentioned in the Evans Genealogy, four sons:

1. Robert, "of Merion," "eldest son and heir," d. 1754.
2. Hugh, "of Merion," d. 1771, aged 92.
3. Evan, of Gwynedd, preacher, b. 1684, d. 1747.
4. Owen, of Gwynedd, d. 1757.

Among these four sons, Thomas Evan seems to have divided up the whole of his tract, during his lifetime, and not many years after the first settlement. They had something like equal shares, and their lands lay in this order: Evan on the Whitpain line, then Robert, then Owen, then Hugh, reaching to the Montgomery line. (But Robert and Hugh and their father were concerned at different times in conveyances of the lands they held, and I have not thoroughly sifted out these

---

[1] This shows where it was that Evan ap Hugh, the first settler, had built his house,—*i. e.*, north-east of the line on which the "great road," now the turnpike, was subsequently laid out.

[2] Robert John's "new house" was no doubt where the borough of North Wales now is,—probably the Jacob Shearer (now Swartley) place, on the west side of the turnpike.

transactions.) The sale of 236 acres by the father to Evan took place in 1713; and in December, 1715, he made a deed for 306 acres to Owen. The latter's plot lay near the middle of the original great tract, the deed showing that it must have been on both sides of where the turnpike now is, and have included the Meredith farm (now Jonathan Lukens' estate), and part or all of that of Algernon S. Jenkins. On the south-western side was property of Robert Evan, and on the north-eastern that of Hugh Evan,— corresponding to the statement made above.

Of these four brothers, Evan and Owen lived and died in Gwynedd. The former, a preacher, will be referred to more fully in a subsequent chapter. Owen lived on the Meredith place, and I think the old house there, still standing, was built by him. It was very old, Margaret Meredith says, when her father, Dr. Joseph Meredith, bought it in 1814. Owen Evans was an active Friend, and has a short memorial in the John Smith manuscript collection. He was a store-keeper by occupation, was a justice of the peace, and for many years a member of the Provincial Assembly; was twice married, and died in 1757.

The other two sons, Robert and Hugh, appear to have lived mostly in Merion, where they both died. Both were men of considerable property. In deeds, 1705 and 1709, Robert is located "of Merion." Further details will be given concerning him and his brother Hugh in the chapter on the Evans Genealogy. Concerning their father, however, it may be here stated that in 1722 he married, for his second wife, Hannah Davies, of Goshen, Chester county. She was then a widow for the second time. Her first husband was Reese John, of Merion (the Reese John William repeatedly mentioned in this volume; by him she was the mother of John Jones, carpenter, of Montgomery, and other children); her second husband, whom she married about 1702, and who died about 1720, was Ellis David, of Goshen; and for her third she took, in 1722, our Gwynedd chief of the clan Evans. He was then 71 years old, and

THE FIRST SETTLERS' HOMES.

she 66.[1] After his marriage he removed to Goshen, and the Friends' records show the certificate of Gwynedd meeting, given for his removal, in which he is called "our antient friend Thomas Evans;" and while it speaks of him very highly, it adds that "many of us were more willing if he could find his way clear to have finished the remainder of his days where he was more conversant."

Thomas, however, lived out his span of life at Goshen. They made him an overseer of the meeting there, from 1735 to 1737; in 1738, the 12th of 10th month, he died, aged 87 years. His widow survived him until 9th mo. 29th, 1741, when she died, aged 85. Her will is on record in Philadelphia, and she leaves bequests to her several children, and to various other persons.[2]

---

[1] His son Hugh had married her daughter Lowry.
[2] See further details in the Jones Genealogy, *post*.

IX.

Establishment of the Friends' Meeting.

IN any narrative of the early life of Gwynedd, the Friends' meeting occupies a conspicuous place. It and the first settlement are associated in all the old accounts. The meeting place is substantially as old as the township; the erection of the meeting-house was almost the first object of the people's common efforts; and for three-quarters of a century it was the only place of public worship within the township. Located at the geographical centre, for the common convenience, it was the centre, likewise, of the most important and serious interests of the community. These fervently religious people held sacred their house of worship, but, besides, it was dear to them as the place where they celebrated their simple but solemn ceremonials of marriage, and where, with repressed but not the less strong sorrow, they committed the remains of their dead to the final rest. Closely attached to each other, not only as countrymen whose race feeling is proverbial, but by ties of kindred which made them almost a single family, they formed in the beginning a singularly compact and united body, and when they gathered at the meeting-house, it was a re-union of members whose interests, feelings, and ideas were all in common. The First-day morning gathering, the exhortation by Robert Evans, or his brother Cadwallader; the greetings when meeting broke, the chat outside, under the white-oaks and buttonwoods, made a most important feature in the quiet life of the little community; while the visit of Friends from Merion or Plymouth, with a sermon by Hugh Roberts, Ellis Pugh, or Rowland Ellis, was

ESTABLISHMENT OF FRIENDS' MEETING. 73

an experience awakening its special interest; and such extraordinary occasions as an appointed meeting by a famous preacher,— Thomas Chalkley, or John Fothergill, perhaps,— were events that stirred it to its depths.

The minute-book of Gwynedd monthly meeting begins in 1714, with several minutes, reciting the authority (from Haverford monthly and Philadelphia quarterly meetings) for organizing the new monthly meeting, and it also gives the following historical account:

"This place hath been originally settled by the present inhabitants, most of them yet living, and called by the name of Gwynedd township, in the latter end of the year 1698, and beginning of the year 1699. The Principal Settlers and Purchasers among others were William Jones, Thomas Evans, Robert Evans, Owen Evans, Cadwallader Evans, Hugh Griffith, John Hugh, Edward Foulke, John Humphrey, and Robert Jones. Amongst all those concern'd in this settlem't, there were but few particulars that publickly appeared for Truth before they came from their Native Country, though several among them were convinced and had a Secret Love to Truth and Its followers, and soon after gave Obedience & Gradually Joined in a new Society. These few mentioned, with the first Conveniency often met together to wait upon the Lord, at the houses of John Hugh and John Humphrey, until more were added to their numbers.

"In the year 1700, two years after our arrival in this land, a Meeting House was Built, and meetings kept therein by the Consent and approbation of Haverford Monthly Meeting, unto which we at first Joyn'd ourselves, and under whose care we were for a time.

"And finding our number to Increase, and Truth prevail, it was thought necessary to Build a new Meeting House, which was erected in 1712, and on the 19th of the Ninth Month in the same year the first meeting of worship was held therein.

"Our numbers still Increasing by many adjacent Settlers Coming in, and a young Generation arising, and not having the opportunity of a Monthly Meeting of worship amongst ourselves, for the benefit of the People in General, more especially the young and rising Generation, yt are not so well acquainted with the Discipline of Truth, a Consideration arose in the minds of Fr'ds belonging to Gwynedd and Plymouth Meetings, and a religious concern to have the same settled among us, and in order thereto profess'd their Inclination to Haverford Monthly Meeting for their approbation. The which was obtained, Together with the Concurrence of the Quarterly Meeting att Philadelphia, and immediately was put In practice."

This minute contains the substance of the history of the meeting, from the arrival of the settlers until 1714, but some further details may conveniently be added. The following is from the records of Philadelphia Monthly Meeting:—

10th mo. 4th, 1699. Rowland Ellis, in behalf of Haverford Monthly Meeting, having acquainted this meeting that several Welsh people, Friends and others, are lately settled on ye East side of Scuylkill, in this county, about 20 miles off from this place, who for some time have had a First day's meeting by ye advice and consent of ye sd meeting of Haverford, which is also a Third day's weekly meeting, being brought hither for ye concurrence of the meeting, is approved, and in regard ye said people understand not ye English tongue, they desired to be joyned to Haverford Monthly Meeting for ye present, which is also approved of."

Minutes on the Haverford records are as follows:

1699.— There is a General Meeting appointed at Gwynedd, the second weekly Third-day [*i. e.* the second Tuesday] of every month, at the desire of Friends there.

1703.— Gwynedd Friends desire their Preparative Meeting removed from their General Meeting day to the last Third-day in the month ; which was approved.

1714.— At the Monthly Meeting held at Radnor meeting-house, the 9th day of the 10th month, it is left for further consideration what time to appoint the monthly meetings of Gwynedd and Plymouth; which was left to the appointment of this meeting by the Quarterly Meeting [of Philadelphia].

Gwynedd and Plymouth Friends, after consideration what day is suitable for their Monthly Meeting, propose the last Third-day in every month ; which this meeting acquiesces with.

But, returning to the time of the settlers' arrival, it must be understood that most of them were not then avowed Quakers. The language of the first minute quoted above is that there were "but few" who had publicly appeared as such, before coming over, though "several" had been "convinced," and

ESTABLISHMENT OF FRIENDS' MEETING. 75

had "a secret love" for the Friends, etc. Of those who composed the "few" we are left uncertain, beyond the names of John Hugh and John Humphrey, but I am inclined to think that Hugh Griffith was another. The other settlers were still nominally members of the Established Church of England. It therefore resulted that at first the Friends met for religious service (as is stated in the minute) at the houses of John Hugh and John Humphrey; while the others held a meeting on each Sabbath at the house of Robert Evans. The latter had no ordained minister, but Cadwallader Evans in part supplied the place of one by reading to them, as tradition says, from his Welsh Bible,— but, as very easily may have been, from the Church service-book itself.[1] This meeting must have been composed, for some time, of a considerable number of persons, for it included most of the colony. In the winter's cold, next after their arrival, it is reasonable to presume that they crowded as best they could inside Robert's dwelling, but as the warmer days of spring came on, it may be believed that they found seats without, where upon the meadow bank that descends from the house to the rivulet below, the Sabbath sun shone down upon them, and as he read, lighted the pages of Cadwallader's book.

Precisely how long this meeting was maintained is not certain, but probably not more than a year. When the first Friends' meeting-house was built, in 1700, it would appear that all joined in the work. The story is well known how, according to tradition, the two bodies of worshipers were united, though there have been, at times, somewhat different

---

[1] The Welsh Bibles of that day had prefixed a number of pages containing the Church of England services. Dr. J. J. Levick has the Bible of Thomas Jones, of Merion (son of John ap Thomas), and it is of this sort. It was "Printeedig yⁿ Llundain gan John Bill, Christopher Barker, Thomas Newcomb, a Henry Hills, Printyr," in 1678; and Cadwallader's volume was probably one of the same.

versions of it, Jesse Foulke, of Penllyn, the great-grandson of Edward, the immigrant, seems to be our best authority. He was born in 1742, and had the society, until he grew to manhood, of his grandfather, Thomas Foulke,— who was nearly grown up, at the time of the settlement, and who lived until 1762, and who could have given Jesse details concerning the early experiences of the settlers. Jesse's account[1] was this:

"But, as Cadwallader Evans himself related, he was going as usual to his brother Robert's, when, passing near to the road to Friends' meeting, held at John Hugh's and John Humphrey's, it seemed as if he was impressed 'to go down and see how the Quakers do.' This he mentioned to his friends at the close of their own meeting, and they all agreed to go to the Friends the next time; where they were all so well satisfied that they never again met in their own worship."

The other form of the story is that one of the brothers Evans was passing near a gathering at which William Penn was preaching, and that, hearing his voice, he paused to listen, and, being deeply impressed, brought over his meeting to the Friends.[2]

But it would be altogether unreasonable to attach very great weight to either of these stories. The first is the more likely,—the second being open to serious criticisms relating to dates, etc. The fact is that the settlement was made under the auspices and by the influence of the Welsh Friends, and must have been from the outset thoroughly sympathetic with them. Its close relationships of all kinds with the Merion Welsh, who were generally Friends, the leadership of Hugh Roberts in the immigration, and facts known concerning the religious inclinations of the settlers,— *e.g.*, Edward Foulke and his wife,— go to show that it was an easy and natural step

---

[1] Watson's Annals, Vol. II., p. 78.
[2] *Ibid.*, p. 79.

ESTABLISHMENT OF FRIENDS' MEETING. 77

for all to unite in one religious body. As to Robert Evans, indeed, the memorial of him by Gwynedd monthly meeting says that "*some time before he left his native country he forsook the national worship, and went to Friends' meetings*, and soon after his arrival entered into close fellowship with Friends." And, as all accounts agree that it was at his house that the settlers who were churchmen assembled, it will be seen how unlikely it was that there was any considerable distance of religious opinion to be traversed between them and the others who were Friends. Robert and Cadwallader no doubt led them over, and the precise manner of the change may easily have been according to the Jesse Foulke tradition.

The first meeting-house, built in 1700, was of logs. It must have been small. It stood on the site of the present house. The ground was part of the tract of Robert Evans. It is nearly the highest spot in the township, and almost exactly in the township's geographical centre. The place was then covered with the original forest, but standing on such an elevation, and looking away to the south and south-east, a beautiful view must then have been enjoyed, as now it is, of the valley lands of the townships below, and of the distant slopes of Chestnut Hill. The height, the prospect, the forest-clad hill-sides, were all elements in the situation agreeable to the Welshmen, natives of a hill country, and lovers of the picturesque.

The second meeting-house, completed in 1712, was of stone, and much larger than the first. It stood, also, upon the same site as the present one, and was torn down when the latter was erected, in 1823. The subscription paper for its erection, long preserved in the family of Edward Foulke's descendants, was in Welsh, with the dates 1710–11, and had sixty-six signers, headed by William John and Thomas Evans. The sums given by each ranged from eleven pounds down to one pound, and aggregated about two hundred. Joseph Foulke, in his Journal, says :

"Hugh Griffith assisted in building the meeting-house, in the years 1711–12. The subscription paper, the preamble of which is in the Welsh language, is yet in our possession ; some of the members contributed as much as the worth of one hundred bushels of wheat in that day. The house they erected was a permanent commodious stone building, with two galleries for the youth, and several principal rafters in a hip-roof, firmly united, so that taking it down in 1823, in order to build a new house, we found no small difficulty in separating the ancient woodwork."

At the time of establishing the monthly meeting, in 1714, Gwynedd must have become a strong meeting. The Friends at Plymouth were not so numerous. The monthly meeting was held at Gwynedd entirely, those from Plymouth attending there. This arrangement continued until 1719, when it was agreed to hold the monthly meeting at Plymouth four times a year,—in the 3d, 6th, 9th, and 12th months.

Before 1714 all the records concerning the Gwynedd Friends — including marriages, births, deaths, removals, etc.— were kept in the Haverford books; after that time, the Gwynedd monthly meeting books preserved such records. The marriage list in the latter begins with the two weddings of 6th month (August) 25th, when two of the Evans daughters, first cousins,— Sarah, the daughter of Thomas, and Ann, daughter of Robert,— married two bridegrooms from the Welsh Tract, beyond Schuylkill,— Edward Jones, son of John Evans, of Radnor, and William Roberts, son of Edward, of Merion. These marriages took place, as was the usage, in the meeting-house, in the presence of a large assembly; and though many others had already been solemnized there (under authority of Haverford monthly meeting) we can easily believe that this was regarded as a remarkable occasion. It needs little imagination to picture the stir the double wedding would cause in the settlement, or how lively a topic of conversation it must have made

ESTABLISHMENT OF FRIENDS' MEETING.

from the hills of Gwynedd away to the farthest farm-houses of Radnor and Haverford; nor is it difficult to see the two young wives, mounting on horseback behind their husbands, and riding down by the rude road through Plymouth, to the ford over the Schuylkill, at Spring Mill, with curious but not unkind eyes gazing upon the cavalcade from every cabin that stood along the way.

The following further extracts from the early minutes of Gwynedd monthly meeting will present some additional facts of interest:

11th mo. 22, 1714-15. It is agreed that the monthly meeting for Gwynedd and Plymouth meetings is to be called by the name of Gwynedd Monthly Meeting, to be held the last Third-day in every month, unless occation appear for another day.

John Evans is appointed by this meeting to be clerk for ye same. Edward Foulke and Robert Jones overseers.

2d mo. 26, 1715. Perquioman [Upper Providence] Friends are granted liberty until the 9th month next, to hold a meeting on the first First-day of every other month.

5th mo. 26, 1715. Perquioman ffrds proposed for Liberty to Build a meeting-house and settle a Burying-Ground: the matter is referred to further consideration.— [Next month:] the matter being considered, Liberty as to the burying-place at present is only granted.

2d mo. 25, 1725. Gwynedd First-day morning meeting to begin at 10 o'clock, by reason of ye afternoon meetting being held at several places.

1722. This meeting hath had in Consideration afternoon meetings, & it is agreed yt our first-day morning's meetting begin at 10 o'clock, and in the afternoon at 4 o'clock.

1725. Gwynedd Friends acquainted this meetting [*i.e.* the monthly meeting, which included also Plymouth and Richland] "of their necessity to enlarge their meeting-house," and inquired whether they might take subscriptions from 'such as are frequenters' of the meeting. The latter question, "after some discourse is referred to ye Quarterly Meetting att Philadelphia;" [and in the month following the report was made that the matter was left by the quarterly to the discretion of the monthly meeting.]

10th mo. 28, 1725. Gwynedd Friends have agreed with John Cadwalader, John Jones, and John Evans to perform ye enlargement of their meeting-house.

4th mo. 29, 1725. The Friends at Swamp [Richland, Bucks county] are granted leave to hold a Preparative Meeting.

1721. John Rumford, from Haverford, and George Boone, from Abington, [present themselves] in order to joyn themselves to this meeting. " The said Friends also requested the concurrence of this meeting to fix a Convenient place for a burial, and liberty to build a Meeting-House thereon to accommodate the few Friends residing in them parts." [This refers to the establishment of the meeting at Oley, Berks county. A little later, on the records, we have mention of " John Rumford, att Oley."]

5th mo. 27, 1725. Friends at Oley granted a Preparative Meeting.

1725. Our Friends at ye Swamp moved att this meetting their necessity to settle a Burying-Ground, that by ye meetting being too rocky; desiring assistance [etc.]. A committee is appointed to consult with them and endeavor to settle a place. [Next month:] The Frds appointed last meeting to assist Swamp Frds, having visited ye place proposed by them, Also concluding in some convenient time ye meeting-house may be removed there, They think it a proper place, and most of ye Frds residing there approve of it, and also this meeting does, too.

7th mo. 27, 1726. A Youths' Meeting is appointed on ye second Third-day of 2d and 8th months.

The quarterly meeting to which the Friends at Gwynedd originally belonged was that of Philadelphia. It was not until 1786 that Abington Quarter, composed of the monthly meetings of Abington, Horsham, Gwynedd, and Richland, was established. This is now (1884) held at four several places once a year: at Abington in the second month, Horsham in the fifth, Gwynedd in the eighth, and Byberry in the eleventh.

From Gwynedd monthly meeting, after its establishment in 1714, other monthly meetings were presently set out. The Friends at Richland, increasing in numbers, and finding it a long distance to come to Gwynedd, had a monthly meeting granted them in 1742. In 1737, the settlement of Friends at Oley, which looked to Gwynedd as its parent, was allowed a monthly meeting. The Friends' settlement at Providence, (called commonly Perkiomen in the early records, and with

the name spelled variously) was also an offshoot from Gwynedd, and Providence meeting, until it was "laid down," some fifteen years ago, belonged to Gwynedd Monthly Meeting. A minute, in 1723, of appointments of persons to keep "true accounts of births and burials," names "Hugh Foulke and John Jones, for Gwynedd meeting, John Rees for Plymouth, George Boone for Oley, Andrew Cramer for Perquioman; none from the Swamp [Richland] being present."

The present meeting-house, much larger than that of 1712, was built in 1823. At the time of its erection, the number of members and others who habitually attended warranted so large a house, but the time is long since past when its benches are filled, except upon very extraordinary occasions. For a number of years it has been the custom to open only half the house — the southern end — on First-days, and even this is more than sufficient for the congregations that usually assemble.

X.

Details Concerning the Early Friends.

THE Friends' meeting was strong in numbers, from the time when all the settlers joined in it, but it was, besides, strong in the character of its membership. The attendance, frequently, of Ellis Pugh and Rowland Ellis, from Plymouth, and the ministry of those who belonged to Gwynedd particular meeting, made the gathering here one of religious life and vigor. "From the first establishment of Gwynedd meeting," says John Comly in his *Friends' Miscellany*,[1] "we notice many Friends, remarkable for great integrity and uprightness, and of deep religious experience."

At first, Robert and Cadwallader Evans were the only preachers. The former perhaps was not so strong a man, intellectually, as the latter, and from the fact that Cadwallader was the reader in the early Sabbath gatherings, we infer the superiority of his education. But both were men of weight, and both deeply respected in the community. Samuel Smith, in his *History of Pennsylvania*, speaks of "Robert and Cadwallader Evans, two brothers, who stood faithful not only in word and doctrine, but their exemplary lives and conversations, and their services among their neighbors, rendered their memories precious to many, though they could neither read nor write in any but the Welsh language."

---

[1] Vol. III., p. 371.

The sermons of both brothers were doubtless delivered in Welsh; this is indicated by Rowland Ellis's statement in Philadelphia Monthly Meeting, quoted in the preceding chapter. In the manuscript collection of memorials, made by John Smith, of Burlington, there is one of Gwynedd Monthly Meeting concerning Robert Evans. Mentioning his birth in Wales, his emigration, and settlement in Gwynedd, it says:

"Some time before he left his native country he forsook the national worship, and went to Friends' meetings, and soon after his arrival he entered into close fellowship and union with Friends. He was a very diligent frequenter of our meetings. * * * * He had a gift in the ministry which was well received, as it was chiefly remarks on his own experience in religion * * * *."

Robert died in the 1st month (March), 1738, and Thomas Chalkley, in his Journal, says: "I was at the burial of Robert Evan, of North Wales. He was upward of four score years of age, and one of the first settlers there;—a man who lived and died in the love of God and of his neighbors, of whom I believe it might be truly said, as our Saviour said of Nathaniel, 'Behold an Israelite indeed, in whom there is no guile.' He was a minister of Christ, full of divine and religious matter."

The printed volume of Memorials published in 1787 by the Yearly Meeting of Philadelphia (frequently referred to in this volume) contains twelve memorials from Gwynedd Monthly Meeting, three of them referring to Friends — Ellis Pugh, Rowland Ellis, and William Trotter — who belonged to Plymouth particular meeting. The other nine were of Gwynedd,— Cadwallader Evans, Evan Evans, Alice Griffith, Ann Roberts, John Evans, Jane Jones, Ellen Evans, Mary Evans, and William Foulke. In the John Smith manuscript collections there are several more memorials,— of Robert Evans, just quoted, Owen Evans, Rowland Roberts, Margaret Jones, John Humphrey, and others.

In relation to Cadwallader Evans, the memorial in the printed volume[1] says: "He was a diligent and seasonable attender of our religious meetings. On First-days particularly he was ready an hour before the time appointed, and then read several chapters in the Bible or some religious book; as the time approached he would frequently observe the time of day, and by means of such watchful care he was seated in meetings one of the first, and scarcely ever after the time appointed. * * He received a gift in the ministry, in the exercise whereof he was generally led to speak of his own experience in religion and the Christian warfare; and his testimony, though short, was instructive, lively, and manifestly attended with divine sweetness. Notwithstanding it was always acceptable, he was very cautious of appearing, lest any, as he often said, should be drawn from a right concern of mind, to place their dependence on words." The memorial further speaks of his usefulness "in many services of the church, especially that weighty one of visiting Friends in their families," and says his endeavors "in that skillful and tender office of healing discord in private families were remarkably successful. In such services he spent much of the latter part of his life, riding about from one house to another; and where no cause of reprehension appeared, he interspersed his discourse on common affairs with useful hints, solid remarks, and lessons of instruction; but where admonition or comfort was necessary, the propriety of his advice, and the uprightness of his life, added weight to his labors and seldom failed of good effects. * * * It was his practice, in winter evenings especially, to read the holy scriptures in his family, and was particularly careful that neither child nor servant should be from home at unseasonable hours, being highly sensible how slippery the paths of youth are, and how numerous the snares which attend them."

It is evident, however, that both Robert and Cadwallader

---

[1] Collection of 1787, p. 130.

DETAILS CONCERNING THE EARLY FRIENDS.

were not frequent or extended in their communications. They were exhorters rather than preachers. The memorial in relation to Ann Roberts (wife of Rowland), says "her first coming among us [1705-10] was seasonable, for we having few ministers, the field before her was extensive, in which she labored fervently."

A little later, other ministers appeared. Prominent among these were two of the second generation — Evan Evans, son of Thomas, and John Evans, son of Cadwallader. From the memorial of the latter, from which I shall presently quote more at length, it seems he must have appeared as a minister about 1712-13, and a passage in the Journal of Jane Hoskens,[1] who, from 1712 to 1716, was a teacher in Friends' families at Plymouth, gives us the impression of a religious awakening during that period. She says:

"About this time, the Lord was graciously pleased to renew his merciful invitation unto the Friends and inhabitants of North Wales and Plymouth. Many of the youth were reached. * * Several were called to the work of the ministry. * * Among the many others favored was our dear and well-beloved friend and brother, John Evans, who was blessed with an excellent gift in the ministry * * * * ."

Concerning John Evans, the memorial[2] says he was "a man of good natural understanding, and favoured early in life to see the necessity of a diligent attention to the voice of Divine wisdom. In the twenty-third year of his age [he was born in 1689] he appeared in the ministry. * * * He had a clear engaging manner of delivery, was deep in heavenly mysteries, and

---

[1] See her Journal, at length, in *Friends' Miscellany*, Vol. III. Jane was an interesting character. She was a young girl, who had come over from London under trying circumstances, and who, in Philadelphia, to pay her passage money, engaged herself for four years as teacher. She began to preach when about 21.

[2] Collection of 1787, p. 175.

plain in declaring them; being well acquainted with the holy scriptures, he was made skillful in opening the doctrines therein contained, and was often led to draw lively and instructive similitudes from the visible creation. He traveled through most of the northern colonies in the service of truth, and several times through this province. He was often drawn to attend general meetings, funerals, and other public occasions, particularly the adjacent meetings after their first establishment.   *   *   *
He was a zealous promoter of visiting Friends in their families, was many times engaged therein, and his labors were awakening and useful; often employ'd in visiting the sick, the widow, and the fatherless and others in affliction; on these occasions he was seldom large in expression, but his silent sympathy and secret breathing for their relief was more consolatory than many words; a considerable part of his time was spent in assisting widows, and the guardianship of orphans, which, though laborious to him, was of much advantage to them."

John Evans died in September, 1756, his ministry having covered about fifty-four years. He was undoubtedly one of the strongest and most influential characters of his time. His cousin Evan probably began to preach a little later than he, but the two for many years were closely associated. Amongst the minutes from the monthly meeting records there are indications of this, and in the memorial of Evan it is said of the two men that "their friendship was pure, fervent, and lasting as their lives, and their separation a wound to the latter [John Evans], the remembrance of which he never wholly survived. They travelled together through many of these colonies in the service of the ministry."

Some extracts from the monthly meeting records may here be presented:

1722. A certificate for Evan Evans, John Evans, Hugh Foulk, and Ellis Hugh, ministers, in order to recommend them to ye Quarterly Meetting of Ministers and Elders att Philadelphia, was read and approved.

1722. Application being made on behalf of Margaret Jones for a few Lines to ye Quarterly Meeting of Ministers, to signifie our unity with her ministry [a committee was appointed].

1723. Evan and John Evans laid before this Meetting a concern they had to visitt some meetings in the Jerseys. They both being young and pretty much unknown they laid it to Consideration whether it be proper to have a few lines with 'em.

1723. Our friend Ann Roberts having returned from her visit to North Carolina and Virginia produced two certificates, which was read and well received.

1724. Hugh Foulke acquainted this meeting a concern lay upon his mind to visit Frds at Long Island. [Rowland Ellis and Cadwallader Evans were appointed to draw a certificate for him.]

1725, 6th mo. 31st. Sarah Davis laid before this Meeting her Concern to visit Frds in Maryland and ye adjacent parts of this Province. [This approved, and in 12th mo. following:] Sarah Davis produced a certificate of her travels in Maryland which was read and received.

30th of ye 9th mo., 1725. It is agreed y^t ye Meeting of Ministers signifie on the behalf of our friends Cadwallader Evans, Row. Robert, Andrew Dean, and Mary Foulke, y^t ye few words dropt by them is in a general way well received.

5th mo. 26th, 1726. It is agreed here with ye concurrence of ye Women's Meeting, that Alice Griffith, Ellin David, and Ellin Evans be constituted and appointed Elders and Assistants in ye affairs of ye ministry.

At precisely what time it was that the meeting was strongest in ministers I am not able to say, but probably between 1725 and 1745. Joseph Foulke in his manuscript Journal speaks of its strength in early times, and says:

"I have heard my parents say that at one time fourteen approved ministers belonged to the [monthly?] meeting, and when the Yearly Meeting was held at Burlington, N. J., the late George Dillwyn remarked that in his youthful days North Wales was called 'the school of the prophets.'"

From the Journal of John Fothergill,[1] of England, we get

---

[1] This John Fothergill (b. 1676; d. 1744), himself an eminent preacher, had two distinguished sons,—Dr. John Fothergill (1712-1780), the physician, of London; and Samuel Fothergill (——-1773), a preacher among Friends. Dr. Fothergill was one of the most successful physicians of his age; he had an income of

some glimpses of the Friends at Gwynedd, about this time. In 1721, accompanied by Lawrence King, he was visiting meetings in America, and we find the following passages in his Journal:

"The 10th of 11th mo. [January] we had a Meeting at Buckingham, and went the 11th to North Wales, where we lodged at John Evan's, and had a good Meeting that Evening with a large Number of Friends who came to see us. The 12th, being accompanied by several of those and some other Friends, we went to a new settled Place called Great Swamp, and tho' the Snow was deep and the Frost very severe, yet thro' the Lord's Goodness we got well through, and had a good little Meeting with some Friends and other People who came in that Evening at Peter Leicester's. The 14th we were [again] at the Meeting at North Wales, which was very large, several other Professors coming in, and the Gospel was preached in its own Authority and Wisdom, and was exalted in many souls, [etc.] We had another Meeting that Evening at the House of Hugh Foulke, which was much to our Satisfaction. The 15th we had a meeting at Plymouth * * and the 16th we were at North Wales meeting again: a large solidly edifying Meeting it was. * * The 17th we had a meeting at Horsham * * * We lodged that night at William Stockdale's, where we had some good service in the Love of the Truth that Evening, among a pretty many Friends."

His Journal continues (after mentioning visits to meetings in New Jersey and the neighborhood of Philadelphia):

"The 17th [of 12th mo., February] we had a Meeting in the Baptist Meeting-house near *Skippolk* [Skippack?], at the Request of some of them, where the Lord * * gave us a comfortable Time to General Satisfaction. We parted lovingly, and came that Night to Evan Evans's, at North Wales, and were the 18th at Friends' Meeting there, which was large, and it being First-day we had another in the Evening."

In 1736, John Fothergill made another visit to this country, and was again at Gwynedd. His Journal says:

"The 27th [of 10th mo., December] I set out again into the Country, and had a Meeting that Day at Plymouth, and a large one the Day

---

£7,000, and he left an estate of £80,000, with part of which he endowed the well-known Friends' School at Ackworth, in Yorkshire. Both he and his brother Samuel wrote several treatises and books.

following at North Wales (it being their Monthly meeting for Business), wherein we were comforted together." * * * [In the following year, having in the meantime visited numerous meetings throughout the country, he was at Goshen, near the end of the 8th month (October), and says: "I went from there to North Wales, and was at two meetings there, wherein Divine Goodness was manifested."]

Returning to our notice of Evan Evans, we find him mentioned by John Churchman as "a grave and solid Friend." Gwynedd Monthly Meeting's memorial[1] speaks of him strongly. One or two passages have already been cited. It says "he was favored with an excellent gift in the ministry, which he exercised in solemn dread and reverence. * * * Besides his travels through many of the colonies, he also frequently visited the several counties in this province, and more particularly many of the adjacent meetings in their infancy; wherein his unwearied labours of love tended much to their comfort, growth, and establishment in the truth." The memorial alludes to his usefulness in the administration of the Society's discipline, and to his consistency of conduct in private life; it adds that "he was abroad in the service of truth when attacked with his last illness; and as the disorder was slow and tedious, he attended several meetings in the fore part thereof," etc. He was about 63 years old when he died,—July 24th, 1747.

Alice Griffith, the wife of Hugh Griffith, is also amongst those who have a memorial in the 1787 Collection. It says that "being a woman of great integrity and uprightness of heart, she became very serviceable in divers respects; zealous for maintaining good order and Christian discipline in the church. She was well qualified for that weighty service of visiting families, having at such opportunities to communicate of her own experience; * * * and * * * would often be drawn forth in opening divine mysteries, as if she had been

---

[1] Collection of 1787, p. 137.

in a large assembly, as many witnesses can testify that have been sensibly reached,— yea, baptized by her religious visits." The language of the memorial does not convey the impression that she was a minister, except in the sense just presented. It speaks of her concern to stir up Friends "to a close attendance of meetings both on First and other days, as also to observe the hour appointed, being herself a good example therein, until, by old age and infirmity of body, she was disabled, which was about three years before her removal." She died April 1st, 1749, but the memorial does not state her age.

William Trotter, whose memorial from Gwynedd Monthly Meeting is also in the Collection of 1787, was a minister at Plymouth. He died on the 19th of 8th month, 1750, aged about 53 years and 6 months. It may be presumed that he was, occasionally at least, an attendant and minister at Gwynedd.

Ann Roberts, who died on the 9th of 4th month, 1740, was a native of Wales, and had been a minister for fifty years. (She was seventy-three at her death.) She was a widow, Ann Bennett, of Abington, when she married Rowland Roberts, and . removed to Gwynedd. The memorial of Gwynedd Monthly Meeting, in the 1787 Collection, says: "Her first coming to reside among us was seasonable, for we having but few ministers, the field before her was extensive, in which she labored fervently," etc. Her usefulness in drawing out younger ministers is noted, and it is added that "she went pretty much abroad, visiting Friends in this and the adjacent provinces, to-wit, the Jerseys, Maryland, Virginia, and Carolina, accompanied to the remotest parts by her near and dear friend Susanna Morris. In her more advanced years she visited Great Britain, accompanied by our esteemed friend Mary Pennel * * *
After her return she met with great difficulties in respect to her outward circumstances, which she sustained with Christian fortitude.   *   *   *   After this, she met with a very heavy

affliction in the loss of her husband, which she likewise bore with becoming resignation," etc. She suffered from the dropsy near the close of her life.

Other memorials are given in the Collection of 1787 concerning Jane Jones, the wife of John Jones, "carpenter," of Montgomery; Ellen Evans, the wife of John Evans, and daughter of Rowland Ellis; Mary Evans, the wife of Owen Evans; and William Foulke, the son of Thomas. John Comly remarks, in *Friends' Miscellany*, what is very noticeable to any careful reader of these and the other memorials referred to, that they are written with unusual merits of composition. He says that "the order, the originality, and perspicuity displayed in these documents furnish a lively evidence of the literary qualifications of the Friends of Gwynedd and Plymouth,"—and the candid reader who is at all in sympathy with their subject matter, must admit that this praise is fairly bestowed.

Jane Jones, Ellen Evans, and William Foulke were valued members, as is clearly apparent from their memorials, but they were not ministers. Mary, the wife of Owen Evans, was born in Philadelphia in 1695, and married Owen in 1736. She died in 1769. Her memorial says[1] "Her public appearances were not very frequent, but when she spoke her testimony was fervent, sound, and edifying * * * She was several times drawn forth in the love of the Gospel to visit Friends in most of the provinces on this continent, also the island of Tortola, which she undertook with the unity of her friends at home, and returned with clear and satisfactory accounts of her labors amongst those whom she visited."

Of Margaret Jones, there is a brief extract from the monthly meeting memorial in the John Smith manuscripts. It says "she received a precious share of Gospel ministry * * * And altho' the latter part of her life was attended with many

---

[1] Collection of 1787, p. 276.

trials and afflictions, nevertheless we believe she held her integrity to the end." Margaret was the wife of John Jones, the son of William John. She died in April, 1743, and was buried at Germantown.

It is impossible to study the records of this early period of the colony's experience without being impressed with the evident strength of character and the sincere religious nature of those who composed it. The tendencies and convictions of the people of Gwynedd, at that time, were obviously those of a simple and sincere body of Christians, closely united in feeling, and maintaining in an unusual degree the primitive virtues of life.

XI.

Narrative of John Humphrey, of Merion.

THE following document refers entirely to occurrences in Wales,—chiefly hardships experienced by the Friends, at certain periods, on account of their religious views. Its relation to the history of Gwynedd, it must be admitted, is not direct. But many of the incidents and details which it embodies concern persons who make a part of this history, and it throws light upon the character of the Welsh people who settled in Merion and Gwynedd, and upon their manner of life in the old country. The document, I believe, has never been printed; I obtained it from a copy preserved amongst the papers of the late Lewis Jones, of Gwynedd.[1] (In Besse's *Sufferings of Friends* some of the incidents here related at length will be found briefly mentioned, but most of the document is unique.)

John Humphrey, who left this account, was not the early Gwynedd settler of that name, as might reasonably be presumed, but another person altogether, and probably not even a kinsman. He was John Humphrey, "of Merion." He came to Pennsylvania in 1683, amongst the first of the Welsh immigrants, and had a considerable tract of land in what is now Lower Merion, directly adjoining the Haverford line. He was a personal friend of Thomas Lloyd, the associate of Penn, and Deputy Governor, and upon the occasion of Thomas's death, in 1694, sent to his brother Charles Lloyd, of Dolobran, Wales,[2]

---

[1] Lewis, I conclude, was the great-great-grandson of Rees John, repeatedly mentioned in John Humphrey's narrative.

[2] The Lloyds were persons of education and wealth. Details concerning them, their family descent, etc., may conveniently be consulted in Keith's *Provincial Councillors of Pennsylvania.*

a well-expressed and impressive letter of condolence, a copy of which is also preserved in the Lewis Jones manuscript, but which I do not think it necessary to reproduce.

John Humphrey[1] was evidently a person of considerable intelligence, and of more than the average education of his time. His Narrative, though quaint, is always perspicuously, and often strongly, composed; and his acquaintance with English was so unusually good, for a Welshman of his period, that he translated into English words and rhyme, Thomas Ellis's "Song of Rejoicing," a Welsh poem of three stanzas.[2]

John Humphrey left no children. But many persons of the same family name are descended from the sons of his brother Samuel.[3]

A Brief Narative of the Sufferings of the Christian People called Quakers at Llwyn Grwill in Merioneth Shire, North Wales, Great Brittain, by John Humphrey.

In the year 1661 our sufferings in Llwyn Grwill was very Cruel, our Persecutors driving us out of our Religious Meetings, and putting us in a Pennfold by the Highway side, while they were drinking and making Merry over us, and over the witness of God in themselves, and in a

---

[1] He came over in 1683, with his wife Joan, and appears to have been, then, of Llwundu, in Merionethshire. Their certificate from the Quarterly meeting of Merionethshire attests that he had been a friend for 23 years (*i. e.* since about 1660, as indicated in his Narrative), that he was faithful in times of great suffering, and that his house "was a free receptacle for Friends." It describes him, also as "a minister, of few words, according to his measure." He died in Merion, on the 28th of 7th month, 1699, aged 66 years. His will was dated in 1699 and published in 1700. His wife had died in 1698. His will shows his interest in literature by a legacy for reprinting an old Welsh book or tract, and he proves his kindly disposition by numerous gifts of remembrance to children of friends and neighbors.

[2] It is given by Dr. Smith, in his *History of Delaware County.* Thomas Ellis was an early settler in Haverford, and a prominent citizen, serving for some time as Register General of the Province. He died in 1688.

[3] Some details as to this family will be found farther on, in a foot-note to the Narrative.

JOHN HUMPHREY'S NARRATIVE. 95

Scoffing way asking if a little Dog that followed us was the Spirit that led us. After they had filled themselves for their work they drove us two Miles by the Sea Shore, Abusing us with their Swords, forcing us to trot before their Horses, it being late & Intending to Oblige the Ferryman to put us on a little Island or bank of Sand in the Sea, where they thought to secure us for that Night, that they might find us safe the next Morning, to drive us 24 miles farther where some of our Friends were in Prison; they having no Warrant or Officer among them; but some of our kind Neighbors overtook us before they had us into the boat, and treated with them between Jest and Earnest, so that they released us out of their hands that Night; but Soon after, the same came in the night time and broke open the House of John William, the Father of Evan John and Rees John,[1] who laid down their Bodies in Pennsylvania,[2] they Violently haled the Family out of their Beds Except their Mother, who was a cripple and could not stir but as she was helped in Bed, they drove them a Mile before Day, slapping them with their Swords (leaving none in the House but the Impotent Woman), and they put them in a Ale-House, while they were Seeking After others. The chief of them went to the house (where my Wife liv'd with her Brother before She was Married), and Knocked at the door; She, supposing who it was, kept the door shut while she dressed herself, knowing he had no good Design. When he came in he took her and sent her to the rest of the Company, and went up and down taking all Sorts that did not go to the Steeple-House, even the Milkmaids from Cottages in their Shifts

---

[1] Evan John and Rees John were early settlers in Merion. The former, (as I have already said in Chapter VIII.) may have been the father of Robert John, one of the first company in Gwynedd. Rees John,—often called Rees John William, *i. e.* Rees, the son of John Williams,—came from Wales in 1684, arriving from Philadelphia on the 17th of 7th month (September), in the ship *Vine*, from Liverpool, William Preeson, master. With him were his wife Hannah and their two sons, Richard and Evan, and daughter Lowry. They had, after their arrival, several other children, one of whom, John, *b.* 1688, removed about 1710 to Montgomery, and was there well known as John Jones, "carpenter." Details concerning him are elsewhere given in this volume, and he will be found often alluded to. His (John's) brother Richard married for his first wife, Jane Evans; their sister Lowry was the second wife of Hugh Evans (son of Thomas), of Gwynedd; and their mother (widow of Rees John), became the second wife of Thomas Evans. So that the connection in different ways between the two Johns named above and the settlers of Gwynedd was very intimate.

[2] Rees John died 11th mo. 26, 1697. John Humphrey's Narrative was therefore written between that time and his own death, in 1699.

and Petticoats, barefooted, driving them 20 miles before their Horses, not Suffering them to go out of the very Channel of the Road. They met an old Woman coming from the Mill with a small bag of Meal on her Head (her Son and Daughter used to come to our Meetings some times), they flung down the bag into the Channel, & made the Old woman trot six Miles before their Horses, untill She was quite tired, there they left her in the Road, and sent the rest to Prison, to a town Called Balla,[1] & there they remained a Considerable time before they were released. I have seen some of these persecutors afterwards come to our Doors & gladly would accept of a Crust of Bread at our hands. Soon after they were Released they were taken by a Warrant & brought before a Justice who tendered the Oath unto them & upon their Refusal they were committed to Prison, & also all sorts of Professors that were under the least Convincement were sent to prison Untill the Prison was filled. There they all Remained till the Assize, where they paid two shillings & sixpence a Week for their Diet besides Duties & Custom which would Amount to a Great Sum of Money in a Year, from every one, which was no small gain to the Gaoler. Then they began to Count the cost & thought what Etsate they had would soon be consumed at that Rate, and that it was better for them to Yield soon than late, & Such that were not willing to part with all went away with the flood at the assize.

But I may not Omit to Record for a Memorial to Posterity, the faithfull Sufferings & sore afflictions in particular of four Friends, to wit, my Brother Samuel Humphrey (who Ran his race and finished his Course in the land of his Nativity, but his Wife and seven Children[2]

---

[1] Bala is an important market town in Merionethshire, on the Dee. It is not, however, the shire-town, Dolgelly having that distinction.

[2] The wife (Elizabeth) came, as here stated, in 1683. But her son Daniel had preceded her, having come the previous year. Elizabeth's certificate is from the Quarterly Meeting of Merionethshire, dated 5th mo. 27th, 1683, and signed by thirteen persons, among whom are Owen Humphrey (brother of her deceased husband, and John, the Narrative author), Rowland Ellis, and two Robert Owens. It refers also to her children, by name Benjamin, Lydia, Amy [or Ann], and Gobitha. (These make, with Daniel, five altogether; John says there were seven; the other two I cannot account for, unless they had accompanied Daniel.) Daniel Humphrey took up land in Haverford, and *m.*, 1695, Hannah, the daughter of Dr. Thomas Wynne, of Wynnewood, in Lower Merion. Daniel and Hannah had ten children, of whom six were sons, and from this couple descended (son) Charles, who was a member of the Continental Congress, 1774-76; (grandson) Joshua, a great ship-builder of Philadelphia, and designer of several ships of the early American navy; (great-grandson) Samuel, who was the Chief Con-

JOHN HUMPHREY'S NARRATIVE.

in the Year 1683 Transported themselves to Pennsylvania); [and] the two Brothers Evan John & Reese John aforementioned, & one John William a poor Husband-man who went through great Conflicts & Suffered the Buffeting of Saten both within and without. These refused to Swear at all and produced a Special Command for it, & by good Authority from the only Law giver who hath Power to kill & to save. This Doctrine indeed was not Preached at large Amongst us in those Days.[1]

It may be said, as before was said of Peter & John, the Innocent Boldness of these Illiterate Men that could not Read nor write save in their own Language, the Court were astonished & mad with fury because they could not make them bow to their Wills, when so many had obeyed their commands & bowed to the Image they had set up and taken the Oath upon their knees. Their Anger was kindled against these faithful sufferers and [they] Commanded them to be Chain'd in Irons, which was Immediately done by the gaoler in Presence of the Court, linking them two and two, & Binding their hands on their backs, then Conveyed them from thence to the gaoler's House, where they remained all Night in that Posture. The County gaol was long 12 Miles distant from that town & [there] happen'd to be exceeding Stormy weather & great floods in their way. When the gaol was Removed they were forced to travel all Coupled in Chains, only their hands were loosed & when they were brought to the Gaol the Gaoler provided Meat & Drink & Beds at the same rate as he Charg'd them and others before Sessions. He put his Victuals on a table and Called some of his Associates to see him tendering his meat to them, Asking them if that was not sufficient for such Men to Eat, & some said it was Sufficient Enough. Then he Vowed with Curses & Oaths, that if they would not take that, he would famish them to Death, & their Blood should be upon their own Heads, & some affirmed that he Might do so, and so he did Endeavour to do for

---

structor in the American navy, from 1815 to 1846; and (great-great-grandson) General A. A. Humphrey, of the U. S. Army, who served with distinction in the War against the Rebellion. Elizabeth Humphrey's son Benjamin, named in the certificate, settled in Haverford, but removed to Merion, where his uncle John, dying childless, had left him his own farm. He *m.*, 1694, Mary Llewellyn, of Haverford, and died in 1738, aged 76. The daughters, named in the certificate, Lydia and Amy [or Ann] *m.* respectively Ellis Ellis and Edward Robert; Gobitha d. 1697, unmarried.

[1] I take this to imply that up to this time it had not been urged by Quaker preachers, in that part of Wales, that it was wrong to take a judicial oath.

a long while, but some means was found in his Absence to Convey a little Victuals through a little hole in the wall on the Point of a pike to keep them alive. They were kept Close Prisoners until the next Assize, then the Judge came that Circuit & they were Released, but the Gaoler being sorely Vexed by the Disappointment he had from the Quakers, after he had Promised himself all they had, he Could get nothing from them, then he devised some Mischief against Samuel Humphrey, Supposing him to be the Author of his Overthrow. He advanc'd some Action Against him in the County Court & got a Writ to the Sheriff and Attacked him on a fair Day when he was about his Business, So that he was Clapt in Prison in depth of winter, having neither fire nor Cloaths for nine Days & Nights, save what he had on when he was taken and those very wet. Neither would he let him have any Repast but what was Conveyed to him in the Gaoler's Absence, and so Kept him close confined for several Months, until a Friend took the cause in Hand, & the Gaoler was cast in the Suit, still wanting advantage.

I Being all this time sick in Bed, several times threatened to be taken out of Bed to Prison, having a Distemper in my Limbs whereby I lost the use of my Right leg and thigh for a time, [when] I Recovered a little & strove to the Bath. In about a Week after I went there, one Day I was Bathing myself and After went to (as their Manner was) Procure Sweat, I Slumbered a little, & Dreamed that the same Gaoler Invited the said four Friends to his House and laid Meat on the Table before them, telling them whether they would Eat or not he would Make them pay. Supposing there was Something in it I took my Pen & Pocket-Book and Entered the Day & hour I saw it. In a little while after I Received an account that Upon the very same Day & Hour they were taken by the same Gaoler with a writ of Quo-Minus from London Upon the Old Action. (I Perceived this was the Lord's doings; therefore I Record It amongst my Memorials.) And so they were kept a long while in prison Untill the Gaoler was weary of them but got nothing. After they were come home from Prison & I from the Bath, Our Meetings were pretty fresh and we did Count the cost & Resolved to keep them up, come what would; so on the first Day of the week those that first Molested us came with Swords and Staves into our Meeting, and took Old & Young, Male and Female, as many as was able to go and haled us before a Justice of the Peace who was a Tender Man and loth to Meddle if he could have his choice. But such was the time that if the least tenderness appeared in any of the Magistrates, the Priests and others would soon charge them with not being faithful to Ceasar; then that would cause them to pass Sentence against their Judgment. The act of Banishment was then in force.[1] The first & Second Offence was fines which was to be Divided between the King and the Informers; and in Case the Parties would not pay the fine they [were] Committed to Prison, & there Remain untill Payment. The third offence was Banishment. So when we came before the Justice he shewed us the Danger we were like to run Ourselves into; but if we would pay the fine and Promise to keep no more Meetings we Should be released; other wise he could do no less than Commit us to Prison. We then in short put them all out of Doubt that we would neither pay nor Promise any such thing on that Account. Then Our Names were taken, and a Commitment in one Altogether, to send us all to Prison; I perceived it then, & do remember that the Justice might be Called a Quaker, [for] his hand did shake till he was Ashamed. When the Commitment was Ready, Old John Williams (the Father of Reese & Evan John) Spoke unto Them on this Wise: " Oh Justice, as thou art to expect Mercy when thou Appearest before the Tribunal Seat of God, for his Sake shew Mercy now, & let this Girl go home to her Mother, who is a Cripple in Bed, and now alone. If the House was on Fire she could not move herself."

One that was Present did Chide the old Man for Speaking after that Manner. The [justice, however,] was then walking up & Down in the Hall, and could not Refrain sheding tears. He said, " Let him alone. He speaks in the Anguish of his Soul," and left the Room, being he Could no longer forbear Weeping. We saw him no more that Night. It was late by that time, & and we had long Eight miles to the County gaol. The Constable was loth to send us there, without leaving us go first to our Houses, so he Dismised [us] upon Conditions that he Could find us the next Day at our Houses. Against Saml. Humphreys went

---

[1] This was the Act of Parliament of 1661, strongly pleaded against by the Friends, Edward Burrough and Richard Hubberthorn appearing at the bar of the House of Commons, and there presenting their arguments. It passed, however, and the King (Charles II.) signed it in May, 1662. It is notable that among the few in the House of Commons who opposed it, and argued for liberty of conscience, was Edmund Waller, the poet. Two other members, Michael Mallett and Sir John Vaughan, took the same side, and were subsequently " convinced" of the Friends' doctrines, the latter being imprisoned with them, and continuing Friendly even when he became Earl of Carberry. The act of 1661 forbade the assembling of five or more Quakers, over 16 years old, under pretence of religious worship, and inflicted fines or imprisonment for the first and second offences, and transportation for the third. A still more severe law was passed in 1664, and while great numbers were imprisoned under them, some were actually banished.

to his Home his Wife was in Labour & was Delivered of two Sons before Morning. He called them Joseph & Benjamin.[1] The Justice had tidings thereof; he sent for the Constable, and took up the Commitment, and wished some of us would Appear before him. The Constable came to stop his Man who was going with some of us to the County gaol, & when he came in Sight he Cry'd with a loud Voice, Saying: "Trowch yn ol! Trowch yn ol! Fe roes Duy ei law argalon y gwr,"—that is to say, "Turn back; turn back; God has laid his hand upon the Man's Heart." So my Brother Owen & Samuel Humphrey went to him the Day following, and as they were going to Hall, they met his [the Justice's] Mother in the Court. She gave them an Account that her Son had been in a sad Condition since they had been there. When they went to him he raised his Spirits & told that his Hand should not be upon them, but he would Bind them over to the Next Quarter sessions, and would venture to Release our Brother Saml., tho' he did know what Danger he Should incur. If he Should be put to it, he knew the Law would not bear him out.

When the Quarter-sessions came the Constable Brought [them] there, according to his orders. There was six Justices on the Bench, & the Sheriff. Some of them were Men of a Thousand Pounds a Year, & the least two Hundred,—most of them in the Prime of their time. When we came before them, they began to deride, mock & Scoff, and in a Scoffing Manner asking if we did know the Ffyold Gatholig &c.,—that is, Catholic faith, &c. Others in a Rage said if we were not Quakers they would make us Quake,—make us their Laughing Stocks,—flinging our hats about. Our friend Evan Ellis said to them that they took more Delight to sit on the Seat of Scorners than on the seat of Justice and Judgment. Then they tendered the Oath to us, which we Refused, then they fined us and upon Default of Payment they Commited us to gaol. It being late and a long way to the County Prison, we were shut up that Night in a Close Room. When it was Night, by the Light of the Moon the whole Bench, with one Accord, Both Sheriff and Justices, save one, came before the door, where we were put in, to make Merry over us & over the witness of God in themselves. Drinking the King's Health, they Commanded the Gaoler to open upon us, & sent in their Parasite to force us to drink the King's health. We, lying upon the Ground like Dead bodies, did not mind what they said. They had Liquor which they Called *Aqua Vita*. They offered us some of it, & in Mocking Manner called it the

---

[1] This was the nephew to whom John Humphrey left his own estate in Merion. He d. 1738, aged 76 years.

JOHN HUMPHREY'S NARRATIVE. 101

water of Life; [saying] it would flow out of our Bellies if we would drink of it. We Still lay Quiet, answering not a Word. Then they sent the fiddler to Play & sing over us and so Continued Tormenting us almost all night, pouring drink in our faces and committed an Indecency hardly fit to be mentioned. We never moved all this while, for all they could do. When it was Day light all was Quiet in Town. I took my Pen & half a Sheet of Paper & wrote what the Lord put in my mind, who I am Satisfied directed my pen to give them a Citation to appear before the Tribunal Seat of God Almighty to Answer not only for their Injury done to us but for Crucifying to themselves the Son of God afresh, and putting of him to open shame. [I] further said that I wished that which they sent to us in a Scoffing Manner calling it aqua Vita might not Prove to be Aqua Mortis to them, &c. This Paper was sent among them that Day & we were sent to the County Gaol.

It may be observed that some of them were never seen on the Bench again, & it was not two Years & a half before the six were in their graves, to Wit, five Justices and the high-Sheriff.

When we came to the Gaol the gaoler after his usual manner Provided Meat & Drink, & laid it upon the Table And told us he would use us as Gentlemen if we would pay, and if not he would use us Otherwise. We Answered we could not Live at that Rate long & would make no bargain with him, he swearing as he used to do that he would Famish us then, and [he] Endeavored so to do as much as he could. However we strove with [it] and lay on the floor untill the Assize. Then the Gaol was to be removed to Bala. I, being lame, was Obliged to Travel a-foot for 12 Miles. (If I had brought a Horse he would have Arrested him for the fees.) When the Assize came, we Presented our Petition to the Judge, and the Second day of the Assize, at Night, as we were going to bed we had it deliver'd to him & he read it, and Delivered it again to the Messenger and Directed that it should be Presented to him the Next day, as soon as he sat on the Bench, which we did Accordingly, at his first Entrance. Then he Read it very serious and Solidly to himself, and handed to the Pathonater to be Read Publicly; so he began to read, untill (when] he came to our Terms of Thee & Thou, he Smiled and Stuttered. The Judge bade him Read on, as he did, after which we were Commanded to be brought to Court. Twelve of the Sheriff's Men came with their holberts to Guard us to the Court. Way was made for us to Stand at the Barr. The Judge asked us why we did not go to Church to worship God and Divine Service. We Replyed that the time was come that they that worshiped God according to His will must worship Him in

Spirit & in Truth, and wheresoever two or three are met together in His Name, He Promiseth to be in the midst of them. Several Questions were asked by several in Court, some in Earnest & some in Jest but we answered them not. Then the Sheriff's Men guard'd us to the gaol again, after they tendered us the Oath, and we Refused. There was a little Paper of George Fox's—sent by Shropshire Friends to us, [upon] hearing that we suffered on the Account of Swearing. The contents thereof was this: "The Cry of the World is 'Swear and kiss the book,' and the Book saith, 'Kiss the Son,' & the Son saith 'Swear not at all.'" We did not know how to get it Published, it being so pertinent to the time & purpose, [but] we offered one six-pence to Nail it on the Court-House door. He concluded he would do it, But his Heart failed him, and he returned it again saying he did not know but they would count it Treason to Publish anything that was against the law. I put it in my Pocket to wait another Opportunity. The Day following the Sheriff and his Train Came to the Gaol and took from amongst us Old John Williams, the Father of Reese John, a short Man with grey hairs & long Beard about Seventy Years of Age. He alone was taken to the Court. The Judge asked if he would Pay the fines. He Answer'd in his own Language that he wronged no Man, he was a poor husbandman, Endeavouring to keep his conscience void of offence towards God & Man, earning his Bread with the sweat of his brow, paying Duties & Customs to whom it was due. Then he was Commanded to be put in a loft at the other End of the Hall, where he was a straight object before the Judge's face, which, as many supposed, Affected his Heart with Pitty to the poor, Innocent, Old Man, for the Judge could not turn his Eyes from him all the while. Then his son, Reese John, was fetched from us to Court; and as they were leading him along they told him that his father had taken the Oath, and promis'd to pay the fine. Howbeit he was so steadfast in his Mind that they Could not move him, altho' he knew not what was become of his Father. The Court Demanded the fine from him, & tendered the oath & he Refused; then he was turned to his Father. The Next was Hugh Price, whom they endeavored to persuade to do as they said the others had done, but to no effect. And when they saw that nothing would prevail, they came in great Rage and fury for us all & and brought us to the Barr. The deputy Sheriff's son had [had] some Quarrel, & my brother [had] taken [part in it] some former time. He was Pricking us with Pins in the Court. We made our Complaint thereof to the Bench; then one of the Lawyers said whosoever abuseth a prisoner at the Barr, the Law was to cut off his Right arm. When to Excuse himself he said he was searching for Treacherous Papers;

JOHN HUMPHREY'S NARRATIVE.

with that he thrust his hand in my pocket, and found that little paper which we could not get any way to Divulge. When he had got it he Proclaimed it to the Court thinking he had got something that would take me by the throat. One of the Lawyers read it and gave it to his Companion, saying "Let it go, my Lord: it will harm no body." So it went to the Judge's hand, & he read it & said nothing to it.

I perceived this to be the Lord's doings, to Cause this Angry fellow to do that service for us, Which we could not have any to do for money, and we were then released from our fines and Imprisonments.

The Gaoler cry'd out Could he keep men in his custody and have nothing for our meat & drink & lodging, The cryer cried out, "Free Men." One of the Justices that Committed us said he would have us here again, ere long, but the Judge said," Let them go now." The Judge sent to us to know [how] it was between us & the Gaoler. We made it appear that we did not partake of any thing that might Be called his, but his cruelty, and that we did Pay, to the utmost — only to the floor which we lay and Trod upon.

JOHN HUMPHREY.

[*A Short Relation omitted in its proper place is here inserted*].

About the Year 1663 the Magistrates of Montgomery Recommended to the Magistrates of Merioneth some vain Sorry fellow that had spent his Estate, urging them to Employ him to suppress the Fanaticks, as they Called them, and Issued forth warrants to bring in all that did not go to the Steeple House; & many was taken in this Net, which they spread, but other Dissenting Professors that had but little Possession in the Truth, [and] Could not stand the Stock — Agreed with the Man to give him some Money, & were Dismissed. None remained Faithful to their Testimony but Friends, and on us he was Resolved to vent his Rage and Cruelty, and locked us up in a Room a Top of the shire hall, and would not as much as allow us a little straw to lay upon. There was a Bundle of Straw in a Window, to stop the wind & rain coming in, which he took away. A Friend said to him, " Thou Canst take out, but thou canst not cause the wind to blow in there." Then we Resolved to suffer, and lie upon the Boards, and the whole Company agreed that one should lay for a Boulster and three lay with their heads upon him, and so all take their turns. Thus we spent several weeks, and He like a severe Master over us, coming to see us Every Day, but after he had spent all he had got from the Dissenting Professors, and could not get any thing from us, he was weary of Friends, and said he would not Trouble himself any farther with us, and so we were Released. JOHN HUMPHREY.

Some Account of the Sufferings of our Ancient friend John Humphreys in Wales in Old England, taken from an old Manuscript.

After I was Married I went to Lanwyddun in Montgomery-shire. There was no Friends' Meetings there before I came; only two Cousins of mine frequented Meetings abroad; but we set up a Meeting, & in a little time a great Concourse of People from the parish about began to come, & our Meetings came to be pretty large. I was several times Apprehended by Warrant and brought to the Assizes in Montgomery but never put to prison but during the Sessions.

There was a Man that lived very near to the place where we kept our Meetings. He was building a house & had many hands from many Parts. Upon our Meeting Day they agreed to come to Disturb our Meetings. So they came to the House after the Meeting was over, & rushed in amongst us, & asked upon what Account so many of us came together. Some of us Asked upon what Account they came amongst us in such a Posture. Upon that one of them steped [up] and took me by the Hair of my Head with the Broad ax in the other hand and Lug'd me towards the door. Some Women throng'd about me and said: "Thou Villain, what dost thou mean?" By that he Answered: "I mean to take off his head."

The Women wrestled and took the Ax from him. He still held me by the hair. They strove with him untill they got his Hands from my head and then cast him out of the door.

As I was going home by the place where they were working, I turned in, thinking to speak with their Master to know whether was it by his Permission they Came, but he not being there the Men came down from the Scaffold and one with a Clift of Wood struck me upon my head untill I was quite dead, Rowling in my Blood. The Woman of the House was an English Woman from London. She cried out with a loud voice and put my head in her apron, & called out for her husband to send away the Wicked Bloody rogue from her House. They abused the friend that was with me also. When my Blood was washed and my wound Dressed I got home. The Rumor was spread abroad; they fled and left the work. The fellow that abused me was never seen again in the country.

In the year 1679 the new Act[1] was in force, and many turned to be

---

[1] This was the revival of the old acts, whose operation had for some time been suspended by the King.

JOHN HUMPHREY'S NARRATIVE.

Informers. Justice Morris came to be an Informer, himself, and Issued out writs & gave them to the Sheriff, who Distrained upon Charles Loyd, Thos. Loyd, Thos. March and others, & took what they could find of their Cattle. The said Friends sought a Replevin, intending to traverse the case to get home the Cattle till the Assize. Charles and Thos. Loyd sent two Men upon two good Horses to Replevin the Cattle. They went to this Morris & shewed their power. He took them to the cattle which was on the other side of the River by his house in a Meadow. When he had them there he took both Horses from them & sent them away, he being Justice of the peace in both Counties, the other side of the River was in Denbighshire. The two Horses were well worth £20 Sterling.

In a few Days after, as the said Justice was going from one place to another on one of these Horses he Stumbled in the river. He fell off & was Drowned before his own door. His warrant was [then] with the Deputy Sheriff to distrain upon us in Lanwyddun. We Expected their coming Every Day, and some [that] were faithless & fearfull did contrive some shift to sell some, & put the rest under the mark of the Landlord. The Sheriff's Wife was very Earnest with her husband to make hay while the Sun shined, for it was thought that if more Writs were Issued forth, [these] if not soon serv'd, would be Void,— the term would Expire. Which made her so Eager, together with the Profit She made of so many Cows that her Husband brought her. But on the Day he intended to come to distrain our Goods he was Taken with a sore fitt in the Morning, & his Man with all speed sent to Thomas Loyd which was about three miles off, to get something for him, but Doctor Loyd was not at home to go with the Man, nor to give him anything. In a little while after the Man returned, the Sheriff Died in his Chair. Had Thos. Loyd been at home & had given him something, Perhaps Some might have Conjectured some ill thoughts of him. However he had the Warrant in his pocket When he Died Intending that morning before the fitt took him to Execute it upon us. The Night before my Wife was Milking the Cows, Saying to us : " I do not know whether I may ever have them to milk again, or no." The first news that I heard was of his Burial. I did Suppose the hand of God was in it working our Deliverance, Therefore I set it down amongst my Memorials.

There was a young man in the Neighborhood about Twenty years of of Age Living with his Father & Mother. As I was agoing before him in the lane, & he a-coming after me with somebody with him, as he came he did go hobbling on one side Crying repeatedly after me : " Quaker! Quaker! Quaker!" I took little notice of him then. But a Few Days after he was Grievously taken with a sore Distemper in his Limbs, so that he Cry'd out with pain and grief. I had never spoke a word to him nor any Body Else, to the best of my Remembrance, of his mocking me, Until his Mother came to my house, with tears, desiring me to forgive him & to pray to God on his behalf. I was seriously Concerned on his Account, and made many a Journey to Visit him in his Sickness. His lower parts was quite benumbed a long time before his Death. He died Sensible, & I believe in peace with God.

XII.

Early Monthly Meeting Records of Marriages: Other Lists of Marriages and Deaths.

ABSTRACTS of the marriage records of Haverford[1] Monthly Meeting (to which the Gwynedd Friends, until 1714, belonged), and of those of Gwynedd Monthly Meeting, are amongst the collections of the Historical Society of Pennsylvania, in Philadelphia. From these I have copied a list, relating to Gwynedd and Montgomery, which follows below. In presenting it, however, I desire to say that while it has been copied with care, and is probably accurate, it is at best but the copy of a copy of the original records, and that these have themselves become, by the passage of time, difficult to decipher, in many instances. Those who may wish to be absolutely certain as to dates, etc., should of course consult the original; otherwise, for ordinary purposes, the list here given will doubtless serve.

List from Haverford Records.

Thomas Siddon, of Dublin township, Philadelphia co., batchelor, to Lowry Evans, of North Wales, spinster, at North Wales meeting place, 5th mo. 28, 1701. [Witnesses: Samuel Siddon, Robert, Thomas, Cadwallader, Elizabeth, Jane, Ann, and Mary Evans, and 28 others.]

Hugh Roberts, of Gwynedd, batchelor, and Ann Thomas, of Upper Merion, spinster, at Merion m. h., 7th mo. 30, 1703.

Alexander Edwards, Jun., of Gwynedd, and Gwen Foulke, of the same township, at Gwynedd m. h., 10th mo. 6, 1703.

---

[1] This is also called Radnor Monthly Meeting. The name at the period of these records was Haverford.

William Lewis, of Newtown, Chester co., and Gwen Jones, of Gwynedd, at Gwynedd m. h., 8th mo. 27, 1704. [Witnesses: Lewis, Evan, Samuel, Seaborn, and Evan Lewis, William, John, Jane, Margaret, and Gainor Jones, and 43 others.]

Francis Dawes, of Gwynedd, and Margaret Griffith, of Philadelphia, at Gwynedd m. h., 9th mo. 27, 1704.

David Jones, of Gwynedd, and Lowry Robert, of the same place, at Gwynedd m. h., 9th mo. 24, 1704. [Witnesses: Griffith, Robert, Margaret and Jane Jones; John, Ellis, William, Evan, Cadwallader, Morris, Nicholas, Rowland, and Jane Roberts, and 20 others.]

Evan Griffith, of Gwynedd, and Bridget Jones, of Radnor, in the Welsh Tract, at Radnor m. h., 3d mo. 3, 1705. [Witnesses: Hugh (his father), David, Edward, Catharine, and Ellin Griffith, Griffith and William John, and 48 others.]

Robert Evan, of Gwynedd, yeoman, and Sarah Evans, of Merion, at Merion m. h., 4th mo. 4, 1705. [Witnesses, Thomas, Cadwallader, Robert, Owen, Hugh, Evan, John, Jane, Ellin, Mary, Jane, Sarah, Gwen, and Margaret Evans; Cadwallader and Jane Morgan, and 71 others.]

Richard Jones, of Meirion, and Jane Evan, of Gwynedd, in the Welsh Tract, at Gwynedd m. h., 4th mo. 6, 1705. [Witnesses: Evan, John, Gainor, and Sarah Jones; Thomas, Anne, Lowry, Robert, Hugh, Evan, and Owen Evans, and 72 others.]

John Davies, of Gwynedd, and Mary James, of Radnor, at Radnor meeting place, 5th mo. 4, 1705.

Robert Humphrey, of Gwynedd, yeoman, and Margaret Evans, of Radnor, spinster, at Radnor m. h., 9th mo. 1, 1705.

Robert Ellis, of Meirion, and Margaret Jones, of Gwynedd, at Gwynedd m. h., 9th mo. 3, 1705. [Witnesses: Rowland, Rowland, Jr., Catharine, and Elizabeth Ellis; William, John, Thomas, Jane, and Richard Jones, and 67 others.]

Hugh Evan, of Gwynedd, and Catharine Morgan, dau. of Cadwallader, of Meirion, of Merion meeting place, 8th mo. 4, 1706. [Witnesses: Thomas, Robert, Evan, Owen, Robert, Owen, Cadwallader, and John Evans; Cadwallader and Jane Morgan, and 68 others.]

Evan Griffith, second son of Griffith John, of Merion, and Jane Jones, step-daughter of John Humphrey, of Gwynedd, at Gwynedd meeting place, 3d mo. 29, 1707. [Witnesses: Griffith and William John, Hugh Griffith, and 51 others.]

LIST OF MARRIAGES AND DEATHS. 109

Robert John, of Gwynedd, and Gaynor Lloyd, of Merion, widow, at Merion m. h., 4th mo. 3, 1706. [Witnesses: William and Griffith John; Thomas, Robert, Eliza, and Hannah Lloyd, and 59 others.]

Ellis Pugh, Jr., of Plymouth, eldest son of Ellis Pugh, of Merion, and Mary Evan, eldest daughter of Owen Evan, of Gwynedd, at a public meeting, 3d mo. 3, 1708.

Rowland Hugh, of Gwynedd, yeoman, and Catharine Humphrey, of Merion, at Merion m. h., 8th mo. 8, 1708. [Witnesses: Ellin and Jane Hugh; John, Robert, and Gainor Humphrey, and 62 others.]

George Lewis, of Gwynedd, batchelor, and Jane Roberts, of the same tp., at Gwynedd m. h., 9th mo. 3, 1708. [Witnesses: Thos. and Richard Lewis; John, Ellis, Wm., and Evan Roberts, and 43 others.]

William Roberts, of Gwynedd, batchelor, and Anne Jones, of the same tp., at Gwynedd m., 12th mo. 4, 1708-9. [Witnesses: Ellis Roberts, and 57 others.]

David Llewellyn, of Haverford, widower, and Margaret Ellis, of Gwynedd, widow, at Gwynedd m., 8th mo. 10, 1709. [Witnesses: Morris and Mary Llewellyn, Rowland Ellis, William and Jane John, and 55 others.]

Edward Parry, eldest son of Thomas, of Huntinton township,[1] Philadelphia co., yeoman, and Jane Evan, second daughter of Robert, of the same place, spinster, at Gwynedd m., 8th mo. 6, 1710. [Witnesses, Thomas, and Thomas Parry, Jr.; Robert, Thomas, and Hugh Evans, and 52 others.]

John Griffith, eldest son of Griffith John, of Meirion, and Grace Foulke, second daughter of Edward, of Gwynedd, at Gwynedd m. h., 3d mo. 6, 1707. [Witnesses: Griffith and William John; Evan Griffith; Edward, Thomas, and Hugh Foulke, and 51 others.]

Hugh Evans, of Gwynedd, yeoman, and Alice Lewis, daughter of James, of Pembrokeshire, Wales, spinster, at Merion m. place, 6th mo. 25, 1710. [Witnesses: Thomas, Robert, Evan, Owen, Jr., and John Evans; David Jones, Cadwallader Morgan, and 67 others.]

Evan Jones, son of John [Evans] of Radnor, dec'd, and Lowry Evans, daughter of Thomas, of Gwynedd, at Gwynedd m. h., 4th mo. 8, 1711.

Thomas Ellis, of Gwynedd, and Jane Hugh, dau. of John, of the same place, at Gwynedd m., 8th mo. 31, 1712.

Rowland Hugh, of Gwynedd, widower, and Ellin Evan, dau. of Thomas, of the same place, spinster, at Gwynedd m., 5th mo. 31, 1712.

---

[1] Thus on the record. Where was this township?

110   HISTORICAL COLLECTIONS OF GWYNEDD.

Thomas Foulke, eldest son of Edward, of Gwynedd, and Gwen Evans, eldest dau. of David, of Radnor, at Gwynedd m. h., 4th mo. 27, 1706.
Humphrey Ellis, of Gwynedd, and Mary Hugh, dau. of John, of Merion, at Radnor m. h., 10th mo. 1, 1708.
Evan Roberts, of Gwynedd, and Jane Evan, dau. of Evan Pugh, of Gwynedd, at Gwynedd m. h., 3d mo. 3, 1709.
Cadwallader Morris, of Gwynedd, and Elizabeth Morgan, of the same place, at Gwynedd m., 3d mo. 24, 1710.
Thomas David, of Gwynedd, yeoman, and Elizabeth Jones, at Gwynedd m., 8th mo. 10, 1711. [Witnesses: John and Robert David, and others.]
John Hanke, of Whitemarsh, yeoman, and Sarah Evans, dau. of Cadwallader Evans, of Gwynedd, spinster, at Gwynedd m., 10th mo. 11th, 1711.
John William, of Montgomery, widower, and Catharine Edwards, of the same place, widow, at Gwynedd m., 3d mo. 12, 1714.
Richard Kenderdine, son of Thomas, late of Abington, dec'd, and Sarah Evans, dau. of Robert, of Gwynedd, at Gwynedd m. h., 10th mo. 2, 1714.
Rowland Roberts, of Montgomery, and Mary Pugh, eldest dau. of Robert Pugh, of Gwynedd, at Gwynedd m., 3d mo. 1, 1713.
Samuel Thomas, of Montgomery, and Margaret Morgan, dau. of Edward, of the same tp., at Gwynedd m., 3d mo. 3, 1713.
Theophilus Williams, son of John, of Montgomery, and Catharine Foulke, dau. of Edward, of Gwynedd, at Gwynedd m., 4th mo. 5, 1713.
Hugh Foulke, son of Edward, of Gwynedd, batchelor, and Anne Williams, dau. of John, of Montgomery, spinster, at Gwynedd m., 4th mo. 4, 1713. [Witnesses: Edward, Thomas, Cadwallader, Evan, Ellin, Jane, and Catharine Foulke; John, William, Thomas and Lewis Williams, and 58 others.]
Ellis Hughs, son of John, of Gwynedd, yeoman, and Jane Foulke, dau. of Edward, of Gwynedd, at Gwynedd m., 4th mo, 5th, 1713. [Witnesses, John and Rowland Hugh, and others.]
John Jones, son of Rees, late of Merion, dec'd, and Jane Edward, dau. of Edward Griffith, late of Llan y Chill, co. of Merioneth, yeoman, dec'd, at Gwynedd m. h., 4th mo. 9, 1713. [Witnesses: Richard and Thomas Jones; Hugh, Evan, and John Griffith, and others.]
Evan Evans, son of Thomas, of Gwynedd, yeoman, and Elizabeth Musgrave, dau. of Thomas, late of or near Halifax, in Yorkshire, Gt. Britain, yeoman, dec'd, at Haverford m. h., 7th mo. 3, 1713.

LIST OF MARRIAGES AND DEATHS.   111

William Morgan, son of Edward, of or near Gwynedd, and Elizabeth Roberts, of Montgomery, at Gwynedd, m. h., 8th mo. 27, 1713.

Cadwallader Roberts, of Gwynedd, yeoman, and Ellen Humphrey, of Merion, at the dwelling place of Rowland Ellis, 4th mo. 9, 1714. [Witnesses: Morris, Nicholas, John, Rowland, Evan, Ellis, and Eliza Roberts; John Humphrey, and 53 others.]

Thomas Williams, of Montgomery, and Catharine Thomas, of Merion, at Gwynedd meeting place, 6th mo. 10, 1714.

Abraham Musgrave, son of Thomas, late of Halifax, Yorkshire, Gt. Britain, yeoman, dec'd, and Gainor Jones, dau. of William, late of Gwynedd, yeoman, dec'd, at Gwynedd m. h., 9th mo. 4, 1714.

Ellis Roberts, of Gwynedd, tailor, and Eliza Thomas, dau. of David, of Radnor, spinster, at Radnor mtg. place, 1st mo., 30, 1715.

Evan Evans, son of Owen, of Gwynedd, yeoman, and Phebe Miles, dau. of Samuel, late of Radnor, dec'd, at Radnor m. h., 2d mo. 13, 1715.

John Evans, son of Cadwallader, of Gwynedd, and Ellin Ellis, dau. of Rowland, of Merion, at Merion m. h., 4th mo. 8, 1715.

Owen Evans, son of Thomas, of Gwynedd, and Ruth Miles, dau. of Samuel and Margaret, of Radnor, at Radnor m. h., 11th mo. 3, 1715-16.

John Hugh, of Gwynedd, widower, and Ellin Williams, of Upper Merion, at Radnor m. h., 12th mo. 12, 1716-17.

Hugh Evans, of Gwynedd, widower, and Lowry Lloyd, of Merion, widow [born Lowry John, dau. of Rees John; wid. of Robert Lloyd], at Merion m. h., 12th mo. 13, 1716-17.

Robert Evan, son of Owen, of Gwynedd, and Ellin Griffith, dau. of Edward, of Upper Merion, at Radnor mtg. place, 3d mo. 30, 1717.

Griffith Hugh, son of Hugh Griffith, of Gwynedd, yeoman, and Jane Roberts, dau. of Robert Ellis, late of Radnor, dec'd, at Gwynedd m. h., 10th mo. 2, 1718.

Thomas Evans, son of Owen, of Gwynedd, yeoman, and Elizabeth Griffith, dau. of Edward, of Merion, dec'd, at Radnor, 4th mo. 30, 1720.

Joseph Ambler, of Montgomery, wheelwright, and Ann Williams, dau. of John, of Meirion, spinster, at Meirion mtg. place, 8th mo. 6, 1720.

John Morgan, son of Edward, of Gwynedd, and Sarah Lloyd, dau. of Thomas, of Merion, at Merion m. h., 9th mo. 8, 1721.

Cadwallader Evans, son of Evan Pugh, of Gwynedd, and Sarah Richard, dau. of Rowland, late of Tredyffrin, Chester co., dec'd, at the house of Katharine Richard, 8th mo. 10, 1722. [Witnesses: "Evan Pugh, his father," Hugh and Ellin Evan, and 41 others.]

112 HISTORICAL COLLECTIONS OF GWYNEDD.

Robert Roberts, son of Edward, of Gwynedd, yeoman, and Jane Evans, dau. of Robert, of Merion, at Merion m. h., 8th mo. 31, 1723, [Witnesses, Robert, Sarah, Thomas, Robert, Owen, Cadwallader, Evan, and Owen Evan, and others.]

Samuel Evans, of Gwynedd, cooper, and Hannah Walker, dau. of Lewis, of Tredyffrin, spinster, at the house of Lewis Walker, 4th mo. 10, 1724.

Lewis Williams, of Gwynedd, and Jane Lloyd, dau. of Thomas, of Merion, at Merion m. h., 8th mo. 8, 1725.

Rees Harry, son of David, of Plymouth, and Mary Price, dau. of Rees, of Haverford, yeoman, at Haverford mtg., 10th mo. 12, 1727.

Joseph Morgan, son of Edward, of Gwynedd, and Elizabeth Lloyd, dau. of Thomas, of Merion, at Merion m. h., 9th mo. 8, 1728.

Robert Evans, son of Owen, late of Gwynedd, dec'd, and Ruth Richard, dau. of Rowland, late of Tredyffrin, Chester co., at Gwynedd m. h., 3d mo. 2, 1729.

Marmaduke Pardo, of Gwynedd, schoolmaster, and Gainor Jones, of Meirion, at Merion m. h., 4th mo. 27, 1729.

William Williams, son of John, of Montgomery, Phila. co., yeoman, and Margaret Longworthy, of or near Radnor, widow, at Radnor meeting place, 6th mo. 10, 1715. [Witnesses: John, Thomas, Davis, Catharine, and Hugh Williams, and others.]

Abraham Evans, of Gwynedd, son of Evan, dec'd, and Lydia Thomas, dau. of William, of Lower Merion, at Radnor m. h., 8th mo. 8, 1747. [Witnesses: Elizabeth, Jonathan, Musgrave, David, Robert, Owen, Jesse, and Anne Evans, and others.]

Musgrave Evans, of Philadelphia, cooper, son of Evan, of Gwynedd, dec'd, and Lydia Harry, dau. of Samuel, of Radnor, at Radnor m. h., 12th mo. 12, 1753.

Amos Griffith, son of Evan, of Gwynedd, and Sarah Lawrence, dau. of Thomas, late of Haverford, dec'd, at Gwynedd m. h., 5th mo. 8, 1755.

John Jones, of Montgomery twp., and Catharine Davis, of Merion, at Merion m. h., 12th mo. 2, 1757.

Evan Jones, son of John, of Montgomery twp., Philadelphia co., and Hannah Lawrence, dau. of Henry, of Haverford, dec'd, at Gwynedd m. h., 6th mo. 10, 1766.

Peter Evans, of Merion, son of Robert and Eleanor, of Gwynedd, dec'd, and Mary Thomas, dau. of William and Elizabeth, of Merion, at Radnor, m. h., 1st mo. 6, 1774.

John Hall, son of Mahlon, of Blockley, and Anne Morris, of the same tp., dau. of Edward, of Montgomery, at Merion m. h., 11th mo. 21, 1783.

Morris Humphreys, of Montgomery tp., farmer, son of Richard, dec'd, and Hannah, dec'd, and Sarah S. Evans, dau. of David and Mary, of Merion, at Merion m. h., 11th mo. 19, 1812.

List from Gwynedd Records.

Edward Jones, son of John Evan, late of Radnor, Chester county, dec'd, and Sarah, dau. of Thomas Evans, of Gwynedd, at Gwynedd m. h., 6th mo. 25, 1715.

William Roberts, son of Edward, of Merion, dec'd, and Anne, dau. of Robert Evans, of Gwynedd, yeoman, at Gwynedd m. h., 6th mo. 25, 1715.

Thomas Edward, son of Alexander, of Montgomery, dec'd, and Mary Price, of Gwynedd, spinster, at Gwynedd m. h., 7th mo. 23, 1715.

Hugh Evan, eldest son of Evan Pugh, of Gwynedd, batchelor, and Mary Robert, dau. of Robert John, dec'd, of Merion, at a public meeting in Gwynedd, 3d mo. 25, 1716.

Benj. Mendinhall, son of Benj., of Chester Co., yeoman, and Lidia Robert, dau. of Owen, of Gwynedd, yeoman, at Gwyn. m. h., 3d mo. 9, 1717.

Nicholas Roberts, son of Robert Cadwalader, of Gwynedd, dec'd, and Margaret Foulke, dau. of Edward, yeoman, at Gwynedd m. h., 3d mo. 23, 1717.

John Roger, son of Roger Roberts, of Merion, and Ellin Pugh, dau. of Robert, of Gwynedd, at Gwynedd m. h., 4th mo. 21, 1717.

Richard William, of Gwynedd, batchelor, and Margaret Eaton, of the same place, at a public meeting in Gwynedd, 10th mo. 7, 1717.

Robert Jones, of Gwynedd, and Anne, dau. of William Coulstone, of Plymouth, at a public meeting in Gwynedd, 8th mo. 22, 1717.

Robert Hugh, son of Hugh Griffith of Gwynedd, and Catharine Evans, dau. of Evan Pugh, of the same place, yeoman, at Gwynedd m. h., 12th mo. 26, 1717.

William Lewis, of Newtown, Chester Co., and Lowry Jones, of Gwynedd, widow, at Gwynedd m. h., 1st mo. 7, 1717-18.

Jenkin Evans, of Montgomery, batchelor, and Alice[1] Morgan, dau. of Edward, of the same place, at Gwynedd m. h., 8th mo. 17, 1718.

---

[1] In the Monthly Meeting minutes, the Clerk writes her name Alce,—*i. e.* the colloquial Ailsie, or Elsie.

Daniel Morgan, son of Edward, "adjacent Gwynedd," yeoman, and Elizabeth Roberts, dau. of Robert, dec'd, of Gwynedd, at Gwynedd m. h., 9th mo. 21, 1718.

Humphrey Jones, son of John [Humphrey] of Gwynedd, and Catherine Jones, dau. of William, dec'd, of the same place, at Gwynedd m. h., 2d mo. 23, 1719.

Rees David, of Upper Dublin, widower, and Margaret Morgan, of Montgomery, at Gwynedd m. h., 3d mo. 9, 1719.

Cadwalader Jones, son of John, of the parish of Llanfawr, Merionethshire, North Wales, Great Britain, dec'd, and Martha Thomas, dau. of David, of Radnor, Chester Co., yeoman, at a public meeting in Gwynedd, 4th mo. 12, 1719.

Cadwalader Foulke, son of Edward, of Gwynedd, yeoman, and Mary Evans, dau. of Robert, of the same place, yeoman, at Gwynedd m. h., 4th mo. 13, 1719.

Hugh Evans, son of Robert, of Gwynedd, and Margaret Robert, dau. of Edward, of the same place, yeoman, at Gwynedd m. h., 8th mo. 23, 1719.

William Morris, son of Morris Richard, of Merionethshire, North Wales, Great Britain, dec'd, and Catharine Pugh, dau. of Richard, of Montgomery, dec'd, at Gwynedd m. h., 8th mo. 26, 1719.

John Webb, of Philadelphia county, and Mary Boone, dau. of George, of the same county, at a public meeting, 7th mo. 13, 1720. [Among the witnesses are George Boon, George Boon, jr., and Benjamin Boone.]

Whereas Squire Boone,[1] son of George Boone, of the county of Philadelphia and Province of Pennsylvania, yeoman, and Sarah Morgan, dau. of Edward Morgan, of the said county and province, having declared their intentions of marriage with each other before two monthly meetings of ye people called Quakers, held at Gwynedd, in ye said county, according to ye good order used among them, whose proceedings therein, after deliberate consideration, and having consent of parents and relations concerned therein, their said proceedings are allowed of by said meeting: NOW THESE ARE TO CERTIFY whom it may concern that for the full accomplishment of their said intentions this 23d day of ye 7th month, in the year of our Lord 1720, the said Squire Boone and Sarah Morgan appeared at a solemn assembly of the said people for that purpose appointed at their public meeting place in Gwynedd aforesaid, and the said Squire

---

[1] This being a somewhat famous couple, I give the certificate.

Boone took the said Sarah Morgan by the hand [and] did in a solemn manner declare that he took her to be his wife, promising to be unto her a faithful and loving husband, until death should separate them, and then and there in the said assembly the said Sarah Morgan did likewise declare [etc., etc., etc.]

        (Signed)   SQUIRE BOONE,
                 SARAH BOONE.

WITNESSES.

Morgan Hugh.	Cad'r Evans.	George Boon.
John Edwards.	Mary Webb.	Edward Morgan.
Thomas Evans.	Eliz. Morris.	Elizabeth Morgan.
Cadw'r Evans.	Dorothy Morgan.	George Boone [Junior].
Robert Evans.	Eliz. Hughes.	Ja : Boon.
Jno. Cadwalader.	Mary Hammer.	Wm. Morgan.
Jno. Williams.	Eliz. Morgan.	Jno. Morgan.
Jno. Humphrey.	Jane Griffith.	Daniel Morgan.
Jno. Jones.	Mary Jones.	Morgan Morgan.
Jno. Jones.	Ellin Evans.	Jos. Morgan.
Owen Griffith.	Gainor Jones.	Jno. Webb.
Rowland Roberts.	Samuel Thomas.	
Amos Griffith.	John Evans.	
	Robert Jones.	

Thomas Williams, of Montgomery, widower, and Jane, dau. of Morris Richard, of Merionethshire, North Wales, Great Britain, dec'd, at Gwynedd m. h., 8th mo. 14, 1720.

John Roberts, son of John, of Abington, and Mary Dawes, dau. of Francis, of Montgomery, yeoman, at Gwynedd m. h., 6th mo. 15, 1723.

John Harris, of Gwynedd, yeoman, and Gainor Hugh, dau. of John, of Gwynedd, at Gwynedd m. h., 10th mo. 5, 1723.

Samuel Richards, son of Rowland, of Tredyffrin, Phila. [Chester] Co., dec'd, and Elizabeth Evans, dau. of Owen, of Gwynedd, dec'd, at Gwynedd m. h., 2d mo. 21, 1726.

Abel Walker, of Tredyffrin, Chester Co., and Sina Pugh, of Gwynedd, at a public meeting in Gwynedd, 4th mo. 13, 1727.

Jonathan Worral, of Marple, Chester Co., and Mary Taylor, of Montgomery, Philada., at Gwynedd m. h., 7th mo. 21, 1727.

Lewis Lewis, son of Ellis Lewis, of Upper Dublin, Phila. Co., yeoman, and Anne Lord, dau. of Henry, of the same county, at Gwynedd m. h., 2d mo. 19, 1728.

John Davies, son of Meredith, of Gwynedd, dec'd, and Mary Bennett, dau. of Henry, of Abington, dec'd, at Gwynedd m. h., 8th mo. 20, 1728.

Peter Jones, son of Peter, of Merion, Phila. Co., and Catharine Evans, dau. of Robert, of North Wales, at Gwynedd m. h., 3d mo. 15, 1740.

Enoch Morgan, son of Edward, of Phila. Co., and Sarah Kenderdine, dau. of Richard, of the same county, at Gwynedd m. h., 3d mo. 14, 1741.

Edmund Phillips, of Richland, Bucks Co., and Elizabeth Davies, of Montgomery, Phila. Co., at a public meeting in Gwynedd, 2d mo. 25, 1729.

William Morgan, of Montgomery, Phila. Co., widower, and Catharine Robeson, of Merion, in said county, at Gwynedd m. h., 10th mo. 7, 1731.

Joseph Davis, of the city of Philadelphia, and Mary Evans of Phila. Co., at Gwynedd m. h., 9th mo. 28, 1732.

William Spencer, son of Samuel, of Horsham, dec'd, and Elizabeth Lewis, dau. of Ellis, of Upper Dublin, at a public meeting in Gwynedd, 3d mo. 24, 1733.

John Jones, son of Robert, of Gwynedd, Phila. Co., and Gainor Humphrey, dau. of Robert, of the same place, at Gwynedd m. h., 4th mo. 7, 1733.

Thomas Williams, of Montgomery Twp., Phila. Co., widower, and Sarah Hank, of Gwynedd, widow, at Gwynedd m. h., 1st mo. 6, 1732–33. [Among the witnesses are John Hank, William Hank, Samuel Hank, John Hank, Jane [or James?] Hank, Elizabeth Hank.]

Moses Peters, son of Garrett, of Montgomery, and Martha Thomas, dau. of Robert, of the same place, at Gwynedd m. h., 3d mo. 17, 1733.

Thomas Lewis, son of Richard, of Montgomery, and Hannah Morgan, dau. of Edward, jr., of the same co., at a public meeting, 3d mo. 7, 1734.

William Foulke, son of Thomas, of Gwynedd, and Hannah Jones, dau. of John, of Montgomery, at Gwynedd m. h., 8th mo. 15, 1734.

Robert Ellis, son of Theodore, of Gwynedd, and Sarah Davis, dau. of Meredith Davis [David] of the same co., dec'd, at Gwynedd m. h., ———, 1734–35.

Edward Evans, of Phila. co., yeoman, and Elizabeth Griffith, dau. of Evan, of the same co., at Gwynedd m. h., 3d mo. 20, 1735.

Robert Lloyd, of Gwynedd, and Catharine Humphrey, dau. of Robert, of the same place, at Gwynedd m. h., 6th mo. 21, 1735.

Griffith Ellis, son of Theodore, of Gwynedd, and Jane Lewis, widow, of the same place, at Gwynedd m. h., 7th mo. 9, 1735.

LIST OF MARRIAGES AND DEATHS. 117

John Forman, son of Alexander, of New Britain, and Elizabeth Nailor, dau. of Joseph, of Montgomery, at Gwynedd m. h., 8th mo. 20, 1735.

William Erwin, of Gwynedd, and Rebecca Roberts, dau. of Cadwalader Robert, of the same place, deceased, at Gwynedd m. h., 11th mo. 13, 1735-6.

William Robert, of Phila. Co., and Mary Pugh, of Gwynedd, widow, at Gwynedd m. h., 9th mo. 16, 1736.

John Robert, son of John, of Montgomery, and Jane Hank, dau. of John, of Whitemarsh, at Gwynedd m. h., 3d mo 13, 1736.

Evan Griffith, of Gwynedd, widower, and Margaret Owen, widow, of the same place, at Gwynedd m. h., 9th mo. 23, 1736.

Owen Roberts, son of William, of Phila. co., and Jane Williams, dau. of John, of Gwynedd, at Gwynedd m. h., 9th mo. 15, 1737.

William Martin, of Gwynedd, Phila. co., and Miriam Morgan, dau. of Edward, jr., late of the same place, at Gwynedd m. h., 3d mo. 25, 1738.

Owen Williams, son of John, of Gwynedd, dec'd, and Mary Meredith, dau. of Meredith David, of Plymouth, at Gwynedd m. h., 10th mo. 22, 1738.

William Edwards, son of John, of Milford, Bucks co., and Martha Foulke, dau. of Hugh, of Richland, at Richland m. h., 8th mo. 24, 1738.

John Williams, son of William Williams, of Philadelphia, and Jane Naylor, dau. of Joseph, of the same county, at Gwynedd m. h., 1st mo. 21, 1740.

Edward Edwards, son of John, of Phila. co., and Elizabeth Robeson, dau. of James, of the same co., at Gwynedd m. h., 5th mo. 7, 1741.

Evan Jones, of Merion, and Priscilla Jones, dau. of John Jones, of Montgomery, at Gwynedd m. h., 3d mo. 20, 1740. [Witnesses: John, Jane, Evan, and Jesse Jones, Jephtha and Ann Lewis, and others.]

David Morris, son of Cadwalader Morris, of Phila. co., and Jane Roberts, of the same county, at Gwynedd m. h., — mo. 20, 1741.

John Roberts, son of William, of Worcester, Phila. Co., and Ann Hughs, dau. of Rowland, of said county, at North Wales m. h., 3d mo. 20, 1742.

William Story, of Phila. Co., and Catharine Morgan, of the same place, at Gwynedd m. h., 6th mo. 17, 1742. [Witnesses: Sarah, Catharine, and Daniel Morgan, and others.]

Joseph Hallowell, of Phila. Co., and Sarah Nanney, dau. of Rees, of the same county, at Gwynedd m. h., 3d mo. 18, 1742.

Robert Roberts, son of Cadwalader, of Gwynedd, Phila. Co., and Sarah Ambler, dau. of Joseph, of the same county, at Gwynedd m. h., 11th mo. 11, 1742-3.

David Humphrey, son of Robert, of Gwynedd, and Elizabeth Roberts, of the same place, at North Wales m. h., 2d mo. 12, 1743.

William Robert, son of William, of Gwynedd, Phila. Co., and Ann Roberts, dau. of William, of Worcester, at Gwynedd m. h., 4th mo. 17, 1746.

Edward Evans, of Dublin, Phila. Co., and Elizabeth Jones, dau. of Humphrey, of the same county, at Gwynedd m. h., 3d mo. 22, 1746.

Nathan Evans, son of Evan, of Gwynedd, dec'd, and Ruth Morgan, dau. of Daniel Morgan, of the same co., at the house of Benjamin Morgan, ———, 1746.

Rowland Edwards, son of John, of Towamencin, Phila. co., and Mary Robeson, dau. of James, of the same co., at Towamencin meeting place, 10th mo. 11, 1746. [Witnesses: John, Mary, Edward, Elizabeth, Robert, and Evan Edwards; James Robeson, Daniel Morgan, Daniel Williams, John and Rowland Evans.]

Robert Jones, of Lower Merion, Phila. Co., and Margaret Evans, widow, of Gwynedd, at Radnor m. h., 11th mo. 5, 1747. [Witnesses: Benjamin and Ann Davids, Robert, Edward, Elizabeth, Jesse and Thomas Evans, and others.]

John Cunrad, of Springfield, Phila. Co., and Elizabeth Shoemaker, dau. of George, of Bucks Co., at Gwynedd m. h., 4th mo. 17, 1748.

Jacob Jones, of Gwynedd, Phila. Co., and Hannah Bennett, of said county, at Gwynedd m. h., 4th mo. 17, 1748.

Rowland Evans, son of John, of Gwynedd, Phila. Co., and Susanna Foulke, dau. of Thomas, of the same place, at Gwynedd m. h., 9th mo. 15, 1748.

Joseph Ambler, son of Joseph, of Montgomery, Phila. Co., and Mary Naylor, dau. of Joseph, of the same place, at Gwynedd m. h., 8th mo. 17, 1749.

Jesse Evans, son of Hugh, of Gwynedd, dec'd, and Catherine Jones, dau. of John, of Horsham, said county, at Gwynedd m. h., 4th mo. 19, 1750.

Edward Foulke, of Gwynedd, Phila. Co., and Margaret Griffith, of the same place, at Gwynedd m. h., 8th mo. 25, 1750.

Thomas Holt, son of Benjamin, of Horsham, Phila. Co., and Sarah Morgan, dau. of Enoch, of Gwynedd, at Gwynedd m. h., 2d mo. 13, 1781.

Thomas Evans, son of Thomas, of Gwynedd, Phila. Co., and Mary Roberts, dau. of John, of Whitpain, at Gwynedd m. h., 11th mo. 19, 1765.

Thomas Shoemaker, son of George, of Warrington, Bucks Co., and Mary Ambler, dau. of Joseph, of Montgomery, Phila. Co., at Gwynedd m. h., 10th mo. 11, 1757.

LIST OF MARRIAGES AND DEATHS.

Joshua Foulke, son of Edward, of Gwynedd, Phila. Co., and Catharine Evans, dau. of Thomas, of the same place, at Gwynedd m. h., 12th mo. 20, 1763.

Jarret Spencer, son of Jacob, of Moreland, Phila. Co., and Hannah Evans, dau. of Thomas, of Gwynedd, at a public meeting in Gwynedd, 11th mo. 22, 1774.

Daniel Evans, of the city of Philadelphia, blacksmith, son of Evan, of Gwynedd, and Eleanor Rittenhouse, dau. of Matthias, of Worcester twp., at a public meeting in Plymouth, 4th mo. 14, 1763. [Witnesses: Matthias, David, and Benjamin Rittenhouse; Jonathan, David, Letitia, Mary, and Thomas Evans, and 27 others.]

Cephas Child, son of Cephas, of Plumstead, Bucks County, and Priscilla, dau. of Joseph Naylor, of Montgomery, at Gwynedd m. h., 2 mo. 16, 1751.

Benjamin Dickinson, son of Joshua, of Whitpain, and Isabel, dau. of John Wright, of Hatfield, at Gwynedd m. h., 10th mo. 23, 1755.

George Morris, of Gwynedd, son of George, of Springfield, Chester [now Delaware] Co., and Jane Foulke, dau. of William, of Gwynedd, at Gwynedd m. h., 12th mo. 6, 1757.

Daniel Jones, son of Isaac, of Montgomery, Phila. Co., and Margaret Moore, dau. of Mordecai, of Norrington, Phila. Co., at Plymouth m. h., 1st mo. 10, 1765.

Edward Ambler, son of Joseph, of Montgomery, Phila. Co., and Ellin Foulke, dau. of Edward, of Gwynedd, said county, at Gwynedd m. h., 5th mo. 14, 1767.

Edward Roberts, son of Robert, of Gwynedd, Phila. Co., and Ellin Lewis, dau. of Enos, of the same place, at Gwynedd m. h., 10th mo. 4, 1764.

Daniel Williams, of North Wales, Phila. Co., and Sarah Meredith, dau. of Meredith Davies, of Plymouth, at North Wales m. h. [date wanting; earlier, probably, than 1764].

John Roberts, son of John, of Whitpain, and Ellin Williams, dau. of Thomas, of Montgomery, dec'd, at Gwynedd m. h., 10th mo. 11, 1764.

Aquila Jones, son of Griffith, of Phila., dec'd, and Margaret Evans, dau. of Owen, of Gwynedd, dec'd, at Gwynedd m. h., 10th mo. 25, 1759.

Matthias Rhodes, of Gwynedd, Phila. Co., and Hannah Hardy, of Horsham, at Gwynedd m. h., 7th mo. 3, 1759. [Witnesses: Mary Hardy, Jane Williams, Elizabeth Humphreys, Mary Jones, Christopher Rhodes, Gwen Foulke, Ann Ambler, and 10 others.]

Thomas Evans, of Gwynedd, and Mary Brooke, of Limerick, at Gwynedd m. h., 10th mo. 9th, 1764. [Witnesses: Hugh and Susanna Evans, Sarah Geary, Anne Evans, Hugh Evans, Robert Jones, Jane Roberts, and 38 others.]

Ezekiel Shoemaker, son of Richard, of Horsham, and Ann Williams, dau. of John, of the same place, at Gwynedd m. h., 11th mo. 10, 1761.

Ellis Lewis, of Upper Dublin, Phila. Co., and Ellin Evans, dau. of John, of Gwynedd, dec'd, at Gwynedd m. h., 12th mo. 18, 1764. [Witnesses: Lewis, Jane, and Ann Lewis, Cadwalader, Jane, Rowland, and Susanna Evans, and 52 others.]

John Robeson, son of James, of Franconia, Phila. Co., dec'd, and Mary Edwards, d. of John, of Towamencin, said county, at Gwynedd m. h., 11th mo. 17, 1761.

William Lewis, son of William, of Newtown, Chester Co., dec'd, and Ruth Jones, dau. of Evan Jones, of Merion, Phila. Co., dec'd, at Gwynedd m. h., 11th mo, 20, 1764.

Robert Rogers, of Norriton, and Jane Roberts, of Gwynedd, at a public meeting at Elizabeth Meredith's, in Plymouth, 11th mo. 4, 1763.

Eldad Roberts, son of Rowland, of Montgomery, and Jane, dau. of Isaac Jones, of the same place, at Gwynedd m. h., 10th mo. 18, 1763.

William Luken, son of Abraham, of Towamencin, and Catharine Evans, dau. of Edward, of the same place, dec'd, at Gwynedd m. h., 10th mo. 20, 1762.

Evan Evans, son of Cadwalader, of Whitpain, and Catharine, dau. of Edward Morris, of Phila., at Gwynedd m. h., 11th mo. 23, 1762.

Nathan Cleaver, son of Peter, of Upper Dublin, and Ruth Roberts, dau. of John, of Whitpain, at a public meeting in Gwynedd, 5th mo. 24, 1768.

Isaac Jones, jr., of Warrington, Bucks Co., yeoman, son of John, and Ann Ambler, dau. of Joseph, of Montgomery, Phila. Co., at a public meeting in Gwynedd, 10th mo. 14, 1766.

Joseph Ambler, son of John, of Montgomery twp., Phila. Co., and Elizabeth Forman, dau. of John, of New Britain, Bucks Co., at Gwynedd m. h., 10th mo. 8, 1776.

Morgan Morgan, son of Edward, of Whitpain, Phila. Co., and Ann Roberts, dau. of John, of the same place, at Gwynedd m. h., 4th mo. 21, 1774.

John Evans, son of John, of Gwynedd, and Margaret Foulke, dau. of Evan, of the same place, dec'd, at Gwynedd m. h., 11th mo. 19, 1754.

LIST OF MARRIAGES AND DEATHS. 121

Jesse Holt, son of Benjamin, of Horsham, Phila. Co., and Sarah Thomas, dau. of John, of Montgomery, said county, at Gwynedd m. h., 11th mo. 21, 1780.

Levi Heston, of Phila., son of John, of Montgomery twp., and Susanna dau. of George Maris, of Gwynedd, at Gwynedd m. h., 4th mo. 21, 1795.

John Wilson, son of John, of Whitemarsh, Montgomery Co., and Hannah Maris, dau. of Geo., of Gwynedd, at Gwynedd m. h., 3d mo. 8, 1796.

Jarret Heston, son of John, of Montgomery twp., and Rebecca Maris, dau. of George, of Gwynedd, at Gwynedd m. h., 5th mo. 17, 1796.

James Wood, jr., son of John, of Plymouth, and Tacy Thomas, dau. of John, of Montgomery, at a public meeting in Gwynedd, 4th mo. 12, 1796.

Joseph Lukens, of Whitemarsh, widower, and Mary Roberts, dau. of Amos, of Gwynedd, dec'd, at Gwynedd m. h., 10th mo. 7, 1794.

William Roberts, son of John, of Lower Milford, Bucks Co., and Rebecca Pennington, dau. of Paul, of Baltimore, at a public meeting in Gwynedd, 11th mo. 11, 1785.

John Evans, son of Edward, of Towamencin, Phila. Co., and Mary Lawrence, dau. of Daniel, of Haverford, Chester Co., at Gwynedd m. h., 11th mo. 19, 1776.

William Hallowell, son of Joseph, of Whitemarsh, Phila. Co., and Mary Roberts, dau. of John, of Whitpain twp., said county, 6th mo. 17, 1777.

Samuel Thomas, of Plymouth, son of John, and Hannah Roberts, dau. of Robert, of Gwynedd, at a public meeting in Plymouth, 7th mo. 7, 1796.

John Lukens, son of John and Rachel, of Towamencin, and Jane Adamson, dau. of John and Ann, of Horsham, at a public meeting in Gwynedd, 11th mo. 14, 1797.

Paul Conard, son of Joseph, of Tredyffrin, Chester Co., and Sarah Roberts, dau. of Joseph, of. Montgomery twp. and co., at Gwynedd m. h., 5th mo. 28, 1793.

John Heston, of Upper Dublin, son of Zebulon, of Upper Makefield, [Bucks Co.], dec'd, and Elizabeth, and Mary Dickinson, widow, dau. of Mordecai Moore, of Montgomery twp., at Gwynedd m. h., 1st mo. 12, 1780.

Cadwalader Child, of Horsham, son of Cephas and Mary, of Plumstead [Bucks Co.], and Elizabeth Rea, of Montgomery twp., dau. of John and Jane, dec'd, of Philadelphia, at a public meeting in Gwynedd, 5th mo. 6, 1800.

Isaac Roberts, of Montgomery twp., son of Joseph, dec'd, and Mercy, and Alice Comfort, dau. of Ezra and Alice, of Whitemarsh, at a public meeting in Plymouth, 3d mo. 13, 1800.

Peter Roberts, son of John, jr., and Elizabeth, of the twp. and co. of Montgomery, and Elizabeth Comfort, dau. of Ezra and Alice, of Whitemarsh, at a public meeting in Plymouth, 11th mo. 20, 1800.

John Thomas, son of John and Mary, of Montgomery twp., and Gainor Forman, dau. of Alexander and Jane, of New Britain, Bucks Co., at Gwynedd m. h., 11th mo. 11, 1800.

James Walton, of Abington, son of Jeremiah and Margaret, and Martha Hughes, dau. of Atkinson and Jane, of Horsham, at a public meeting in Gwynedd, 4th mo. 14, 1801.

Benjamin Morgan, son of Morgan and Ann, of Whitpain twp., and Tacy Stroud, of Montgomery twp., dau. of Edward and Hannah, dec'd, of Motherkill, Del., at a public meeting in Gwynedd, 5th mo. 13, 1800.

Samuel Lovett, of Bristol twp., Bucks Co., son of Joseph, dec'd, and Ann, and Sarah Roberts, dau. of Amos and Sarah, dec'd, of Gwynedd, at Gwynedd m. h., 4th mo. 13, 1802.

Dennis Shoemaker, son of Isaac and Rachel, of Norrington, Montgomery Co., and Sarah Coulston, dau. of James and Rebecca Wood, of Whitpain, at a public meeting in Gwynedd, 11th mo. 16, 1802.

Cadwalader Roberts, of Montgomery twp. and co., son of Cadwalader and Mary, dec'd, and Elizabeth Evans, of Gwynedd, dau. of Thos. and Elizabeth, dec'd, at a public meeting in Gwynedd, 12th mo. 14, 1802.

Isaac Lowry, son of William, of Worcester, Montgomery Co., and Margaret Stroud, dau. of Edward Stroud, of State of Delaware, dec'd, at Gwynedd m. h., 5th mo. 24, 1803.

Amos Griffith, son of Amos and Sarah, dec'd, of Gwynedd, and Phebe Cleaver, dau. of Nathan and Ruth, of Montgomery twp., at a public meeting in Gwynedd, 11th mo. 11, 1794.

Jonathan Cleaver, of Montgomery twp., son of Nathan and Ruth, and Ann Jones, dau. of Isaac and Gainor, of the same place, at a public meeting in Gwynedd, 4th mo. 10, 1804.

Isachar Kenderdine, son of John, dec'd, and Hannah, of Horsham, and Sarah Morgan, dau. of Morgan and Ann, of Whitpain, at a public meeting in Gwynedd, 12th mo. 11, 1804.

Richard Roberts, of Montgomery twp., son of Cadwalader and Mary, dec'd, and Mary Scott, of Worcester, dau. of Alexander and Jane, at a public meeting in Gwynedd, 5th mo. 14, 1805.

LIST OF MARRIAGES AND DEATHS.

Amos Roberts, son of Edward, of Whitpain, and Rachel Morgan, dau. of Daniel, of Gwynedd, at Gwynedd m. h., 2d mo. 8, 1803.

Henry Jones, of Montgomery, son of Evan, dec'd, and Hannah, and Jane Lewis, dau. of Amos and Eleanor, dec'd, of Upper Dublin, at a public meeting in Gwynedd, 11th mo. 12, 1805.

Joseph Shoemaker, son of Thomas, of Gwynedd, and Martha Lukens, dau. of Peter, of Towamencin, at a public meeting in Gwynedd, 4th mo. 15, 1788.

Thomas Shoemaker, of Gwynedd, son of Thomas and Mary, dec'd, and Hannah Iredell, of Montgomery, dau. of Robert and Susanna, at a public meeting in Gwynedd, 11th mo. 11, 1806.

George Roberts, of Montgomery twp., son of Joseph, dec'd, and Mercy, and Phebe Scott, dau. of Alexander and Jane, of Worcester twp., at a public meeting in Gwynedd, 12th mo. 16, 1806.

Charles Mather, of Cheltenham, son of Isaac and Mary, dec'd, and Jane Roberts, dau. of Job and Mary, of Whitpain, at a public meeting in Gwynedd, 5th mo. 12, 1807.

Samuel Conrad, of Horsham, son of Samuel and Hannah, dec'd, and Sarah Hallowell, of Montgomery twp., dau. of William and Mary, dec'd, at a public meeting in Gwynedd, 11th mo. 17, 1807.

John Ambler, jr., of Montgomery twp., son of Joseph and Sarah, and Ann Morgan, dau. of Morgan and Ann, of Whitpain, at a public meeting in Gwynedd, 12th mo. 8, 1807.

Edward Spencer, of Horsham, son of Job and Hannah, and Mary Roberts, dau. of Cadwalader and Mary, dec'd, of Montgomery twp., at a public meeting in Gwynedd, 4th mo. 12, 1808.

Charles Jones, of Montgomery twp., son of Isaac and Gainor, and Ann Jones, dau. of Jonathan and Susanna, dec'd, of Whitemarsh, at a public meeting in Gwynedd, 12th mo. 5, 1809.

Isaac Jeanes, of Whitemarsh, son of Joseph and Mary, and Lydia Shoemaker, dau. of Joseph and Martha, of Gwynedd, at a public meeting in Gwynedd, 12th mo. 12, 1809.

Cadwalader Foulke, of Gwynedd, son of Hugh and Ann, and Ann Shoemaker, dau. of David, dec'd, and Jane, of Whitemarsh, at a public meeting in Plymouth, 11th mo. 27, 1810.

Nathan Evans, of Gwynedd, son of Thomas and Elizabeth, dec'd, and Ann Shoemaker, dau. of Joseph and Tacy, of the same place, at a public meeting in Gwynedd, 12th mo. 4, 1810.

Edward Foulke, of Gwynedd, son of Amos, dec'd, and Hannah, and Tacy Jones, dau. of Isaac and Gainor, of Montgomery twp., at a public meeting in Gwynedd, 12th mo. 11, 1810.

Evan Jones, of Montgomery twp., son of Evan, dec'd, and Hannah, and Lowry Miles, dau. of Caleb, dec'd, and Jane Foulke, of Gwynedd, at a public meeting in Gwynedd, 4th mo. 9, 1811.

William Robinson, of Providence twp., Montgomery Co., son of Nicholas and Elizabeth, and Jane Evans, dau. of Thomas and Elizabeth, dec'd, of Gwynedd, at a public meeting in Gwynedd, 11th mo. 12, 1811.

Jacob Styer, of Whitpain, son of John and Tacy, and Ann Lukens, dau. of Jesse and Susanna, of Gwynedd, at a public meeting in Gwynedd, 12th mo. 3, 1811.

Isaac Warner, jr., son of Isaac, of Moreland, Montgomery Co., and Martha, and Elizabeth Hughes, dau. of Atkinson and Jane, of Horsham, at Gwynedd m. h., 4th mo. 14, 1812.

Alexander Forman, jr., of New Britain, Bucks Co., son of Alexander and Jane, and Sarah Foulke, dau. of Hugh and Ann, of Gwynedd, at a public meeting in Gwynedd, 10th mo. 6th, 1812.

Samuel Lukens, of Gwynedd, son of Jesse and Susanna, and Mary Farra, dau. of Atkinson and Elizabeth, of Norriton, at a public meeting in Plymouth, 11th mo. 19, 1812.

Thomas Jacobs, of Providence twp., son of Thomas and Lydia, dec'd, and Sarah Fussell, dau. of Bartholomew and Rebecca, of Whitpain, at a public meeting in Gwynedd, 12th mo. 8, 1812.

Thomas Foulke, of Richland, Bucks Co., son of Israel and Elizabeth, and Sarah Lancaster, dau. of Thomas, dec'd, and Ann, of Whitemarsh, at a public meeting in Plymouth, 3d mo. 10, 1814.

Joseph Fussell, of East Fallowfield, Chester Co., son of Bartholomew and Rebecca, and Rebecca Moore, dau. of Henry and Priscilla, of Montgomery twp., at a public meeting in Gwynedd, 6th mo. 14, 1814.

Israel Scott, of Worcester twp., son of Alexander, and Jane, and Edith Lukens, dau. of Jesse and Susanna, of Gwynedd, at a public meeting in Gwynedd, 11th mo. 15, 1814.

William Ellis, Jr., of Whitpain twp., son of William and Sarah, and Sarah Jones, dau. of David and Esther, of Montgomery twp., at a public meeting in Gwynedd, 12th mo. 13, 1814.

Ashton Roberts, of Gwynedd, son of Nathan and Margaret, and Sarah Wilson, dau. of Joseph and Ann, dec'd, of Bristol twp., Bucks Co., at a public meeting in Gwynedd, 2d mo. 14, 1815.

Amos Wilson, of Whitemarsh, son of John and Elizabeth, dec'd, and Catharine Lukens, dau. of Abraham and Martha, of the same place, at a public meeting in Gwynedd, 5th mo. 9, 1815.

LIST OF MARRIAGES AND DEATHS. 125

John Forman, of New Britain, Bucks Co., son of Alexander and Jane, and Eleanor Shoemaker, of Gwynedd, dau. of Joseph and Tacy, at a public meeting in Gwynedd, 10th mo. 3, 1815.

David Ambler, of Montgomery twp., son of Joseph, dec'd, and Sarah, and Margaret Hallowell, dau. of William and Susanna, of Abington, at a public meeting in Plymouth, 11th mo. 16, 1815.

Solomon Fussell, of Providence twp., son of Bartholomew and Rebecca, and Milcah Martha Moore, dau. of Henry and Priscilla, of Montgomery twp., at a public meeting in Gwynedd, 2d mo. 6, 1816.

Richard M. Shoemaker, of Cheltenham, son of Robert, dec'd, and Martha, and Sarah Cleaver, dau. of Ellis and Elizabeth, dec'd, of Gwynedd, at a public meeting in Gwynedd, 2d mo. 13, 1816.

Ezekiel Shoemaker, of Gwynedd, son of Joseph and Tacy, and Margaret Weber, of Whitpain, dau. of Jacob and Tacy, at a public meeting in Plymouth, 2d mo. 15, 1816.

Amos Bailey, son of John, dec'd, and Edith, of Falls twp., Bucks Co., and Esther Adamson, dau. of Robert and Tabitha, of Horsham, of Gwynedd m. h., 12th mo. 9, 1817.

Jonathan Ellis, of Whitpain, son of William and Sarah, and Elizabeth Jones, dau. of David and Esther, of Montgomery twp., at a public meeting in Gwynedd, 11th mo. 18, 1818.

Emmor Kimber, jr., of Richland, Bucks Co., son of Richard and Susanna, dec'd, of Radnor, Delaware Co., and Lydia Shoemaker, dau. of Jacob, dec'd, and Sarah, at a public meeting in Gwynedd, 11th mo. 17, 1818.

Ellis Cleaver, of Gwynedd, son of Ezekiel and Mary, dec'd, and Tacy Evans, dau. of Thomas and Elizabeth, dec'd, of the same place, at a public meeting in Gwynedd, 7th mo. 6, 1819.

John H. Cavender, of Abington, son of William and Elizabeth, dec'd, and Hannah Shoemaker, dau. of Joseph and Tacy, of Gwynedd, at a public meeting in Gwynedd, 10th mo. 12, 1819.

Jesse Tyson, of Upper Providence twp., son of Robert, dec'd, and Mary, and Maria Heston, dau. of Levi and Susanna, dec'd, of Gwynedd, at a public meeting in Gwynedd, 4th mo. 18, 1820.

William Zorns, of Gwynedd, son of Jacob and Hannah, and Mary Righter, dau. of John, dec'd, and Elizabeth, of Roxborough, Phila. Co., at a public meeting in Plymouth, 5th mo. 11, 1820.

Caleb Evans, of Whitpain, son of Thomas and Elizabeth, both dec'd, and Agnes Roberts, dau. of Cadwallader and Mary, both dec'd, of Montgomery twp., at a public meeting in Gwynedd, 6th mo. 13, 1820.

Joseph Shoemaker, of Gwynedd, son of Joseph and Tacy, and Phebe Hallowell, dau. of William and Susanna, of the same place, at a public meeting in Gwynedd, 4th mo. 10, 1821.

Jesse Spencer, of Gwynedd, son of John, dec'd, and Lydia, and Mary Custard, of Gwynedd, dau. of Joseph and Amelia, both dec'd, of Richland, Bucks Co., at a public meeting in Gwynedd, 4th mo. 24, 1821.

Jesse Shoemaker, of Gwynedd, son of Joseph and Martha, and Sarah Ambler, dau. of Edward and Ann, of Montgomery twp., at a public meeting in Gwynedd, 12th mo. 11, 1821.

John Ambler, of Montgomery twp., son of John and Ann, dec'd, and Mary Thomas, dau. of John and Mary, of Plymouth, at a public meeting in Gwynedd, 11th mo. 12, 1822.

John Lloyd, of Moreland, Montgomery Co., son of Benjamin and Sarah, both dec'd, and Lydia Spencer, dau. of John, dec'd, and Lydia, of the same place, at a public meeting in Gwynedd, 4th mo. 8, 1823.

Aaron Lukens, of Plymouth, son of David and Mary, dec'd, and Anna M. Foulke, dau. of William and Margaret, dec'd, of Gwynedd, at Gwynedd m. h., 4th mo. 13, 1824.

Alexander Forman, of New Britain, Bucks Co., yeoman, son of Alexander and Jane, both dec'd, and Mary Ambler, dau. of Joseph, dec'd, and Sarah, of Montgomery, at a public meeting in Gwynedd, 2d mo. 15, 1825.

Edward Ambler, jr., of Montgomery twp., son of Edward and Ann, and Mary Roberts, dau. of George and Rachel, of Gwynedd, at a public meeting in Gwynedd, 10th mo. 18, 1825.

Silas Walton, of Upper Dublin, son of Jeremiah and Rachel, of Horsham, and Priscilla Ambler, dau. of John and Priscilla, dec'd, of Montgomery twp., at a public meeting in Gwynedd, 10th mo. 7, 1826.

Israel L. Tennis, of Towamencin, son of Samuel and Mary, and Elizabeth Lukens, dau. of Enos and Ann, of the same place, at a public meeting in Gwynedd, 12th mo. 12, 1826.

Jonathan Maulsby, of Plymouth, Montgomery Co., son of Samuel and Susanna, and Jane Jones, dau. of Evan and Sarah, of the same county, at a public meeting in Gwynedd, 4th mo. 8, 1828.

Jesse Shoemaker, of Gwynedd, son of Joseph, dec'd, and Martha, and Sarah Lukens, dau. of Enos and Ann, of Towamencin twp., at a public meeting in Gwynedd, 6th mo. 10, 1828.

Justinian Kenderdine, son of Joseph, dec'd, and Hannah, of Horsham, and Tacy Thomas, dau. of John, dec'd, and Sarah, of Whitpain, at a public meeting in Gwynedd, 12th mo. 9, 1828.

LIST OF MARRIAGES AND DEATHS.

Jonathan Lukens, of Gwynedd, son of Jesse and Susanna, dec'd, and Elizabeth Righter, jr., dau. of John, dec'd, and Elizabeth, of Roxborough, Philadelphia Co., at a public meeting in Gwynedd, 4th mo. 15, 1825.

Isaac Ellis, of Whitpain, Montgomery Co., son of William and Sarah, and Margaret Thomson, dau. of John and Mary, of the same county, at a public meeting in Gwynedd, 6th mo. 9, 1829.

John Rutter, of Upper Dublin, son of James and Mary, and Elizabeth Ambler, dau. of Edward and Ann, dec'd, of Montgomery twp., at a public meeting in Gwynedd, 12th mo. 8, 1829.

Thomas Bancroft, of Delaware Co., son of John and Elizabeth, and Lydia Ambler, dau. of John and Priscilla, dec'd, of Montgomery Co., at a public meeting in Gwynedd, 4th mo. 12, 1831.

David Jones, son of David and Esther, of Montgomery twp , and Hannah Conrad, dau. of Thomas, dec'd, and Mary, of the same place, at a public meeting in Gwynedd, 4th mo. 19, 1831.

Evan G. Lester, of Richland, Bucks Co., son of Thomas and Hannah, both dec'd, and Cynthia E. Jones, dau. of Evan and Sarah, dec'd, at a public meeting in Gwynedd, 2d mo. 14, 1832.

Lewis Jones, of Upper Dublin, son of Henry, dec'd [of Montgomery twp.], and Jane, and Mary Livezey, dau. of Samuel and Mary, of the same county, at a public meeting in Plymouth, 3d mo. 15, 1832.

Joseph Zorns, of Upper Dublin, son of Jacob and Hannah, and Ann Hallowell, dau. of William, dec'd, and Susanna, of Horsham twp., at a public meeting in Gwynedd, 4th mo. 3, 1832.

Joseph W. Conrad, of Montgomery twp., son of Thomas, dec'd, and Mary, and Hannah S. Meredith, dau. of David and Rachel, of said county, at a public meeting in Plymouth, 5th mo. 16, 1832.

David Thomas, of Whitpain, son of Evan and Christiana, both dec'd, and Sarah Gibson, dau. of John, dec'd, and Elizabeth, of Roxborough, at a public meeting in Gwynedd, 12th mo. 4, 1832.

Charles Evans, of Gwynedd, son of Nathan, dec'd, and Ann, and Mary Morgan, dau. of Benjamin and Tacy, of Whitpain, at Gwynedd m. h., 3d mo. 12, 1833.

Edwin Moore, of Upper Merion, son of Richard, dec'd, and Abigail, and Phebe Foulke, dau. of Joseph and Elizabeth, of Gwynedd, at a public meeting in Gwynedd, 5th mo. 13, 1834.

William Lukens, of Philadelphia, son of Amos and Sarah, and Edith Lukens, dau. of George and Esther, of Montgomery Co., at a public meeting in Gwynedd, 12th mo. 9, 1834.

John Rich, of Byberry, son of Joseph and Elizabeth, dec'd, and Ann B. Cooper, of Gwynedd, dau. of Mahlon and Jane, of Horsham, at a public meeting in Gwynedd, 4th mo. 7, 1835.

John Clifton Lester, of Richland, Bucks Co., son of John and Abigail, both dec'd, and Hannah B. Mather, of Whitpain, dau. of Charles, dec'd, and Jane, at a public meeting in Gwynedd, 9th mo. 15, 1835.

Thomas Shoemaker, of Gwynedd, son of Thomas and Mary, both dec'd, and Margaretta Farra, dau. of Atkinson and Elizabeth, dec'd, of Montgomery Co., at a public meeting, 10th mo. 13, 1835.

Robert Shoemaker, of Montgomery twp., son of Thomas and Hannah, dec'd, and Sarah Roberts, dau. of George, dec'd, and Rachel, of Gwynedd, at a public meeting in Gwynedd, 4th mo. 12, 1836.

Watson Comly, of Byberry, Phila. Co., son of Joseph and Rachel, and Mary G. Lester, dau. of Thomas and Hannah, both dec'd, at a public meeting in Gwynedd, 4th mo. 18, 1837.

John W. Hamton, of Plymouth, son of James and Harriet, both deceased, and Tacy S. Morgan, dau. of Benjamin and Tacy, of Whitpain, at a public meeting in Gwynedd, 3d mo. 13, 1838.

Benjamin G. Foulke, of Richland, Bucks Co., son of Caleb and Jane, dec'd, and Jane Mather, dau. of Charles, dec'd, and Jane, of Whitpain, at a public meeting in Gwynedd, 3d mo. 6, 1838.

John Walton, of Moreland, Montgomery Co., son of Jeremiah and Hannah, dec'd, and Mary Thomson, dau. of John and Mary, dec'd, of Gwynedd, at a public meeting in Gwynedd, 11th mo. 13, 1838.

James Hall, of Blockley, Phila. Co., son of John and Ann, and Sarah J. Ellis, widow, of Whitpain, dau. of David, dec'd, and Esther Jones, at a public meeting in Gwynedd, 12th mo. 3, 1839.

John T. Michener, of Plumstead, Bucks Co., son of Abraham and Jane, and Elizabeth Forman, dau. of John and Eleanor, of said county, at Gwynedd m. h., 5th mo. 4, 1842.

Charles Hall, of Blockley, Phila. Co., son of James and Hepzibah, dec'd, and Sarah Lukens, dau. of Nathan and Matilda, both dec'd, at the house of Ezekiel Cleaver, in Gwynedd, 2d mo. 16, 1843.

Hugh Forman, of New Britain, Bucks Co., son of Alexander and Sarah, dec'd, and Jane Hallowell, dau. of William and Catharine, dec'd, of Plymouth, at a public meeting in Plymouth, 3d mo. 16, 1843.

Josiah Cleaver, of Montgomery twp., son of Salathiel and Mary, and Martha P. Lukens, dau. of Peter, dec'd, and Mary, at the house of Evan Jones, in Gwynedd, 4th mo. 11, 1844.

Nathaniel F. Kinsey, of Milford twp., Bucks Co., son of John and Elizabeth, dec'd, and Elizabeth Morgan, dau. of Morgan and Ann, of Montgomery twp., at the house of Morgan Morgan, 4th mo. 16, 1844.

LIST OF MARRIAGES AND DEATHS.

Samuel J. Levick, of Richland, Bucks Co., son of Ebenezer and Elizabeth W., of Philadelphia, and Susanna M. Mather, dau. of Charles, dec'd, and Jane, of Whitpain, at the house of Job R. Mather, 11th mo. 17, 1844.

Ellis Cleaver, of Gwynedd, son of Ellis and Elizabeth, both dec'd, and Hannah Pugh, dau. of Jonathan, dec'd, and Esther, of the same co., at the house of Ellis Cleaver, 4th mo. 9, 1846.

Penrose Mather, of Cheltenham, son of Bartholomew and Ann, dec'd, and Lydia Shoemaker, dau. of Thomas and Hannah, dec'd, of Gwynedd, at the house of Thomas Shoemaker, 11th mo. 12, 1846.

Daniel Foulke, of Gwynedd, son of Joseph and Elizabeth; and Elizabeth C. Foulke, dau. of William and Susanna, of the same place, at the house of William Foulke, 4th mo. 8, 1847.

William Walmsley, of Philadelphia, son of Joseph and Ann, and Letitia Mather, dau. of Charles and Jane, both dec'd, at the house of Job R. Mather, 6th mo. 10, 1847.

Anthony C. Michener, of Abington, son of John and Martha, and Hannah W. Jones, dau. of Charles and Ann, of Montgomery twp., at the house of Charles Jones, 1st mo. 6th, 1848.

Eli Simmers, of Upper Dublin, parents deceased, and Mary L. Walton, dau. of Jeremiah and Rachel, both dec'd, at the house of Silas Walton, 12th mo. 6, 1849.

Charles Conard, of Whitpain, son of John and Sarah, and Lydia Ann Walton, dau. of Silas and Priscilla, of Montgomery twp., at the house of Silas Walton, 2d mo. 14, 1850.

George A. Newbold, of Byberry, Phila. Co., son of Samuel and Abigail, dec'd, and Hannah C. Foulke, dau. of William and Susanna C., of Gwynedd, at the house of William Foulke, 10th mo. 10, 1850.

Cadwallader R. Evans, of Gwynedd, son of Caleb and Agnes, and Ellen H. Shoemaker, dau. of Joseph and Phebe, of the same place, at the house of Joseph Shoemaker, 2d mo. 13, 1851.

David Cleaver, of Montgomery twp., son of Nathan and Martha, and Hannah Holt, dau. of John and Rachel, of the same co., at the house of John Holt, in Whitemarsh, 4th mo. 10, 1851.

Ellwood Cleaver, of Gwynedd, son of Ellis and Sarah L., dec'd, and Martha Ann Lukens, dau. of Jonathan and Elizabeth, of the same place, at the house of Jonathan Lukens, 10th mo. 9, 1851.

Comly Lukens, of Towamencin, son of George, dec'd, and Esther, and Lydia Acuff [wid. of William], dau. of Jonathan and Elizabeth Ellis, of Norriton twp., at the house of Jonathan Ellis, 2d mo. 16, 1853.

Ezekiel Shoemaker of Gwynedd, son of Joseph and Phœbe, and Hannah H. Meredith, dau. of John and Rachel, both dec'd, of Plymouth twp., at the house of William P. Ellis, 1st mo. 11, 1854.

Joseph M. E. Ambler, of Upper Dublin, Montgomery Co., son of Andrew, dec'd, and Mary I., and Hannah Cleaver, dau. of Solomon and Lydia, of [Gwynedd] the same co., at the house of Solomon Cleaver, 2d mo. 16, 1854.

Isaac Conard of Whitemarsh, son of John, dec'd, and Sarah, and Mary Walton, dau. of Silas and Priscilla, of Montgomery twp., at the house of Silas Walton, 4th mo. 6, 1854.

Jacob Beans, of Baltimore, Md., son of Jonathan and Elizabeth, and Sarah C. Smith, dau. of John and Betsy Rich, of Gwynedd, at the house of Benjamin C. Rich, in Horsham, 1st mo. 8, 1857.

Milton Darlington, of West Marlboro, Chester Co., son of Richard and Edith, and Sarah Forman, dau. of Alexander, dec'd, and Mary, of New Britain, Bucks Co., at the house of Hugh Forman, 6th mo. 10, 1858.

Jonathan Thomas, of [Upper Dublin], Montg. Co., son of Spencer [dec'd], and Hephziba, and Margaretta N. Phipps, dau. of Peter and Lydia, [of Whitemarsh], at the house of Peter Phipps, 10th mo. 11, 1860.

Lewis J. Ambler, of Upper Dublin, son of Andrew, dec'd, and Mary, and Rachel Walton, dau. of Silas and Priscilla, of Montgomery twp., at the house of Silas Walton, 9th mo. 25, 1862.

John Stackhouse, of Falls twp., Bucks Co., son of Thomas and Phœbe K., dec'd, and Anna Shaw, dau. of Lewis B. and Esther, of Gwynedd, at the house of Lewis B. Shaw, 1st mo. 8, 1863.

Charles E. Ambler, of Plymouth, son of Edward and Mary R., and Pamela F. Shaw, dau. of Lewis B. and Esther, of Gwynedd, at the house of Lewis B. Shaw, 2d mo. 12, 1863.

Edwin Mullin, of Gwynedd, son of Robert and Phœbe [of Horsham], and Anna R. Conrad, dau. of Peter and Sarah, of Horsham, at the house of Peter Conrad, 2d mo. 19, 1863.

Chalkley Ambler, of Philadelphia, son of John and Ann, both dec'd, and Catharine C. Evans, dau. of Peter C. and Margaret [of Whitpain], at the house of Chalkley Ambler, 6th mo. 4, 1863.

Edward Pickering, of Bensalem, Bucks Co., son of Samuel W. and Elizabeth L., both dec'd, and Rebecca Rowlett, dau. of John and Drucilla P., of Gwynedd, at the house of John Rowlett, 4th mo. 6, 1864.

James Quinby Atkinson, of Upper Dublin, son of Thomas and Hannah, and Margaretta Foulke, dau. of William and Susanna C., of Gwynedd, at the house of William Foulke, 11th mo. 17, 1864.

LIST OF MARRIAGES AND DEATHS. 131

Jesse James, jun., of Byberry, son of Jesse and Martha, and Sarah J. Cleaver, dau. of Nathan, jr., and Deborah, of Gwynedd, at the house of Nathan Cleaver, jr., 10th mo. 26, 1865.

Aaron Ambler, of Whitemarsh, son of David and Margaret, and Mary M. Conard, dau. of Meredith and Rachel, dec'd, of Whitpain, at the house of Meredith Conard, 1st mo. 17, 1867.

James Q. Atkinson, of Upper Dublin, son of Thomas and Hannah, and Mary Cleaver, dau. of Nathan jr., and Deborah [formerly of Gwynedd], at the house of Jesse James, Bensalem, Bucks co., 5th mo. 20, 1868.

[The following are from the records of the Orthodox monthly meeting of Gwynedd:]

Jacob T. Lukens, of Horsham, Montg. Co., son of William and Martha, and Jane Roberts, dau. of George and Phœbe, of Worcester twp., at a public meeting in Gwynedd, 2d mo. 18, 1832.

James C. Jackson, of Hockessin, New Castle Co., Del., son of Thomas and Jane, and Amelia Spencer, son of Jesse, dec'd, and Mary C., of Gwynedd, at a public meeting in Gwynedd, 5th mo. 16, 1844.

Thomas Wistar, of Montgomery Co., son of Thomas, jr., and Elizabeth B., and Priscilla Foulke, dau. of Edward and Tacy, of the same co., at Gwynedd m. h., 4th mo. 26, 1849.

Samuel Morris, of Philadelphia, son of Samuel B. and Hannah P., dec'd, and Lydia Spencer, dau. of Jesse, dec'd, and Mary C., of Montgomery Co., at Gwynedd m. h., 2d mo. 17, 1853.

Lists of Marriages and Deaths, from Samuel and Cadwallader Foulke's Memorandum Books.

The following lists are made up from memoranda found in two almanac memorandum books that were amongst the papers of Cadwallader Foulke (surveyor), of Gwynedd. The larger of the two is *Aitken's General American Register and Calendar, for the Year 1774*, printed at Philadelphia by R. Aitken; the other is *The Lancaster Pocket Almanack, for the Year 1778*, "by Anthony Sharp, Philom.," printed at Lancaster by Francis Bailey. The two contain blank leaves on which the memoranda appear. Both of them no doubt were originally the property of Samuel Foulke, of Richland (son of Hugh and

132   HISTORICAL COLLECTIONS OF GWYNEDD.

Ann), and the memoranda, begun by him, were added to by his son Cadwalader. Most of the marriages and a large part of the deaths are those of persons living at Richland, but as it would be difficult to select strictly those belonging to Gwynedd, and as there were so many ties of kindred and acquaintance with the Richland people, I have thought it altogether proper to give all that are found in both books. The marriage list is as follows. (For convenience of reference I have prefixed to the entries a series of numbers.)

1. Samuel Foulke and Ann Greasley, married 9th mo. 24, 1743.
2. Abel Roberts and Gainor Morris, 2d mo. 17, 1744.
3. Joseph Green and Catharine Thomas, 3d mo. 10, 1744.
4. Edward Thomas and Alice Roberts, 10th mo. 21, 1749.
5. Samuel Thomas and Phebe Lancaster, 10th mo. 19, 1752.
6. John Roberts and Margaret Gaskill, 5th mo.—, 1753.
7. John Lancaster and Elizabeth Barlow, 12th mo.—, 1753.
8. Jonathan Heacock and Susanna Morgan, 3d mo. 9, 1745.
9. Isaac Lester and Eleanor Thomas, 8th, mo.—, 1746.
10. Charles Dennis and Sarah Morgan, 4th mo. 11, 1747.
11. John Thomas and Elizabeth Lewis, 4th mo. 23, 1748.
12. Thomas Roberts and Lett'a Rhea, 9th mo. 14, 1750.
13. Joseph Dennis and Hannah Lewis, 5th mo. 20, 1752.
14. Thomas Christie and Martha Ashton, 5th mo.—, 1753.
15. George Hoge and Elizabeth Blackledge, 12th mo. 9, 1756.
16. Joseph Rakestraw and Rachel Ogilby, 11th mo. 7, 1757.
17. John Morgan and Mary Gaskill, 11th mo. 2, 1758.
18. Thomas Casner and Ann Thomas, 7th mo. 2, 1761.
19. Thomas Ashton and Mary Chapman, 1st mo. 13, 1763.
20. Thomas Stalford and Eliz. Wright, 5th mo. 12, 1763.
21. Abra'm Ball and Ann Adamson, 11th mo. 10, 1763.
22. David Roberts and Phebe Lancaster, 5th mo. 2, 1754.
23. Thomas Foulke and Jane Roberts, 10th mo. 10, 1754.
24. John Foulk and Mary Roberts, 10th mo. 14, 1755.
25. John Greasley and Jane Foulke, 11th mo. 17, 1756.
26. Abra'm Roberts and Cathar'ne Lester, 12th mo. 9, 1756.
27. Wm. Foulke and Priscilla Lester, 5th mo. 12, 1757.
28. Wm. Blackledge and Ann Lewis, 6th mo. 15, 1757.
29. Theophilus Foulke and Margaret Thomas, 11th mo. 10, 1757.

LIST OF MARRIAGES AND DEATHS. 133

30. Thos. Blackledge and Margaret Wright, 5th mo. 11, 1758.
31. Jonathan Penrose and Martha James, 5th mo. 10, 1759.
32. Joseph Rawlings and Ann Hilles, 6th mo. 20, 1759.
33. Robert Ashton and Sarah Thomas, 11th mo. 8, 1759.
34. Wm. Thomas and Ann Foulke, 10th mo. 9, 1760.
35. Benj'n Fell and Sarah Rawlings, 11th mo. 3, 1757.
36. Wm. Hicks and Hannah Shaw, 11th mo. 13, 1760.
37. Everard Robert and Ann [Hole?] 6th mo. 11, 1761.
38. John Lester and Jane Antram, 10th mo. 7, 1762.
39. Wm. Burr and Ann Edwards, 8th mo. 3, 1763.
40. Isaac Samuel and Eleanor Lester, 11th mo. 23, 1763.
41. James Walton and Margaret Lewis, 12th mo. 8, 1763.
42. Everard Foulke and Ann Dehaven, Sept. 29, 1778.
43. James Green and Martha Foulke, 5th mo. 6, 1779.
44. John Penrose and Ann Roberts, 11th mo. 8, 1764.
45. Will'm Edwards and Meribah Gaskil, 4th mo. 24, 1766.
46. Will'm Clark and Hannah Loyd, 5th mo. 1, 1766.
47. Joseph Shaw and Rachel Griffith, 6th mo. 4, 1767.
48. Sam'l Nixon and Susanna Roberts, 5th mo. 11, 1769.
49. Robert Fisher and Martha Edwards, 5th mo. 18, 1769.
50. Thomas Strawhen and Mary Heacock, 6th mo. 8, 1769.
51. Lewis Lewis and Mary Burson, 10th mo. 12, 1769.
52. Abra'm Walton and Rachel Heacock, 10th mo. 12, 1769.
53. George Michener and Hannah Carr, 10th mo. 19, 1769.
54. John Chapman and Hannah Antram, 11th mo. 30. 1769.
55. John Roberts, sen., and Martha Edwards, sen., 11th mo. 1, 1770.
56. Will'm Penrose and Mary Roberts, 11th mo. 8, 1770.
57. Randal Iden and Eleanor Foulke, 1st mo. 9, 1772.
58. John Thompson and Abigail Roberts, 3d mo. 25, 1773.
59. John Hallowell and Martha Roberts, 11th mo. 3d, 1774.
60. Edward Fell and Mary Penrose, 12th mo. 8, 1774.
61. Benjamin Green and Jane Roberts, 11th mo. 9, 1775.
62. Amos Roberts and Margaret Thomas, 11th mo. 30, 1775.
63. Isaac Burson and Elizabeth Blackledge, 2d mo. 29, 1776.
64. Joseph Speakman and Catharine Dennis, 11th mo. 14, 1776.
65. Will'm Shaw and Sarah Carr, 4th mo. 17, 1777.
66. Sam'l Penrose and Sarah Roberts, 10th mo. 9, 1777.
67. Jeremiah Williams and Mary Blackledge, 4th mo. 22, 1779.
68. Abrah'm Roberts and Penninnah Thomas, 10th mo. 7, 1779.
69. Edward Roberts and Marah Lewis, 9th mo. 30, 1779.
70. Asher Foulke and Alice Roberts, 11th mo. 11, 1779.

134   *HISTORICAL COLLECTIONS OF GWYNEDD.*

71. Samuel Shaw and Susanna Wray, 11th mo. 25, 1779.
72. Moses Shaw and Mary Carr, 6th mo. 1, 1780.
73. George Williams and Abigail Lancaster, 10th mo. 17, 1780.
74. Edw'd Foulke and Elizabeth Roberts, 11th mo. 1, 1781.
75. George Iden and Hannah Foulke, 1st mo. 24, 1782.
76. Israel Roberts and Ann Foulke, jr., 6th mo. 6, 1782.
77. Israel Foulke and Elizabeth Roberts, 11th mo. 14, 1782.
78. John Griffith and Rachel Greasley, 1st mo. 2, 1783.
79. David Stokes and Anne Lancaster, 4th mo. 15, 1784.
80. Joseph Rawlings and Anne Heacock, 11th mo. 25, 1784.
81. John Greasley and Margaret Roberts, 5th mo. 5, 1785.
82. Hugh Foulke and Sarah Roberts, 4th mo. 8, 1785.
83. Jesse Hicks and Mary Ball, 5th mo. 26, 1785.
84. Eli Kennard and Eliz'th Blackledge, 6th mo. 8, 1786.
85. Joseph Custer and Amelia Foulke, 10th mo. 20, 1786.
86. Judah Foulke and Sarah McCarty, 10th mo. 20, 1786.
87. Jona'n Griffith and Sarah Burson, 11th mo. 2, 1786.
88. Daniel Walton and Martha Green, 10th mo. 2, 1788.
89. Benj'n Foulke and Martha Roberts, 3d mo. 26, 1789.
90. Joseph Heston and Anne Thomas, 10th mo. 15, 1789.
91. John Foulke and Letitia Roberts, 10th mo. 29, 1789.
92. Israel Penrose and Susanna Foulke, 10th mo. 21, 1790.
93. Nathan Roberts and Margaret Ashton, 5th mo. 5, 1791.
94. Shipley Lester and Marg't Nixon, 11th mo. 24, 1791.
95. Samuel Shaw and Elizabeth Ball, 12th mo. 6, 1792.
96. Will'm Samuel and Mary Foulke, 5th mo. 25, 1793.
97. Josiah Dennis and Alice Wilson, 11th mo. 28, 1793.
98. Lewis Lewis and Abigail Roberts, 3d mo. 26, 1795.
99. Amos Richardson and Martha Penrose, 4th mo. 23, 1795.
100. Levi Roberts and Phebe McCarty, 6th mo. 4, 1795.
101. Thos. Penrose and Rachel Hillman, 3d mo. 31, 1796.
102. George Shaw and Rachel Penrose, 11th mo. —, 1795.
103. Thos. Lester and Mary Stokes, 12th mo. 22, 1796.
104. Jacob Beans and Hannah Iden, 8th mo. 31, 1797.
105. Moses Wilson and Jane Lester, 11th mo. 2, 1797.
106. Israel Lancaster and Hannah Nixon, 2d mo. 22, 1798.
107. Hugh Foulke and Sarah Lester, 12th mo. 27, 1798.
108. Isaiah Jemison and Margaret Ball, 4th mo. —, 1798.
109. George Hicks and Ann Penrose, 4th mo. 4, 1799.
110. William Edwards and Susanna Nixon, May 2, 1799.
111. Thos. Gibson and Margaret Foulke, April 25, 1792.

LIST OF MARRIAGES AND DEATHS.

112. Edw'd Jenkins and Sarah Foulke, April 26, 1792.
113. Theo's Foulke and Hannah Lester, May 31, 1792.
114. Cadwallader Foulke and Margaret Foulke, jr., Nov. 14, 1792.
115. Evan Foulke and Sarah Nixon, 4th mo. 7, 1794.
116. Nathan Edwards and Lydia Foulke, April 3, 1800.
117. Evan Roberts and Abigail Penrose, October —, 1799.
118. Joseph Penrose and Margaret Jameson, May 20, 1802.
119. Joseph Meredith and Rachel Foulke, Nov. 5, 1803.
120. Hugh Foulke and Catharine Johnson, Jan. 17, 1804.
121. Abiah Thomas and Sarah Ashton, April 10, 1804.
122. William Green and Mary Roberts, April —, 1804.
123. Job Watson and Gulielma Shaw, Jan. 6, 1794.
124. David McCord and Ann Shaw, Jan. —, 1795.
125. Wm. Manning and Hannah Shaw, April —, 1795.
126. Will'm Nixon and Martha Roberts, 1st mo. —, 1800.
127. Enoch Penrose and Martha Edwards, 11th mo. 26, 1801.
128. Timothy Smith and Rachel Stokes, 12th mo. 3, 1801.
129. Abel Penrose and Kezia Speakman, 4th mo. 1, 1802.
130. Joel Edwards and Ann Green, 3d mo. 31, 1803.
131. George Child and Ann Iden, 1st mo. 5, 1804.
132. David Roberts, jun., and Elizabeth Stokes, 3d mo. 22, 1804.
133. John Shaw, jun'r, and Elizabeth Ball, 11th mo. 22, 1804.
134. Abel Penrose and Abigail Foulke, 5th mo. 2, 1805.
135. Thomas Lester and Hannah Green, 11th mo. —, 1805.
136. John Lester and Abigail Wilson, 2d mo. 27, 1806.
137. Jonathan Evans and Elizabeth Iden, 10th mo. 5, 1809.
138. Thomas Thorp and Mary Foulke, 11th mo 2, 1809.
139. Morgan Morgan and Ann Custer, 11th mo. 15, 1810.
140. Sam'l Iden and Elizabeth Chapman, 11th mo. —, 1810.
141. David Foulke and Mariann Shaw, — mo. —, 1811.
142. John Kinzey and Elizabeth Foulke, Nov'r —, 1816.
143. Thomas Iden and Rachel Parry, Dec'r 10, 1816.
144. Jesse Iden and Ann Wright, Oct'r 9, 1817.
145. Samuel Foulke and Ann Heacock, Dec'r —, 1818.
146. Greenfield Iden and Ann Hartley, April 14, 1819.
147. Jesse Tyson and Maria Heston, April 24, 1818.
148. Samuel Shaw and Sidney Foulke, Dec'r 14, 1822.
149. Dr. James Green and Ann Foulke, Dec'r 14, 1822.
150. Jesse Spencer and Mary Custer, April 24, 1821.
151. Franklin Foulke and Maria H. Tyson, Nov'r 20, 1827.
152. Jesse Jenkins and Mary Ambler, Oct'r 20, 1828.

153. Meredith Conrad and Rachel Jenkins, April 9, 1829.
154. Thomas Strawn and Jane Foulke, April 30, 1829.
155. Peter C. Evans and Margaret Jenkins, October 20, 1831.
156. Dan'l L. Downing and Sarah Iden, 5th mo. 18, 1820.
157. James Boon and Mary Foulke, married 15th May, 1735.
    Their daughter Ann, born 3d April, 1737.
                  Mary, " 17th Jan., 1739.
                  Martha, " 30th June, 1742.
                  James, " 26th Jan., 1744.
                  Judah, " 8th Dec'r, 1746.
                  Joshua, " 24th March, 1749.
                  Rachel, " 10th April, 1750.
                  Moses, " 23d July, 1751.
    The mother's [Mary's] decease, 20th Feb., 1756.
    The father's [James'] second marriage, 20th Oct., 1757.
    Moses Boon and Sarah Griffith married 10th Jan., 1779.
    The father's [James'] decease, Sept., 1785.
    The second wife's [of James] decease, July, 1790.

List of Deaths.

The following is the list of deaths from the two memorandum books. As they had been inserted irregularly, on the various pages, and have been copied nearly in order from the beginning forward, the dates are to some extent intermingled:

Lewis Lewis Died Feb. 16, 1778, aged 72 yrs.
Edward Thomas Died April 4, 1782, aged 62.
12th Oct., 1780, Dyed Thos. Thomas.
21st Feb., 1781, Dyed Sam'l Shaw.
7th Dec., 1790, Dyed Thomas Blackledge, aged 83 yrs.
26th Feb., 1791, Dyed John Lancaster.
12th Feb, 1792, Dyed James Burson, aged 73 yrs.
31st Oct., 1792, Dyed Joseph Ball, aged 74.
12th mo. 23, 1794, Dyed Mary Shaw, aged about 82 yrs.
3d mo. 20, 1796, Dyed Sara Ball, aged 72 yrs.
2nd mo. 2d, 1797, Dyed John Roberts, aged 80.
8th mo. 23d, [1797] Dyed Phebe Roberts, aged 62.
8th mo. 25th, [1797] Dyed John Dennis, aged 18.
1803, Jan. 15, Died Kezia Dennis, aged 87.
Rebekah Bryan, July 23d, 1796, aged 80.
Deb'h Carr, 17th July, 1796, aged —.

LIST OF MARRIAGES AND DEATHS.

Joseph Rawlings, 22d Dec., 1796.
Mary Shaw, Dec'r 23, 1794, aged 82.
Ann Lewis, Nov'r 8, 1785, aged 78.
Thos. Roberts, May 30th, 1786, aged 66.
1797, July 28th, Died Theophilus Foulke, in his 37th year. [This was the son of Theophilus, and father of Dr. Antrim. He was accidentally killed].
April 12th, 1800, Died Wm. Heacock, aged 83.
June 6th [1800], Died Ellin Samuels, aged 76 yrs. 4 mos. and 7 days.
December 20th [1800], Died Jacob Strawhan, of Haycock, aged 8 years.
Feb. 12th, 1795, Dyed the Widow Snodgrass, aged 96 years.
Dec'r 1st, 1798, Dyed Hannah Foulke, of North Wales, in her 85th year [widow of William, the son of Thomas].
October 1st, 1798, Died Robert Kirkbride, of New Britain, with the yellow fever.
John Iden, son of Randal & Eleanor Iden, died 4th April, 1779.
Jan. 21st, 1797, Dyed Samuel Foulke, aged 78 years, 10 months, 17 days. [Member of the Provincial Assembly, father of Cadwalader].
May 12th, 1797, Dyed Ann Foulke, aged 70 years and 9 months. [Wife of Samuel, just mentioned.]
1801, Aug. 29, Died Everard Roberts, aged —.
August 31st [1801], Died Evan Jones, of Northwales, aged near 80 yrs.
Oct. 4th [1801] Died John Roberts Cadw'r, of Northwales, in the 89 year of his age.
Oct'r 7th [1801], Died Elizabeth Thomas, wife of John Thomas, aged 74 yrs.
March 29th, 1802, Died Margaret Foulke, aged near 68 years.
June 23d, 1802, Died Margaret Greasley, aged —.
Oct. 22, 1802, Died John Edwards, aged 78.
1803, Aug't 20, died George Maris, of Northwales, aged —.
June 14th, 1801, Died John Lester, aged 64.
Nov. 6th, 1816, died Gouverneur Morris, of the city of New York.
1811, Aug. —, died Amelia Custer.
1812, May 16th, died Randal Iden, aged 76 yrs.
1815, April 12, at his residence, Richland township, —— county, Ohio, William Thomas, formerly of Bucks co., Pa., aged 81.
1815, Died Levi Foulke, of Gwynedd.
April, 1833, at his residence, Hilltown, Bucks co., Benjamin Morris, in his 86th year.
1805, Aug. 14, died David Roberts, aged 83.
1806, December, died Nathan Roberts, aged 7-.

1807, January 8th, died Jane Maris, widow of George Maris, aged 7- years.
1807, Jan. 13th, died Joseph Custer.
1807, February 16th, died Ann Heacock.
Aug. 23d, 1816, died Elizabeth Stalford, aged 91 years.
Sept'r 6th, 1816, died Caleb Jenkins, aged about 11 years.
Sep. 11th, 1816, died Mary Roberts, wife of Job Roberts, Esq., aged about 57 yrs.
1819, Jan'y 10, died Evan Lloyd, aged about 73 years.
1821, Jan'y —, died Priscilla Foulke, aged — years.
1821, Feb'y 28, died at Harrisburg, Benjamin Foulke, Esq., aged 54 years.
1821, March, died Jesse Foulke, of Northwales.
1822, July 25th, died Jane Foulke, widow of Thomas Foulke, of Richland.
Octo'r 25th, 1820, died Nicholas Gerhart, of Whitpain, aged 105 years, 5 mos., and 29 days, the oldest person, perhaps, in the county, at the time of his decease. He was born in Germany.
July 29th, 1822, died Robert I. Evans, of Philadelphia, son of John Evans, of Northwales, aged about 36 yrs., esteemed for his amiable manners, bright talents, and excellent principles.
July 31, 1822, died Walter Evans, of Mont'y township.
Nov'r 24th, 1822, died Sarah Foreman, dau. of Hugh and Ann Foulke, Gwynedd.
1823, Jan'y, 20, died Joseph Lester, aged — yrs.
1823, Jan'y 21st, died Tabitha Thomas, aged 83 years, the last 40 yrs. of which time she labour'd under a partial Derangement, living entirely alone, a monument of human patience under suffering.
1823, Feb'y 15, died Michael Baum.
1823, Feb'y 26th, died Susanna Lukens, wife of Jesse Lukens.
1823, May 7th, died Edward Morgan, of Montgomery, aged — yrs.
1823, June 17th, Died John Roberts, Esq., of Montgomery, aged near 73.
1823, July 8th, died Daniel Sutch, of Gwynedd, aged about 58.
1823, Sept'r , died Joseph Shoemaker, of Gwynedd.
1823, Nov'r , died Robert Iredell, of Montgomery.
1823, Dec'r 6, died Ann Foulke, wife of Hugh, of Gwynedd.
1823, Dec'r 14, died Jesse Tyson, of Providence.
1824, Jan'y 19th, died Hugh Lloyd, of Horsham, in the 80th year of his age.
1824, Jan'y 20th, died Elizabeth Evans (late Iden), aged 39 yrs. and 11 mos.
1823, July , died Moses Boon, of Exeter [Berks Co.], aged 72.
[1823], August, died Mary Lee, late Boon, wife of Thomas Lee, of Oley, aged 84.
[1823], Nov'r, died Joshua Boon, of Exeter.
1824, Feb'y 6th, died Daniel Morgan, of North Wales, aged   yrs.

1824, Aug't 24, died Martha Walton (late Foulke), aged 68.
[1824], Sept'r   , died Israel Roberts, formerly of Richland.
[1824], Sept. 27th, died Israel Foulke, of Richland, aged 64 yrs. and 7 mos.
[1824], Dec'r 7th, died Abel Penrose, of ditto, aged 46 yrs.
1824, Dec'r 25th, died John Jones, Esq., of Lower Merion township, for many years Associate Judge of Montgomery county.
1825, Jan'y 4th, died Alexander Foreman.
1825, Oct'r 18th, died Hannah Jones, of Northwales, aged 96 yrs.
Nov'r 8th, 1825, died Nicholas Rile, aged 81 years. (9th of Nov'r, 1819, his wife, Margaret, died).
July 16, 1826, died Hannah Kirkbride, aged 79.
1826, Sept. 24, died John Shaw, aged 84.
1826, about the beginning of October, died Hannah Harlan, wife of Caleb Harlan, of Newlin township, Chester county, late Edwards, granddaughter of Hugh Foulke, of Richland, by his daughter Martha.
1826, Dec'r 15th, died Hannah Beans, late Iden, aged 89 years nearly.
Same day, died John Elliott, Esq., of Lower Merion, aged about 50.
1826, Nov'r   , died Asher Foulke, aged 69 yrs.
1827, March   , died Ann Foulke, wife of Everard, in her 69th year.
1827, August 3, died Frederick Conrad, Esq., of Norristown, aged 69 yrs.
September 5th, 1827, died Everard Foulke, Esq., of Richland, aged 72 yrs.
February 7th, 1828, died David Roberts, of Milford, Bucks county.
April 16, 1828, died David Lukens, of Plymouth, aged about 63.
1828,   , died Tho's Lester, of a pulmonary consumption, aged 58.
May 23, 1828, died Benjamin Green, of Richland, aged 78 yrs.
1828, Jan. 12, died Tacy Shoemaker, late Ambler, aged   .
Feb. 7th, 1829, died Hannah Shoemaker, wife of Thomas Shoemaker.
Feb. 12th [1829], died Maria H. Foulke, wife of Franklin Foulke.
Feb. 14th [1829], died Massey Roberts, aged about 83 yrs.
1828, Feb'y 16th, died William Lowry, of Worcester, aged 84 yrs, and his brother John a few days before, aged 81.
Feb. 19th [1828], died Joseph Lewis, Esq. [of Gwynedd], aged 83 yrs.
Feb. 19th [1828], died Isaac Jeans, of Whitemarsh, in the prime of life, of a deep consumption.
1829, August [24th], died Milcah Martha Moore,[1] at Burlington, N. J., widow of Dr. Charles Moore, of Montgomery Square, aged upwards of 90 years.

---

[1] This lady was the daughter of Dr. Richard Hill, a famous physician, first of Maryland, afterward of Funchal, Madeira, and finally of Philadelphia, where he d. 1762. She was born in Madeira, the youngest of twelve children, Sept. 29, 1740,

August 31st [1829], died Edward Jenkins, of Gwynedd, aged 71.
October 14th [1829], died Ellis Cleaver, of Gwynedd, aged 70 years.
Same date [Oct. 14th, 1829], died Jacob Kirk, of Upper Dublin, aged about 100 years.
1829, Oct. 31st, died Ellen Foulke, daughter of Franklin Foulke, aged 10 mos., of consumption.
Dec'r 4th [1829], died Hannah Foulke, of Gwynedd, widow of Amos Foulke, aged 81.
February 22d, 1830, died Everard Bolton, of Gwynedd, aged 9- years.
February 24th [1830], died Ruth Jones, of Montgomery.
Nov'r 24th, 1805, died Jane Lester, aged .
March 4th, 1805, died Elizabeth Evans, of North Wales, aged 79 years, a Remarkable Instance of Longevity that may be attained in female Celibacy.
Nov'r 30th, 1805, died John Thomas, aged 86.
January 16th, 1806, died Jonathan Carr.

List of Deaths from Lewis Jones' Memorandum Book.

Lewis Jones, of Gwynedd (b. in Montgomery, d. in Gwynedd, son of Henry), left in a memorandum book a list of deaths, which I present below. In some cases he had added obituary notices, the bulk of which I have not thought it necessary to present:

Lewis, Amos, d. Oct. 15, 1821, bd. at Gwyn. 16th.
Lukens, Jesse, d. 6, 2, 1822, 38th yr., bd. at U. Dub.

---

and m. 1767, Dr. Charles Moore, the son of Richard Moore (and uncle of Henry Moore, farmer and blacksmith, in Montgomery, where C. S. Knapp lives, 1884). Dr. Charles was a distinguished physician. He had graduated at the University of Edinburgh (Scotland), in 1752, and located to practice in his profession at Montgomery Square, where he d. Aug. 19, 1801, in his 78th year. He was buried at Gwynedd. After his death his widow removed to Burlington, N. J., and died there, without issue, as stated above, Aug. 24, 1829, her age being a little under 89, and not "upwards of 90." She left a bequest for educational purposes to Gwynedd meeting, and was a woman long remembered in the neighborhood. A grand-niece, the daughter of her husband's nephew, Henry (mentioned above), was named after her, Milcah Martha, and married Solomon Fussell, of Chester county.

LIST OF MARRIAGES AND DEATHS. 141

Cleaver, Ellis, sen., d. 10, 14, 1829. (He would have been 71, on the day of his funeral. Bd. at Gwynedd, " surrounded by a great assemblage of friends and acquaintances.")
Zorns, Phebe, dau. Jacob, d. 8, 4, 1819, aged abt. 20 yrs.
Griffiths, Howel, d. 8, 25, 1819.
Lukens, Harriet, 11, 22, 1819.
Mann, John, sen., of Up. Dub., d. 11, 7, 1819, aged 78.
Shay, John, sen., of Up. Dub., d. 11, 16, 1819.
Conrad, Saml, sen., of Horsham, d. 11, 21, 1819.
Detwiler, Martin, of U. D. (likewise his grand-child), d. 11, 24, 1819.
Ambler, Hannah, dau. Edward & Ann, d. 2d mo. , 1820.
Evans, Mary, sen., wid. Amos, d. 4, 21, 1820.
Meredith, Dr. Joseph, d. August 7, 1820.
Cleaver, Sarah, d. 9, 15, 1820, at her nephew's in Shoemakertown.
Paul, Hannah, sen., d. 9, 14, 1820 ; bd. Horsham, 16th.
Dull, Christian, sen., d. 9, 27, 1820.
Foulke, Priscilla, d. 1, 25, 1821 (in her 77th year), bd. at Gwynedd 28th. "Remains were followed by a numerous circle of relations and friends."
Foulke, Jesse, d. 3, 15, 1821, bd. Gwynedd 18th.
Rausberry, John, of Montgomery tp., d. June , 1821, "from injuries occasioned by a bull, a few days previous."
Harrar, Rebecca, wife Nathan, d. 8, 25, 1821, of consumption.
Bates, Thomas, jr., d. 8, 24, 1821. Bd. at Baptist burying-ground at Montgomery, 25th. Sermon by [Rev.] Joseph Mathias.
Weber, Jacob, jr., d. 9, 11, 1821 (about 5 yrs. old), of dysentery.
Burney, Hannah, jr., dau. of Wm. Burney, d. 9, 12, 1821, of dysentery.
Kneedler, Catharine, dau. of Jacob Kneedler, sen., d. 9, 16, 1821, of dysentery,—" on which evening she was to have been married."
Hallowell, Thos., sen., d. Oct. 10, 1821. Bd. at Horsham, 12th.
Moore, Priscilla, wife of Henry, d. 10th mo. , 1821.
Foulke, Anna, wife of Levi, d. 11, 21, 1821. Bd. Gwynedd, 23d.
Shoemaker, Thomas, of Upper Dublin, d. (suddenly) 7, 21, 1822. Bd. at U. D. 22d.
Ramsey, Elizabeth, 1, 18, 1825, aged about 59. Bd. at Montgomery Baptist Church, 20th.
Shoemaker, Phebe, jr., d. 8, 19, 1827, in 68th yr. Bd. at Upper Dublin, 20th.
Shoemaker, Margaret, wife of Jonathan, d. 8, 21, 1827.
Morgan, Edward Stroud, d. 8, 10, 1827. Bd. Gwynedd, 11th.

Shoemaker, Jonathan (son of Phebe just above, and husband of Margaret, just above), d. 9th mo. , 1827. Bd. Upper Dublin.

Moore, Henry, formerly of Montg. twp. [husband of Priscilla, mentioned above], d. 10 mo. , 1829. Bd. in Chester co., where he had lived for some years. [L. J. adds an obituary notice at length, speaking of him as one advanced in years, of much benevolence, sweetness of disposition, excellent memory, interesting conversation, etc.]

Acuff, Jacob, d. 4, 2, 1829. Bd. at Whitemarsh, 7th.

Shoemaker, Hannah, wife of Thos. of Gwynedd, d. 2, 7, 1820, bd. at Gwynedd 9th.

Lewis, Joseph, Esq., d. 2, 19, 1829.

Hugh, John S., d. 9, 14, 1829,

Kirk, Wm. J., d. 10, 14, 1829. } Bd. at Gwynedd, on same day; one
Kirk, Jacob, sen., d. 10, 14, 1829. } at 9, and one at 10 o'clk. Jacob the grandfather of W. J.

Foulke, Cadwallader, d. 3, 22, 1830. Bd. at Gwynedd, 24th.
 [L. J., speaking of "very large assemblage at funeral," expresses the general feeling of loss of one so highly useful.]

Mather, Charles, d. 11, 12, 1830. Bd. at Gwynedd, 14th.

Maulsby, Jane, wife of Jonathan Maulsby, of Plym., aged 28 yrs. 1 mo. 28 d. Died at residence of her father in Gwynedd. [Evan Jones's dau.]

XIII.

Evans Family Genealogy.[1]

IT is intended to present, here, systematically, all the ascertained facts concerning Thomas, Robert, Owen, and Cadwalader Evans, of Gwynedd, and their descendants. The details given are by no means complete: some of the branches of the family could not be traced beyond the early generations; and in some cases information asked for was not furnished; yet the mass of facts given is extensive, and may serve as the basis of for fuller work by any one who is particularly interested in the family.

The origin of the Evans family, in Wales, is indicated by notes given on a following page by the late Mrs. William Parker Foulke, the ancestress of her husband[2] having been the daughter of Robert Evans. Her facts are drawn from a very elaborate family document prepared by the late Rowland E. Evans, son of Cadwalader of Philadelphia. It traces the descent of the four brothers of Gwynedd back to Mervyn Vrych, King of Man, who was killed in battle with the King of Mercia, A. D. 843. Mervyn married Essylt, daughter and sole heiress of Conan Tyndaethwy, King of Wales (who d. 818 or 820). Both Mervyn and Essylt traced their descent from Lludd, King of Britain, brother of Caswallon, the chief who resisted the invasion of Cæsar, before the Christian era.

---

[1] This and the Genealogies immediately following are inserted at this place in the volume because they begin with the first settlers, and present a large part of the available details in relation to them and to the early history of the township. The fact that they continue to the present time is unavoidable, and probably not seriously objectionable,—even if a more strenuous attempt had been made to give a strictly consecutive arrangement to all the contents of the book.

[2] Mary Foulke, wife of Cadwallader.

Passing over, however, a number of intermediate generations, from Mervyn Vrych, the following may be noted:

I. David Goch, of Penllech, appears to have been a lessee of crown lands in Caernarvonshire, in the 18th year of Edward II., and to have been living on November 9, 1314. He m. Maud, dau. of David Lloyd (who traced descent from Owen Gwynedd, Prince of Gwynedd), and had three sons, one being

II. Ievan Goch, of Graianoc and Penllech, who appears as one of the jury to take the extent of the hundred of Cymytmaen, in 1352. His ownership of certain lands is shown in titles of that period. He m. Eva, dau. of Einion ap Cynvelyn (who traced descent from Bleddyn, Prince of Wales); and had two sons, the eldest being

III. Madoc, who appears in the Cwn Amwlch pedigree as "ancestor of the gentlemen of Ysbitty Evan," in Denbighshire. His son was

IV. Deikws ddu, who m. Gwen, dau. of Ievan ddu (who traced his descent to Maelor Crwm, head of the 7th of the noble tribes of Wales), and had a son,

V. Einion, who m. Morvydd, dau. of Matw ap Llowarch, and had a son,

VI. Howel, who m. Mali, dau. of Llewellyn ap Ievan, and had a son,

VII. Griffith, who m. Gwenllian, dau. of Einion ap Ievan Lloyd, and had four children, the third being

VIII. Lewis, who m. Ethli, dau. of Edward ap Ievan, and had six children, the fourth being

IX. Robert, who m. Gwrvyl, dau. of Llewellyn ap David, of Llan Rwst, Denbighshire, and had by her six sons and six daughters, the fourth being

X. Ievan, known as Evan Robert Lewis. He was living, probably a young man, in 1601. He removed from Rhiwlas (or its neighborhood), in Merionethshire, to Vron Goch (probably in Denbighshire), and there passed the remainder of his life.[1] He had five sons, all taking for themselves, in the Welsh manner, the surname ap Evan:

    1. John ap Evan.
    2. Cadwalader ap Evan.
    3. Griffith ap Evan.
    4. Owen ap Evan.
    5. *Evan ap Evan.*

---

[1] In the genealogy of the Owen Family, descended from his son Owen, it is said he was "an honest sober man," and was born "near the end of the reign of Queen Elizabeth."

XI. Evan ap Evan was the father of the four brothers who came to Gwynedd in 1698 (and of Sarah, their sister, who came with them, and m. Robert Pugh). He was twice married; by his first wife he had two daughters, by his second four sons,—the Gwynedd settlers.

From the other sons of Evan Robert Lewis, others of the Welsh settlers in Pennsylvania were descended. John ap Evan, it is stated, had several children, and one account[1] says that two of them were William John, of Gwynedd (the purchaser, with Thomas Evans, of the township), and Griffith John,[2] of Merion, (who d. 1707). This would make William John and Thomas Evans first cousins, and such a relationship is very probable.

Cadwalader ap Evan, the second son of Evan Robert Lewis, it is stated, left no children. "Of Griffith ap Evan nothing is known." The descendants of Owen ap Evan are very numerous; they form the Owen Family, the posterity of Robert and Jane Owen, of Merion,[3] who came from Wales in 1690, and d. 1697; and the Cadwalader family are his descendants also, in the female line.

Beginning, then, the account of the Evans family in this country,[4] and making the immigrants the First Generation, we have the following

---

[1] A MS. in the possession of Hannah Evans, Moorestown, N. J.

[2] Griffith John was the father of John Griffith, who m. Grace Foulke, dau. of Edward, and of Evan Griffith, who married John Humphrey's step-daughter, Jane Jones.

[3] I have consulted freely a MS. Genealogy of the Owen Family, belonging to George S. Conarroe, Esq., of Philadelphia. (It is a copy of one originally made by Rowland Evans). Owen ap Evan had three sons, Robert, Owen, and Evan, and two daughters, Jane, who m. Hugh Roberts, the Merion settler and preacher, and Ellen, who m. ---- Cadwalader. Ellen's son, John Cadwalader, "schoolmaster," came to Merion, from Pembroke, Wales, and m., 1699, Martha Jones, dau. of Dr. Edward Jones, of Merion. His son was Dr. Thomas Cadwalader, of Philadelphia, father of General John, and Lambert, of the Revolution.

[4] Several copies of the Evans Family Record (mentioned on p. 58), begun in 1797, by Cadwalader Evans, son of Rowland, are extant. They vary in the extent of the information they present (having been added to, probably, each by its own

Genealogical Sketch.

[NOTE. The surname, in this Genealogy, of all whose names are given with Arabic figures on the left, is EVANS, except where otherwise explicitly stated. Female lines are not followed out. The character ❧, at the end of a paragraph, means that the son mentioned is again taken up as the head of a family, and fuller details given concerning him. The Roman numerals at the beginning of paragraphs, and at the head of lists of children, show the *generation;* the Arabic numbers, running through the Genealogy, are distinctive, each person having his own, by which he may be identified wherever named subsequently.]

Children of Evan ap Evan, of Wales:
1. Thomas ap Evan. ❧
2. Robert ap Evan. ❧
3. Owen ap Evan. ❧
4. Cadwalader ap Evan. ❧
5. Sarah ap Evan. ❧

I. (1.) THOMAS EVANS, eldest of the four brothers, son of Evan ap Evan, immigrated from Wales, 1698. His first wife was ANN, who d. in Gwynedd, 1st mo. 26, 1716. He m., 2d, at Goshen meeting, Chester county, 10th mo. 14, 1722, HANNAH DAVIES, widow, of Goshen. (HANNAH was then the widow of Ellis David, or Davies, of Goshen, who died 1st mo. 17, 1720. But before marrying him she was the widow of Reese John William, of Merion, who d. 11th mo. 26, 1697.— See Jones Genealogy, in this volume). In 1723, THOMAS EVANS removed from Gwynedd to Goshen, and died 10th mo. 12, 1738, "aged 87 years,"—which would make his birth in 1651. His wife survived until 9th mo. 29, 1741, when she d., "aged 85 years." All the children of THOMAS EVANS were by his first wife, as follows:

II. Children of Thomas and Ann:
6. Robert d. 1754, m. Jane ——, and Sarah Evans. ❧

---

copyist), but they differ very little, if any, on points of importance. One of these is in the possession of Charles J. Wister, Esq., of Germantown; another, of Jonathan Evans, of Germantown; a third, somewhat different, of Mr. Allen Childs, of West Philadelphia; a fourth was furnished the writer by Susan Y. Foulke, of Norristown; and still others would no doubt be brought to light by more extended search.

7. Hugh, d. 1772, m. Catharine Morgan, Alice Lewis, Lowry Lloyd. ℬ
8. Owen, d. 1757, m. Ruth Miles, Mary Nicholas. ℬ
9. Evan, d. 1747, m. Elizabeth Musgrave. ℬ
10. Ann.
11. Lowry, m. Evan Jones, son of John, of Radnor, dec'd, at Gwynedd m. h., 4th mo. 8, 1711.
12. Ellin, m. Rowland Hugh, yeoman, of Gwynedd, widower, at Gwynedd m. h., 5th mo. 31, 1712. (Rowland's first wife was Catharine Humphrey, of Merion, whom he m. 8th mo. 8, 1708).
13. Sarah, m. Edward Jones, son of John, of Radnor, dec'd, at Gwynedd m. h., 6th mo. 25, 1715.

I. (2.) ROBERT EVANS, of Gwynedd, brother to Thomas, son of Evan ap Evan, immigrant from Wales, 1698. He was a preacher among Friends. His wife's name was ELLEN.[1] He died in the 1st month (March), 1738, "aged about 80 years," which would have made his birth about 1658, and was bu. at Gwynedd. There is a brief memorial of him in the John Smith MS. collection of Philadelphia (Orthodox) Yearly Meeting, and numerous details concerning him are given elsewhere in this volume.

II. Children of Robert and Ellen :
14. Hugh, d. 1734, m. Margaret Roberts. ℬ
15. Evan, " father of Edward Evans, late of South st. [Phila.], and of Jane Much." (Family Record, 1797–1815.) ℬ
16. Lowry, m. at Gwynedd m. h., 5th mo. 28, 1701, Thomas Siddon, son of Anthony Siddon, of Upper Dublin. "She left a daughter, Susanna Swett, lately deceased in Phila., and Anthony Siddons, lately deceased, was a grandson of said Thomas." (Family Record.)
17. Mary m. Cadwallader Foulke, Thomas Marriott. (For details her line, see Foulke Genealogy.)
18. Ann, m. William Roberts, blacksmith, son of Edward, of Merion, dec'd, at Gwynedd m. h., 6th mo. 25, 1715. "She was the mother of Robert Roberts and Evan Roberts, both dec'd about 1780 or 1790 in North Wales" [Gwynedd].
19. Sarah, m 10th mo. 2, 1714, at Gwynedd m. h., Richard Kinderdine, "son of Thomas, late of Abington, dec'd." "She was the mother

---

[1] I should feel uncertain as to this, but I have for it the authority of so careful an investigator as the late Mrs. William Parker Foulke.

of Sarah Morgan, widow of Enoch Morgan, dec'd. Some of her children are now [1797] living in or near North Wales."
20. Jane, m. at Gwynedd m. h., 8th mo. 6, 1710, Edward Parry.

I. (3.) OWEN EVANS, of Gwynedd, third of the brothers, son of Evan ap Evan, immigrant from Wales, 1698, d. 10th mo. 7, 1723, in his 64th year, which would make his birth 1659. His wife's name was ELIZABETH. His will is dated 10th mo. (December) 4, 1723, and was proved December 20; he gives his son John a tract of 160 acres, " being on the south-west end of my land, with the house and plantation thereunto belonging." He makes bequests to his children, Cadwallader, Elizabeth, Evan, Robert, Thomas, and Mary, and mentions Jane as dec'd. He names two grandsons, Owen, the son of Robert, and Owen, the son of Thomas. He appoints his wife Elizabeth executrix, and for overseers "my two brothers Robert and Cadwalader, my two sons, Evan and Robert, and my two cousins [nephews] Evan, son of Thomas, and his brother Owen."

II. Children of Owen and Elizabeth:

21. Thomas, d. 1760, m. Elizabeth Griffith. ℔
22. John, d. unmarried, 1762. His will was probated Sept. 26. He leaves legacies to his sister Elizabeth Richards, his nephews Rowland and Samuel Richards, his sister-in-law, Elizabeth Evans, and her daughter Mary, his nephews Edward, Thomas, and Griffith Evans. He appoints his nephew, John Evans, executor and residuary legatee.
23. Robert, d. September, 1746, m. Ellen Griffith, Ruth Richards. ℔
24. Cadwallader, d. unmarried. (The Family Record calls him "Cadwallader Owen").
25. Evan, d. 1728, aged 44, m. Phœbe Miles. ℔
26. Mary, m. 1st, 3d mo. 3, 1708, Ellis Pugh, jr., of Plymouth, eldest son of Ellis Pugh, of Merion, 2d, 9th mo. 16, 1736, William Roberts. She survived her second husband, and her will was made 3d mo. (May) 1748, and proved in August. She mentions her grandsons Ellis and Elijah Pugh, her granddaughter Mary Pugh, her "only daughter" Sina Walker (Abel Walker, of Tredyffrin, m. Sina Pugh, of Gwynedd, 4th mo. 13, 1727); her grandson, Isaac Walker,

the daughters of her son, Ellis Roberts, her brothers John, Cadwallader and Thomas.
27. Elizabeth, b. 8th mo. 20, 1700, at Gwynedd, m., 2d mo. 21, 1726, Samuel Richards, son of Rowland, of Tredyffrin.
28. Samuel, m. 4th mo. 20, 1724, Hannah Walker, dau. of Lewis, of Merion.
29. Jane, d. before 1723. (As appears by her father's will).

I. (4.) CADWALADER EVANS, of Gwynedd, son of Evan ap Evan, youngest of the four brothers, immigrant, 1698, b. in Merionethshire, Wales, in 1664, d. at Gwynedd, 3d mo. 30, 1745. He m. in Wales, ELLEN, dau. of John Morris, of Bryn Gwyn, [White Hill], Denbighshire. He was a preacher, after joining the Friends. A memorial concerning him, by Gwynedd monthly meeting, has already been cited (p. 84).

II. Children[1] of Cadwallader and Ellen.
30. John, b. 1689, d. 1756, m. Ellen Ellis.
31. Sarah, m. at Gwynedd m. h., 10th mo. 11, 1711, *John Hanke*, of Whitemarsh, yeoman ; and had issue several children : John, b. 1712 ; William, b. 1720 ; Samuel, b. 1723 ; Joseph, b. 1725 ; Jane, b. 1714, m. John Roberts (see Roberts Genealogy); Elizabeth, b.1716; Sarah, b. 1728. *John Hanke* made his will Dec. 12, 1730, and it was proved in May, 1731; he leaves his wife, Sarah, executrix, and mentions his " seven children," all named above ; also his cousin John Hank, to whom he leaves 8 pounds. He appoints his brother [in-law] John Evans, and his friends, Thomas Evans, son of Owen, of Gwynedd, and Jonathan Robeson, trustees. His will indicates that he had real estate in Whitemarsh.

I. (5.) SARAH EVANS, sister of the four brothers, dau. of Evan ap Evan, m. ROBERT PUGH (the marriage, doubtless, in Wales). She appears to have come over with her brothers.

II. Children of Robert and Sarah (surname Pugh) :
32. Sarah, m. Samuel Bell. " They left one daughter, Hannah, who m. Evan Rees, of Providence township, near Perkiomen ; and had several children, one of whom, Samuel, m. a daughter of Colonel

---

[1] Two children, a son and daughter, died on the voyage from Liverpool to Philadelphia, in 1698.

150   HISTORICAL COLLECTIONS OF GWYNEDD.

Jacob Stroud, of Northampton county; he [Samuel] lived lately in Providence, and was a few years ago a member of Assembly for Montgomery county;[1] he now lives beyond the Blue Mountains, in Northampton county, where his father-in-law, Stroud, lived. His brothers, Evan and Daniel, and sister Sarah, still live in Providence, and are of the Baptist church."—(Doc. 1797).

33. Evan. " He went to Virginia to live. One of his sons became a Baptist minister, and one a justice of the peace, in good circumstances." (Doc. 1797).

34. Ellen. "She m. first, John Rogers, and was the mother of Sidney Pickering, a Public Friend." (Doc. 1797). Gwynedd records show marriage of " John Roger, son of Roger Roberts, of Merion," and Ellen Pugh, dau. of Robert, of Gwynedd, at Gwynedd m. h., 4th mo. 21, 1717. The will of Roger Roberts, 1720, mentions his son John Rogers (above) as then living.

35. Sarah, m. Rowland Roberts. " They had a son Eldad, who was the father of John Roberts, Esq., now a justice of the peace, in Montgomery township." (Doc. 1797). (See Roberts Genealogy).

II. (6.) ROBERT EVANS, "of Merion," son of Thomas, b. in Wales, lived for some time in Gwynedd, moved to Merion, and d. there late in 1753 or early in 1754, "aged about 80." In June, 1705, his father conveyed him 298 acres in Gwynedd (part of his tract, and apparently the part adjoining Montgomery), which subsequently he sold to his brother Hugh. In these and other conveyances he is called "eldest son and heir," and "son and heir apparent" of Thomas, and in the later deed (conveying to Hugh), the recital, after stating his purchase from his father in 1705, says he " built a messuage and other edifices, and made a plantation and other improvements" on the tract. In 1705 he is recorded as " of Gwynedd, yeoman." In 1709, however, in a conveyance from his father, he is described as " of Merion," so that apparently he moved there between 1705 and 1709. He appears to have been twice married: first, to JANE ———; and, second, to

---

[1] He was a member in 1805. (This illustrates the later information than 1797 contained in this document.)

Sarah Evans, of Merion, 4th mo. 4, 1705. (Haverford Records). His will, dated May 1, 1753, was proved Jan. 22, 1754; he mentions his daughter Catharine Evans, his daughters Anne Tillbury and Jane Roberts, his son Cadwalader, his grandsons Robert Evans and Amos Roberts, and his granddaughters Sarah and Catharine Evans, daughters of Thomas. He appoints his oldest son, Thomas Evans, executor, and leaves him the farm he now lives on, in Merion, 315 acres. He appoints his brother Hugh and his friend Robert Roberts, " both of Merion," and his brother Owen, of Gwynedd, overseers.

III. Children of Robert and (1st wife) Jane:
36. Elizabeth, b. 9th mo. 3, 1703. (Gwynedd Records.)

Children of Robert and (2d wife) Sarah.
37. Jane, b. 1st mo. 20, 1706, m. 8th mo. 31, 1723, Robert Roberts, son of Edward, of Gwynedd; and had issue a son, Amos, whose son, George, occupying the old Robert Evans place, d. about 1831.
38. Thomas, b. 1707, m. Katherine Jones.
39. Cadwalader, b. 4th mo. 7, 1709, d. about 1770, m. Ann, dau. of Joseph and Alice Pennell.
40. Catharine, b. 11th mo. 28, 1710, d. unm., in Philadelphia. Her will is dated in 1749, and was probated Feb. 2, 1758. She appears to have been housekeeper for her father, who lived in Philadelphia at the time of his death. Her will makes bequests to her sister Anne Tillbury, her nephew Robert Evans, son of Cadwallader; her niece Catharine, dau. of Thomas; and residue to her brothers Thomas and Cadwalader. She appoints Owen Jones executor, and Anthony Benezet and Isaac Zane trustees.
41. Hugh, b. 3d mo. 6, 1715.
42. Ann, b. 1st mo. 23, 1717, m. Thomas Tillbury, of Philadelphia, baker.

II. (7). Hugh Evans, of Merion, son of Thomas, b. in Wales, lived for many years in Gwynedd, d. in Philadelphia, 4th mo. 6, 1772, aged 90 yrs. 2 mos. In 1716 he is recorded as "of Gwynedd, yeoman," and his removal to Merion must have been later. A minute of Gwynedd Monthly Meeting, 10th mo. 27, 1715, says: " Our friend Hugh Evans, who Lately took a Trading Voyage to Great Britain, being returned, brought a Certificate from Haverford-West, which was read and gave a good acc't of his life and Conversation whiles in them parts." It was HUGH who related the incident of seeing William Penn on his knees at prayer, as mentioned elsewhere. He was a member of the Provincial Assembly, in 1722, and from 1746 to 1754 continuously. His will, dated 10th mo. 18, 1771, describes him as "of the city of Philadelphia," and "far advanced in years." He mentions his daughters Ann Howell and Susanna Jones, his grandson Hugh Howell, and granddaughter Abigail Howell, and appoints Samuel Howell and Ann executors. (June 25, 1772, his two sons-in-law took out letters of administration, also). He m., 1st, 8th mo. 4, 1706, CATHERINE MORGAN (d. 6th mo. 11, 1708), dau. of Cadwallader, of Merion; 2d, 6th mo. 25, 1710, at Merion, ALICE LEWIS, dau. of James, of Pembrokeshire, Wales; and, 3d, 12th mo. 13, 1716, LOWRY LLOYD, of Merion, widow of Robert Lloyd, and dau. of Reese John William. Of his children by his first wife, if any, we have no account.

III. Children of Hugh and Alice:

43. James, b. 6th mo. 29, 1711.

Children of Hugh and Lowry:

44. Ann, b. 1st mo. 23, 1718, m. 1st mo. 8, 1744-5, Samuel Howell, son of Jacob, of the Boro' of Chester, and had issue: Hugh, Samuel (or Jacob?), Ann, m. Aaron Ashbridge; Deborah, m. Daniel Mifflin.

45. Susanna, b. 11th mo. 25, 1719-20, d. May 4, 1801, m. May 30, 1740, Owen Jones, Sen. (b. Nov. 13, 1711, d. Oct. 9, 1793), son of Jonathan[1] and Gainor (born Owen), of Merion. The children of Susanna and Owen, were as follows, surname *Jones*:

   1. Jane, b. 1741, m. Caleb Foulke. (See Foulke Genealogy.)

---

[1] Jonathan Jones was born in Wales, in 1680, the son of Edward Jones, "chirurgeon," and Mary Wynne, dau. of Dr. Thomas Wynne, one of the first settlers in Merion. Edward d. 1737, aged about 92; Jonathan lived to be over 90.—See Dr. Levick's paper on old Merion families, *Penna. Mag.*, Vol. IV.

2. Lowry, b. 11th mo. 30, 1742, m. May 5, 1760, Daniel Wister,[1] merchant, of Philadelphia, (b. Feb. 4, 1738-9, d. Oct. 27, 1805), son of John and Anna Catharina; and had issue nine children, including Sally,[2] Elizabeth ("Betsy"). John, m. Elizabeth Harvey; Susan, m. John Morgan Price; Charles J., m. Rebecca Bullock.
3. Owen,[3] b. 1st mo. 15, 1745, m. 1st, Mary Wharton, and had issue six children, all d. in infancy; 2d, Hannah Smith, widow, who had by her former marriage four children.
4. Susanna,[4] b. Sept. 4, 1747, d. Feb. 5, 1828, at Burlington, N. J., m. Sept. 2, 1779, John Nancarro; and had issue John, jr., who m. Miss Quarles, of Baltimore.
5. Hannah, b. 1749, m. Amos Foulke. (See Foulke Genealogy.)
6. Rebecca, m. John Jones, of Lower Merion; no issue. (J. J. had children by a former wife.)
7. Sarah, m. Samuel Rutter, and had issue: Thomas, Martha, m. Howell Hopkins; and Rebecca.
8. Martha, d. unm.
9. Ann, d. unm.
10. Jonathan, m., 1st, Mary Potts, of Plymouth, who died about a year after her marriage; 2d, Mary McClenaghan, widow (dau. of William Thomas, of Lower Merion), and had issue: Owen Jones, who was member of Congress 1857-59, and Col. of the 1st Penna. Cavalry, 1861-63. (Owen's son, J. Aubrey Jones, Esq., now occupies the old Jones homestead, Wynnewood, Lower Merion.)

46. Abigail, prob. d. unm. (In 1745, she signs the certificate of the marriage of her sister Ann.) As she is not named in her father's will, she was prob. d. before 1771.

II. (8). OWEN EVANS, of Gwynedd, son of Thomas, b. in Wales, d. at Gwynedd, 3d mo. 1, 1757, "aged 70," which would fix his birth in 1687.[5] A brief memorial of him in John Smith's

---

[1] See details Daniel Wister and his progenitors, *Penna. Mag.*, Vol. V., p. 385.

[2] It is her Revolutionary Diary, kept at Gwynedd, that is given elsewhere in this volume.

[3] He was a distinguished citizen, Provincial Treasurer of Pennsylvania from 1769 to 1776; his name was placed with those of Col. Samuel Miles, and William Wister, on much of the Provincial paper money. In Sept., 1777, he was one of the Friends arbitrarily arrested and sent to Winchester, Va.—See Gilpin's *Exiles*.

[4] She is repeatedly quoted by Watson in his *Annals*.

[5] "He died," says one of the Evans MS. genealogies, "where Caleb Foulke, sen., now lives" (1797),—*i. e.* the old Meredith house; now (1884) the estate of Jonathan Lukens.

manuscript collection says: "His education was amongst Friends. He was of an honest and sincere disposition, a lover of truth . . . zealous, active, and serviceable in our meetings of discipline. He was an elder about 14 years." In a deed to his son Samuel he describes himself as "storekeeper." His will, dated 2d mo. 18, 1754, was proved May 2, 1757. He leaves his son Samuel a lot of land, "adjoining a tract that I have already conveyed to him, containing 82 acres." To his "eldest son" Amos, he leaves a small legacy, "having provided well for him before." He mentions his daughter Margaret (a minor), and his granddaughters the children of Amos. He appoints his wife Mary executrix, with his loving cousins Thomas Evans, jun., Rowland Evans, and Evan Jones, overseers. OWEN was for many years a justice of the peace, by appointment of the Governor: his first commission appears to be that of August 25, 1726, and he probably served (by numerous re-appointments) to 1752, though it is not easy to distinguish him (in the record in the Penna. *Archives*), from Owen Evans, of Limerick, who was contemporary and also a J. P. OWEN was also a member of the Provincial Assembly, from 1739 to 1750 inclusive. He m., 1st, at Radnor m. h., 11th mo 3, 1715–16, RUTH MILES, dau. of Samuel and Margaret of Radnor; and, 2d, at Philadelphia m., 2d mo. 29, 1736, MARY NICHOLAS, dau. of Samuel, yeoman, deceased. MARY survived him; she d. 5th mo. 20, 1769, and was bu. at Gwynedd. She was a preacher, and the memorial of Gwynedd m. m. concerning her is in the Collection of 1787. "She was born in Philadelphia, in or about the year 1695, her father dying when she was young." After her husband's death, "she lived some years with her daughter, who was married and settled in Philadelphia, but returned back again within the compass of this meeting. . . . Her last illness was lingering."

III. Children of Owen and Ruth:
47. Ann, b. 4th mo. 9, 1717, d. (before 1754).
48. Owen, b. 5th mo. 18, 1719, d. (before 1754).
49. Amos, born 4th mo. 25, 1721, m. Elizabeth Lewis. ⚹
50. Samuel, b. 3d mo. 29, 1729; " he kept school at North Wales some time ago," the Family Record of 1797 says. He owned, for some time, the place (now Fritz Hartman's) where his grandfather, Thomas, had lived.

Children of Owen and Mary:
51. Margaret, (a minor in 1754), m. Aquilla Jones, son of Griffith, of Phila., dec'd, at Gwynedd m. h., 10th mo. 25, 1759. " She left one daughter [Mary, b. 10th mo. 29, 1760], who married Marmaduke Cooper, of New Jersey, and she left one dau., now the wife of [Israel] Cope, in Arch St. near 8th." (Evans Rec., 1797.) Margaret and Aquilla Jones also had a son, Aquilla, b. 3d mo. 9, 1763.

II. (9). EVAN EVANS, of Gwynedd, son of Thomas, b. in Wales, 1684, d. 5th mo. 26, 1747, m. at Haverford m. h., 7th mo. 13, 1713, ELIZABETH MUSGRAVE, dau. of Thomas, dec'd, yeoman, of Halifax, England. He was a preacher among the Friends, and a memorial of him by Gwynedd monthly meeting, in the collection of 1787, has already been cited (p. 89). He lived by the present mill on the Wissahickon, now (1884) belonging to Henry Mumbower. His will, dated 5th mo. 3, 1747, was proved Aug. 3 of that year. He leaves bequests to his sons Abraham, Jonathan, Musgrave, David, and Daniel, and his dau. Barbara. He mentions his wife's uncle, Jonathan Cockshaw. He appoints his wife Elizabeth and son Jonathan his executors, with authority to sell the farm he lives on, about 200 acres. He appoints his brother, Owen Evans, his cousin, Thomas Evans, jr. (son of Owen), and William Foulke, trustees for his children.

III. Children of Evan and Elizabeth:
52. Jonathan, d. 1795, m. 1740, Hannah Walton. ⚹
53. Abraham, m. 1747, Lydia Thomas. ⚹
54. Daniel, m. 1763, Eleanor Rittenhouse, (sister of David). ⚹
55. Barbara, m. Isaiah Bell.
56. Musgrave, d. 1769, m. 1753, Lydia Harry. ⚹

57. David, d. 1817, aged 84, m. 1755, Letitia Thomas. ℔
(Three other children are mentioned in the Gwynedd Records: Hannah, d. 1720; William, d. 1745; Hannah, d. 1745).

II. (14). HUGH EVANS, of Gwynedd, son of Robert, d. 1734, m. 8th mo. 23, 1719, MARGARET ROBERTS, dau. of Edward. He received, 1719, from his father, a deed for 275 acres of land, in the north-eastern part of Robert's original great tract— the part next the meeting-house. He lived probably at his father's house, now (1884) belonging to Silas White, and in his will, (dated May 2, 1734, probated Oct. 1, same year) makes provision for his parents living there. He leaves to his son Robert, the west side of his farm, " with the buildings and improvements; extending eastward to a fence about 20 perches westward of the Great Road," and to his son Jesse the remainder of the farm, eastward of this fence. He names his sons Hugh, jr., and Edward, and daughters Anne, Sarah, and Mary. He appoints his wife executrix, and names as trustees for his minor children, his brother-in-law, Robert Roberts, his cousins, Evan Evans, Owen Evans, John Evans, and Thomas Evans; and John Jones. MARGARET, his widow, m. 1747, Robert Jones, of Merion.

III. Children of Hugh and Margaret:
58. Robert, b. 5th mo. 26, 1720. (Was living 1748.)
59. Ann, b. 5th mo. 26, 1720 (twin with Robert). She m. Benjamin Davids, "the father of Hugh Davids, late dec'd, of Rahway, N. J., also of Hannah Jenks, Tacy Ogden, and others."—*Evans Record, 1797.*
60. Edward, b. 3d mo. 5, 1723. (Was living 1748.)
61. Jesse, m. Catharine Jones. ℔
62. Hugh. (Was living, a minor, 1748.)
63. Sarah, d. 5th mo. 31, 1745.
64. Mary, d. 5th mo. 31, 1745.

II. (15). EVAN EVANS, son of Robert, the immigrant. He m. and had ten children, of whom the fullest account I have found is in the copy of the Evans Genealogy in the posses-

EVANS FAMILY GENEALOGY. 157

sion of Mr. Allen Childs. It (with some aid from Mr. Charles J. Wister's copy), refers to five of them as follows:

III. Children of Evan and ———— :

65. Jane, m. —— Much.
66. Robert.
67. Edward, " late of South street" (1797), who had six children, as follows:
    1. Francis, d. infancy.
    2. Mary, d. infancy.
    3. Samuel, of N. Y., Captain U. S. N.
    4. George, of N. C., Captain U. S. N.
    5. John, Sackett's Harbor, N. Y., midshipman U. S. N.
    6. Thomas, a sailor on brig *Rattlesnake*, Captain Moffatt.
68. Thomas,
69. Katherine, m. —— Jones, son of G. Jones, and they had a son Samuel, who m. Rebecca Morgan; whose dau. Sarah m. John Childs, of North Carolina. A son of this last couple, also named John Childs, m. Mary Treby, dau. of Rev. Thomas and Margaret Allen; and had issue nine children, of whom the second is Allen Childs, b. in North Carolina, 1844, now (1884) of Philadelphia. He m. 1878, Katherine, dau. of Col. John D. Kurtz, U. S. Engineer Corps, and has issue.

II. (21). THOMAS EVANS, of Gwynedd, son of Owen and Elizabeth, d. 5th mo. 22, 1760, m. at Radnor m. h., 4th mo. 30, 1720, ELIZABETH GRIFFITH, dau. of Edward, of Merion, dec'd. In his will, dated March 13, 1760, and proved May 26, same year, he describes himself[1] as "innkeeper." He leaves his eldest son Owen 10 pounds, " he having received his portion heretofore," provides for his wife, ELIZABETH, and makes bequests of 20 to 50 pounds each to his daughter Mary, and sons Edward, Griffith, and John. He mentions his grandson William, son of his eldest son Owen, appoints his son Thomas executor, and says: " I direct him to sell all my land the east side the Philadelphia road, situate between ye lands of Rowland Evans, on the one side, and

---

[1] The Evans document of 1797 says he "was a farmer and kept a tavern in the same place"— where his father, Owen, lived.

Peter Lukens, Cadwallader Jones, and Ballas Wick on the other." He also names his cousins John Jones, Rowland Evans, and Samuel Evans, overseers.

III. Children of Thomas and Elizabeth :

69½. Jane, b. 11th mo. 15, 1723.
70. Owen, "the father of Isaiah Evans, who d. in 1808, in Philadelphia; of Jane, who m. Alexander Scott, of Elizabeth, who d. unm.," (making her home, at her decease, " at the house of John Evans, sen., at North Wales,") and of William, named in his grandfather's will.
71. Griffith, b. 5th mo. 29, 1735.
72. John, b. 10th mo. 1, 1737.
73. Thomas, b. 1st mo. 24, 1733, m. Elizabeth Roberts.
74. Edward, b. 9th mo. 4, 1730.
75. Mary, b. 1728, d. unm.

(The Gwynedd records shows the deaths of children of Thomas and Elizabeth, as follows : Edward, 1728; Elizabeth, 5th mo. 5, 1745).

II. (23.) ROBERT EVANS, of Gwynedd, son of Owen, d. September, 1746, m. 1st, at Radnor mtg., 3d mo. 30, 1717, ELLEN GRIFFITH, dau. of Edward, of Upper Merion ; 2d, at Gwyedd m. h., 3d mo. 2, 1729, RUTH RICHARD, dau. of Rowland, late of Tredyffrin, Chester county. ROBERT'S will was dated 7th mo. (September) 8, 1746, and probated October 1, indicating very closely the time of his death. He leaves to his two sons, Evan and Robert, "the messuage and tract of land situate the west side [of] and divided from my other land by the road leading from North Wales meeting-house to Plymouth meeting-house," containing about ten acres, his wife, RUTH, to have a right to live on it, however, till his said sons were of age. He makes bequests to his "eldest son" Owen, to his son Peter, and to his daughter Catharine, wife of Peter Jones, and names as his "minor children" Evan, Robert (both named above), Ellin, Sarah, Elizabeth, Ruth, and one yet unborn, but expected. He appoints his wife RUTH executrix, with power to sell the farm he lives on, about 150 acres. He appoints his brothers John and Thomas Evans, his brother-in-law Samuel Richards, and his uncle, Joseph Jones and his cousin John Evans, overseers and trustees. He describes himself in his will as " of Gwynedd, yeoman."

III. Children of Robert and Ellen:

76. Catharine, b. 1st mo. 9, 1718, m. 3d mo. 15, 1740, at Gwynedd m. h., Peter Jones, son of Peter, of Merion.
77. Owen, b. 1st mo. 9, 1719–20. (Living in 1746.)
78. Peter, b. 1722, m. Mary Thomas. ₱
79. James, b. 1st mo. 14, 1724 : d. prob. before 1746.

[The above children were living when their mother d.; in 1727, their father, in a deed as administrator of her estate, names them as her heirs. James, not being named in his father's will, 1746, was probably then d.]

Children of Robert and Ruth:

80. Evan,
81. Robert, " a house-carpenter, living in 5th St., Philadelphia [1797], d. prior to 1820. He had a son John, who lived in 6th St. above Race, and had two sons, Robert and William."
82. Ellin, m. Jeremiah McVeagh, " and has left several daughters in Pikeland, and one son."
83. Sarah, d. 8th mo. 6, 1759, *unm.*
84. Elizabeth.
85. Ruth, m. —— Scotten. " She is the mother [1797] of Priscilla and —— Scotten, now bonnet-makers in Strawberry alley." (Fam. Rec., 1797–1815).
86. (Posthumous). This was probably Jane, b. 1st mo. 22, 1747, d. 3d mo. 23, 1832, m. Atkinson Hughs, father of Atkinson Hughes, of Horsham.

II. (25.) EVAN EVANS, of Gwynedd, son of Owen, d. 8th mo. 7, 1728, " aged 44," which would make his birth in 1684. He m., 2d mo. 13, 1715, PHŒBE MILES, (b. 4th mo. 20, 1690), son of Samuel (dec'd), and Margaret of Radnor. His will is dated 8th mo. 4, 1728, and was proved Oct. 22, same year. He gives to his two sons Samuel and Nathan "the plantation and tract of land " he lives on, his wife PHŒBE to have " her lawful thirds." He names also his sons Joseph and Miles, and dau. Elizabeth. He appoints as trustees his three brothers,

John, Robert, and Thomas, his two brothers-in-law, Thomas Thomas, and Owen Evans,[1] and his cousin John Evans. PHŒBE, with her children, removed after her husband's death within the limits of Haverford monthly meeting, as is shown by their certificate from Gwynedd, presented at Haverford, 2d mo. 29, 1729.

III. *Children of Evan and Phœbe:*

87. Elizabeth, b. 11th mo. 26, 1715, m. —— Meredith. "She had one daughter, Phebe, who m. Isaac Williams, of Whitemarsh, and is now dec'd. She [Phebe Williams] now dec'd, left two daughters, one of whom m. a son of Isaac Potts."—*Doc't of 1797.*[2]
88. Samuel, b. 6th mo. 17, 1718, d. 8th mo. 14, 1728.
89. Nathan, b. 1720, d. 1758, or '59, m. Ruth Morgan.
90. Joseph, b. 9th mo. 18, 1723, "the father of William Ashby's wife."
91. Miles (named in his father's will).

II. (30.) JOHN EVANS, of Gwynedd, son of Cadwalader, b. in Denbighshire, Wales, 1689, d. at Gwynedd, 9th mo. 23, 1756, m. ELEANOR ELLIS, dau. of Rowland,[3] of Merion, at Merion m. h. 4th mo. 8, 1715. ELEANOR, b. near Dolgellan, Merionethshire, Wales, 1685, d. 4th mo. 29, 1765. JOHN was a preacher of eminence among the Friends: details concerning him in that capacity have been elsewhere given in this volume (p. 85). His will, dated 9th mo. 16, 1756, was proved June 22, 1757. He leaves to his dau. Jane Hubbs the life right, with remainder to her children, of a lot of 2½ acres, "part of the tract of 100 acres which I hold, to be laid out for her the west side of Montgomery road, adjoining George

---

[1] This was Owen Evans (8), the J. P., son of Thomas; he m. Ruth Miles, sister to PHŒBE, here mentioned.

[2] It is necessary to caution the reader that this Record of 1797 was added to somewhat later, as appears by the memorandum made upon it by Charles Evans, (and referred to in this volume at p. 58), and that when it mentions things as "now" existing, or as having occurred, it cannot be strictly depended upon to mean the year 1797, but may mean a date later,—say as late as 1815.

[3] Rowland Ellis traced his descent, through a long line, including the Nannau family, of Wales, back to Henry III., of England.

Maris's field." He gives his daughters, Margaret, Ellen, and Elizabeth, 50 acres, "to be divided off the upper end, next Owen Evans's land." He mentions his sons Rowland and John, and appoints them and his son Cadwalader executors.

III. Children of John and Eleanor:

92. Cadwalader, b. 1716, d. 1773, m. Jane Owen.
93. Rowland, b. 1717–18, d. 1789, m. Susanna Foulke.
94. Margaret, b. 5th mo. 26, 1719, m. Anthony Williams; but left no issue.
95. Jane,[1] b. 1st mo. 30, 1721, m. John Hubbs. "She left two sons, John and Charles, and three [2] daughters, Rachel, Ellen, and Mary. Ellen m., 1781, Amos Lewis, of Upper Dublin [son of Ellis Lewis, 2d, and his first wife Mary], and Rachel also m., 1785, Amos Lewis.— (See Lewis Genealogy).
96. Ellen, b. 11th mo. 21, 1722, m., at Gwynedd m. h., 12th mo. 18, 1764, Ellis Lewis, 2d [widower], of Upper Dublin. *Ellis* d. 1783; *Ellen* survived him.— (See Lewis Genealogy.)
97. John, b. 1724, d. 1727.
98. Elizabeth, b. 6th mo. 26, 1726, d. 3d mo. 6, 1805, unmarried. She is mentioned as living with her bro. John, and giving the information embodied by her nephew in the Evans Record. Her will, dated 5th mo. 13, 1804, was proved March, 1805. She mentions her niece, Margaret Hubbs, to whom she leaves her "chest of drawers" and wearing apparel. She devises to Jesse Foulke and William Foulke, of Gwynedd, and John Jones, of Montgomery, in trust, a lot of land, in Gwynedd, purchased of Jesse Evans, for the use of Gwynedd Preparative Meeting. To her brother John Evans she leaves the residue of her estate, real and personal, appointing him executor.
99. John, b. 1730, d. 1807, m. Margaret Foulke.

---

[1] A letter from Eleanor Evans, of Gwynedd, to Mary Pemberton, of Philadelphia, dated 20th of 7th mo., 1762, preserved among the Pemberton papers, says; "I should take it kind [if] any of my good friends, of Philadelphia, particularly thyself, would call to see my Daughter, Jenny Hubbs. I know thou, dear friend, Loves ye afflicted, such an one indeed is she. [She] lives now at Kinsington. It's but short step from ye great road to her house, when thou art going up to thy countrey seat at Germantown. She had her certificate read and signed here. I suppose she will produce It at your next monthly meeting."

[2] See Elizabeth Evans' mention of her niece Margaret Hubbs. This appears at first sight to indicate a fourth daughter of Jane, but probably she was Elizabeth's grand-niece.

III. (38.) THOMAS EVANS, of Gwynedd, son of Robert, "of Merion," and Sarah, b. 4th mo. 22, 1707, m. 1st, 1730, KATHERINE JONES (who d. 11th mo. 21, 1732), dau. of Robert, of Merion; 2d, HANNAH ——— (who d. 6th mo. 22, 1760); 3d, 10th mo. 9, 1764, MARY BROOKE, of Limerick (who d. 7th mo. 14, 1805, aged 84). THOMAS appears to have received from his father the latter's land in Gwynedd, 230 acres, lying along the Swedes' Ford road (now the property, chiefly, of Jacob B. Rhoads), it being that which Thomas, the original purchaser, had sold to Robert, when he was dividing up his great tract. THOMAS d. in 1784; his will is dated 1st mo. 6, and was proved May 3, in that year. He leaves his wife MARY £250 in "good money," exclusive of an annuity of £12 derived from lands in Limerick township; and numerous other bequests and privileges of residence, etc. To his son Hugh, "my messuage and plantation in Gwynedd, where I now dwell, about 230 acres." He leaves legacy to his daughter Sarah, widow of George Geary; mentions her three children; also the two sons of his daughter, Catherine Foulke, Thomas and Samuel (they both minors); his daughter Mary, his daughter Susanna, and her children. He makes his son Hugh and his daughters Susanna, Ann, Mary, and Hannah residuary legatees. MARY EVANS, his widow, survived him over twenty years; her will, dated May 25, 1802, was proved in August, 1805, at Norristown. In it she describes herself as "of Gwynedd, widow," and "advanced in years." She leaves numerous bequests: to the children of her sister, Ann Hilles, £20 each; to the children of her sister Margaret £20 each; her "ten plate stove for the use and benefit of the school under the direction of Friends' Preparative Meeting of Gwynedd"; to Hannah Spencer £10; to niece Phebe Wood, £10; to Sarah Geary, £10; to Samuel Evans, £10; to Sarah Evans, relict of Hugh Evans, £10; to her [Sarah's] son, Hugh Evans, £5 and "my

EVANS FAMILY GENEALOGY.   163

Franklin stove in the front parlor"; to Thomas Evans, £8; to Thomas Foulke, son of Joshua, £5; to Abraham Updegrave, £10; to John Barlow, of Limerick township, "one moiety of all the annuities that may be due and unpaid, arising from the premises on which he resides." She appoints Levi Foulke and Joseph Shoemaker executors.

IV. Children of Thomas and Katherine:

100. Sarah, b. 6th mo. 8, 1731, d. 9th mo. 25, 1808, m. George Geary, who d. before 1784, and had issue 3 children.
101. Katherine, b. 11th mo. 14, 1732, m. 12th mo. 20, 1763, Joshua Foulke, of Gwynedd, son of Edward, and had issue. (See Foulke Genealogy.)

Children of Thomas and Hannah:

102. Susanna, b. 1st mo. 3, 1737, m. and had issue, and was living in 1784 (as appears by her father's will).
103. Ann, b. 7th mo. 21, 1740, m. Levi Foulke. (See Foulke Gen'gy).
104. Mary, b. 10th mo. 31, 1741, m. 6th mo. 10, 1784, " Richard Humphreys, the elder, son of John and Mary, late of Oxford twp., dec'd," and, subsequently (according to the Record of 1797), William Wilson.
105. Hannah, b. 5th mo. 26, 1745, m. 11th mo. 22, 1774, Jarret Spencer, son of Jacob, of Moreland.
106. Hugh, b. 8th mo. 9, 1747. He m. Sarah ——, and d. in 1792. His estate was settled by his widow, and George Maris and Levi Foulke, adm'rs. The farm which he had inherited from his father was divided between Joseph Evans and Thomas Evans, by a survey made in October, 1812, by Cadwallader Foulke. They were sons of *Hugh* and *Sarah:* Joseph, b. 12th mo. 11, 1785; Thomas, b. 8th mo. 8, 1787.

III. (49). AMOS EVANS, of Merion, son of Owen and Ruth, of Gwynedd, b. 4th mo. 25, 1721, m. ELIZABETH LEWIS. They removed within the limits of Haverford m. m., presenting a certificate from Gwynedd m. m., dated 9th mo., 1742.

IV. Children of Amos and Elizabeth:

102a. Owen, b. 4th mo. 18, 1746.
103a. Ruth, b. 10th mo. 28, 1749.
104a. Ann, b. 2d mo. 2, 1752, m. Dr. John Davis.

105*a*. Lydia, b. 10th mo. 23, 1754.
106*a*. Rebekah, b. 6th mo. 4, 1757.
107. Hannah.
108. Rose, d. before 1794, m. Charles Willing,[1] son of Thomas, and had issue: Elizabeth, m. Marshall B. Spring, of Boston, Mass.; Thomas, d. 1834; Richard, d. 1833.

III. (52.) JONATHAN EVANS, of Philadelphia, son of Evan and Elizabeth, of Gwynedd, m. 4th mo. 19, 1740, HANNAH WALTON, dau. of Michael, of Philadelphia. JONATHAN d. 2d mo. 3, 1795, aged 81. HANNAH d. 4th mo. 23, 1800, aged 85.

IV. Children of Jonathan and Hannah:
109. Elizabeth, b. 1741, d. 1746.
110. Samuel, b. 1742, d. 1744.
111. Joel, b. 12th mo. 24, 1743, d. in Jamaica, date not known. He is probably the Joel, "merchant," of Philadelphia, mentioned Vol. II., Sabine's *Loyalists*.[2]
112. Mary, b. 10th mo. 7, 1746, d. 6th mo. 14, 1794, m. Adam Hubley.
113. William, b. 3d mo. 4, 1749. He went with the Loyalists, in the Revolution, and his property was confiscated. See Sabine, Vol. II.
114. Benjamin, b. 9th mo. 16, 1751, d. 1793.
115. John, b. 3d mo. 30, 1753, d. 1798, in New York. He is probably the John mentioned with Joel and William above, in Sabine, Vol. II.
116. Jonathan, b. 1759, d. 1839, m. Hannah Bacon.

III. (53.) ABRAHAM EVANS, of Merion, son of Evan, m., at Radnor m. h., 8th mo. 8, 1747, LYDIA THOMAS, dau. of William, of Lower Merion.

IV. Children of Abraham and Lydia:
117. Evan, m., 1771, Mary Harmon.

---

[1] See Keith's *Prov. Councillors of Penna.* (p. 97).

[2] Joel's property, an undivided half of an estate in Blockley, Philadelphia county, was confiscated by the Executive Council of Penna., and sold for £15,000 Continental money. (*Colonial Records*, Vol. XII., p. 617). His brother William's property, a two-story carpenter shop, and lot of ground, on the north side of Pine St., between 3d and 4th, Philadelphia, was confiscated and sold to Benjamin Evans. (*Colonial Records*, XII., p. 97.) In these sales, one-fourth of the money was retained to become the principal of a ground rent, the annual income of which was payable to the University of Pennsylvania. On Joel's land the rent was to be 7½ bushels, and on William's property, 4½ bushels, per annum, of "good merchantable wheat."

EVANS FAMILY GENEALOGY.

118. Elisha,[1] "who keeps tavern at Norristown" [1797].
[And other children; names not obtained].

III. (54.) DANIEL EVANS, of Philadelphia, blacksmith, son of Evan, of Gwynedd, m. "at a public meeting in Plymouth," 4th mo. 14, 1763, ELEANOR RITTENHOUSE, dau. of Matthias, of Worcester township. (She was a sister of David Rittenhouse, the mathematician, who signs as one of the witnesses of the marriage). I have no data concerning their children, if they had any.

III. (56.) MUSGRAVE EVANS, of Philadelphia, cooper, son of Evan, of Gwynedd, m. at Radnor m. h., 12th mo. 12, 1753, LYDIA HARRY, dau. of Samuel, of Radnor.

IV. Children of Musgrave and Lydia:

119. Sarah.
120. Martha.
121. Ann.
122. Thomas.

III. (57.) DAVID EVANS, "of Spruce St.," Philadelphia, house carpenter, son of Evan, of Gwynedd, m. Aug. 10, 1755, LETITIA THOMAS, of Radnor. DAVID d. 1817, aged 84, and was bu. at Friends' ground, 4th and Arch Sts.[1] This couple had a large family of children, but only part of their names, as follows, have been obtained.

IV. Children of David and Letitia:

123. Letitia, b. 10th mo. 15, 1759, d. 1780, m. Richard Moore, son of Mordecai and Elizabeth, and had issue one child, Letitia, who m. her first cousin, Levin H. Jackson. (Richard Moore, b. 1745, d. 1829.)
124. Gulielma, b. 12th mo. 14, 1762.

---

[1] Cadwalader Evans, now [1884] of Bridgeport, Montg. Co., is a son of Elisha. See Auge's *Men of Montgomery County*, p. 460.

[1] Was it this David Evans who went with Dr. Parrish to New England, in the winter of 1775-6, to distribute supplies to the people around Boston, destitute by reason of the siege?—See *Penna. Mag.*, Vol. I., p. 168.

125. Charles, b. March 30, 1768, d. Sept. 5, 1847. (He was the seventh child of his parents.) Settling in Reading, Penna., he became a prominent lawyer, acquired wealth, and founded the beautiful cemetery of that city now known by his name. He d. unmarried.
126. David, b. 6th mo. 26, 1770.

III. (61.) JESSE EVANS, of Gwynedd, son of Hugh, m. 4th mo. 19, 1750, CATHARINE JONES, dau. of John, of Horsham. The Family Record of 1797 refers to him as having "formerly lived where George Maris lives." He was a tailor by trade, as well as a farmer, and, in 1755, sold the 55½ acres left him by his father (which included the present dwelling of Dr. M. R. Knapp, the dwelling and store of Wm. H. Jenkins, and the Acuff hotel property), to George Maris, for 270 pounds. He then bought of Hugh Evans, of Merion, Thomas's son, the property now owned by Jacob B. Bowman. Of his children no list has been obtained.

III. (73.) THOMAS EVANS, of Gwynedd, son of Thomas, b. 1st mo. 24, 1733, d. 9th mo. 3, 1818, m. 1765, ELIZABETH ROBERTS (b. 11th mo. 19, 1740, d. 1794), dau. of John and Jane Roberts, of Whitpain. (See Roberts Genealogy.) The Family Record of 1797 speaks of him as living where his father did (the farm now occupied by Ellen H. Evans), and calls him familiarly, "Tommy Evans."

IV. Children of Thomas and Elizabeth:
127. Jane, b. 11th mo. 13, 1766, d. 5th mo. 18, 1781, *unm.*
128. Caleb, b. 1768, d. 1855, m. Catharine Conrad, Agnes Roberts. ₰
129. Tacy, b. 1st mo. 10, 1770, d. 5th mo. 4, 1840, m. 1819, Ellis Cleaver (d. 1829), son of Ezekiel and Mary.
130. Nathan, b. 1772, d. 1826, m. Ann Shoemaker. ₰
131. Thomas, b. 1774, d. same yr.
132. John, b. 1775, d. 1777.
133. Jonathan, b. 1778, d. 1844, m. Elizabeth Iden. ₰
134. Elizabeth, b. 1st mo. 31, 1781, m. 1802, Cadwalader Roberts, of Gwynedd. (See Roberts Genealogy.)

EVANS FAMILY GENEALOGY.   167

135. Jane, b. 12th mo. 24. 1784, d. 7th mo. 3, 1876, m. 1811, William Robinson, of Providence (b. 1777, d. 1859), son of Nicholas and Elizabeth. William and Jane removed to Ohio, in 1816 or 1817. Their children were; Elizabeth, b. 1814, d. 1847; Tacy, b. 1818; Samana, b. 1818, m. George P. Clark.

III. (78.) PETER EVANS, of Merion, son of Robert, of Gwynedd, b. 1st mo. 20, 1722, m. MARY THOMAS, dau. of William and Elizabeth, of Merion.[1] PETER appears to have removed to Merion; the births of his children, as here given, are from the Haverford records.

IV. Children of Peter and Mary:

136. Jonathan, b. 7th mo. 2, 1745.
137. Ezekiel, b. 5th mo. 27, 1747.
138. Hannah, b. 10th mo. 7, 1748.
139. Rachel, b. 1st mo. 21, 1751.
140. Levi, b. 7th mo, 18, 1753.
141. Priscilla, b. 9th mo. 30, 1755.
142. Zachariah, b. 3d mo. 8, 1758.
143. Margaret, b. 3d mo. 2, 1760.
144. Mary, b. 12th mo. 17, 1761.

III. (89.) NATHAN EVANS, of Gwynedd, son of Evan and Phebe, b. 11th mo. 17, 1720, d. 1758 or '59, m. "at the house of Benjamin Morgan," 1746, RUTH MORGAN, dau. of Daniel. In 1758, he obtained a certificate for his removal to Wilmington, Del., and the records of the monthly meeting there show the presentation of it, 6th mo. 8, in that year, for himself, wife, and the four children named below. But in 1759 (10th mo. 11), his widow requested a certificate for her return to Gwynedd.

IV. Children of Nathan and Ruth:

145. Daniel.
146. Lemuel.

---

[1] There is some confusion of dates, (and possibly of identity), concerning PETER. According to the Historical Society's abstract of Haverford records, his marriage occurred in 1774. (See p. 112, this volume.) But the dates of his children's births indicate 1744 as the correct date.

147. Elijah.
148. Samuel.

III. (92.) Dr. CADWALADER EVANS, of Philadelphia, son of John and Eleanor, b. at Gwynedd, 1716, d. 6th mo. 30, 1773, m. 1st mo. 22, 1760, JANE OWEN, dau. of Owen Owen, of Philadelphia, dec'd. CADWALADER was bu. at Gwynedd; he left no children. A more particular sketch of him will be elsewhere given.

III. (93.) ROWLAND EVANS, of Gwynedd, son of John and Eleanor, b. 1718, d. 8th mo. 8, 1789, in Philadelphia. He m. at Gwynedd m. h., 9th mo. 15, 1748, SUSANNA FOULKE (b. 1st mo. 17, 1720, d. 3d mo. 1, 1787), dau. of Thomas and Gwen. (See Foulke Genealogy.) A sketch of him will be separately given.

IV. Children of Rowland and Susanna:

149. Cadwalader, born Dec. 7, 1749, merchant in Philadelphia, d. Feb. 21, 1821, unmarried.
150. John, d. 10th mo. 1, 1772, in his 20th year, unmarried.
151. Sarah, b. April, 1751, d. Jan. 27, 1831, unmarried.
152. Ellin, d. unmarried, 182-.
153. Charles, married, but left no issue.
154. David, d. unmarried.

III. (99.) JOHN EVANS, of Gwynedd, son of John and Eleanor, b. 12th mo. (February), 1730, d. 9th mo. (September), 1807, m. Nov. 19, 1734, MARGARET FOULKE, dau. of Evan and Ellen, of Gwynedd. (MARGARET b. 4th mo. 19, 1726, d. 3d mo. 6, 1798.— See Foulke Genealogy.) It was this JOHN who furnished Cadwalader, his nephew (son of Rowland), with the family data which form the basis of the 1797 Record. He was known in Gwynedd as "John Evans, the elder" (though his own father's name was John), in order to distinguish him from his son John. He was a prominent and active member of Gwynedd meeting. Joseph Foulke (elsewhere in this volume) gives some interesting reminiscences of him. He lived all his life at the old home of his father and grandfather, in Gwynedd (now the Bellows place). " From letters in my possession, written to his son," says Rowland Evans, Esq., now [1884] of Lower Merion, " he seems to have been an earnestly religious man." His will, which presents him as quite a rich man, was probated November 6, 1807. He gives his son John the "plantation, consisting of three tracts, where he now dwells," in Gwynedd, about 192 acres; directs his son Cadwalader to release any supposed claim he may have on the fee or title, in consideration of bequests now made him; leaves two tracts (homestead) to his son Cadwalader, one 245 acres, the other 36, he to pay £500 to his [the testator's] grandsons John and Robert; bequeaths to his friends Levi Foulke, Jesse Foulke, and John Jones, jr., son of Evan, or their survivors, £20 in trust to keep up the burial ground enclosure at Gwynedd meeting, the fund to be used in the discretion of Gwynedd preparative meeting; gives his son Cadwalader two undivided thirds in 50 acres of land adjoining the homestead, " late estate of brother Cadwalader," gives son Cadwalader the half residue of estate, the other half to grandson Robert; gives £200 to son John; gives £200 to grandsons Rowland and Evan in equal shares; appoints son Cadwalader and grandson Robert executors.

IV. Children of John and Margaret :

155. Evan, d. 1757, aged 9 mos.
156. John, b. Sept. 7, 1759, d. 1814, m. Gaynor Iredell, Eleanor Ely. ℔
157. Cadwalader, b. 1762, d. 1841, m. Harriet V. Musser. ℔
158. Rowland, b. 1762 [twin brother to Cadwalader] ," a merchant in Philadelphia," d. 10th mo. 10, 1793, of yellow fever, unmarried.

IV. (116.) JONATHAN EVANS, of Philadelphia, carpenter, son of Jonathan and Hannah, b. 1st mo. 25, 1759, m. 4th mo. 13, 1786, HANNAH BACON, dau. of David and Mary. A memorial of him, by the Southern District m. m. of Philadelphia, will be found reprinted in the collection of 1879. " His parents gave him a liberal education at the schools under the care of Friends in this city, and possessing strong mental powers and quick perceptions, he made considerable profiiciency in most of the branches of useful learning. He was placed apprentice to the carpenter's trade, and afterwards followed that business many years." At the period of his religious convincement " it was a time of great civil commotion, ... and about this period he was drafted as a soldier for the war of the Revolution. While many of the younger members of the Society were caught with the martial spirit of the day, he was constrained to maintain his testimony, in support of which he suffered an imprisonment of sixteen weeks." " Having scruples respecting the propriety of doing the ornamental work that was put on buildings, and persons generally declining to meet his scruples by giving him such parts as he was easy to do, he was many times under great difficulty in relation to the means of living, particularly when there was little building of any kind to be done." (The memorial says, however, in a later passage, that he retired from business many years before his death, having acquired a competence.) He was an overseer (in the Society of Friends) at the age of 24, and an elder at 36. In the 12th mo., 1826, after a sermon by Elias Hicks, to a very large congregation at 12th st. meeting in Philadelphia, JONATHAN EVANS arose and declared at some length that the doctrines preached by Elias were not those held by the Society of Friends.[1] He subsequently took a prominent part in the movements of the "Separation." In 1837, in correspondence with John Wilbur, he reviewed sharply the positions taken by Joseph John Gurney.[2] He d. in Philadelphia, 2d mo. 8,

---

[1] His remarks are given at length in the memorial. For a statement friendly to E. H., see Janney's *History of Friends*, Vol. IV., p. 155, et. seq.

[2] See John Wilbur's Journal, p. 228.

1839. Hannah, b. 3d mo., 1765, d. 2d mo. 27, 1829. She was a minister among Friends, and there is a memorial of her in the collection of 1879.

V. Children of Jonathan and Hannah:

159. William, b. 1787, d. 1867, m. Deborah Musgrave, Elizabeth Barton. ℞
160. Joseph, b. 1789, d. 1871, m. Grace Trimble. ℞
161. Mary, b. 9th mo. 25, 1791, d. 1st mo. 28, 1859.
162. Hannah, b. 9th mo. 7, 1793, d. 8th mo. 21, 1865, m. at Pine St. m. h., Philadelphia, 11th mo. 4, 1818, Joseph Rhoads, "of Marple twp., Delaware county, tanner," son of Joseph, dec'd, and Mary. Joseph d. 1st mo. 16, 1861, in his 75th year. Issue of Joseph and Hannah (surname Rhoads): Mary, m. Dr. Wm. E. Haines, and has issue; Deborah; Joseph, m. Elizabeth Snowden, and has issue; Hannah, d. young; Elizabeth; Dr. James E. (editor of *Friends' Review*, and now (1884) president of Bryn Mawr Female College under care of Friends), m. Margaret W. Ely, and has issue; Charles, of Haddonfield, N. J., conveyancer, m. Anna Nicholas, and Beulah S. Morris, and has surviving issue by first wife; Jonathan E., of Wilmington, Del., m. Rebecca C. Garrett, and has issue.
163. Joel, b. 1796, d. 1865, m. Hannah Rhoads. ℞
164. Thomas, b. 1798, d. 1868, m. Catharine Wistar. ℞
165. Charles, b. 1802, d. 1879, m. Mary Lownes Smith. ℞

IV. (117.) Evan Evans, of Philadelphia, house-carpenter, son of Abraham and Lydia, m. 4th mo. 1, 1771, Mary Harmon, dau. of Tubal, of Philadelphia.

V. Children of Evan and Mary:

166. Jacob, b. 2d mo. 8, 1772.
167. Sarah, b. 12th mo. 27, 1773.
168. Francis, b. 10th mo. 12, 1780.

IV. (128.) Caleb Evans, of Gwynedd, son of Thomas and Elizabeth, b. 2d mo. 16, 1768, d. 7th mo. 3, 1855, m., 1st, 1798, Catharine Conrad, dau. of Peter, of Whitpain; 2d, 1820, Agnes Roberts (b. 1783, d. 1872), dau. of Cadwalader and Mary. (See Roberts Genealogy). Caleb lived for many years, and died, at the home of his father (now the Ellen H. Evans place). He had but two children who grew up,— one by each wife.

V. Children of Caleb and Catharine:
169. Peter C., b. 1799, d. 1880, m. Margaret Jenkins.

Children of Caleb and Agnes:
170. Cadwalader R., b. 1821, d. 1861, m. Ellen H. Shoemaker.
171. Elizabeth, b. 1824, d. 1825.

IV. (130.) NATHAN EVANS, son of Thomas and Elizabeth, b. 1st mo. 25, 1772, d. 1st mo. 19, 1826, m. 12th mo. 14, 1810, ANN SHOEMAKER (b. 1786, d. 1863), dau. of Thomas and Tacy.

V. Children of Nathan and Ann:
172. Charles, b. 1811, m. Mary M. Morgan, Sarah M. Harris.
173. Edmund, b. 1816, d. 1847, m. Jane R. Smith; no issue.

IV. (133.) JONATHAN EVANS, son of Thomas and Elizabeth, b. at Gwynedd, 6th mo. 26, 1778, d. 4th mo. 7, 1844, m. at Richland, Bucks co., 10th mo. 5, 1809, ELIZABETH IDEN (d. 1st mo. 23, 1824), dau. of George and Hannah.[1] JONATHAN taught school "near Everard Foulke's," at Richland (half a mile from Bunker's Hill), for two years after his marriage, and then removed to Gwynedd, where he taught for several years. In 1816 or '17 he removed to Sandy Hill (Whitpain), where he remained teaching until after the death of his wife, in 1824, and then discontinued housekeeping. In 1832 and '33 he was in Ohio, near Mt. Pleasant, with his son, and then returned to Gwynedd, where he made his home[2] with his brother Caleb.

V. Children of Jonathan and Elizabeth:
174. Thomas I., b. 1810, d. 1883, m. Ann Worthington.
175. George I., b. 1812, m. Sarah Griffith, Mary P. Richards.

---

[1] Hannah was the dau. of Samuel and Ann Foulke; see Foulke Genealogy.
[2] Some further details will be given hereafter concerning Jonathan's work as a teacher, at Gwynedd and Montgomery.

176. Caleb, b. 1815, m. Sarah Black. ⓟ
177. William R., b. 1817, m. Mary W. Allen, Martha S. Carr. ⓟ
178. Job, b. 1820, d. same year.
179. Hannah I., b. 1821, m. Thomas D. Tomlinson, of Marietta, Iowa, and has issue 9 children.

IV. (156.) JOHN EVANS, of Gwynedd, son of John and Margaret, b. September 7, 1759, d. 1814, m., 1st, GAYNOR IREDELL (d. 12th mo. 12, 1785), dau. of Robert, of Montgomery; 2d, ELEANOR ELY,[1] dau. of —— and Esther. (Esther was the dau. of Evan Foulke by his second wife; Margaret Evans, mother of this JOHN, was Evan's daughter by his first wife; this couple were therefore nearly first cousins, their mothers being half sisters. (See Foulke Genealogy.) JOHN received by the will of his father, part of the Evan Foulke tract on the Penllyn road, adjoining Spring-House. (See No. 99, this Genealogy.) ELEANOR survived him.

V. *Children of John and Gaynor:*

180. John F., b. 9th mo. 3, 1784. He was living as late as 1814, and had been a clerk or assistant in business to his uncle Cadwalader (No. 157).
181. Robert I., b. 11th mo. 14, 1785, d. July 29, 1822. It will be seen by the date above that his mother d. when he was but a few weeks old. He engaged successfully in business in Philadelphia, and d. unm., July 29, 1822. There is a letter from him among the Cadwallader Foulke papers, dated July 21, 1818, in which he regrets his present inability to visit Gwynedd, as he is about leaving for Montreal and Quebec, by way of Ballston and Saratoga, intending to be absent a month. His estate was settled by Roberts Vaux, Esq., of Philad'a, administrator. An obituary article in MS., among the Cadw. Foulke papers (taken apparently from a Philadelphia newspaper) says he was brought up by his grandfather (John Evans, No. 99, who left him valuable bequests), and lived

---

[1] Eleanor's mother, Esther Foulke, m. an *Ely*, according to good authority; but some accounts call her husband Yearsley; and in a bond dated March 26, 1800, ELEANOR herself is called YAXLEY, and signs her name to a receipt for interest on the back of it "Nelly Yaxley,"—which seems to be conclusive that her own name was neither Ely nor Yearsley, when she m. John Evans.

with him till 1805, when he engaged as an apprentice to a mercantile house in Philadelphia. The article describes him in terms of warm praise as a very exemplary and much beloved man, devoted in his leisure to literature and scientific studies, and with "talents and acquirements remarkably devoted to the good of his fellow creatures." He was one of the Directors of the Public Schools; of the Pennsylvania Institution for the Deaf and Dumb; a Manager of the Apprentices' Library, and actively interested in other public institutions. (See Cadwallader Foulke's allusion to his death, p. 138.)

Children of John and Eleanor:

182. Rowland, b. 11th mo. 18, 1802. He was living in 1809.
183. Evan C., b. 8th mo. 29, 1805. He was living at the time of his father's death, 1814, and later, but d., probably unm., before 1828. Cadwalader Roberts was his guardian, and Cadwallader Foulke adm'r of his estate.
184. Randolph W.
185. Esther.
[Both the last named probably d. young.]

IV. (157.) CADWALADER EVANS, junior, son of John and Margaret, of Gwynedd, b. at Gwynedd, Dec. 25, 1762, d. Oct. 26, 1841, m. HARRIET VERENA MUSSER, dau. of John, of Lancaster, Pa. A sketch of CADWALADER will be given elsewhere.

V. Children of Cadwalader and Harriet:

186. Juliana Doddridge, d. 1866, unm.
187. Margaret Eleanor, unm.
188. John Glendour, d. 1827, unm.
189. Rowland Edanis, d. 1866, unm.
190. Edmund Cadwalader, b. 1812, d. 1881, m. Mary Louisa Allen. ₱
191. William Elbert, b. 1816, d. 1869, m. Anna Smith, Emma Fotterall. ₱
192. Cadwalader, d. 1861, unm.
193. Manlius Glendower, b. 1821, d. 1879, m. Ellen Kuhn. ₱
194. Harriet Verena, m. Gouverneur Morris Ogden, Esq., of New York (d. July, 1884), and had issue: Cadwalader E., David B., Gouverneur Morris, all living in New York (1884).

V. (159.) WILLIAM EVANS, of Philadelphia, son of Jonathan and Hannah, b. 10th mo. 5, 1787, d. 5th mo. 12, 1867, m., 1st,

1811, DEBORAH MUSGRAVE (d. 6th mo. 27, 1815, in her 28th year), dau. of Aaron and Abigail; and 2d, 12th mo. 23, 1824, ELIZABETH BARTON (b. in Newton, Camden Co., N. J., 1st mo. 2, 1794, d. 11th mo. 14, 1861), dau. of John and Rebecca. Of WILLIAM and both his wives there are memorials, published in the volume issued in 1879 by Philadelphia Yearly Meeting (O.) WILLIAM, "during his whole life was a member of this [Southern District] monthly meeting." He appeared as a minister in 1817; was recommended in 1822. He traveled considerably in religious work, and was much interested in education amongst Friends. In connection with his brother, Thomas Evans, he edited a series of fourteen volumes of the "Friends' Library," made up of "journals, doctrinal treatises, and other writings of Friends," the series being begun in 1837, and one volume issued each year. WILLIAM and Thomas also edited, 1854, a new edition of "Piety Promoted," a "Collection of Dying Sayings of Many of the People called Quakers." (Part of this was originally edited by John Tomkins, London, 1701, and successive parts were added by John Field, John Bell, Josiah Wagstaffe, Josiah Forster, and others.) For many years he was clerk of Philadelphia Yearly Meeting [O.] His journal was published in 1870, edited by his brother, Dr. Charles Evans. DEBORAH died at the early age of 28. ELIZABETH was a minister; she first spoke as such in the meeting at Newton, N. J., in 1815; in 1818, Haddonfield monthly and quarterly meetings acknowledged her ministry. She d. somewhat suddenly while on a visit to Salem, N. J.

VI. Children of William and Deborah:

195. Abigail, b. 10th mo. 1, 1812, m. Horatio C. Wood, and had issue: William E., b. 1854.
196. Jonathan, b. 4th mo. 29, 1814, d. 7th mo. 5, 1841. (He was a druggist, at 3d and Spruce Sts., Philad'a, the stand previously occupied by his uncle Thomas Evans.)

Children of William and Elizabeth :

197. Rebecca, b. 10th mo. 5, 1825, d. 11th mo. 13, 1836.
198. Hannah, b. 6th mo. 7, 1827.
199. Elizabeth R., b. 7th mo. 4, 1830.
200. William, b. 8th mo. 1835, m. Rebecca Carter; and has issue: John C., b. 1868; Charles, b. 1870; Alice C., b. 1872; Grace, b. 1874; William B., b. 1875; Ruth, b. 1877. (*William* is of the firm of Evans & Yarnall, Philadelphia, and resides at Moorestown, N. J.)

V. (160.) JOSEPH EVANS, of Delaware county, son of Jonathan and Hannah, b. 9th mo. 28, 1789, d. 2d mo. 10, 1871, m. 5th mo. 26, 1814, at Uwchlan m. h., GRACE TRIMBLE (b. 12th mo. 24, 1789, d. 8th mo. 17, 1867), dau. of William and Ann. They resided in Springfield township, Del. Co. " They were much esteemed and exemplary members of the Society of Friends, in which she [as well as her husband] was for many years an elder."

VI. Children of Joseph and Grace:

201. Ann C., b. 3d mo. 21, 1815, m. 5th mo. 6, 1847, Isaac C. Evans, (b. 3d mo. 23, 1818), son of Isaac and Mary, and has issue : Mary, Joseph, Isaac, Anne, Lydia, Rowland, William.
202. Hannah, b. 1817, d. 1826.
203. William, b. 1819, d. 1821.
204. Mary, b. 5th mo. 23, 1823, m. 11th mo. 7, 1844, William Mickle, of New Jersey (b. 7th mo. 24, 1813, d. 6th mo. 16, 1856), son of George and Mary, and has issue: Anne, Mary, Sarah, Joseph, William.
205. Joseph, b. 1825, d. 1826.
206. Thomas, b. 8th mo. 24, 1830, m. and has issue : Charles, Mary, Grace. (Howard Co., Maryland.)
207. John, b. 1833, d. 1851.

V. (163.) JOEL EVANS, son of Jonathan and Hannah, b. 3d mo. 7, 1796, d. 5th mo. 13, 1865, m. HANNAH RHOADS. He was an elder in the Society of Friends, and for some time (after the service of his brother William in that capacity) clerk of Philadelphia Yearly Meeting (O.)

EVANS FAMILY GENEALOGY.

IV. Children of Joel and Hannah:

208. Mary, d. 8th mo. 27, 1850, in her 29th year, m. William Rhoads, jr., and had issue: Mary.
209. William, d. 1st mo. 24, 1843, in his 20th year.
210. Owen, m. Lydia Thompson, and has issue: Mary, Beulah T., Edwin, and William.
211. Hannah, b. 1830.
212. Charles, m. Anne ———, and has issue: Wistar, and two who d. young.
213. Samuel, m. Anne Taylor, and has issue: Mary, Eleanor, Caroline, Albert.
214. Joel, m. Emma Stokely, and has issue.

[Three children of JOEL and HANNAH, named Joel, Elizabeth, and Elizabeth, d. young.]

V. (164.) THOMAS EVANS, of Philadelphia, son of Jonathan and Hannah, b. 2d mo. 23, 1798, d. 5th mo. 25, 1868, m. CATHARINE WISTAR, dau. of John and Charlotte, of Salem, N. J. She d. 12th mo. 5, 1871, in her 70th year. THOMAS EVANS was an eminent minister among Friends, whose preaching was characterized by "winning eloquence." An extended memorial of him is in the collection published by Phila. Y. M. (O.) in 1879. He received a strong religious impression in his youth; at 21 he began business; at 23 he went, as companion to George Withy, an English minister, and traveled four months in the Southern and Western States. At the time of the Separation in the Society of Friends, 1827–8, he took an active and very prominent part [on the side of the body distinguished as Orthodox]. He first spoke in the ministry in 1832, while on a religious visit to Virginia, but did not again speak for some years,—about 1838. In 1844 his ministry was approved. About this time his health became much impaired, and he fixed his residence for four years in the country, after which he returned to the city. In 1837 he joined his brother William in editing "Friends' Library," a series of fourteen volumes, and later, "Piety Promoted," in four vols. (Philadelphia: 1854.) He wrote, besides, "A Concise Account of the Religious Society of Friends," "An Exposition of the Faith of the Religious Society of Friends," "Youthful Piety," etc. His feeble health was occasioned in part, if not entirely, by an injury to his spine caused by extreme exertions on board a ship, during a storm, on a voyage to Charleston, S. C.,—his errand being to look after the Friends' meeting property in that city.[1]

VI. Children of Thomas and Catharine:

215. John Wistar, b. 4th mo. 7, 1836, d. 12th mo. 29, 1873, m. Eleanor Stokes, and had issue: Elizabeth W., Thomas, J. Wistar, Eleanor.
216. Thomas Wistar, b. 12th mo. 15, 1837, d. 2d mo. 16, 1857.
217. Hannah Bacon, b. 9th mo. 19, 1839.
218. Katharine, b. 7th mo. 14, 1841, m. Francis Stokes, and has issue: Katharine E., Henry W., Esther, Edith, Francis Joseph.
219. Jonathan, b. 8th mo. 16, 1843, m. Rachel R. Cope, and has issue: Anna C., F. Algernon, Edward W. *Jonathan* resides at Germantown; was some time of the firm of Cooper, Jones & Cadbury, Philadelphia.

---

[1] An elaborate obituary notice of THOMAS EVANS, published in the Philadelphia *North American*, June 22, 1868, and ascribed to Edward Hopper, contains these passages: "This [the So. of Friends] was to him a most precious communion. His affections, his time, his talents, were all given without stint to the support of this body of Christians, whose principles, testimonies, and we might say minute peculiarities, were subjects of his entire approval, and whose tenets found an unqualified response in his religious convictions." [Having referred to his clearness of view, and acumen in expression, with reference to the history, doctrine, and discipline of Friends; and to the fact that, although quite a young man, he was a leading witness in the great New Jersey chancery suit, in 1829-33, the article says:] "His testimony as presented to the Court, and which has been preserved in printed records, exhibits a knowledge of the points involved, and a power of ready expression, with a thorough understanding of everything that had a bearing upon the subject connected with the issue, unsurpassed by anything which is to be found in the annals of religious litigation." [Of his character as a preacher the notice says:] "His manner, though often much subdued by a sense of personal unworthiness, was animated, and the messages which he bore were often beautifully illustrated by apt and facile expression and striking analogies; and, while retaining all the simplicity and earnestness of an apostle, he was eloquent in a high degree, and withal there was a baptizing unction attending his ministry, which reached the hearts and minds of many."

V. (165) CHARLES EVANS, M. D., of Philadelphia, son of Jonathan and Hannah, b. 12th mo. 25, 1802, d. 4th mo. 20, 1879, m. MARY LOWNES SMITH, who survives him. CHARLES was an elder in the Society of Friends, conspicuous for his exertions in the interests of that religious society, and much engaged in benevolent and philanthropic labors. He was for many years attending physician at the Frankford Asylum for the Insane, and strongly interested in the treatment of mental diseases, on the care of which he was much consulted. He was some time editor of *The Friend*. He edited, in 1870, the Journal of his brother William, and wrote "Friends in the Seventeenth Century." (*New ed.*, Philad'a, 1876.) He left no issue.

V. (169.) PETER C. EVANS, of Whitpain, son of Caleb and Catherine, b. 1st mo. 24, 1799, d. 2d mo. 24, 1880, m. October 20, 1831, at Doylestown, Pa., by Josiah Y. Shaw, Esq., MARGARET JENKINS (b. 3d mo. 6, 1800, d. 10th mo. 8, 1872), dau. of Edward and Sarah, of Gwynedd. (See Jenkins Genealogy.)

VI. Children of Peter and Margaret:

220. Catharine, b. 10th mo. 21, 1834, m. 1863, Chalkley Ambler, now (1884) of Philadelphia, and has issue.
221. Sarah, b. 9th mo. 7, 1836.
222. Charles Edward, b. 8th mo. 9, 1838, m. Arabella G. Green, dau. of Carlo and Hannah R., and has issue: Edward J., b. 1877; William S., b. 1879; Harry S., b. 1882.

V. (170.) CADWALADER R. EVANS, of Gwynedd, son of Caleb and Agnes, b. 5th mo. 17, 1821, d. 5th mo. 23, 1861, m. 2d mo. 13, 1851, ELLEN H. SHOEMAKER (b. 10th mo. 24, 1823), dau. of Joseph and Phebe, of Gwynedd. CADWALADER lived at the original home of his ancestor, Owen Evans.[1]

VI. Children of Cadwalader and Ellen:

223. Joseph S., b. 11th mo. 17, 1851.

---

[1] See statement concerning this property at p. 59 of this volume.

224. Elizabeth, b. 10th mo. 31, 1853.
225. Anna, b. 1st mo. 29, 1856.
226. Mary E., b. 11th mo. 5, 1858.
227. Caleb, d. in infancy.

V. (172.) CHARLES EVANS, of Philadelphia, son of Nathan and Ann, b. 9th mo. 30, 1811, m., 1st, 1833, MARY M. MORGAN, (b. 1807, d. 1862), dau. of Benjamin and Tacy; 2d, 1876, SARAH M. HARRIS, dau. of Jonas.

VI. Children of Charles and Mary:

228. Tacy A., b. 1833, d. 1st mo. 25, 1884, m. 1865, Benjamin O. Loxley, son of Benjamin R., of Philadelphia; and had issue two sons.
229. Morris J., b. 1837, d. 1870, m. 1861, Elizabeth T. Hayhurst, dau. of Thomas; and had issue: Mary J., b. 1863, Charles W., b. 1865.
230. Charles W., b. 5th mo. 24, 1842, d. 8th mo. 31, 1864, unm.

V. (174.) THOMAS I. EVANS, carriage and wagon maker, of Mt. Pleasant, Ohio, son of Jonathan and Elizabeth, b. 7th mo. 22, 1810, d. 2d mo. 23, 1883, m. ANN WORTHINGTON (b. 9th mo. 3, 1811).

VI. Children of Thomas I. and Ann:

231. Mary E., b. 9th mo. 8, 1838, d. 9th mo. 21, 1864, m. 6th mo. 3, 1856, Dr. Jonathan Taylor Updegraff (b. 5th mo. 13, 1822, d. 11th mo. 30, 1882, elected Representative from the 18th district of Ohio, in the U. S. Congress, 1878, and re-elected 1880 and 1882); and had issue.
232. Rebecca J., b. 9th mo. 28, 1840.
233. George W., b. 2d mo. 3, 1843, m. 1874, Pocahontas R. Lunsford, and has issue: Blanche L., b. 1875; Murkland G., b. 1876; Claude I., b. 1879; Minnie M., b. 1881. (Stafford Co., Va.)

V. (175.) GEORGE I. EVANS, of Emerson, Ohio, son of Jonathan and Elizabeth, b. at Gwynedd, 8th mo. 31, 1812, m. 1st, 1834, SARAH GRIFFITH (b. 1814, d. 1846), dau. of Evan and Elizabeth, of Mt. Pleasant, O.; 2d, 1848, MARY P. RICHARDS (b. 1810, d. 1876), dau. of Samuel and Ann, of Mt. Pleasant. GEORGE removed from Gwynedd to Ohio in 1830.

EVANS FAMILY GENEALOGY.

VI. Children of George I. and Sarah:

234. Elizabeth E., b. 1835, m. 1853, John Scott; and has issue.
235. Julia A., b. 1837, m. 1859, Thos. McMillan.
236. Evan G., b. 1840, m. 1862, Rebecca Craft, dau. William and Rachel, and has issue: Arthur W., George M., Sarah E., Ellery Channing.
237. Sarah E., b. 1842, d. 1863.
238. Mary A., b. 1844, m. 1870, Geo. W. Michener.

Children of George I. and Mary:

239. Hannah J., b. 1849.

V. (176.) CALEB EVANS, of Bucks Co., Pa., son of Jonathan and Elizabeth, b. 4th mo. 8, 1815, m. 4th mo. 26, 1837, SARAH C. BLACK (b. 3d mo. 15, 1818).

VI. Children of Caleb and Sarah:

240. Wilson C., b. 1st mo. 23, 1838, m. 9th mo. 1, 1870, Mary Jane Lande (b. 4th mo. 6, 1848), and has issue: Adah S., b. 1871, Stanley C., b. 1873, Emma D., b. 1877.
241. Mary Emma, b. 11th mo. 19, 1848, m. 9th mo. 19, 1872, Edward R. Doan, of Carversville, Bucks Co., and has issue.

V. (177.) WILLIAM R. EVANS, of Carversville, Bucks Co., son of Jonathan and Elizabeth, b. 9th mo. 19, 1817, m., 1st, 10th mo. 16, 1839, MARY W. ALLEN (d. 7th mo. 17, 1842), 2d, 10th mo. 15, 1846, MARTHA S. CARR (b. 4th mo. 25, 1822). By his first wife he had no children.

VI. Children of William R. and Martha:

242. Mary W., b. 8th mo. 1, 1847, m. Joseph Roberts, son of Charles and Sarah, of Upper Dublin. (See Roberts Genealogy).
243. Macre J., b. 11th mo. 5, 1850, m. 9th mo. 19, 1872, William H. Robinson; and has issue.
244. Anna H., b. 1853, d. 1857.
245. Willett D., b. 11th mo. 28, 1855.
246. Howard P., b. 4th mo. 28, 1860.

V. (190.) EDMUND CADWALADER EVANS, M. D., son of Cadwalader and Harriet V., b. at Gwynedd, August 12, 1812. He graduated at the Univ. of Penna., studied medicine, took his degree of M. D., and practiced his profession near Paoli, in Tredyffrin, Chester Co., for several years. Later, he resided near West Chester, but in 1865 removed to Lower Merion, in his native county, near the original home of his ancestor Rowland Ellis. He d. May 20, 1881. He m. April 17, 1844, MARY LOUISA ALLEN, dau. of Rev. Benjamin Allen, of Hyde Park, N. Y. She d. 1861. (Four children d. in infancy; the survivors are here given).

VI. Children of Edmund C. and Mary Louisa:

247. Rowland, b. July 12, 1847, in Tredyffrin; now a member of the Philadelphia bar, residing in Lower Merion; he m., 1878, Mary Binney Montgomery, dau. of Richard R. Montgomery, Esq., of Philadelphia, and has issue: Edmund C., Elizabeth Binney, Alice, Mary, Essyllt.

248. Allen, b. Dec. 8, 1849, in Tredyffrin; an architect in Philadelphia; resides in Lower Merion. He m. 1876, Rebecca Lewis, dau. of John T. Lewis, Esq., of Philadelphia, and has issue: Mary Allen, John Lewis, Margaret Eleanor.

V. (191). WILLIAM ELBERT EVANS, son of Cadwalader and Harriet V., b. in Philadelphia, 1816, where he resided all his life. He m. 1st, ANNA SMITH, dau. of Jacob Smith, Esq., of Philadelphia, and 2d, EMMA FOTTERALL, dau. of William Fotterall, Esq., who survives, without issue. WILLIAM E. d. 1869. His children, besides others who d. in infancy, were two in number.

VI. Children of William E. and Anna:

249. Emily, m. John Henry Livingston, of Dutchess co., N. Y.

250. Glendower, graduated with distinction at Harvard University; a member of the bar in Boston, Mass.; m. Bessy, dau. of Edward Gardiner, Esq., of Boston.

V. (193.) MANLIUS GLENDOWER EVANS, son of Cadwalader and Harriet V., b. in Philadelphia, 1821, and resided there most of his life; m. ELLEN KUHN, dau. of Hartman Kuhn, Esq., of Philadelphia. In 1870 he removed to New York, and in 1875 went to Europe for his health, where he continued to reside until his death in 1879. He left four children, besides others who d. young. His wife survives.

VI. Children of Manlius G. and Ellen:

251. Cadwalader, b. 1847, in Philadelphia, d. in New York, 1880, m. Angelina B., dau. of Israel Corse, Esq., of New York, and had issue: Lena, and Edith Wharton.
252. Ellen Lyle, m. Alfred T. Mahan, Commander U. S. N., and has issue: Helen Evans, Ellen Kuhn, Lyle Evans.
253. Rosalie, unm., resides with her mother, in N. Y.
254. Hartman Kuhn, b. in Philada., 1860, unm. Returning to the United States, after the death of his father, he engaged in sheep ranching in Wyoming Ter.

The records of Gwynedd, Haverford, and Philadelphia meetings, the will lists in the Registers' offices at Philadelphia and Norristown, and other documents, supply many names of persons surnamed Evans, who, it is probable, should have been included in this chapter, at one place or another. I have preferred, however, not to build up with materials which I could not regard as fairly certain. I therefore present, below, a list of some who should probably have been included, leaving it to some one interested in completer work to search out the proper connection:

1. Joseph M. Evans, d. about 1830, in Gwynedd. Andrew Ambler was executor of his estate. In a bond given him in 1829, by Cadwallader Foulke, he is described as "of Gwynedd, gentleman." (Was he the son of Hugh? and heir, with his brother Thomas, of what is now the Rhoads farm, on Swedes Ford road?)
2. Edward Evans, of Philadelphia, a prominent man there, who d. 10th mo. 13, 1771 (Friends' m. records), may have been Edward, "of South street" (No. 67 in Genealogy), son of Evan. The meeting records also show the marriage of Edward Evans, of Philadelphia, and Rebecca Clark, dau. of William, dec'd, at Philad'a mtg., 3d mo. 5, 1757; and that Rebecca, "widow of Edward," d. 1st mo. 1, 1785, aged "about 80 years."
3. The MS. family record preserved by Hannah Evans, Moorestown, N. J., says that Edward Evans, who lived about 1800 or 1808 at s. e. corner of 4th and Vine Sts., Philad'a, was grandson or great-grandson of Robert, of Gwynedd, the first settler.

4. The Gwynedd Records show the following births:

   Children of Hugh and Mary Evans:
 Evan, b. 1st mo. 16, 1717.
 Robert, b. 7th mo. 1, 1719.
 John, b. 2d mo. 2, 1721.

   Children of George and Susanna Evans:
 Daniel, b. 2d mo. 3, 1752.
 Amos, b. 10th mo. 17, 1754, d. 10th mo. 12, 1759.
 Anne, b. 2d mo. 12, 1757, d. 9th mo. 30, 1759.
 William, b. 9th mo. 4, 1759.

   Children of Samuel and Lydia Evans:
 Mary, b. 2d mo. 8, 1754, d. 10th mo. 1, 1827.
 Owen, b. 7th mo. 15, 1756, d. 8th mo. 24, 1820. (Whitpain.)
 Rees, b. 12th mo 4, 1758.
 Ruth, b. 5th mo. 7, 1762.

   Children of Jehu and Mary Evans:
 Elizabeth, b. 8th mo. 28, 1762.
 Sarah, b. 8th mo 6th, 1777, d. 3d mo. 8, 1786.
 Phebe, b. 3d mo. 3, 1782.
 Jehu, b. 3d mo. 2, 1787.

5. Gwynedd records also give these deaths:

 Mary, d. 5th mo. 16, 1745, wife of Robert.
 Mary (Worcester), d. 3d mo. 28, 1802, dau. Thos. and Elizabeth. (This was probably No. 75 in the Genealogy.)
 Elizabeth (Worcester), d. 9th mo. 13, 1841, aged 82 yrs. 6 mos.

6. Haverford records show the births and deaths of numerous Evanses, among them six children (1747-1759) of John and Sarah; one, (1761) of Griffith and Hannah; one (1785) of David and Elinor. Other Evans parents mentioned are John and Mary, and David and Adah. The records of Haverford show that in 1749, Nathan Evans removed there from Gwynedd; in 1756, Nathan Evans and wife removed to Gwynedd; in 1752, Hugh Evans came from Gwynedd.

7. The Philadelphia records show births (1772-1780) of three children of Evan and Mary Evans; also, among others, the following deaths:

 Joseph, d. 10th mo. 5, 1779, aged 34.
 David, d. 11th mo. 20th, 1783, aged 40.
 Elizabeth, d. 4th mo. 28, 1788, wife of Benjamin.
 Evan, d. 6th mo. 23, 1793, aged 45.
 Benjamin, d. 1st mo. 5, 1793, aged 41.
 Ann, d. 9th mo. 17, 1793, aged 25.

EVANS FAMILY GENEALOGY.

Mary, d. 10th mo. 13, 1793, aged 40.
Susanna, d. 9th mo. 22, 1799, aged 15, dau. of Edward.
Lydia, d. 4th mo. 11, 1800, aged 85, of Radnor.
Ann, d. 12th mo. 20, 1802, aged 17, dau. of Benj'n, dec'd.
Francis, d. 9th mo. 20, 1807, aged 27 [son Evan and Mary].
Jacob, d. 7th mo. 5, 1807, aged 35 [son Evan and Mary].
Joshua, d. 2d mo. 11, 1771, aged 25.
Thomas, d. 5th mo. 26, 1771, aged 56.
Thomas, d. 4th mo. 16, 1778, aged 30.

8. John Evans, yeoman, who was in Davidson Co., North Carolina, in 1790, gave a power of attorney to John Roberts and Christian Dull, of Gwynedd, to collect rents from sixty acres of land in Upper Dublin, which had descended to him "as eldest brother and heir at-law" of David Evans.

9. David Evans, of Philadelphia, gentleman, "being aged and infirm of Body," made his will Sept. 27, 1745. He mentions his wife *Elizabeth*, his brother-in-law, John Owen, of Chester county, the six children of his daughters Susanna and Margaret, "whom had by a former wife," and his four children by his present wife, Evan, Rebecca, Sidney, and Sarah. He appoints Evan Jones, of Merion, son of Thomas, dec'd; Owen Jones, of Philadelphia, and John Owen, guardians and overseers. *Elizabeth* was the dau. of Robert and Jane Owen, of Merion. Her (and David's) son Evan "was the father of David Evans, joiner, who lived in Arch street, between 6th and 7th." Their daughter Sarah, "spinster," made her will July 14, 1762, and it was proved December 21 of that year. She makes bequests to her sister Sydney Howell, wife of Joseph Howell, and to the children of her brother Evan, dec'd, Sidney, David, and Rebecca, the last two minors. (Philad'a meeting records show the marriage of Joseph Howell, of Philadelphia, tanner, son of Jacob (and Sarah, dec'd), of New Garden, Chester Co., and Sydna [Sydney] Evans, dau. of David, of said city, of Philadelphia, m. 4th mo. 26, 1759.)

XIV.
Roberts Family Genealogy.

IT is designed in this chapter to give systematically what is known concerning the descendants of Robert Cadwalader, of Wales, whose children, in the Welsh manner, took the surname Robert, subsequently changed to Roberts. His sons were Cadwalader, Morris, Nicholas, John, and Rowland, and he had one daughter, Elizabeth. All these, as well as their father, were in Gwynedd or Montgomery, within a few years after the earliest company of settlers.

Cadwalader is said to have come with the first settlers, in 1698, and there is reason to believe that he was accompanied by Morris. That they were among the company on the *Robert and Elizabeth* is not certain, but the family tradition is that upon the ship which brought them there was much sickness, and that Cadwalader, who was noted for his kind and benevolent character, was active in assisting those who were ill.[1] Subsequently, the father, Robert Cadwalader, came over with his wife, and their other children: Nicholas, John, Rowland, and Elizabeth. Some of them, certainly John, settled first near Philadelphia, in Oxford township, but all of them had located in Gwynedd or Montgomery, within a few years after the first settlement. An old account book of Ellis Roberts, of Gwynedd, tailor (not of this family), shows that Morris Roberts bought buttons (Ellis spells it "butnes") of him, in the 9th mo., 1704, and that he had other dealings with Nicholas Roberts, as early as the 5th mo., 1705. Cadwalader bought land of Robert John, in 1710, and his name is on

---

[1] The definite statement is ascribed to George Roberts, of Gwynedd (No. 58 in this Genealogy), that Cadwalader "came over in company with Edward Foulke and Cadwalader Evans" — *i.e.* on the *Robert and Elizabeth*, with the original company.

the subscription paper for building the new meeting-house of 1712, — the subscriptions for the purpose being raised in 1710-11.

The parents, Robert Cadwalader and his wife, were old people when they came, and did not long survive. In the marriage certificate of their daughter Elizabeth, and Daniel Morgan, in 9th mo., 1718, Robert is spoken of as "late of Gwynedd," showing his death to have occurred previous to that time.

It is the tradition that none of the family were Friends at the time of their immigration, but if not, they soon joined the Society. John was married according to the order of Friends in 1706; Rowland and Elizabeth, in like manner, in 1713; Cadwalader, in 1714; Nicholas, in 1717; and Morris, in 1718. Rowland was a minister among the Friends, and so also was Elizabeth, as well as her husband, Daniel Morgan.

Genealogical Sketch.

[The general plan of this Genealogy is precisely the same as that preceding, in Chap. XIII. See details in NOTE, on p. 146.]

I. (1.) ROBERT CADWALADER, a man advanced in years, from one of the northern counties of Wales, immigrated with his wife (whose name is not definitely ascertained) and three sons and a daughter (two sons having previously come), and settled about 1700, at Gwynedd. Both he and his wife survived their removal but a few years.

II. Children of Robert Cadwalader — (surname Roberts):

2. Cadwalader, b. 1673, d. 1731, m. Eleanor Ellis.
3. Morris, m. Elizabeth Robeson.
4. Nicholas, d. 1733, m. Margaret Foulke.
5. John, d. 1772, m. Elizabeth Edward.
6. Rowland, b. 1685, d. 1749, m. Mary Pugh, Ann Bennett.
7. Elizabeth, m. 9th mo. 21, 1718, Daniel Morgan, son of Edward. Both she and her husband were ministers in Society of Friends. Daniel d. at an advanced age, 1773. Their children were Benjamin, b. 1719, m., 1744, Sarah Davis; Ruth, b. 3d mo. 15, 1721, m., 1746, Nathan Evans. (See Evans Genealogy).

II. (2.) CADWALADER ROBERTS, eldest son of Robert Cadwalader, b. in Wales, in 1673, immigrated, probably, in 1698, and settled in Gwynedd. In 1710, he bought land, 140 acres, of Robert John, on or closely adjoining the site of the borough of North Wales.[1] All the accounts and traditions describe him as a man highly esteemed for his benevolence. He m., 4th mo. 9, 1714, ELEANOR ELLIS (b. 8th mo. 17, 1693), dau. of Humphrey and Jane Ellis, of Merion (she is called in the marriage certificate Ellin Humphrey),[2] and he (CADWALADER) d. 3d mo. 7, 1731, of small-pox, at Gwynedd.[3] His estate

[1] A memorandum upon a copy of the poem given below says: "His residence was on the North Wales road, about two miles above Gwynedd meeting-house, east side, since occupied by Everard Bolton, H. Beaver, Dr. Meredith, and others."

[2] The wedding took place at Rowland Ellis's house, in Merion, afterward the residence of Charles Thomson, Sec. of the Continental Congress.

[3] The following poem on the death of C. R. is doubtless the earliest specimen of verse relating to Gwynedd. Its internal evidence shows that it must have been written soon after the death of C. R., in 1731. The poet is otherwise unknown.

VERSES WRITTEN ON CADWALADER ROBERTS, WHO DIED IN GWYNEDD, IN 1731. BY ROBERT SIMMONS, POET.

(*Drawn out of the Old, by Cadwalader Roberts, jr., 3d mo. 30, 1767.*)

You Christians all of North Wales hark with speed,
I have a line or two for you to read,
Ponder them o'er, consider well your state
Before you come unto your God so great.
  *   *   *   *

These lines I send you as a pattern given,
That you may know the way that leads to Heaven.
Follow the steps of him that's gone before;
Do you but this, you need not do no more.

Cadwalader Roberts, who was a man of fame,
Well known in town and country by his name,
Who lived to the age of sixty, lacking two,—
But now his death severely we shall [rue?]

On May the seventh he resign'd his breath,
And on the ninth he was laid under the earth.
It was in the year of our Lord alone,
One thousand seven hundred and thirty one.
  *   *   *   *

was settled by his widow, as administratrix, letters being issued to her, dated May 31, 1731. ELEANOR m. a second time, Rowland Hugh, of Gwynedd, and d. 1755.

III. Children of Cadwalader and Eleanor:

8. Rebecca, b. 3d mo. 14, 1715, d. 12th mo., 1795; m. William Erwin, and had issue 10 children.
9. Robert, b. 1719, d. 1760, m. Sarah Ambler.

II. (3.) MORRIS ROBERTS, son of Robert Cadwalader, b. in Wales, immigrated, probably with his brother Cadwalader, about 1698, settled in Gwynedd (where he was, from the entries in Ellis Roberts's mem. book, as early as 1704), m. 2d mo. 18, 1718, ELIZABETH ROBESON, of Abington. In 1734, he applied to Gwynedd monthly meeting for a certificate to remove to North Carolina, and probably went there.

> A loving husband and a father dear,
> Thou wast unto thy wife, and children fair.
> O, thou art gone who would have been their stay,
> Which did prove to them a mournful day.
>
> Thy brothers all which are in number four,
> Each day thy death they sorely do deplore.
> Also, thy only sister, whom thou so dearly loved,
> With grief of heart each day for thee she's moved.
> Thy friends and neighbors all are grieved in heart,
> Since cruel death did thee and them impart.
>
> Thou charitable was unto the poor,
> Nor didst thou let any pass by thy door,
> But some relief unto them did give,
> In money or in meat, while thou did live.
>
> It is enough to pierce the ardent skies,
> To hear the lamentable moans and cries,
> Of the poor for their great loss so sore,
> Say: "Blest Cadwalader we shall see no more."
>
> *   *   *   *
>
> All people of North Wales weep and lament,
> Since the days of our great friend are spent,
> For few like him is there now left behind,
> So low, so meek, so courteous, and so kind,
> In entertaining friends, and strangers too,
> But now they are crying: "Lord, what shall we do?"
>
> *   *   *   *

III. Children of Morris and Elizabeth :

10. Susanna, m. Jacob Zimmerman.
11. Hannah, m. William Howe, "and moved to back country."
12. Sophia, m. John Cadwalader, and had issue : John, b. 1755; Elizabeth, b. 1760. The parents removed to Oley, and from there John, jr., rem. to Virginia, about 1786.
13. Lydia, m. Joseph Jones.
14. Morris, d. young.
15. Nehemiah, d. at "Squire" Job Roberts's. (He is said to have been mentally impaired.)

II. (4.) NICHOLAS ROBERTS, son of John Cadwalader, d. 1733, immigrated from Wales with his parents, m. MARGARET FOULKE, dau. of Edward, of Gwynedd. (See Foulke Genealogy.) His estate was settled by Evan Foulke and John Roberts, administrators, to whom letters of administration were issued, April 14, 1733.

III. Children of Nicholas and Margaret:

16. Jane, b. 1718, d. 1790, m. 8th mo. 20, 1741, David Morris, son of Cadwalader, of Philadelphia ; and had issue 5 children : Elizabeth, Eleanor, Nicholas, Edward, Jane. (Elizabeth m. David Jackson. Jane m. Abiah Cope, of Chester county, from whom are numerous members of the Cope family.)
17. Ellen, b. 1720, m. John Siddons ; and had issue.
18. Elizabeth, b. 6th mo. 11, 1723, d. 5th mo. 29, 1790, m. David Humphrey, of Gwynedd, son of Robert and Margaret, and had issue eight children. They removed south, to Maryland, and had many descendants in Baltimore, and elsewhere, surname Dukehart, Riley, Pope, Fowler, Jones, Davenport, Roberts, Ball, Balderson, Matthews, etc.

II. (5.) JOHN ROBERTS, of Montgomery, son of Robert Cadwalader, b. abt. 1680, d. 1773, immigrated, from Wales, with his parents. He settled, first, in Oxford twp., near Philadelphia, and while there m. 6th mo. 7, 1706, ELIZABETH EDWARD, of Merion. He subsequently removed to Montgomery, and his name is attached in 1711 to a petition of Gwynedd and Montgomery residents for the legal settling of the route of a road to the mills on Pennypack. (See chapter, *post*, on Early Roads.) His will, dated 5th mo. 15, 1763, was proved Sept. 30, 1773. He leaves his grandson, John Jones, a tract, 100 acres, "where he now liveth," in Montgomery, subject to a payment to his (John's) brother, Evan; his son John Roberts, a tract, 162 acres, adjoining the above, and lands of Isaac Jones; he mentions his grandson John Roberts; he leaves his dau. Elizabeth Blair, bed, furniture, etc., and remission of "all bonds, bills, notes, and book debts contracted or entered into by her former husband, John Jones, or by herself within the time of her widowhood." To his granddaughter, Jane McKinley, he leaves an obligation given him by John McKinley. He leaves £5 "to the Hospital in Philadelphia," and to his dau. Elizabeth Blair an annuity of £2 10s., but this to cease, "if the place she formerly lived on comes to her possession again." He mentions his grandchildren (some of them minors), Elizabeth, Ruth, Sarah Ann, Jane, Margaret, and Job Roberts; Margaret, Ellinor, and Ann Jones; and Jonathan Blair. As will be noticed from the dates of his birth and death, JOHN lived to be over ninety years of age.[1]

  III. Children of John and Elizabeth:

18. Elizabeth, b. 6th mo. 15, 1707, m. 1st, John Jones,[2] by whom she had issue: Jane, John, Mordecai, Evan, Margaret, Ellen, Ann; and 2d (earlier than 1763), John Blair, by whom she had issue: Jonathan.
20. Mordecai, b. 1709, d. 1745.
21. James. [Jane?]
22. John, b. 1714, d. 1801, m. Jane Hank, Eleanor Williams.

II. (6.) ROWLAND ROBERTS, of Montgomery, fifth son of Robert Cadwalader, b. 1685, in Wales, d. 7th mo. 22, 1749; immi-

---

[1] His son John (No. 16) d. at 87 years; and his grandsons, John (33) and Job (40) d. at 84 and 94 respectively.

[2] From this marriage descended a considerable family, of whom Mordecai Jones, now [1884] and for many years living on the turnpike near the Treweryn bridge, is presumed to be one.

grated with his father, m. 1st, 3d mo. 1, 1713, MARY PUGH, eldest dau. of Robert and Sarah, of Gwynedd (see Evans Genealogy); and, 2d, ANN BENNETT, widow, of Abington. ROWLAND was a preacher amongst the Friends. A short memorial of him, by Gwynedd monthly meeting, in the John Smith MS. collection, says: "He received a gift in the ministry, and visited his native country in the service of truth, and returned with certificates giving a good account of his services there. Altho' he was not of ready utterance, yet his matter was often weighty and instructive, savoring of love and good-will to mankind." ANN, his wife, was also a preacher, and is referred to in this volume (p. 90). ROWLAND seems to have been an energetic and substantial business man. His will shows that, prior to 1749, he had established a tavern in Montgomery. It is dated 7th mo. 12, of that year, and was probated October 10. He leaves to his "daughter-in-law" Hannah Jones, two small lots of land, "part of the tract I now live on; one on the west side of the great road, over against the tavern erected on my said premises, taking all the land appertaining to me on the said side of the great road;" and the other situated between another road and Joseph Ambler's house; "provided always, and I do hereby direct that neither the said Hannah nor any other person claiming under her shall at any time hereafter erect and set up a tavern in opposition to the one that is already on my premises, while it continues in my family unsold." He mentions also Mary Davis, another "daughter-in-law," his son-in-law James Williams, to whom he leaves "one dun filly, according to my promise by word of mouth;" and makes provision for his dear wife, ANNE ROBERTS, who is to have the right to occupy during her life-time "the old house where we now live." His son Eldad is appointed executor, and is left, besides other property, "all the plantation and tract of land where I now live."

ROBERTS FAMILY GENEALOGY. 193

III. Children of Rowland and Mary:
23. Eldad, b. 1713, d. 1789, m. Elizabeth Mitchell, Jane Jones. ☙
24. Sarah, b. 1715.

III. (9.) ROBERT ROBERTS, carpenter, of Gwynedd, son of Cadwalader, b. 10th mo. 18, 1719, d. 1760, bu. at Gwynedd, m. 11th mo. 11, 1742, SARAH AMBLER (b. 5th mo. 25, 1721), dau. of Joseph and Ann. (Joseph was a wheelwright; his wife, Ann, was a Williams, before marriage; they were married in 1720.) ROBERT'S will is dated 8th mo. 14, and was proved 10 mo. 29, 1760. He leaves to his dau. Ellen a lot of 15 acres, in Gwynedd, part of a lot of 25 acres, "to be divided off the west end thereof, next to Wissahickon creek," and orders his executor, his brother-in-law, Edward Ambler, to sell the remainder of his property, about 50 acres. He names his children Cadwalader, Joseph, Ann, Mary and Hannah. His widow SARAH survived until 4th mo. 22, 1796, and d. of palsy.

IV. Children of Robert and Sarah:
25. Cadwalader, b. 1743, d. 1816, m. Mary Shoemaker. ☙
26. Ann, b. 1745, d. 1823, m. Hugh Foulke, and had issue. (See Foulke Genealogy.)
27. Joseph, b. 1747, d. 1799, m. Sarah Shoemaker, Mercy Pickering. ☙
28. Ellen, b. 1st mo. 15, 1749, d. 2d mo. 25, 1827, unm.
29. Rebecca, b. 1752, d. same year.
30. Mary, b. 1753, d. 1825, m. Jacob Albertson, of Cheltenham, and had issue: Hannah, m. Jesse Williams; Rebecca; Josiah, m. Alice T. Maulsby; Jacob, m. Martha Livezey;[1] Benjamin, m. Amy Haines;[2] Rebecca, m. George Shoemaker.
31. Hannah, b. 4th mo. 5, 1756, d. 9th mo. 27, 1825, m. Samuel Thomas, son of John; d. without issue.

III. (16.) JOHN ROBERTS, of Whitpain, son of John and Elizabeth, b. 5th mo. 28, 1714, d. 10th mo. 8, 1801,[3] m. 1st, 3d mo.

---

[1] J. Morton Albertson, Norristown, b. 1826, m. Sarah P. Lee, is son of Jacob and Martha.
[2] Charles Albertson, Philadelphia, b. 1833, m. Mercie Eastburn, is son of Benjamin and Amy.
[3] Cadwallader Foulke, recording his death (see p. 137), calls him "John

13, 1736, JANE HANK, dau. of John and Sarah; 2d, 10th mo. 11, 1764, ELEANOR WILLIAMS, dau. of Thomas. (JANE b. 1714, d. 1762; ELEANOR d. 1796.)

IV. Children of John and Jane:

32. Cadwalader, b. 1737, d. 1748.
33. John, b. 1738, d. 1824, m. Elizabeth Cleaver. ⚏
34. Elizabeth, b. 1740, d. 1794, m. Thomas Evans. (See Evans Genealogy).
35. Ruth, b. 3d mo, 1743, d. 12th mo. 1820, m. Nathan Cleaver, son of Peter and Elizabeth, of Upper Dublin; and had issue 5 children: Phebe, m. Amos Griffith; David; Jonathan, m. Nancy Jones; Nathan, m. Martha Shoemaker; Salathiel, m. Mary Shoemaker.
36. Sarah, b. 5th mo. 1745, d. 1st mo. 1837, unm.
37. Ann, b. 1748, d. 1808, m. Morgan Morgan; and had issue 7 children: Benjamin, m. Tacy Stroud; Elizabeth; Sarah, m. Issachar Kenderdine; Morgan, m. Ann Custer; Ann, m. John Ambler; David, m. Sarah Kenderdine; Mary.
38. Jane, b. 3d mo. 1751, d. 11th mo. 1, 1821, m. 10th mo. 22, 1778, David Shoemaker, and had issue 5 children: Ellen, m. Jonathan Taylor; Margaret, m. Ezra Comfort, of Plymouth, preacher (b. 1777, d. 1847); John, d. in childhood; Ann, m. Cadwallader Foulke (see Foulke Genealogy); Mary, m. John Jones.
39. Mary, b. 11th mo. 5, 1753, d. 9th mo. 23, 1786, m. 6th mo., 1777, William Hallowell, son of Joseph, of Whitemarsh; and had issue 5 children: John, m. Alice Potts; Job, m. Hannah Thomas; Sarah, m. Samuel Conrad; William, m. Catharine Shoemaker and Jane Richards (born Walker); and one child, d. in infancy.
40. Job, b. 1757, d. 1851, m. Mary Naylor, Sarah Thomas. ⚏
41. Jonah, b. 1760, d. 1761.

IV. Child of John by 2d wife, Eleanor:

42. Eleanor, b. 1768, m. Richard Shoemaker; and had issue 5 children: John; Hannah, m. Isaac Moore; Job; Ann, m. John Shay; Charles.

III. (23.) ELDAD ROBERTS, of Montgomery, son of Rowland and Mary, b. 12th mo. 19, 1713, d. 1789, m. 1st, 1747, ELIZABETH MITCHELL, dau. of Richard, of Wrightstown, Bucks

---

Roberts Cadwalader," showing the persistency with which the Welsh names were maintained, in some cases.

Co. (the marriage "very disagreeable to our discipline," says a minute of Gwynedd monthly meeting,—though all parties appear to have been Friends). ELIZABETH d. 5th mo. 1760, and ELDAD m. 2d, 10th mo. 18, 1763, JANE JONES, dau. of Isaac, of Montgomery. By each wife ELDAD had two children. His will, dated 1st mo. 29, 1789, was probated March 26 of the same year, at Norristown. He gives his wife JANE all household goods, furniture, etc., "that she brought to me," and £20 a year "in gold or silver." To his son Mordecai he leaves £250 "in current gold," also his desk and silver watch; to his dau. Elizabeth Mullen £120, and his dau. Mary Roberts £150. To his son John (afterwards "Squire" John), "the plantation where I live," in Montgomery, 200 acres, also the residuary personal estate, and he to be executor of the will.

IV. Children of Eldad and Elizabeth:

43. John, b. 1750, d. 1823, unm.—See biographical sketch, and other details, elsewhere in this volume.
44. Mordecai, b. 1753, m. Ellen Decker.

Children of Eldad and Jane:

45. Elizabeth, b. 1764, m. Isaiah Mullen; and had issue, John.
46. Mary, b. 3d mo. 23, 1766, d. 1st mo. 1859 (bu. at Gwynedd, 1st mo. 18). She lived with her uncle, Isaac Jones (usually called Isaac, Senior, though he was himself the son of Isaac), of Montgomery, and is elsewhere mentioned.

IV. (25.) CADWALADER ROBERTS, of Montgomery, farmer, son of Robert and Sarah, b. 10th mo. 18, 1743, d. 2d mo. 7, 1816, m. 5th mo. 24, 1768, MARY SHOEMAKER, dau. of Richard and Ann. (MARY b. 3d mo. 14, 1744, d. 12th mo. 23, 1795.)

V. Children of Cadwalader and Mary:

47. Edward, b. 1771, d. 1850, m. Rebecca Phillips.
48. Ezekiel, b. 1775, d. 1856, m. Ann Doyle.
49. Cadwalader, b. 1777, d. 1871, m. Elizabeth Evans.
50. Joseph, b. 1779, d. 1859, m. Elizabeth Rubencamp.

51. Richard, b. 1782, d. 1860, m. Mary Scott.
52. Agnes, b. 1783, d. 1872, m. Caleb Evans. (See Evans Gen'y.)
53. Mary, b. 1786, d. 1830, m. 1808; Edward Spencer, son of Job and Hannah, of Horsham; and had issue 2 children: Cadwalader R.; and Agnes S., m. Josiah E. Willis.

IV. (27.) JOSEPH ROBERTS, of Montgomery, son of Robert and Sarah, b. 8th mo. 27, 1747, d. 1st mo. 12, 1799. He is called "cordwainer" in a deed, 1769, when he bought of Henry McQuoin a farm on the Horsham road (known in later years as "White Cottage Farm"), in Montgomery. He was known as a man of unusual physical strength, but d. comparatively young, the tradition being that he injured himself by excessive effort, such as lifting a wagon, and removing a fallen tree from the road. He was twice married: 1st, 5th mo. 22, 1770, to SARAH SHOEMAKER (b. 1748, d. between 1771 and 1774), dau. of Richard and Agnes; and 2d, 5th mo. 11, 1774, to MERCY PICKERING, dau. of Isaac and Sarah,[1] of Solebury, Bucks Co. MERCY b. 8th mo. 27, 1745, survived her husband thirty years, continuing the charge of her farm in her advanced age. (A note in the memorandum book of her son Joseph (No. 63) says: "8th mo. 27, 1825.—This day my mother is 80 years old. She attends entirely to the affairs of the family, such as getting meals, making bread, etc. She got dinner for Israel Lancaster and Isaiah Jones [visitors], and for Hugh and myself." Again: "8th mo 27, 1826.—At mother's. This day she was 81 years old. She attended to

---

[1] Sarah Pickering was the dau. of Joseph Lupton, the elder, a weaver by occupation, and a man of good education, who came from Yorkshire, England, and settled in Bucks county. He m., 1st, Mercy Twining, from near Newtown, and 2d, Mary Pickering (b. Scarborough, widow Samuel, who came from England), and after this second marriage removed to Virginia. William, Samuel, and Grace Pickering, Mary's children, also removed there. Grace Pickering m. in Virginia William Lupton, and lived in Frederick Co., in 1787, and their son Asa [or Asahel?], b. 1757, m. 1787, Hannah Hank, dau. of John, of Rockingham Co., Va., of the same family, no doubt, as President Lincoln's mother and the Hanks mentioned in the Evans Genealogy, in this volume.

the affairs of the family, as usual; health good, recollection sound.") MERCY d. of palsy, 2d mo. 14, 1829.[1]

---

[1] In the volumes of *Penna. Archives* and *Colonial Records*, will be found details of a trying experience in Joseph's life. Petitions were presented to the Supreme Executive Council of the State in January and March, 1783, asking the remission of a fine of £150 imposed upon Joseph Roberts, of Montgomery township, cordwainer. He had been convicted of a "misdemeanor," at a preceding Court of Oyer and Terminer, his offence being, as charged, "aiding British prisoners to escape." The first petition, dated "Montgomery, Jan. 27, 1783," recites that he has been adjudged to the payment of the fine—

"—— for giving some Directions concerning their Road to a few travelers asking for them at his Door. That the said Travelers were absolute Strangers to your Petitioner, and neither from their Habit nor their discourse gave him any reason to suspect they were British soldiers. That your petitioner was wholly ignorant at this Time of any act of Assembly against giving Food or information of their Road to strangers requesting them, and so far from knowing that he thereby incurred a fine, that he believed he was only performing a common act of hospitality. That your petitioner is but a young Man and except his Trade and Industry has little in the world to support a wife and five children, who must with himself be reduced to great Distress, if not Ruin" [unless the fine be remitted].

Accompanying this petition was another from "Neighbors and Acquaintances of Joseph Roberts." The signers (whose names follow) "certify that he is a sober industrious young Man, of good Character among us; and that we have no doubt of the truth of the several allegations" in his petition.

Hezekiah Williams. Archibald McClean, Surgeon, 1st Batt'n, P. C. M. David Evans.
Ed. Bartholomew.   William Mullen.   Caleb Foulke.
Chas. Moore, M. D. Charles Stedman.   Samuel Wheeler.
Evan Jones.   Eliz: Ferguson.   Zebulon Potts, Esq.
Mordecai Moore.   Robert Loller, Surveyor.   Thos. Franklin.
Wm. McClean.   Seth Quee, Esq.
   William Roberts.

These petitions were read in the Council, Feb. 20, 1783, and their prayer rejected. On March 18, other petitions were presented of like character, one of them from prominent citizens of Philadelphia, supported by letters from Colonel William Bradford, jr., and from Chief Justice Thomas McKean. Colonel Bradford says he is informed from credible authority that Joseph had "sustained the character of a sober, industrious, and peaceable citizen, no ways inimical to the Liberties of America." The Chief Justice says that "he has heretofore supported the character of a quiet and inoffensive man, and that he has but little knowledge of public affairs, and is but a weak Politician."

Upon this re-hearing of the case by the Council, the petition was granted, and the fine remitted. The costs of the trial, it appeared, were £32 13s. 6d. There were three indictments, and the witnesses were: Noah Lee, 7 days [attendance]; James Burt, 7 days; Ebenezer Archibald, 7 days.

V. *Children of Joseph and Sarah:*

54. Sarah, b. 8th mo. 27, 1771, d. 10th mo. 31, 1854, m. 1st, Paul Conrad, by whom she had 4 children: Jesse, Mary, Sarah, and Rebecca; and 2d, at Valley meeting, 10th mo. 25, 1815, Isaac Walker, of Tredyffrin, son of Joseph and Sarah, by whom she had one son, Isaac R. Walker.

Children of Joseph and Mercy:

55. Isaac, b. 1775, d. 1851, m. Alice Comfort.
56. Jonathan, b. 4th mo. 19, 1777, d. 8th mo. 25, 1832, unm., of consumption, in Bucks co., "eight miles beyond Buckingham," and was bu. at Buckingham. A shoemaker by trade.
57. Hugh, also a shoemaker, b. 3d mo. 28, 1779, d. 3d mo. 18, 1848, unm., and bu. at Gwynedd.
58. George, b. 1781, d. 1851, m. Phebe Scott.
59. John, b, 1783, d. same year.
60. Charles, b. 1784, d. 1845, m. Hannah White, Anna Maria Hoskins.
61. Septimus, b. 9th mo. 30, 1786, d. 1st mo. 6, 1826, unm. He was one of the earliest students at Westtown, his name being on the roll in 6th mo., 1803. Subsequently, from 5th mo., 1809, to 9th mo., 1812, he was a teacher there. He also taught in Philadelphia (previous to 1809), having charge of the Friends' school for colored children, and a portrait of him, by one of his pupils, is extant.[1] He had gone to Mauch Chunk, as a clerk in the offices of the Lehigh Coal and Navigation Co., and was living there when he d. of a hemorrhage.
62. Mercy, b. 9th mo. 14, 1789. d. 1st mo. 26, 1870, unm.
63. Joseph, b. 3d mo. 22, 1793, d. 8th mo. 25, 1835, unmarried. A sketch of him will be placed separately in this volume.

IV. (33.) JOHN ROBERTS, son of John and Jane, b. 9th mo. 30, 1738, d. 8th mo. 11, 1824, m. 1772, ELIZABETH CLEAVER, dau. of Peter, of Upper Dublin. (ELIZABETH d. 5th mo. 24, 1808.)

V. *Children of John and Elizabeth:*

64. Peter, b. 4th mo. 7, 1773, d. 2d mo. 2, 1801, m. 1800, Elizabeth Comfort; no issue. (She subsequently m. Benjamin White.)

---

[1] A copy is in possession of Charles Roberts, of Philadelphia. It is a spirited picture, showing the costume of a plain young Friend of 1805, and interesting also as exhibiting the artistic talent of the colored lad who produced it.

65. Ruth, b. 8th mo. 28, 1775, d. 9th mo. 1857, m. 1803, Jesse Ambler, son of John and Ann; no issue. (Jesse d. 1851, aged 75.)

IV. (40.) JOB ROBERTS, of Whitpain, son of John and Jane, b. 3d mo. 23, 1757, d. 8th mo. 20, 1851, m. 1st, 1781, MARY NAYLOR (b. 1758, d. 1816); 2d, SARAH THOMAS, widow (born Williams, dau. of Joseph). A biographical sketch of "Squire" JOB will be found elsewhere in this volume. He had no children by his second wife.

V. Children of Job and Mary:

66. Hannah, b. 1783, d. 1785.
67. Jane, b. 3d mo. 1, 1785, d. 2d mo. 1, 1847, m. 5th mo. 12, 1807, Charles Mather, son of Isaac and Mary; and had issue: Job R., Mary Morris, Hannah B., m. John C. Lester, of Richland; Jane, m. Benjamin G. Foulke, of Richland (see Foulke Genealogy); Susanna M., m. Samuel J. Levick; Letitia, m. Wm. Walmsley; Charles, Lydia T.

IV. (44.) MORDECAI ROBERTS, son of Eldad and Elizabeth, b. 7th mo. 11, 1753, m. ELLEN DECKER. The tradition is that MORDECAI served in the Revolutionary army, probably as a private soldier, and that during the Battle of Germantown, in which he was engaged, his father, then an old man, lay on his bed at Montgomery, listening to the cannonade (which could be heard at that distance), in great distress of mind about "Mord." The monthly-meeting records have an entry in the 11th mo., 1776, that MORDECAI ROBERTS "has joined the military men in their exercise, and wholly neglects the attendance of meetings." After carrying the case for some months, in the 6th mo., 1777 (four months before Germantown), the meeting disowned him.

V. Children of Mordecai and Ellen:

68. Eleanor.==69. John.==70. Eldad.==71. Medad, d. young.==72. Charles.==73. Mordecai.==74. Martha.==75. James.==76. Mary.==77. Ann. ==77½. Jane.

V. (47.) EDWARD ROBERTS, son of Cadwalader and Mary, b. 3d mo. 9, 1771, d. 10th mo. 25, 1850, m. 1796, REBECCA PHILlips, dau. of David. He was a farmer, and settled, about 1795, at Catawissa, on the North Branch of the Susquehanna, in which locality many of his descendants now live.

VI. Children of Edward and Rebecca:
78. Cadwalader, b. 1800, d. 1876, m. Ann Phillips. ℬ
79. Hannah, b. 1802, d. 1803.
80. William, b. 1804.
81. Hannah, b. 1806, m. Edward Shay, of Horsham; and had issue: John, b. 1835, m. Hannah Haupt.
82. Edward, b. 1808, m. Annie Bartholomew. ℬ
83. David, b. 1811, d. 1877, m. Frances Sanders. ℬ
84. Stephen F., b. 1814, m. Margaret George. ℬ
85. Josiah A., b. 1820, m. Anna M. Clewell. ℬ

V. (48.) EZEKIEL ROBERTS, son of Cadwalader and Mary, b. 12th mo. 19, 1775, d. 2d mo. 13, 1856. He was a farmer, and removed first to near Toronto, Canada, where part of his family were born, then later to Ohio. He is buried at Belmont, O. He m. ANNE DOYLE (b. 8th mo. 28, 1777, d. 2d mo. 2, 1827).

VI. Children of Ezekiel and Ann:
86. Joseph, b. 1799, d. 1830, m. Esther Scott. ℬ
87. Mary, b. 1801, d. 1856, m. Abraham Griffith; and had issue: Elma, m. John Cooper (Cedar Falls, Ia.); Anna R., m. Wm. Giffen, (Newport, Ohio); Rees L., m. Catharine Seal (Morning View, O.); Charles, m. Sarah J. Peck (New Jersey); Ruth, m. Reuben Creighton (Mt. Horeb, Ohio).
88. Agnes, b. 1803, m. Rees Larkin, and had issue 9 children, mostly settled in Missouri, Iowa, Kansas, Nebraska, and Illinois, with numerous descendants.
89. George, b. 1805, d. 1827. (Bu. at Hainsville, O.)
90. Charles, b. 1808, d. 1875, m. Sarah Harris. ℬ
91. John, b. 1810, m. Susanna Metz, Elizabeth Wilson. ℬ
92. Nancy, b. 1812, m. John Taggart (St. Clairsville, O.); and had issue 8 children, residents of Illinois, Ohio, and Minnesota. (Agnes D., m. Wm. P. Roberts, 179 this Genealogy.)
93. Esther, b. 1815, d. 1878, m. David Smith, and had issue 7 children, residents of Ohio, Iowa, Kansas, and Missouri.

V. (49.) CADWALADER ROBERTS, of Gwynedd, son of Cadwalader and Mary, b. 11th mo. 3, 1777, d. 2d mo. 19, 1871, m. 12th mo. 14, 1802, ELIZABETH EVANS (b. 1781, d. 1842), dau. of Thomas and Elizabeth. CADWALADER was a tailor and farmer; he is elsewhere mentioned in this volume. For many years he had charge of the meeting property at Gwynedd, and was sexton of the burial-ground. He lived on the turnpike below Acuff's, on a small farm which after his death was added by sale to the John Gilbert estate.

VI. Children of Cadwalader and Elizabeth :

94. Job, b. 1814, d. 1858, m. Hannah Pickering.
 (Two children older than Job d. in infancy).

V. (50.) JOSEPH ROBERTS, son of Cadwalader and Mary, b. 11th mo. 2, 1779, d. 4th mo. 11, 1859, m. ELIZABETH RUBENCAMP (d. 1840). He was a farmer; was buried at Horsham.

VI. Children of Joseph and Elizabeth :

95. Agnes, b. 1804, d. 1882, m. Jonathan Jarrett; and had issue: J. Roberts, Elizabeth, Mary, Tacy A., m. Jesse Ambler.
96. Charles, b. 1807, d. 1866, m. Sarah A. Kenderdine.
97. Mary, b. 1810, m. Henry Magee; and had issue: Martha W., Charles R., Elizabeth, Agnes J., m. Charles H. Kehr; J. Roberts, Henry.
98. Jesse, b. 1812, d. 1819.

V. (51.) RICHARD ROBERTS, son of Cadwalader and Mary, b. 1st mo. 1, 1782, d. 9th mo. 17, 1860, m. 1805, MARY SCOTT, dau. of Alexander. (MARY d. 1828, and bu. at Horsham.) RICHARD was a farmer; lived in Ohio; was buried at Emerson, in that State.

VI. Children of Richard and Mary :

99. Israel, b. 1806, d. 1849, m. Sarah T. Ward.
100. Alexander S., b. 1809, d. 1850, m. Mary Fort.
101. Mary, b. 1811.
102. Ezekiel, b. 1813, m. Eliza Ann Griffith, Eliz. P. Harrison.
103. John C., b. 1815.
104. Rowland, b. 1817, m. Mary Ann Humphreys.

105. Phebe, b. 1820, d. 1879, m. William Waterman; and had issue: George (Ohio); Israel R. (W. Va.); Charles R. (Ohio).

V. (55.) ISAAC ROBERTS, of Whitemarsh, son of Joseph and Mercy, b. at Montgomery, 4th mo. 27, 1775, d. 8th mo. 13, 1851, m. 3d mo. 13, 1800, ALICE COMFORT, dau. of Ezra. (ALICE b. 4th mo. 23, 1779, d. 2d mo. 22, 1841.) Isaac was a farmer; both he and his wife were buried at Plymouth.

VI. Children of Isaac and Alice:

106. Mercy, b. 6th mo. 3, 1801, d. 4th mo. 26, 1873.
107. Elizabeth, b. 7th mo. 10, 1803, d. 12th mo. 23, 1825.
108. Ezra, b. 1805, d. 1854, m. Lydia Passmore. ⚘
109. Charles W., b. 1807, m. Martha Walker. ⚘
110. { Joseph V., b. 6th mo. 16, 1810, d. 3d mo. 12, 1834.
111. { Jacob, b. 1810, m. Phebe Williams. ⚘
112. Isaac, b. 2d mo. 1, 1814, m. 1850, Mary H. Bacon (b. 1818), dau. of John, of Greenwich, N. J. No issue.
113. Hiram, b. 8th mo. 28, 1816; unm.
114. Hannah, b. 4th mo. 30, 1819; d. 6th mo. 16, 1882.

V. (58.) GEORGE ROBERTS, of Gwynedd, farmer, son of Joseph and Mercy, b. at Montgomery, 3d mo. 10, 1781, d. 6th mo. 16, 1851, m. 12th mo. 16, 1806, PHEBE SCOTT, dau. of Alexander and Jane. (PHEBE b. 1st mo. 12, 1783, d. 8th mo. 16, 1860.) Both were buried in the ground near Penllyn, belonging to (O.) Friends.

VI. Children of George and Phebe:

115. Jane, b. 6th mo. 22, 1809, m. 12th mo. 18, 1832, Jacob T. Lukens, son of William and Martha; and had issue: Phebe, Willet, Martha T., m. Richard T. Shoemaker; George R., Jonathan R., Elizabeth L., m. Jonathan P. Iredell; Joseph R., Hannah W., Mary Anna.
116. Jonathan, b. 4th mo. 9, 1811, unm.
117. Elizabeth, b. 12th mo. 21, 1817.
118. Joseph, b. 5th mo. 12, 1820, m. 3d mo. 10, 1859, Alice P. Hallowell; no issue.
119. Septimus, b. 1826, m. Ellen H. Ambler. ⚘

V. (60.) CHARLES ROBERTS, of Philadelphia, son of Joseph and

ROBERTS FAMILY GENEALOGY. 203

Mercy, b. at Montgomery, 7th mo. 26, 1784, d. 7th mo. 9, 1845; m., 1st, 11th mo. 1, 1810, HANNAH WHITE (b. 8th mo. 16, 1789, d. 12th mo. 4, 1830), dau. of Solomon, of Philadelphia; and 2d, 10th mo. 16, 1834, ANNA MARIA HOSKINS (b. 7th, mo. 11, 1794, d. 12th mo. 5, 1869), dau. of Joseph, of Radnor. A sketch of CHARLES will be separately given in this volume.

VI. Children of Charles and Hannah:

120. Solomon W., b. 1811, d. 1882, m. Anna S. Rickey, Jane E. Shannon. ⚭
121. Elihu, b. 1813, m. Anne Petit. ⚭
122. Samuel A., b. 1816, d. 1817.
123. Caleb C., b. 1821, m. Helen S. Bingham. ⚭
124. Henrietta, b. 1st mo. 26, 1824, d. 1st mo. 17, 1877; m. 1st mo. 9, 1854, Dr. Richard J. Levis, of Philadelphia; and had issue: Anna R. (d.); Louise, m. John Thompson; Mary H. (d.), Henrietta R. (d.), Minford, Alice (d.)

VI. (78.) CADWALADER ROBERTS, tailor, son of Edward and Rebecca, b. 1st mo. 12, 1800, d. 5th mo. 20, 1876, m. 10th mo. 25, 1842, ANN PHILLIPS (b. 3d mo. 14, 1819; d. 8th mo. 22, 1864). CADWALADER was buried at Catawissa, Pa.

VII. Children of Cadwalader and Ann:

125. Rebecca A., b. 10th mo. 16, 1845, d. 6th mo. 9, 1859.
126. Edward C., b. 5th mo. 19, 1848, d. 2d mo. 4, 1866.
127. David B., b. 1st mo. 26, 1850, d. 2d mo. 22, 1877.
128. Ruth H., b. 9th mo. 24, 1853, d. 7th mo. 5, 1879, m., 1875, William U. John, farmer, of Bear's Gap; and had issue: Mary A., Rebecca A., Rachel E., Ruth H.
129. Sarah E., b. 1858, m. 1880, James Crawford.
130. Rachel A., b. 1860.

VI. (82.) EDWARD ROBERTS, of Bloomfield, Ind., physician, son of Edward and Rebecca, b. 12th mo. 29, 1808, m. ANNIE BARTHOLOMEW.

VII. Children of Edward and Annie:

131. Josiah.==132. Petrican.==133. Charles H.==134. Caroline. ==135. Rebecca.==136. Cordelia.==137. Agnes.==138.

Edward (twin with Agnes). == 139. Josephine. == 140. Hannah.==141. Vilaria. (Most of these children of EDWARD and ANNIE are married, and live in Indiana, near Bloomfield.)

VI. (83.) DAVID ROBERTS, mason, son of Edward and Rebecca, b. 8th mo. 19, 1811, m. 1835, FRANCES SANDERS (b. 1817).

VII. Children of David and Frances:
142. Alfred, b. 1837, m. Eliz. R. Richel, and has issue.
143. Rebecca R., b. 1839, m. 1865, Aaron Sechler ; and has issue.
144. Hannah, b. 1842, m. Geo. W. Mowrer, and has issue.
145. Josiah R., b. 1844, m. Eliz. J. Clawson ; and has issue.
146. John E., b. 1847, m. Laura Derling ; and has issue.
147. Margaret S., b. 1851, m. Peter A. Richel ; and has issue.
148. Fannie, b. 1854, m. Theodore C. Reese ; and has issue.
149. Sarah E., b. 1857.

VI. (84.) STEPHEN F. ROBERTS, farmer, son of Edward and Rebecca, b. 7th mo. 10, 1814, m. MARGARET GEORGE.

VII. Children of Stephen F. and Margaret:
150. Eli W., m. Kate Machimer.
151. George E., m. Ella M. Jacobs.

VI. (85.) JOSIAH A. ROBERTS, of Columbia Co., Pa., son of Edward and Rebecca, b. Feb. 2, 1820, m. 1845, ANNA M. CLEWELL.

VII. Children of Josiah A. and Anna M.:
152. William H., b. 1846, m. Ellen Barndt, and has issue.
153. Harvey, b. 1848, m. Maria L. Fenstermacher.
154. Arthur, b. 1850, m. Mary E. Rauch, and has issue.
155. Sarah A., b. 1852, m. Charles Decker, and has issue.
156. Edward, b. 1854, m. Rettie Lewis, and has issue.
157. { Anna M., b. 1857. }
158. { David, b. 1857. }
159. { Clarence, b. 1860. }
160. { Clay, b. 1860. } Died in infancy.
161. { Clara, b. 1860. } Died in infancy.
162. Joseph E., b. 1862.

VI. (86.) JOSEPH ROBERTS, of Ohio, son of Ezekiel and Anna, b. 1799, d. 1830, m. ESTHER SCOTT (b. 1809, d. 1883).

ROBERTS FAMILY GENEALOGY. 205

VII. Children of Joseph and Esther:

163. Amanda, b. 1830, m. Jephtha Kinsey, and has issue.

VI. (90.) CHARLES ROBERTS, of Iowa, farmer, son of Ezekiel and Anna, b. 1808, d. 1875, m. SARAH HARRIS. They had issue 13 children, of whom two d. in childhood.

VII. Children of Charles and Sarah:

164. John, m. Mary Barrett, Sarah A. McKee; and has issue. ℔ == 165. Martha A., m. Jas. H. Lounsberry; and has issue. === 166. Levi m. Mary J. Rogers; and has issue. === 167. Ezekiel, m. Samantha Jackson; and has issue. === 168. Theudas, m. Mary A. Noe. ===169. Wright, m. Samantha Severe. == 170. Frances M., d. ===171. Emanuel N., m. Eleanor Frazier; and has issue. === 172. Charles H., m. Mary J. Hagan: and has issue.=== 173. Amanda, m. John D. Oden. === 174. Sarah J., m. Anthony M. James.
[These families lived, 1883, in Iowa and Missouri.]

VI. (91.) JOHN ROBERTS, manufacturer, Henry, Ill., son of Ezekiel and Anna, b. 1810, m. 1837, SUSANNA METZ; and, 1857, ELIZABETH B. WILSON. By his first wife he had issue six children, who all d. in childhood.

VI. (94.) JOB ROBERTS, farmer, son of Cadwalader and Elizabeth, b. at Gwynedd, 4th mo. 1, 1814, d. 8th mo. 31, 1858, in Harford Co., Md. (bu. at Fallston Friends' ground). He m. HANNAH PICKERING (b. 7th mo. 23, 1811), dau. of Yeomans, of Bucks Co.

VII. Children of Job and Hannah:

175. William P., b. 6th mo. 16, 1845, m. 1869, Anna M. Pugh (b. 1846, d. 1870), dau. of Abner, of Oxford, Pa.; 2d, 1876, Agnes D. Taggart (b. 1854), dau. of John (see No. 92, this Genealogy), by whom he has issue: Horace W., b. 1877; Roy G., b. 1880. *William* graduated, 1869, from the Law Dep't, Univ. of Michigan; served in Union Army, in 47th Regt. P. V. M., and as officer 45th Regt. U. S. Colored Troops. Now member of the bar, Minneapolis, Minn.

176. Ellwood P., b. 9th mo. 30, 1847, d. 11th mo. 23, 1864, in U. S. Military Hospital, Philadelphia, member 195th Regt. P. V. (Bu. at Gwynedd.)

177. Horace W., b. 12th mo. 5, 1850, m. Edith R. Hooper.
178. Richard J., b. 1854, m. Martha C. Shoemaker.

VI. (96.) CHARLES ROBERTS, of Upper Dublin, farmer, son of Joseph and Elizabeth, b. 1807, d. 1866, m. SARAH A. KENDERDINE (b. 1807, d. 1871).

VII. Children of Charles and Sarah E.:
179. Elizabeth, b. 1832, d. 1862, unm.
180. Gulielma, b. 1834, d. 1865, without issue, m. Edwin Thomas.
181. Jesse, b. 1837, m. Sarah E. Skirving; and has issue.
182. George K., b. 1840, m. Elizabeth E. Shay; and has issue.
183. Richard K., b. 1843, m. Ruth A. Michener; and has issue.
184. Anna J., b. 1845, d. 1866, unm.
185. Joseph, b. 1848, m. Mary W. Evans (see No. 242, Evans Genealogy); and has issue.

VI. (99.) ISRAEL ROBERTS, of Ohio, merchant, son of Richard and Mary, b. 1806, d. 1849, m. SARAH T. WARD (b. 1809, d. 1880).

VII. Children of Israel and Sarah T.:
186. Frances L., Chicago, Ill., b. 1834. === 187. Josephine, b. 1838, m. Eber B. Ward (Capt. 34th Ill. Vols., d. 1863); and had issue two children, who d. young.===188. Mary A., b. 1842, d. 1855.

VI. (100.) ALEXANDER S. ROBERTS, son of Richard and Mary, b. 1809, d. 1850, Captain Ill. troops in Black Hawk War, d. in Texas, m. MARY FORT; and had issue: (189.) Amanda, (Liberty, Texas).

VI. (102.) EZEKIEL ROBERTS, of Ohio, son of Richard and Mary, b. 1813, a minister in the Society of Friends, m. ELIZA ANN GRIFFITH (b. 1817, d. 1867), and, 2d, 1876, ELIZABETH P. HARRISON. Issue by his first wife: (190.) Richard E., m. Mira G. Smith.

VI. (104.) ROWLAND ROBERTS, of Short Creek, O., miller, son of Richard and Mary, b. 1817, m. 1843, MARY ANN HUMPHREYS (b. 1819).

VII. Children of Rowland and Mary Ann:

191. Charles H. (lawyer, Chicago).=== 192. Sarah Irene.=== 193. Richard A., m. Catharine P. Barnes.=== 194. Mary Eliza.=== 195. Agnes E.

VI. (109.) CHARLES W. ROBERTS, of West Chester, Pa., son of Isaac and Alice, b. 1807, m. MARTHA W. WALKER (b. 1808, d. 1877), widow, dau. of James Cresson.

VII. Children of Charles W. and Martha W.:

196. Martha C.=== 197. James C., m. Elizabeth L. Garrett.=== 198. Mercy Anna.

VI. (111.) JACOB ROBERTS, of Chester Co., Pa., son of Isaac and Alice, b. 1810, m. 1837, PHEBE WILLIAMS (b. 1810).

VII. Children of Jacob and Phebe:

199. Josiah A.===200. Joseph.===201. Hannah W.===202. Alice, d. ===203. Sarah W.

VI. (119.) SEPTIMUS ROBERTS, of Worcester, son of George and Phebe, b. 7th mo. 15, 1826, m. ELLEN H. AMBLER, dau. of David and Margaret.

VII. Children of Septimus and Ellen H.:

204. Phebe A. === 205. Margaret A., d. === 206. Elizabeth. === 207. Sue.===208. Jane.

VI. (120.) SOLOMON W. ROBERTS, of Philadelphia, civil engineer, son of Charles and Hannah, b. 8th mo. 3, 1811, d. 3d. mo. 20, 1882, m. 1st, 1851, ANNA S. RICKEY (b. 1827, d. 1858), dau. of Randal H.; 2d, 1865, JANE E. SHANNON (b. 1834, d. 1869), dau. of Ellwood. After some preparatory education in Philadelphia, SOLOMON went, at sixteen years old, to Mauch Chunk, where he was, first, an assistant to his uncle, Josiah White, then directing the works of the Lehigh Navigation Co., and later served as assistant engineer on the canal, which in the autumn of 1829 was opened from Mauch Chunk to Easton. (In the spring of 1827, when the railroad at Mauch Chunk, from Summit Hill down to the river, was opened, he rode on the first train, it being the first railway train run in Penna.) Entering the State service, he had charge of the construction of a division of the canal on the Conemaugh, and then was principal assistant to Sylvester Welch in locating and constructing the Portage railroad over the Alleghenies. His division, on the west side, included a tunnel, 901 feet long, the first railroad tunnel in America; and the splendid stone viaduct over the Conemaugh near Johnstown, now used by the Penna. R. R., is his design and construction. Remaining in the State service until 1836,[1] he visited Europe,[2] and upon returning was chief engineer of the Catawissa Railroad from 1838 to 1841; president of the Philad'a, Germ'n & Norr'n R. R. in 1842; president of the Schuylkill Navigation Co. from 1843 to 1846; member of Penna. Legislature in 1846; and from 1848 to 1856 engaged in locating, constructing, and operating the railroad (now the E. division of the Pittsburg, Fort Wayne & Chicago) from Pittsburg to Crestline. In 1856 he returned to Philadelphia to live, and being then chosen chief engineer and general superintendent of the North Penna. railroad, retained the place twenty-two years, and resigned in January, 1879.[3] He was a member of the American Philosophical Society, and active in the work of the Franklin Institute; a great reader, he wrote verse with facility, and took a deep interest in art. (In his youth he had painted a portrait in oil, of his mother, and had a different direction been given his talents, he might have made a fine artist.)

---

[1] See his Reminiscences of this period, *Penna. Mag.*, Vol. II.

[2] During his stay in Wales, he learned from George Crane, the famous ironmaster of Yniscedwin, near Swansea, the process of smelting ore by anthracite and hot blast, and this, communicated by him to Josiah White, led to the establishment of the great Crane Iron Works, at Catasauqua.

[3] See sketch of his work, *Railway World*, Philad'a, Feb. 1879.

VII. Children of Solomon W. and Anna S.:
209. Anna H.==210. Alfred R., m. Emily I. Lewis, and has issue: Sidney L., b. 1881.==211. Elizabeth W., d.==212. Edith C., d.==213. Arthur W., d.

Children of Solomon W. and Jane:
214. Ellwood S., d.==215. Mary E.

VI. (121.) ELIHU ROBERTS, of Philadelphia, son of Charles and Hannah, b. 10th mo. 2, 1813, m. 1838, ANNE PETIT (b. 3d mo. 11, 1817), dau. of Woodnutt, of Salem, N. J.

VII. Children of Elihu and Anne:
216. Charles, b. 8th mo. 21, 1846. A. B., Haverford College, 1864. Member Common Council, Philadelphia, 1882–84. Of Whitall, Tatum & Co., mfrs.
217. Hannah White, b. 11th mo. 30, 1848, m. 1880, Chas. E. Hopkins, of Philadelphia; and has issue.
[Two children (Charles E., b. 1841, Woodnutt P., b. 1845) d. in infancy].

VI. (123.) CALEB C. ROBERTS, of Philadelphia, son of Charles and Hannah, b. 1821, m. 1849, HELEN S., dau. of Col. John Bingham.

VII. Children of Caleb C. and Helen S.:
218. John B., physician, A. B., Univ. of Penna., b. 1852.
219. Mary B., m. Theodore Kitchen; and has issue.

VII. (164.) JOHN ROBERTS, of Nebraska, a pioneer in that State, son of Charles and Sarah, b. 1831, m. MARY BARRETT (d. 1853), and, 2d, SARAH A. MCKEE.

VIII. Children of John and Mary:
220. Mary, b. 1853, m. Charles Martley.

Children of John and Sarah A.:
221. Charles H.==222. S. Elizabeth, m. Charles S. Wright, and 2d, George O. Hoffman.==223. I. Frances, m. Henry Christie.==224. E. Dell.==225. Eda B. (twin with preceding), m. Chas. W. Fleming.==226. John, d.==227. Dwight J.

XV.

Foulke Family Genealogy.

THE details concerning Edward Foulke's ancestry, his removal, etc., have already been fully given.¹ It is intended in this chapter to present what is known to the author concerning his descendants.

Genealogical Sketch.

I. (1.) EDWARD FOULKE, of Gwynedd, immigrant from Wales, 1698, b. 5th mo. 13, 1651, d. 1741. (There is also a statement that he was 88 yrs. 5 mos. old at his death, which, the date of his birth being fixed according to his own narrative, in 1651, would place his death in 1739.) He m. ELEANOR HUGH, dau. of Hugh Cadwalader. She d. at Gwynedd in the 1st mo., 1733.

II. Children of Edward and Eleanor:

2. Thomas, d. 1762, m. Gwen Evans. ℔
3. Hugh, b. 1685, d. 1760, m. Ann Williams. ℔
4. Cadwallader, b. 1691, d. 1743, m. Mary Evans. ℔
5. Evan, d. 1745, m. Ellen Roberts, Anne Coulston. ℔
6. Gwen, m. 10th mo. 6, 1703, Alexander Edwards, jun., son of Alexander Edwards, of Montgomery twp., and had five children, surname *Edwards*: Edward, Alexander, Thomas, Joseph, and Jane. She survived her husband, as is shown by mention of her in her brother Thomas's will.
7. Grace, m. 3d mo. 6, 1707, John Griffith, eldest son of Griffith John, of Merion, and had issue, surname *Griffith*: Griffith, John, Evan, Susanna.
8. Jane (her birth is given in the Exeter monthly meeting records as 11th mo. 10, 1684, but this clashes with the date assigned as the birth of her brother Thomas, by other authority, — 6th mo. 7, 1685). She m. 4th mo. 5, 1713, Ellis Hugh (Hughes), son of John

---

¹ See *ante*, p. 32, *et seq.*

Hugh, of Gwynedd. They removed to Oley, now Berks county. "From them are descended the numerous families of that name spread through Oley, Exeter, Maidencreek, and the settlements on the north branch of the Susquehanna." Jane d. 8th mo. 7, 1766, at the home of her son-in-law, Samuel Lee, in Oley. She had been "an Elder of Exeter m. m. for about thirty years." Her husband, Ellis, b. 1687, d. 1st mo. 11, 1764. Exeter records show the following children of this couple: John, b. 3d mo. 19, 1714, m. Hannah Boone; William, b. 1716, m. Amy Willits; Rowland, b. 1720, d. 1738, unm.; Samuel, b. 1722, d. 1796, m. Elizabeth Willits, Margaret May; Edward, b. 1724, d. 1791, m. Elizabeth ——; Margaret, b. 1726, d. 1810, m. Samuel Lee.

9. Catharine, m. 4th mo. 5, 1713, Theophilus Williams, son of John, of Montgomery, and had issue, surname *Williams*: John, Benjamin, Mary, Eleanor.

10. Margaret, m. 3d mo. 23, 1717, Nicholas Roberts, son of Robert Cadwalader, of Gwynedd, and had issue three daughters: Jane, Eleanor, Elizabeth. (See Roberts Genealogy.)

II. (2.) THOMAS FOULKE, of Gwynedd, son of Edward and Eleanor, born in Merionethshire, Wales, immigrant to Gwynedd, 1698, with his parents, m., at Gwynedd m. h., 4th mo. 27, 1706, GWEN EVANS (d. 12th mo. 6 [or 3?], 1760), eldest dau. of David, of Radnor. They settled at Gwynedd, on part of the Edward Foulke tract (see p. 61). THOMAS FOULKE d. 8th mo. 15 [or 10th mo. 10?] 1762; his will, dated June 11, 1757, was proved October 24, 1762. He appoints his son William executor, and leaves him his real estate, 213 acres (subject to certain charges of annuities, legacies, etc.), except that he gives his eldest son Edward 25 acres (or £100 in cash, instead), "part of the tract I now own, to be surveyed off the north-east end by a line from Hannaniah Pugh's land to my son William's, and parallel to the line now dividing the lands of my son Edward and me." He reserves certain rights of residence in his house, with annuities, etc., to his wife, "Gwen," and gives to his sister Gwen Edwards, "the use of the house she now lives in," with fire-wood, etc., and a small annuity. He also leaves legacies to his daughters Eleanor, Sarah, wife of William Jones, and Susanna, wife of Rowland Evans.

III. Children of Thomas and Gwen:

11. Edward, b. 1707, d. 1770, m. Gainor Roberts, Margaret Griffith. ℬ
12. William, b. 1708, d. 1775, m. Hannah Jones. ℬ
13. Ellin, b. 6th mo. 18, 1710, d. later than date (1757) of her father's will, which speaks of her as then living. She m. William Williams, and had 8 children: Susanna, Hugh, Margaret, Sarah, Thomas, Hannah (m. John Stoy, and had issue 5 children); Samuel, Elizabeth (m. Samuel Davis, and had issue 5 children: Cadwallader, William, Thomas, Evan, Anne).
14. Evan, b. 6th mo. 27, 1712. (The Gwynedd list of deaths mentions Evan Foulke, 12th mo. 11, 1748, and it probably refers to him).
15. Margaret, b. 3d mo. 22, 1715, d. 9th mo. 23, 1734, unm.
16. Susanna, b. 1st mo. 17, 1720, m. Rowland Evans. (See Evans Genealogy).
17. Sarah, b. 1st mo. 17, 1720, m. William Jones, and had issue, Sarah, who m. David Green.
18. Caleb, b. 6th mo. 13, 1722, d. 7th mo. 7, 1736.

II. (3.) HUGH FOULKE, of Richland, Bucks county, the second son of Edward and Eleanor, m., 1713, ANN WILLIAMS (b. 11th mo. 8, 1693, d. 9th mo. 10, 1773), dau of John, of Montgomery. HUGH removed from Gwynedd to Richland, probably about the time of his marriage. A memorial of Richland m. m. says: "He was a member of our meeting for about thirty years, the latter part of his life. He had a good gift in the ministry, which we believe he endeavored faithfully to discharge. . . . . . His last illness, which was very sharp, he endured with much patience and resignation. . . . . . He died on the 21st of 5th mo., 1760, in the 75th year of his age, and the 40th of his ministry." From HUGH are descended all the Foulkes whose origin is traceable to Richland, and no doubt a majority of the members of this family now living are of his line. A family memorandum says: "All their [Hugh and Ann's] children lived

FOULKE FAMILY GENEALOGY. 213

to marry and raise families, except Edward. In seventy years after their marriage, the number of their posterity was 343, and in 1810 was estimated at upward of 500, of whom 115 bore the name of Foulke."

III. Children of Hugh and Ann:

19. Mary, b. 7th [or 9th?] mo. 24, 1714, d. 2d mo. 20, 1756, m. James Boon, of Exeter, Berks county, son of George, the elder, and brother to Geo. Boone, and of Squire Boone, father of Daniel, of Kentucky. *James* was b. 5th mo. 7, 1709, and d. 9th mo. 1, 1785. He had issue by Mary Foulke, 12 children, of whom three (Joshua, b. 1748; Hannah, b. 1752; Nathaniel, b. 1753) are recorded as dying in infancy. The others were as follows, (surname *Boone*):
    1. Ann, b. 2d mo. 3, 1737, d. 4th mo, 4, 1807, m. Abraham Lincoln (of the family of Abraham Lincoln, President of the United States) a member of the Penna. Const. Conv. of 1787, and of the Penna. Legislature, etc. (The marriage was not "according to the order" of the So. of Friends; 8th mo. 27, 1761, Ann Lincoln makes acknowledgment to Exeter monthly meeting for marrying "out.") *Abraham* d. 1st mo. 31, 1806, in his 70th year.
    2. Mary, b. 11th mo. 17, 1738, m. Thomas Lee, son of Samuel, of Oley, 5th mo. 14, 1778.
    3. Martha, b. 1742.
    4. James, jr., b. 1743 (distinguished in his time as a mathematician).
    5. John, b. 1745.
    6. Judah, b. 10th mo, 10, 1746, m. Hannah Lee, dau. of Samuel and Margaret, of Oley, 11th mo. 15, 1770.
    7. Dinah, b. 1748.
    8. Rachel, b. 1751.
    9. Moses, b. 5th mo. 23, 1751, m. 1779, Sarah Griffith.
20. Martha, b. 5th mo. 22, 1716, d. 4th mo. 17, 1781, m. 1st, Oct. 4, 1738, William Edwards, of Milford, Bucks co., and, 2d, John Roberts, son of Thomas.
21. Samuel, b. 1718, d. 1797, m. Ann Greasly. ℔
22. Ellen, b. 1st mo. 19, 1720, m. John Lloyd, of Horsham, at Richland m. h., 8th mo. 21, 1742.
23. John, b. 1722, d. 1787, m. Mary Roberts. ℔
24. Thomas, b. 1724, d. 1786, m. Jane Roberts. ℔
25. Theophilus, b. 1726, d. 1785, m. Margaret Thomas. ℔
26. William, b. 1728, d. 1796, m. Priscilla Lester. ℔
27. Edward, b. 10th mo. 19, 1729, d. March 1st, 1747, unm.

28. Ann, b. 1st mo. 1st, 1732, m. William Thomas.
29. Jane, b. 1st mo. 3d, 1734, d. 8th mo. 1771, m. John Greasly.

II. (4.) CADWALLADER FOULKE,[1] of Gwynedd, third son of Edward and Eleanor, b. in Wales 7th mo. 13, 1691. He lived at Gwynedd until 1731, when he removed to Philadelphia, and d. there 7th mo. 17, 1743, " after a short illness." The memorial of Philadelphia m. m. concerning him says : " He was born in Wales, and came over to this Province with his parents, when young; married and settled at Gwynedd, where he lived most of his time; and from thence about twelve years before his decease removed to this city. He was of an open generous disposition, and useful and active in the support of the discipline and good order of the church, an Elder well respected and exemplary in his life and conversation." In Gwynedd he was a " yeoman"; he bought, 1718, land, 307 acres, of Hugh Pugh, son of Evan ap Hugh, and sold it, 1732, to Robert John.[2] In his deed to the latter he is described as " late of Gwynedd, but now of Philadelphia, shop-keeper." His residence, and probably place of business, are shown by a deed from Edward Cotteral to him, in 1740, for a "lot adjoining the house where he [C. F.] lives, on the north side of High street, near the Court House." He was appointed a justice of the peace for Philadelphia Co., Nov. 22d, 1738. The Philadelphia Co. records show acknowledgments of deeds, etc, before him, in 1739, '40, and '41 (and probably later). CADWALLADER m. at Gwynedd m. h., 4th mo. 13, 1719, MARY EVANS, dau. of Robert.[3]

---

[1] The matter immediately following, the genealogy of the line of CADWALLADER FOULKE, was especially prepared for me by the late Mrs. William Parker Foulke, of Philadelphia, and is here inserted bodily, nearly as she wrote it, the whole being given together directly to the latest generation.

[2] See details about this property at p. 69.

[3] Robert Evans [says Mrs. W. P. F.'s MS.] was the third son of Evan, ap Evan, ap Robert, ap Lewis, ap Griffith, ap Howel Gôch, ap Einion, ap Deikws ddu, ap Madoc, ap Ievan Gôch, ap David Gôch, ap Trahnarn Gôch, ap Madoc, ap Rhys

FOULKE FAMILY GENEALOGY. 215

(See Evans Genealogy.) MARY was a minister among Friends, and made a number of journeys of religious duty, among others to Barbadoes, Nantucket, and Rhode Island. She m., 2d, at Philadelphia meeting, 11th mo. 31, 1744, Thomas Marriott, of Bristol, Bucks co., and d. 1747. A memorial in the John Smith MS. collection says: "Her corpse was taken to Phila., and, after a solemn meeting held on that occasion at the Bank Meeting House, she was buried in Friends' burying ground there." CADWALLADER and MARY had ten children, but one only, Judah, second born, lived to adult age.

III. Children of Cadwallader and Mary:

30. Judah, b. 1722, d. 1776, m. Mary Bringhurst. See following:

III. (30.) JUDAH FOULKE, of Philadelphia, b. at Gwynedd, 7th mo. 30, 1722, d. January 24, 1776, m. 12th mo. 16, 1743, MARY BRINGHURST, of Philadelphia, dau. of John.[1] JUDAH was a prominent and active citizen; that he loved letters, the well-cherished and well-used volumes of classics which were owned by him attest. From 1745 to 1750 he was Collector of Excise for Philadelphia. In 1770, he was sheriff of the city and county of Philadelphia, and again in 1771 and 1772. A quaint document, dated December 11, 1773, recites that His Excellency John Penn, "with the advice of the Council, constitutes and appoints JUDAH FOULKE, gentleman, Keeper of the Standards of Brass for weights and measures for the county of Philadelphia." His will, written 1774,

---

Gloff, ap Rhys Vaughan, ap Rhys Mechyllt, ap Rhys Grûg, ap Rhys, ap Griffith, ap Rhys ap Tewddur Mawr, ap Einion, ap Owen, ap Howel ddu, ap Cadelh, ap Rodri Mawr, ap Mervyn Vrych. (The mother of Mervyn Vrych, King of Man, was Nest, grand-dau. of Brockwell Yscithiog, Prince of Powis, who defeated Ethelred K. of Northumberland on the Dee near Bangor, about the year 607. One of Brockwell's sons was Bishop Tysillis, the opponent of St. Augustine.)

[1] John was the son of John and Rosina Bringhurst, and was b. in Amsterdam, Holland. His wife, Mary, was the daughter of James Claypoole, merchant, of London, and Mary his wife.

makes his wife sole legatee, "in full confidence of her maternal affection for our children," and appoints his brother-in-law Joseph Bringhurst, and his friends Abel James and Joseph Fox, executors. His dwelling was No. 34 Front St., North, where d. his widow, Jan. 22, 1798, aged nearly 77 yrs.

IV. Children of Judah and Mary :

31. John, b. 1757, d. 1796, m. Eleanor Parker. ℔
32. Elizabeth, d. unm. ℔
33. Mary, d. April 5, 1807, unm. ("Aged 54 years.")
34. Deborah, b. 9th mo. 28, 1764, m., 1st, Oct. 16, 1788, William Pearson, son of William and Ann, dec'd, of Northern Liberties; and, 2d, 11th mo. 2, 1809, Isaac Tyson, of Philad'a, son of James and Sarah, of Springfield, Del. Co. By her first husband she had issue, surname *Pearson :* Mary, b. Feb. 10, 1791, d. Feb. 2, 1813, unm.

IV. (31.) JOHN FOULKE, of Philadelphia, son of Judah and Mary, was a physician, a man of learning, and of high repute in his profession, while of his generous practical humanity and thorough accomplishments, much interesting testimony exists. A memorandum of April 6, 1767, has : " John Foulke entered at Robert Proud's school, to learn Latin ;" and this is the earliest noteworthy record we have of him. The late Joseph Carson, M. D., writes: " Dr. Foulke presented himself for graduation in 1779, and was prevented from receiving his degree, in consequence of the abrogation of the charter of the college, from the political excitement of the Revolution.[1] Dr. Foulke was an honored member of the profession, and one of the first elected members of the College of Physicians." His diploma of Fellowship bears date January 2, 1787.[2] By means of his private school for

---

[1] He received his diploma as Bachelor of Medicine in 1780. This degree of B. M. was discontinued after the union, Sept. 30, 1791, of the Phila. College of Medicine and the University of Penna.

[2] In 1789 appeared the "Oration which might have been delivered to the Students in Anatomy, on the late Rupture between the Two Schools in this City."

medical instruction, conducted at 107 North Front Street [his residence] he educated many members of the profession most distinguished both here and elsewhere. In one especial line, Dr. Foulke preceded both Dr. James and Dr. Dewees, for he it was who gave in Philadelphia the first systematic instruction in obstetrics."

During the prevalence of the yellow fever epidemic in Phila., he fearlessly devoted himself to the aid of the sufferers, and was frequently absent for days in the infected districts.

He set sail from Phila. May 4, 1780, for Port l'Orient, in the brig Duke of Leinster; Mr. George Fox accompanied him. They were the bearers to Benj. Franklin, then American Minister to France, of letters introductory from Thomas Bond and Joseph Wharton. Mr. Bond describes the travelers as "the sons of our worthy deceased Friends Judah Foulke and Joseph Fox. They have both had a liberal education, and are now in the laudable pursuit of further useful knowledge in Europe. Mr. Foulke has deservedly obtained in the Philadelphia University, a Diploma of Batchelor of Medicine." Mr. Wharton's letter of the same date, April 27, 1780, says:

The bearer, my friend Dr. John Foulke, is a Whig in his principles, has subscribed the Test to this State, and though, from the singularity of the tenets of the Quakers, he has not been active in the

---

It begins with a mock-solemn adjuration to the adherents of the leaders of the adverse factions, Drs. Shippen and Foulke:

"Friends and associates! lend a patient ear,
Suspend intestine broils, and reason hear.
Ye followers of F―― your wrath forbear ―
Ye sons of S―― your invectives spare."

This grotesque satire was written by Francis Hopkinson, "with a view to appease the dissension that arose from abrogating the charter of the college, then renewing it, and leaving the University in existence. It may have contributed to the coalition in 1791." [Dr. Jos. Carson.]

field, yet in the line of his physical profession, has been useful in the hospitals.[1] His intention in visiting France is to improve himself in Surgery and Physic; but being a perfect stranger in Paris, will stand in need of recommendations to the most eminent in the medical branches, as well as for favorable introductions into the hospitals. Will you therefore, my good Sir, as my friend is of unimpeached morals, and his relatives long known for good citizens, take him by the hand, and recommend him to those gentlemen who can be most useful to him? I know you will, and in this happy thought, I subscribe myself,

Respectfully, etc.,
JOSEPH WHARTON.

His Excellency DR. FRANKLIN.

Before his return to America, Dr. Foulke visited Germany and Holland, and the stay abroad was rich in experiences, in added friendships, and in knowledge gained. At a lecture on Pneumatics, which he delivered at the old Hall of the College, Fourth St. below Arch, in May, 1784, he exhibited to his friends the first balloon seen in this country. He had been greatly interested by the subject of aerostation, while in France, where the invention of the balloon had been lately made public. An autograph note to Dr. Foulke from General Washington states that "he would with great pleasure attend the lecture on Pneumatics, but the business which brought him to the City does not leave him at liberty, as the Members of the Cincinnati are anxious to bring it to a close."

Dr. Foulke was elected to membership of the American Philosophical Society in 1784, and in 1786 became one of its Secretaries, Benjamin Franklin being President.

He m., May 8, 1788, ELEANOR, dau. of Richard[2] and

---

[1] In the "Diary of Robert Morton," *Penna. Magazine*, Vol. I., he says: "Oct. 8th [1777] . . . I went to see Dr. Foulke amputate an American soldier's leg, which he completed in twenty minutes, while the physician at the military hospital was forty minutes performing an operation of the same nature."

[2] Richard Parker was the son of Richard, the son of Richard, of Rolgley, Lincolnshire, Eng., who emigrated in 1684: see Proud's *History of Pennsylvania*, Vol. II p. 218, notes.

Lydia Parker, dec'd, of Phila. She survived until the summer of 1860.[1] The following were the

V. Children of John and Eleanor Foulke:

35. Richard Parker, b. 1789, d. 1860, m. Anna Catharine Ströhn.
36. Mary, b. Aug. 1, 1790; d. unm.
37. Eleanor Parker, b. April 6, 1792; d. 1882; m. Burgess B. Long; no children.

IV. (32.) ELIZABETH FOULKE, dau. of Judah and Mary, b. 28 9th mo., 1758. A notice, written in 1820, says of her: "She was possessed of a strong and active mind, which was improved by cultivation, and of manners cheerful and engaging; and although deprived by death of most of her near relations, she had collected around her a large circle endeared to her by the most tender ties of friendship. Her house was the loved resort of persons of both sexes and all ages, to whom she adapted her conversation with remarkable facility. . . . . By the Society of Friends in this city, her loss will long be felt; she was an active member, and for nearly thirty years a minister of the Gospel. . . . . The Prison, the Public Alms House, and the Asylum for Widows all engaged her attention, and in each of them her voice was raised in endeavors to reclaim the wanderer and comfort the afflicted." There is a letter from her to Sarah Harrison, in *Friends' Miscellany* (Vol. XI., p. 185), dated at Philadelphia, 11th mo. 29, 1793, in which she speaks of the recent terrible visitation of yellow fever. She had been absent from the city ten weeks, but seems to have been well informed of the condition of affairs within it: "Outward circumstances," she says, "concurred to heighten the virulence of the disease and increase its progress. The coming of rain and cold weather, towards which the minds of many were too much turned as a source of relief, was withheld, and the

---

[1] Her married life was a little more than 8 years, her widowhood 64 years,—a very remarkable instance.

parched earth seemed to mourn with its inhabitants. * * It is impossible for tongue or pen to give a just idea of the awfulness of the scene, or of our feelings through the course of it. It seemed at times as tho' the Almighty would utterly desolate the city." She d. unmarried, at Burlington, N. J., October 19, 1820, and was there interred.

V. (35.) RICHARD PARKER FOULKE, b. April 5, 1789, m. August 6, 1812, ANNA CATHARINE STRÖHN, dau. of Philip and Anna Catharine Ströhn, b. May 17, 1792, d. January 30, 1856. He had no bent towards a profession, and his early establishment in business was due to the affectionate interest in him of his uncle, Mr. William Parker. He d. at the summer residence of his son, William Parker Foulke, near West Chester, Pa., August 22, 1860.

VI. Children of Richard P. and Anna C.:
(The children of Richard Parker and Anna Catharine Foulke were eleven in number: all of them d. young, except):
38. Elizabeth, 2d dau., b. March 25th, 1814, d. May 4, 1864. She m. May 12, 1855, Patrick Beirne, of Lewisburg, W. Va., b. in County Roscommon, Ireland, and had, surname *Beirne*: (1.) Richard Foulke, b. 1856, m. in 1877, Clara Haxall, dau. of Thomas Billopp Grundy, of Baltimore, Md. (and has issue: Clara, b. Nov. 4, 1878; Elizabeth Foulke, b. Nov., 1879; Richard Foulke, b. August 25, 1882); and (2) William McDermott, b. 1858, d. 1859.
39. William Parker, b. 1816, d. 1865. See below.
40. Francis Edward, youngest child, b. May 17, 1834.

VI. (39.) WILLIAM PARKER FOULKE, b. May 31, 1816, m. April 26, 1855, JULIA DE VEAUX POWEL, dau. of Col. John Hare Powel,[1] of Philadelphia. She d. April 30, 1884. WILLIAM PARKER FOULKE early showed the philanthropic spirit by which he was distinguished. Well read in the law, he prac-

---

[1] His name was originally John Powel Hare, but, as the adopted son of his mother's sister, Mrs. Powel, he caused it to be changed by Act of Assembly to John Hare Powel. His father, Robert, who was the son of Richard Hare (of Limehouse, near London, Eng.), came to Pennsylvania, June 4, 1773.—See Keith's *Provincial Councillors of Pennsylvania*, pp. 129, 133-134.

ticed for a time at the Philadelphia Bar. In 1845 he appears as a member of the Phila. Society for Alleviating the Miseries of Public Prisons; and in 1846 as one of the Visiting Committee for the Eastern Penitentiary. In his endeavor "to reconcile the highest interests of the Commonwealth with the utmost exhibition of humanity towards offenders," he struggled long with popular prejudice and indifference. His writings on the various branches of penal administration and reform and his efforts during nearly half of his life, identify his name with the Pennsylvania system of separate imprisonment. The late Frederick A. Packard, his fellow-laborer, writes of "the weeks and months and years devoted by Mr. Foulke to journeys and examinations, consultations, discussions, conferences with strangers from other States and from foreign countries, correspondence, reports, addresses, memorials, besides the constant active duties of personal inspection in Philadelphia, and attendance upon legislation at Harrisburg." In 1858 Mr. Foulke first proposed the appointment of a Commission to revise the Penal Code of Pennsylvania. His memorial, which was adopted by the Society, led in due time to the necessary legislation, and he was made one of a committee to confer with the Commissioners, and to suggest such changes as the experience of the Society approved. The Commissioners were appointed in 1859, and in 1860 a report of the Conferences appeared, the Code itself being enacted the same year.— In 1845, Mr. Foulke became a Manager of the Penna. Colonization Society; in 1853, '54, '55, he was sent a delegate to the meetings of the parent society at Washington. The Society's influence, through his urgency, was exerted to procure a Government survey of the country interior of Liberia, with the view of directing settlement to the more healthy region.[1]— Three years of serious effort

---

[1] Commander Lynch, U. S. N., made his report of the partial completion of this survey, Sept. 5, 1853. See H. R. Doc. 1, 54 pp.

were given by Mr. Foulke to the promotion of the Arctic Expedition of 1860, under Dr. I. I. Hayes, and his labors in this behalf are perpetuated in the name — Port Foulke — given to the winter harbor of the explorers in North Greenland. — He was an ardent and serviceable member of the Academy of Natural Sciences. His discovery, in the summer 1858, in the green-sand formation at Haddonfield, N. J., of a gigantic fossil extinct reptile marked his labors in that field.[1] Associated with the Pennsylvania Historical Society, in 1842, he took an active interest in its work; he was in 1850, with Hon. Jos. R. Ingersoll, Rev. Albert Barnes, Bishop Potter, and others, charged with the preparation of a series of historical papers, and his essay "On the Right Use of History," was published 1856. — Prof. J. P. Lesley, chief of the present (Second) Geological Survey of Pennsylvania, speaks in high terms of his services in procuring the publication of the Report of the First Survey. He says: "Among the few men in the Commonwealth who knew either the character of the Report, or the actual value of the Survey, Mr. Foulke occupied the most prominent position, and it was he who finally succeeded in dragging the buried manuscript into notice and in so stimulating public opinion in its favor as to get an act passed for its publication, in 1851."[2] He was one of the three earliest projectors of the Philadelphia Academy of Music and the fine proportions of that building are largely due to him. He desired, indeed, that it should be of yet greater size, "that the many might be attracted at reasonable rates." His hope was, by elevating the standard of popular amusements, dramatic, operatic, and musical, to aid in the purification of tastes and manners among the people at large. He thought

---

[1] In Nov., 1868, a restoration of the skeleton was made by Prof. Waterhouse Hawkins, the English scientist, and presented to the Academy.

[2] Prof. Lesley's memorial address of W. P. F. (Owing to delays the Report did not finally appear until 1859).

also that to lay the foundation of such a school for complete education in music, as should be included by the ultimate scheme, " would enable us hereafter to command the best musical talent of the world, and also to provide for the cultivation of such talent among ourselves." Prof. J. P. Lesley read before the American Philosophical Society, Nov. 6, 1868, a Memoir of Mr. Foulke, which is found in Volume X. of its proceedings, and which was prepared at its instance. William Parker Foulke's connection with this body was of long duration, and he was a member of its Council at the time of his death, which took place on June 18, 1865.

Children of William Parker and Julia de Veaux :
VII. 41. Julia Catharine, b. Jan. 22, 1856, m. May 3, 1882, Henry Carvill Lewis,[1] M. A., Univ. of Penna., Prof. of Mineralogy A. N. S., of Phila., and has, surname *Lewis*, Gwendolen de Veaux, b. Mar. 21, 1883.
42. William de Veaux, b. June 9, 1857.
43. Richard Parker, b. Aug. 30, 1858, d. Jan. 7, 1865.
44. Lisa de Veaux, b. March 8, 1860.
45. John Francis, b. Nov. 26, 1861, B. A. and B. L., Univ. of Penna., Member of Phila. Bar.
46. Sara Gwendolen, b. June 26, 1863.
47. George Rhyfedd, b. Aug. 16, 1865.
[Thus the living representatives of Cadwallader Foulke's line to-day, Sept. 28, 1883, are twelve in number, as follows : Francis Edward Foulke, youngest son of Richard Parker Foulke ; Richard Foulke Beirne and his three children ; three sons and three daughters as above named of William Parker Foulke ; and Gwendolen de Veaux Lewis, child of the eldest of these.—J. de V. F.]

II. (5.) EVAN FOULKE, of Gwynedd, son of Edward, b. in Wales, immigrant, 1698, with his parents, d. 1745. He received from his father, in 1725, 250 acres of the eastern side of the latter's original tract, the east corner of which was almost

---

[1] Henry Carvill is the son of F. Mortimer, son of John F., son of Johann A. P. Ludwig (of Crailsheim, Wurtemburg), who came to Philadelphia June 3, 1777, and Anglicised his name to Lewis.

precisely at the present village of Spring-House, and he lived near that place. He m., 1st, ELLEN ROBERTS, dau. of Edward, of Gwynedd, and, 2d, ANNE COULSTON, widow. Sept. 20, 1745, letters of administration were granted upon his estate to his widow, ANNE FOULKE.

III. Children of Evan Foulke by his two wives :

48. Margaret (dau. of ELLEN), b. 4th mo. 19, 1726, d. 3d mo. 6, 1798, m. John Evans, of Gwynedd, son of John and Eleanor. (See Evans Genealogy).

49. Esther (dau. of ANNE), b. 1st mo. 16, 1744, m. 1st, —— Yaxley,[1] and had issue (surname Yaxley): Eleanor, and Ann; m., 2d, —— Johnson, and had issue two children, surname *Johnson*, Samuel and Mary. (Eleanor Yaxley, m. John F. Evans, son of John and Margaret; Mary Johnson m. Thomas Scarlett, and had issue two children, Robert and Mary.)

[The Gwynedd monthly meeting records show the death of the following children of Evan Foulke: Edward, son of Evan and Ellen, 5th mo. 29, 1745; Anne, dau. Evan and Ellen, 6th mo. 4, 1745; Ellen, dau. Evan and Anne, 6th mo. 15, 1745].

III. (11.) EDWARD FOULKE, of Gwynedd, son of Thomas and Gwen, b. 1707, d. 10th mo. 10, 1770, m., 1st, GAINOR ROBERTS, dau. of Edward, of Gwynedd. GAINOR d. 7th mo. 14, 1741; he m., 2d, MARGARET GRIFFITH, dau. of Hugh, of Gwynedd, 8th mo. 25, 1750. MARGARET survived him: her will was probated Sept. 26, 1781; she names her dau. Hannah and her son Cadwalader, leaving them legacies in money, and leaves to her son Hugh, whom she appoints executor, "all my plantation where he now dwells," 180 acres, mostly in Gwynedd, partly in Horsham, but lying contiguous. (This is the present property [1884] of Daniel Foulke, and estate of Thomas S. Foulke). EDWARD had part of the land of his father, Thomas Foulke; it lay to the eastward of the latter's (given by will to William), towards the Spring-House, and Thos. S. Foulke regarded it as the

---

[1] I think the name here given is correct, and not Ely or Yearsley. See *ante*, p. 173.

same which has been in recent time the place of Albert Hoover, and John Murphy. EDWARD was a man of education and business capacity. He was some time engaged in Philadelphia, as clerk to the Pennsylvania Commissioners of Loans (his brother-in-law, Rowland Evans, being one of the Board).

IV. Children of Edward and Gainor:

50. Joshua, b. 1731, m. Catharine Evans, Hannah Jones. ₱
51. Ann, b. 6th mo. 22, 1732, m. John Ambler, and had issue seven children, surname *Ambler:*
    1. Joseph, m. Elizabeth Forman: no issue.
    2. Edward, m. Ann Mather, and had issue: Edward, Hannah, Sarah, Elizabeth, Ann, and others.
    3. John, jun., m., 1st, Priscilla Naylor, and had issue: Naylor, Charles, Priscilla, Mary, Lydia, and others; (Priscilla m. Silas Walton, Mary m. Jesse Jenkins: see Jenkins Genealogy; Lydia m. Thomas Bancroft); 2d, m. Mary Thomas, who left no issue.
    4. Jesse, m. Ruth Roberts; no issue. (See Roberts Genealogy).
    5. Gainor, m. Isaac Jones, of Montgomery, and had seven children: John, Ann, who m. Jonathan Cleaver; Charles, George, Tacy, who m. Edward Foulke; Jesse, Isaac.
    6. Tacy, m. Joseph Shoemaker, and had issue six children: Ezekiel, who m. Margaret Weaver; Joseph, who m. Phebe Hallowell; Jesse, d. unm.; Ann, who m. Nathan Evans; Hannah, who m. John Cavender, of Philadelphia; Ellen, m. John Forman, of New Britain.
    7. Susanna, m. Jesse Lukens, of Towamencin, and had nine children: (1) Samuel, m. Mary Farra, no issue; (2) Charles, d. unm.; (3) Ann, m. Jacob Styer, and had issue John F., Samuel L., Albanus, (4) Martha, m. Isaac Jones, of Plymouth; (5) Edith, m. Israel Scott, of Towamencin, and had issue: Jesse, Jane, Job; (6) Cadwallader d. unm.; (7) Peter, m. Elizabeth Wilson, and had issue: Algernon, Susan, Elizabeth, Martha; (8) Jonathan, m. Elizabeth Righter, and had issue: Jesse, Martha Ann, Mary F.; (9) Hugh, m. and had issue.
52. Eleanor, b. 7th mo. 15, 1735, m., 5th mo. 14, 1767, Edward Ambler, son of Joseph, of Montgomery.

IV. Children of Edward and Margaret:

53. Hugh, b. 1751, d. 1831, m. Ann Roberts. ₱
54. Alice, b. 7th mo. 15, 1754, d. in infancy.
55. Hannah, b. 9th mo. 20, 1755, d. 6th mo. 24, 1781, m. Edward Stroud, and had issue: Edward, Margaret, Tacy,
56. Cadwallader, b. 1758, d. 1808, m. Phebe Ellis, Ann Chirington. ₱

III. (12.) WILLIAM FOULKE, of Gwynedd, son of Thomas and Gwen, b. 1708, d. 1775; m. HANNAH JONES, dau. of John ("carpenter"), of Montgomery, at Gwynedd m. h., 8th mo. 15, 1734. The memorial of Gwynedd m. m. says: "He was born of religious parents, early settlers of Gwynedd," and "in the station of elder and overseer, which he filled for a number of years, he was exemplary and serviceable." HANNAH d. 12th mo. 1, 1798. The will of WILLIAM, probated Nov. 6, 1775, names his wife, Hannah, and appoints his sons Caleb and Jesse executors. To his son Jesse he gives "the plantation where I now dwell;" to his son Levi "the plantation where he now dwells," containing about 100 acres; to his son Levi and daughter Jane a lot of 25 acres, near Levi's farm, to be equally divided between them, Levi's share to be the end next Joshua Foulke's, and Jane's the end next William Williams's; to his son Jesse he gives "a narrow strip of land which I hold, between the tract I sold George Maris, and lands of one Roil;" to his sons Levi and Jesse his right to a share in a lime-kiln, in Plymouth; to his sons Caleb and Amos, and daughters Jane, Priscilla, and Lydia, bequests of money.

IV. Children of William and Hannah:

57. Jane, b. 6th mo., 22, 1735, m. 1757, George Maris, of Gwynedd, son of George, of Springfield, Chester [now Delaware] county. This couple lived where now Jacob Acuff's hotel is. George Maris d. Aug. 20, 1803, leaving a large estate, mostly in land. His children were ten in number, including Amos, Jesse, Ann, Jane, and George, who all d. unmarried; the others were (surname *Maris*):

   1. William, who received the homestead by his father's will, but d. the next year, 1804, unm., leaving it to his nephew, Jesse J.
   2. Jonathan, who m., 1792, Judith McIlvaine, dau. of John and Susanna, and had issue one son, Jesse J., b. 1793, who m. Mary West, dau. of Saml. and Mary, and had issue: Hannah, who m. John Stokes; John M., Samuel W., William, Jesse Emlen, Edward, Sarah Ann, and Mary W.

FOULKE FAMILY GENEALOGY. 227

3. Susanna, m. 1795, Levi Heston, of Philada., son of John, of Montgomery twp., and had issue : Maria m. Jesse Tyson, of Upper Providence, and Franklin Foulke, of Gwynedd, —No. 125, this Genealogy; (2) Jane, m. Robert Tyson.
4. Hannah, m. 1796, John Wilson, son of John, of Whitemarsh, and had issue: George, Ann, m. Benjamin Jones; Susan (the poet), m. Solomon Lukens; Rebecca.
5. Rebecca, m. 1796, Jarrett Heston, son of John, of Montgomery.

58. Caleb, b. 1736, d. 1811, m. Jane Jones. ℔
59. Levi, b. 1739, d. 1815, m. Ann Evans. ℔
60. Amos, b. 1740, d. 1793, m. Hannah Jones. ℔
61. Jesse, b. 11th mo. 9, 1742, d. 3d mo. 16, 1821, unm. He and Priscilla occupied the old homestead, at Penllyn, and lived, greatly esteemed, to advanced years. (See mention of their deaths, in Cadw. Foulke's and Lewis Jones's lists ; also, repeated allusions to them in the Sally Wister diary.)
62. Priscilla, b. 10th mo. 3, 1744, d. 1st mo. 25, 1821, unm.
63, 64, 65, Margaret, b. 1746; Sarah, b. 1748; Judah, b. 1751 ; all d. in infancy.
66. Lydia, b. 4th mo. 9, 1756, m. John Spencer[1] (b. 1756, d. 1799), son of Jacob and Hannah, of Moreland, and had issue, surname *Spencer:*

1. Susan, b. 4th mo. 10, 1784, d.   , unm.
2. Edith, b. 12th mo. 16, 1785, d. 1865, unm.
3. George, b. 4th mo. 29, 1787, m. Mary Thomas, of Cayuga Co., New York, and d. without issue. His widow survives. He was a well known and much esteemed resident of Horsham.
4. Priscilla, b. 8th mo. 27, 1788, d. 6th mo. 8, 1865, unm.
5. Jesse,[2] b. 12th mo 22, 1790, d. 9th mo. 30, 1841, m. Mary Custard, and had issue : (1) Amelia, m. James C. Jackson, of Hockessin, Del., and has issue; (2) John, m. Mary J. Rhodes, and has issue; (3) George, m. Ella L. Shoemaker, and has issue : (4) Lydia, m. Samuel Morris, of Olney, Philadelphia, and has issue; (5) Anna; (6) William F., m. Christiana Bradley, and has issue.

---

[1] John Spencer was the son of Jacob and Hannah (Jarrett), and the brother of Jarrett Spencer, who m. Hannah Evans [see p. 163]. Jacob was the son of Samuel, of Upper Dublin, who m. Mary Dawes, dau. Abraham and Edith of Whitemarsh. Samuel was the son of Samuel and Elizabeth, who came to Pennsylvania from Barbadoes, about 1700. — See details Spencer Family, *post.*

[2] Jesse Spencer lived at Penllyn in the old Foulke mansion, a much esteemed man.

6. Jonathan, b. 8th mo. 18, 1792, d. 4th mo. 6, 1867, m. Sarah Harris and Sarah Lang. By his second wife he had issue: Florence, m. Samuel E. Stokes; John E. and George E. d. young.
7. Rebecca, b. 7th mo. 19, 1794, d.   , unm.
8. Rachel, b. 11th mo. 12, 1796, d. 4th mo. 8, 1851, unm.
9. Lydia, b. 8th mo. 10, 1799, d. 12th mo. 30. 1823, m. John Lloyd; left no issue.

III. (21.) SAMUEL FOULKE, of Richland, son of Hugh and Ann, b. 12th mo. 4, 1718, d. 1st mo. 21, 1797; m. 1743, ANN GREASLEY (d. 5th mo., 1797). He was a prominent member of the Society of Friends, was appointed clerk of Richland monthly meeting at its first establishment, in 1742, and continued in that capacity "about thirty-seven years, and nearly thirty years served as clerk to the meeting of ministers and elders." From 1761 to 1768 inclusive he was a member of the Provincial Assembly of Pennsylvania, and fragments of his journal kept during that time have been printed.[1] In 1781, notwithstanding his prominence in the meeting, he was disowned, with other members of Richland meeting,[2] for having taken the oath of allegiance to the Colonies. He made the translation from Welsh into English of Edward Foulke's narrative. Several obituary notices, and a letter to a minister, by him, will be found in *Friends' Miscellany*, Vols. III., IV.

IV. *Children of Samuel and Ann:*
67. Eleanor, b. 1744, d. 7th mo. 6, 1833, m. Randall Iden.
68. Thomas, b. 4th mo. 11, 1746, d. 10th mo. 7, 1784, unm.
69. Amelia, b. 1753, d. 8th mo. 7, 1811, m. Joseph Custer.
70. Hannah, b. 9th mo. 15, 1756, d. 3d mo., 1840, m. George Iden.
71. Israel, b. 1760, d. 1824, m. Elizabeth Roberts.
72. Judah, b. 1st mo. 18, 1763, m. Sarah McCarty. They had a large

---

[1] *Penna. Mag.*, Vol. IV.

[2] Including his brothers, John, Thomas, and Theophilus, and his nephew, Everard. It is said that this disciplinary procedure could only be accomplished with help from other meetings, directed from Philadelphia, and that Samuel Foulke, who had for many years sat "at the head of the meeting," continued to do so to his death.

family, 13 children being recorded on Richland m. m. records. In 1818 they removed to Miami, O., and they have numerous descendants in the West.
73. Cadwallader, b. 1768, d. 1830, m. Margaret Foulke. ⓟ
74. John, b. 1767, m. Letitia Roberts. ⓟ
[Israel, b. 1749, and Judah, b. 1752, d. young].

III. (23.) JOHN FOULKE, of Richland, son of Hugh and Ann, b. 12th mo. 21, 1722, d. 5th mo. 25, 1787, m. MARY ROBERTS (b. 4th mo. 26, 1730, d. 10th mo. 2, 1787), dau. of Edward, of Richland. JOHN was a member of the Provincial Assembly from Bucks County from 1769 to 1775.

IV. *Children of John and Mary:*
75. Edward, b. 7th mo. 16, 1758, m. Elizabeth Roberts, Ann Roberts. ⓟ
76. Anne, b. 10th mo. 27, 1760.
77. Jane, b. 8th mo. 2, 1763, d. 3d mo. 18, 1780.
78. Aquila, b. 3d mo. 2, 1766. He m. his first cousin, Amelia Roberts, and for this breach Richland m. m. disowned them, 1789.
79. Margaret, b. 10th mo. 17, 1768, m. ——— Gibson.
80. Evan, b. 5th mo. 6, 1771, m. Sarah Nixon, and had issue : Olivia, Charles, Asenath (m. Samuel Foulke, son of Judah, No. 99); Susanna, Samuel, Edward and others. This family removed to Ohio, except Charles, who m. Catherine P. Edkins, and lived near Stroudsburg, where he d. 1883.
81. Lydia, b. 10th mo. 2, 1775, m. Nathan Edwards.

III. (24.) THOMAS FOULKE, of Richland, son of Hugh and Ann, b. 1st mo. 14, 1724, d. 3d mo. 31, 1786, m. JANE ROBERTS (b. 11th mo. 3, 1732, d. 7th mo. 25, 1822), dau. of Edward, of Richland.

IV. *Children of Thomas and Jane:*
82. Everard, b. 1755, d. 1827, m. Ann Dehaven. ⓟ
83. Abigail, b. 10th mo. 4, 1763.
84. Susanna, b. 11th mo. 5, 1766.
85. Samuel, b. 11th mo. 19, 1767.
[Edward, b. 1756, Samuel, b. 1761, d. in infancy].

III. (25.) THEOPHILUS FOULKE, of Richland, son of Hugh and Ann, b. 12th mo. 21, 1726, d. 11th mo. 4, 1785, m. MAR-

GARET THOMAS, dau. of Samuel and Margaret. They had twelve children, of whom four (Benjamin, b. 1763, Rachel and Charles, twins, b. 1773, and Charles, b. 1777), d. in infancy; and one, Benjamin, b. 1768, d. 1784, unmarried. The survivors are given below. Theophilus, like his brothers, fell under the censure of the meeting, for departure from strict peace principles.

IV. Children of Theophilus and Margaret:

86. Hugh, b. 8th mo. 29, 1758, d. 9th mo., 1846, m. Sarah Roberts, Sarah Lester, Catharine Johnson. By his second wife he had no children; by his first wife: Joseph, Martha, Joseph ; by his third wife: Deborah, Sarah, Hugh, Theophilus, Caspar, Benjamin.
87. Jane, b. 8th mo. 22, 1759, d. 3d mo. 16, 1816.
88. Theophilus, b. 1761, d, 1798, m. Hannah Lester.
89. Sarah. b. 1764, d. 1828, m. Edward Jenkins (See Jenkins Gen'y).
90. Benjamin, b. 11th mo. 19, 1766, d. 2d mo. 28, 1821, m. Martha Roberts (b. 1764, d. 1831), dau. of John and Margaret, and had issue: Hannah, m. George Custard; Jane, m. Thomas Strawn; Charles (d. 1857, unm.); Rachel, Rachel, 2d. *Benjamin* was a member from Bucks Co. of the House of Representatives of Pennsylvania, for several years, being elected in 1816, 1817, 1819 (?), and 1820. He d. at Harrisburg, while in attendance upon the session.[1]
91. Margaret, b. 1771, d. 1845, m. Cadw. Foulke. (See No. 73, this Genealogy.)
92. Rachel, b. 3d mo. 17, 1775, d. 3d mo. 3, 1850, m. Dr. Joseph Meredith, of Gwynedd. They lived after their marriage in the house afterward Fredk. Beaver's, where North Wales now is, and in 1814, bought of Jane Foulke, Caleb's widow, the property, now Jonathan Lukens' estate, where both d. (Dr. M. d. August 7, 1820). Their children were : (1) Hannah Hough, d. March 6, 1870, unm.; (2) Charles F., of Quakertown, physician, b. June 1, 1808, m. Olivia Weisel, and has issue ; (3) Margaret; (4) Edward J., b. Dec. 20, 1811, d. April 5, 1865, at Gwynedd.

---

[1] The Journal of the House shows the action of that body in reference to his decease, including a resolution to wear crape during the remainder of the session, with an official funeral procession, including members of both Houses, the Governor, heads of dep'ts, etc.

FOULKE FAMILY GENEALOGY.

III. (26.) WILLIAM FOULKE, b. 12th mo. 10, 1728, d. 4th mo. 11, 1796, son of Hugh and Ann, m. PRISCILLA LESTER (b. 1st mo. 18, 1736, d. 3d mo. 17, 1795), dau. of John.

IV. Children of William and Priscilla :

93. Asher, b. 1758, m. 1779, Alice Roberts, and had issue : Phebe, Anthony, William, Anne, Elizabeth.
94. Issachar, b. 1760, m. Jane ———, and had issue : Priscilla, Bathsheba, Mary, Sarah, Rebecca, Jane, Aaron, Mercy, Barton. They removed to the West, and have numerous descendants there.
95. Jesse, b. 1762, m. Sarah ——— (d. 9th mo. 21, 1791), and had issue : Ellen, Hannah, Rachel, William.
96. John, b. 1764, d. in infancy.
97. Mary, b. 1766.
98. Phebe, b. 1769, d. in infancy.

IV. (50.) JOSHUA FOULKE, of Gwynedd, son of Edward and Gainor, b. 2d mo. 15, 1731, m. 1st, 1763, CATHARINE EVANS (see No. 101, Evans Genealogy), dau. of Thomas and Katharine. CATHARINE d. 5th mo. 11, 1769, after a lingering illness of six months, and left issue two children, Thomas and Samuel, both of whom d. unmarried. JOSHUA m., 2d, HANNAH JONES, dau. of John, of Gwynedd.

V. Children of Joshua and Hannah :

99. Judah, m. Sarah Richards, dau. of Rowland and Lydia, of Waynesville, O., and had issue several children, five of whom reached married life : (1) Samuel, eldest son, m. Asenath Foulke, dau. Evan, from Richland, Bucks Co., and had issue ; (2) Margaret, m. Ezra Smith, son of Jacob, from Loudoun Co., Va., and had issue ; (3) Thomas, m. Hannah Moore, dau. Benjamin B. and Lydia, and had issue ; (4) Lydia, m. Isaac A. Ogborn, son of Joseph and Elizabeth, and d., leaving one dau. ; (5) Sarah, m. Joseph Ogborn, son of John and Mary, from Maryland (distantly related to Lydia's husband), and had issue.
100. John E., m. Hannah Conard, in Belmont Co., O., but left no issue.
101. Margaret, m. 1815, George Hatton,[1] of Indiana, and had one son,

---

[1] George Hatton was b. at Uwchlan, Chester Co., Pa., 10th mo. 28, 1790, the son of Robert Hatton (b. in Ireland, 7th mo. 14, 1746), who was the son of Joseph and Susanna Hatton. (Joseph d. at Waterford, Ireland, in 1759; Susanna came to this country, and m. ——— Lightfoot, and d. 1781, aged 61 years. Her maiden name was Hudson.)

Robert, who m. Susanna Evens, dau. of Edmund and Elizabeth (who were originally from the north of England, but had lived near Baltimore, and moved to Indiana in 1832). The children of Robert and Susanna E. are, surname *Hatton :* Joseph, Elizabeth E., Sarah, Margaret, Eliza, Robert, Willets, Lorenzo, and Edmund. *Robert* is a minister amongst Friends; resided some time at Easton, Md., now (1884) in Chester Co., Pa.

IV. (53.) HUGH FOULKE, of Gwynedd, son of Edward and Margaret, b. 2d mo. 21, 1752, d. 2d mo. 23, 1831, m. ANN ROBERTS (b. 1745, d. 12th mo. 7, 1823), dau. of Robert and Sarah (see No. 26, Roberts Genealogy). The memorial of Gwynedd m. m. concerning him says he suffered much during the Revolution "on account of his faithfulness in the support of our peaceable testimony against war. * *
For above forty years he bore a faithful testimony, both by precept and example, against the use of spirituous liquors, He was one of the first in his neighborhood who abandoned the use of them in hay-time and harvest. He labored much on the subject both publicly and privately." For many years he was an elder, and member of the Yearly Meeting Representative Committee. In 1816, in consequence of a fall, he became lame, so as to be confined to the house for months.[1]

V. Children of Hugh and Ann:

102. Ellen, b. 4th mo 16, 1775, d. 11th mo. 18, 1846, unm.
103. Mary, b. 1st mo. 1, 1777, d. 7th mo. 12, 1855, unm.
104. Cadwallader, b. 1778, d. 1858, m. Ann Shoemaker.

---

[1] Hugh lived on the property occupied later by his two sons, Joseph and Hugh, jr. (it had been left him by his mother, Margaret Griffith,—see *ante*), now Daniel Foulke's and the estate of Thos. S. Foulke. Joseph Foulke says in his Journal that of his father's children five sisters and two brothers "all remained until the youngest was 22 years old, without a death or marriage in the family. One sister, however, was several years a teacher at Westtown." Joseph also says, concerning his father (Hugh, 53): "I think I never saw him fail, when he undertook: his wisdom and discernment preserved him from entering upon a fruitless undertaking. But wherever he saw his way, he persevered, and would not — using his own words — let 'either the love of ease or the dread of conflict' hinder him from a faithful discharge of duty."

FOULKE FAMILY GENEALOGY. 233

105. Hannah, b. 8th mo. 14, 1780, d. 12th mo. 12, 1837, unm. She was a teacher at Westtown School from 1807 to 1815.
106. Sarah, b. 6th mo. 13, 1783, d. 4th mo. 25, 1822, m., 1812, Alexander Forman, of New Britain, son of Alexander and Jane, and had issue: Gainor, b. 1813, d. 1833; Joseph, b. 1815, d. 1881; Hugh, b. 1818, m. Jane Hallowell; Mary, b. 1823, d. in inf.
107. Joseph, b. 1786, d. 1863, m. Elizabeth Shoemaker. 𐰁
108. Hugh, b. 1788, d. 1864, m. Martha Shoemaker. 𐰁

IV. (56.) CADWALLADER FOULKE, son of Edward and Margaret, b. at Gwynedd, 1758, d. 2d mo. 27, 1808, m. 1st, PHŒBE ELLIS, dau. of John and Lucy. PHŒBE was b. 1765, and d. 9th mo., 1802 ("having been married 16 years"), of yellow fever, in Philadelphia. Her husband, leaving the city, took their daughter, Sarah (see below) to his brother Hugh's, at Gwynedd; and went, himself, in 1806, to Wheeling, Ohio, where he m. ANN CHIRINGTON. Subsequently, he went on a trading voyage, down the Ohio river, and it was believed was robbed and thrown overboard by river pirates. (His death, as above, was fixed as occurring Feb. 27, 1808.)

V. Children of Cadwallader and Phœbe:

109. Sarah, b. 4th mo. 27, 1787, d. 7th mo. 27, 1849. She was placed, after her mother's death, at Joshua Woolston's boarding-school, Fallsington, Bucks Co., and, later (1805), took charge of a school at Mansfield, N. J. Having gone West, with her father, she m. 12th mo., 1809, Wm. Farquhar, who d. 11th mo. 8, 1810, and her child d. near the same time. She was a teacher at Westtown from 1811 to 1816, and m. 1st mo. 11, 1816, James Emlen, of Philadelphia, by whom she had issue, surname *Emlen:*

1. James, b. 10th mo. 16, 1816, d. young.
2. Mary, b. 3d mo. 2, 1818, m. Chalkley Bell.
3. Phœbe, b. 4th mo. 12, 1820, m. John Rowland Howell.
4. Sarah Cresson, b. 4th mo. 19, 1822, m. Wm. P. Bangs.
5. Anne, b. 1st mo. 7, 1824, m. Joseph Howell.
6. Susan, b. 9th mo. 20, 1826, unm.
7. Samuel, b. 3d mo. 23, 1829, m. Sarah Williams.

IV. (58.) CALEB FOULKE, son of William and Hannah, b. at Gwynedd, 12th mo. 5, 1736, d. 1st mo. 25, 1811, m. in Philadelphia, 1st mo. 21, 1762, JANE JONES, eldest dau. of Owen and Susanna. (See Evans Genealogy.) CALEB was a merchant in Philadelphia; he doubtless went there early in life, and engaged in business. His name is among the signers to the non-importation agreement of October, 1765. For many years his firm consisted of himself and his younger brother Amos, the name being "Caleb and Amos Foulke." (Papers thus signed I have, of 1774.) Later, however, Amos seems to have retired, as the firm in 1790 (and perhaps earlier), was "Caleb and Owen Foulke," the junior partner being Caleb's eldest son. The latter firm did a large foreign trade; among other things they exported flaxseed and imported linens from Newry, Belfast and Cork. These operations were, however, finally disastrous; at CALEB's death his estate was heavily involved, a debt to a London firm being large. In 1766 he had bought the Owen Evans farm, on the Swedes Ford road (now the estate of J. Lukens), and this he made his home during the British occupation of Philadelphia, and at other times, and perhaps permanently resided there toward the close of his life. In 1813, the Sheriff of Montgomery county, Isaiah Wells, sold it in the hands of his executors, his sons Caleb and Charles, and it was bought by his widow, JANE, who sold it to Dr. Joseph Meredith in 1814. JANE d. in Germantown in 1815; her will was proved December 14th. She appoints her sons Caleb and Charles executors, and names her daughters Lowry Jones [wife of Evan, of Gwynedd] and Hannah and Jane Foulke.

V. Children of Caleb and Jane:

110. Owen.
111. Caleb, m. Mary Cottinger, [Margaret Cullen?] Sarah Hotchkiss.
112. Charles, m. Eliza Lowery. No issue.
113. Hannah, d. unm.
114. Jane, d. unm.
115. Lowry, m. Samuel Miles, Evan Jones. (See Jones Family).

IV. (59.) LEVI FOULKE, of Gwynedd, son of William and Hannah, b. 3d mo. 20, 1739, d. 6th mo. 27, 1815, m. ANN EVANS (No. 103, Evans Genealogy), dau. of Thomas and Hannah. LEVI received from his father that part of William's estate which was occupied in recent years by William Foulke, Levi's grandson, and has lately belonged to D. C. Wharton. He built the eastern — stone — end of the house, there, and the date-stone is marked "L. & A. F." They had but one child who lived beyond infancy.

V. Child of Levi and Ann:

116. William, b. 1767, d. 1833, m. Margaret McIlvaine. ℬ

IV. (60.) AMOS FOULKE, of Philadelphia, merchant, son of William and Hannah, of Gwynedd, b. 11th mo. 5, 1740, d. 1793, m. 5th mo. 20, 1779, HANNAH JONES, dau. of Owen and Susanna, of Philadelphia. He was associated in business with his eldest brother, Caleb, by the firm name of "Caleb and Amos Foulke," and d. in the yellow fever visitation of 1793.

V. Children of Amos and Hannah:

117. Susan, b. 10th mo. 11, 1781, d. 2d mo. 1, 1842, unm.
118. Edward, b. 1784, d. 1851, m. Tacy Jones. ℬ
119. George, b. 7th mo. 23, 1786, d. 7th mo., 1848, unm.

IV. (71.) ISRAEL FOULKE, son of Samuel and Ann, b. 2d mo. 4, 1760, d. 9th mo. 27, 1824, m. ELIZABETH ROBERTS, dau. of David. (ELIZABETH d. 12th mo. 17, 1831, aged 71.) Their children are named on the Richland m. m. records; four dying in childhood, the others are given below.

V. Children of Israel and Elizabeth:

120. Thomas, b. 12th mo. 31, 1784, d. 6th mo. 4, 1832, m., 1814, Sarah Lancaster, (d. 1869, aged 71 years), dau. of Thomas and Ann, of Whitemarsh, and had issue: (1.) Anne, m. Edward Thomas, (d.) of Richland, and has issue: Lancaster, of Philadelphia, druggist; Edwin, d.; Irvine, Ellwood, Sallie; and (2.) Letitia, m. Jehu J. Roberts, (d.) of Cheltenham, and has issue: Thomas F., d.; Annie L. m. Robert Croaseale, (d.); Caroline; Sarah m. John

Walton, and has issue two daus.; Tacy, m. Charles Knight, and has issue, two sons and four daus.
121. David, b. 12th mo. 21, 1786, m. Miriam Shaw, dau. of John and Phebe, and had issue: Israel, b. 1814, John R., b. 1818. *David* m., 2d,—— Roberts, of Byberry, and had issue, with others: Jane, m. Israel J. Grahame, druggist, Philadelphia.
122. Hugh, b. 9th mo. 8, 1793, d. 4th mo. 3, 1853, m. Elizabeth Roberts, dau. of Levi and Phebe, and had issue 12 children: Amos, Barton L., Phebe R., Jordan, Elizabeth, m. Penrose Hicks; Thomas M., Sarah E., Franklin, Abigail Jane, Franklin, 2d, Jane R., Susan J.
123. Phebe, b. 12th mo. 7, 1795, d. unm.
124. Amos, b. 8th mo. 10, 1798.

IV. (73.) CADWALLADER FOULKE, of Gwynedd, surveyor, son of Samuel and Ann, b. at Richland, 7th mo. 14, 1765, d. 3d mo. 22, 1830, m. his first cousin, MARGARET FOULKE (b. 1771, d. 1845), dau. of Theophilus and Margaret. CADWALLADER removed to Gwynedd about 1805, and bought the farm where Gwynedd station now is, belonging in recent time to Rodolphus Kent. He was an active and useful man, well known as a surveyor; a sketch of him will be separately given. He and his wife had but one son.

V. Child of Cadwallader and Margaret:

125. Benjamin Franklin, b. May 25, 1796, d. Sept. 30, 1845, m. Maria Heston Tyson (widow of Jesse), dau. of Levi and Susanna Heston. (Maria, b. Dec. 29, 1799, d. Feb. 12, 1829. By her first husband she had one son, Jesse Maris Tyson.) *Benjamin Franklin* and *Maria* had issue one child, Eleanor, b. 1828, d. in infancy.

IV. (74.) JOHN FOULKE, of Richland, son of Samuel and Ann, b. 12th mo. 6, 1767, d. 4th mo. 5, 1840, m., 1789, LETITIA ROBERTS (b. 9th mo. 10, 1767, d. 10th mo. 18, 1854), dau. of Thomas, Jr., and Letitia. A memorial of Richland m. m. concerning JOHN says he was a minister, who frequently attended adjacent meetings, visiting most of those in Philadelphia, Baltimore, Ohio, and Indiana Yearly Meetings. He was particularly zealous for the testimonies of Friends against slavery and intemperance. "Being a faithful advocate for those held in slavery, he pleaded their cause where and when ever opportunity offered; and, at different times, with the approbation of his own meeting, he visited the city of Washington, while Congress was in session . . . . . . [having there] many interesting interviews with those high in office," to urge the injustice of slavery, and to ameliorate the condition of the slaves.

V. Children of John and Letitia:

126. James, b. 1790, d. 4th mo. 8, 1866, m. 1815, Hannah Shaw, and has issue: (1) Abby Ann, b. 1816, d. 1859; (2) Stephen, b. 1819, m. Matilda Penrose, and has issue; (3) Sarah, b. 1822; (4) John, b. 1830.
127. Sidney, b. 1791, d. 12th mo., 1862, m. 1822, Samuel Shaw.
128. Abigail, b. 1794, m. 1833, Thomas Wright.
129. Elizabeth, b. 1795, m. 1816, John Kinsey, Jr.
130. Ann, b. 1797, m. 1822, James R. Green.
131. Hannah, b. 1799, m. 1848, Bartholomew Mather.
132. Kezia, b. 1804.
133. Mary, b. 1806, m. 1847, Joseph Paul.

IV. (75.) EDWARD FOULKE, of Richland, son of John and Mary, b. 7th mo. 16, 1758, m., 1st, ELIZABETH ROBERTS, dau. of Thomas, jr., and Letitia (ELIZABETH d. 7th mo. 25, 1793); and, 2d, m. ANN ROBERTS, dau. of same parents.

V. Children of Edward and Elizabeth:

134. Jane, b. 1782, m. William Fussell.
135. Rowland, b. 12th mo. 29, 1783, m. Eliza Maus, and removed to Philadelphia. He had issue: including Charles M., Richard, and Edward. (Henry B. Foulke, real estate agent, Philad'a., is the son of Richard).
136. Agnes, b. 1785, d. unm.
137. Mary R., b. 1787, d. 1847.
138. John, b. 1789, d. unm.
139. Edward, b. 1792, d. 1859, m. Matilda Green.

Children of Edward and Ann:

140. Joshua, b. 1797, m. Caroline Green (b. 1805), dau. of William

and Mary, and had issue : Missouri G., m. Milton Roberts ; Cornelia, m. David R. Jamison ; Matilda G., m. same ; Jane, m. Lewis Roberts ; Edward, d. in childhood ; Alice, d. in infancy.
141. Elizabeth, m. Anthony Johnson.
142. Penninah, m.

IV. (82.) EVERARD FOULKE, of Richland, son of Thomas and Jane, b. 9th mo. 8, 1755, d. 9th mo. 5, 1827, m. 1778, ANN DEHAVEN. By appointment of the governor, he was many years a justice of the peace, and he was one of the assessors of the United States taxes in 1798, when John Fries raised his " rebellion" in the upper end of Bucks, and in Northampton cos., against the collection of the tax, and attacked, in Lower Milford and at Quakertown, 'Squire EVERARD and other assessors, forcing them to desist from the performance of their duty.[1]

V. *Children of Everard and Ann :*
143. Abigail, b. 5th mo. 18, 1779, m. Abel Penrose.
144. Eleanor, b. 7th mo. 18, 1781, d. 4th mo. 28, 1815.
145. Caleb, b. 1783, d. 1852, m. Jane Green.
146. Samuel, b. 3d mo. 28, 1786, m. Elizabeth Johnson, and had issue : Joseph J., Abigail, Jesse D.
147. Thomas, b. 4th mo. 13, 1789, d. in Kentucky ; issue two dau's.
148. Susanna, b. 9th mo. 18, 1791, d. 1883, m. David Johnson.
149. Anna, b. 5th mo. 3, 1794, d. 9th mo. 16, 1820.
150. Margaret, b. 12th mo. 24, 1796, m. Peter Lester, and had issue : Anna, m. Aaron B. Ivins ; Mary d. unm.
151. Everard, b. 7th mo. 21, 1800, m. Frances Watson, dau. of John, of Buckingham (Frances d. 2d mo. 11, 1868, aged 71), and removed to Ohio, and then to Illinois. (In 1883 he was living with his son Thomas D. Foulke, at Arthur Springs, near Sidney, Ill.) Issue of Everard and Fanny : (1) Watson, b. 1826 ; (2) William D., b. 1828, m. Alice G. Thomas ; (3) Jonathan Ingham, b. 1830 ; (4) Thomas D., m. Maria Whiteman ; (5) Lester E.

IV. (88.) THEOPHILUS FOULKE, of Richland, son of Theophilus and Margaret, b. 8th mo. 26, 1761, d. 7th mo. 28, 1798, m.

---

[1] The details of this episode will be found in the Report of the Trial, 1799, when Fries was convicted of treason ; printed in Philadelphia, 1800.

HANNAH LESTER, dau. of John and Jane, of Richland. (HANNAH, b. Feb. 2, 1767, d. July 4, 1850.) THEOPHILUS was accidentally killed by falling from a tree, which he had climbed to release an entangled fishing-line. He was a justice of the peace, by appointment of the governor, and also a member of the House of Representatives of Penna., elected in 1794, '95, '96, and '97.

V. Children of Theophilus and Hannah:

152. Antrim, b. 1793, d. 1861, m. Letitia Lancaster.
153. Sarah, b. 1st mo. 10, 1797, d. 10th mo. 25, 1852, m. 1819, Richard Moore (b. 4th mo. 20, 1794, d. 4th mo. 30, 1875), son of Henry and Priscilla, of Montgomery, and had issue; surname *Moore*:
   1. John Jackson, of Richland, b. 11th mo. 17, 1819, m. Jane, dau. of Isaac and Elizabeth Warner, and has issue: Alfred, of Philadelphia, member of the bar, trustee of the gas works of the city, etc.; Ellen; Arthur, member of the Philadelphia bar.
   2. Hannah, b. 7th mo. 27, 1821, m. 10th mo. 5, 1843, William M. Levick, of Philadelphia, member of the bar, son of Ebenezer and Elizabeth W., and has issue: Anna F., Elizabeth J.

V. (104.) CADWALLADER FOULKE, of Whitemarsh, son of Hugh and Ann, b. 10th mo. 28, 1778, d. 6th mo. 7, 1858, m. ANN SHOEMAKER (d. 10th mo. 13, 1821, aged 36), dau. of David and Jane, of Whitemarsh.

VI. Children of Cadwallader and Ann:

154. David, b. 11th mo. 24, 1811, m. 1867, Susan Y. Michener (widow of Lea), dau. of Silas and Hannah Shoemaker, of Upper Dublin.
155. Hannah, b. 2d mo. 16. 1814, m. 1863, Mordecai Price, of Little Falls, Md., son of Mordecai and Mary D.
156. Samuel, b. 2d mo. 25, 1816, m. 1849, Anne Jones, dau. of Jonathan and Eliza, of Plymouth. Samuel d. 4th mo. 23, 1857.
157. Josiah, b. 1st mo. 19, 1819, d. 8th mo. 10, 1848, unm.

V. (107.) JOSEPH FOULKE, of Gwynedd, son of Hugh and Ann, b. 5th mo. 22, 1786, d. 2d mo. 15, 1863, m. 1810, ELIZABETH SHOEMAKER, dau. of Daniel and Phebe, of Upper Dublin. (ELIZABETH b. 8th mo. 29, 1791, d. 8th mo. 1, 1873.) JOSEPH was a prominent Friend, a minister of the Society, and for many years conducted in Gwynedd a private school for boys. A sketch of him will be separately given.

VI. Children of Joseph and Elizabeth:

158. Phebe, b. 11th mo. 28, 1811, d. 7th mo. 5, 1876, m. 1834, Edwin Moore, of Upper Merion (b. 1811); and had issue: Eliza, m. Isaac E. Ambler, of Gwynedd; Joseph F. (of New York); Richard F., d.; Daniel F., m. Melissa Conrad, Emily Ashenfelter; Edwin, jr., m. M. Clarissa Buckwalter, Emma Lukens.
159. Daniel, b. 1814, m. Elizabeth Foulke, Lydia Walton.
160. Thomas, b. 1817, m. Hannah Shoemaker.
161. Ann, b. 4th mo. 6, 1820, d. 7th mo. 5, 1847, m. 1840, Samuel Moore, of Upper Merion, and had issue: Richard, m. Elizabeth Carver; Elizabeth F., m. Benj. L. Hilles; Henry C., m. Hannah Jones; Hannah, m. Edwin P. Hollingsworth; Thomas F., d. in infancy.
162. Sarah, b. 1823, d. 1840, unm.
163. Joseph, jr., M. D., of Buckingham, Bucks Co., b. 1827, m. Caroline Chambers, and has issue: Elizabeth C., Phebe F., Caroline, Hannah, William D., Melissa E.

V. (108.) HUGH FOULKE, of Gwynedd, son of Hugh and Ann, b. 6th mo. 18, 1788, d. 5th mo. 1, 1864, m. MARTHA SHOEMAKER (b. 3d mo. 6, 1790, d. 4th mo. 11, 1868), dau. of Thomas and Mary, of Abington.

VI. Children of Hugh and Martha:

164. Thomas S., b. 2d mo. 1, 1829, d. 4th mo. 10, 1884, m. 1855, Phebe W. Shoemaker, dau. of Silas and Hannah, of Upper Dublin. Thomas was b. at Abington, but in his childhood his parents removed to the family homestead, at Gwynedd. He took an active part in township affairs; was many years clerk of Gwynedd monthly meeting; for some years was clerk in Bank of Northern Liberties, Philadelphia: in 1870 became Superintendent of Swarthmore College, which place he held at his decease.
165. Hugh, jr., b. 1st mo. 13, 1831. He was for a number of years principal of the boarding-school for boys at Gwynedd (established originally by his uncle Joseph), and went in 1861 to New York, where he was, first, an assistant, but afterwards for several years principal teacher of the large school for both sexes, in charge of Friends. Impaired health compelled him to give up this engagement in 1879.

FOULKE FAMILY GENEALOGY. 241

V. (111.) CALEB FOULKE, JR., son of Caleb and Jane. He was twice married, and had by his first wife five children. Her name is given as MARGARET CULLEN;[1] his second wife was SARAH HOTCHKISS.

VI. Children of Caleb and Margaret:

166. Louisa, d. unm.
167. Jane, m. Alexander Hall.
168. Ellen, m. —— Hatfield, of Philadelphia; no children. (Her husband, by a former wife, was the father of Dr. Nathan Hatfield, sen.)
169. William, m. Lucy Dickinson (who d. Feb. 6, 1871), and had issue: William H. H., Margaret. *William* d. December 2, 1847, and was bu. (as also his wife, subsequently) in the burial ground at Gwynedd meeting. He was then ticket agent for the Philada., Germ'n, and Norristown R. R., at 9th and Green sts., and lived on Green st., just below.

V. (116.) WILLIAM FOULKE, of Gwynedd, son of Levi and Ann, b. 10th mo. 7, 1767, d. 4th mo. 6, 1833, m., 1793, MARGARET McILVAINE, dau. of John and Lydia. (MARGARET b. 2d mo. 14, 1771, d. 2d mo. 4, 1809.)

VI. Children of William and Margaret:

170. John M., born 1st mo. 18, 1795, d. 3d mo. 13, 1874, m. Ann Sinclair. He went to Baltimore, and thence to Cincinnati, engaging extensively in business, though not ultimately with success. His children were (1) Edward, of Emory, Ill., who m. Adelaide Colladay, dau. of Jacob and Julia, and has issue: Anna, m. Arthur Pinkham, John, Edward, William Llewelyn, Carrie C.; and (2) Lydia A., who m. David Wilson, of Evans, Ill. (She was sometime a teacher of the Friends' school at Gwynedd.)
171. Levi, b. 4th mo. 6, 1796, d. 1st mo. 4, 1878, m. Eliza White, of Washington, D. C., and had issue: William L., Eliza, m. William Augustus; Virginia, m. Robert Kirby; Ella, m. Joseph Dill.
172. Anna, b. 4th mo. 9, 1798, d. 11th mo. 19, 1873, m. Aaron Lukens, and had issue: William, d. unm.; Elizabeth, d. unm.; David, Margaret A., m. Albin Smedley; Mary; Edward, d., m. Sarah ——; Ellen, Henry, d. unm.
173. William, b. 1802, d. 1882, m. Susanna Conrad.

---
[1] Also by some family authority as Mary Cottinger.

V. (118.) EDWARD FOULKE, of Gwynedd, son of Amos and Hannah, b. in Philadelphia, 11th mo. 17th, 1784, d. at Gwynedd, 7th mo. 17th, 1851, m. 12th mo. 11, 1810, TACY JONES, dau. of Isaac and Gainor, of Montgomery. His father dying (of yellow fever, in Philadelphia, 1793), when he was but nine years old, he was brought up by his uncle and aunt, Jesse and Priscilla Foulke, at Penllyn, in Gwynedd. " He was of a cheerful disposition, and greatly beloved by all who knew him,— kind to the poor, to whom he never turned a deaf ear."

VI. *Children of Edward and Tacy:*

174. Ann J., b. 9th mo. 15, 1811, m. December 26, 1832, Dr. Hiram Corson (b. Oct. 8, 1804), son of Joseph and Hannah, of Plymouth; graduate, 1828, of the medical department University of Pennsylvania; and has issue, surname *Corson*, as follows :

1. Edward F., b. Oct. 14, 1834, d. June 22, 1864, graduate, M. D., Univ. of Penna., assistant surgeon U. S. N., previous to and during War of Rebellion.
2. Joseph K., b. Nov. 22, 1836, graduate in pharmacy, and of medicine, assistant surgeon U. S. Vols., and U. S. A.; m. Ada, dau. of Judge Wm. Carter, of Wyoming Territory.
3. Caroline, b. April 2, 1839, d. unm.
4. Tacy F., m. William L. Cresson, son of James; and has issue.
5. Charles Follen, graduate Univ. of Penna., member of the bar of Philada., m. 1876, Mary, dau. of Lewis A. Lukens, of Conshohocken.
6. Susan F., m. Jawood Lukens, of Conshohocken.
7. Bertha, m. James Yocom, of Philadelphia.
8. Frances S., m. Richard Day, of Philadelphia.
9. Mary.

175. Jesse, b. 6th mo. 23, 1813.
176. Charles, b. 1815, d. 1871. m. Harriet M. Corson.
177. Susan, b. 7th mo. 18, 1818.
178. Owen, b. 1820, d. in infancy.
179. Priscilla, b. 10th mo. 10, 1821, m. Thomas Wistar, son of Thomas, and has issue: Priscilla F. Wistar, d. 12th mo. 28, 1882.
180. Jonathan, b. 1825, d. in infancy.
181. Lydia, b. 2d mo. 18, 1827, m. Charles W. Bacon, son of John.
182. Rebecca, b. 5th mo. 18, 1829, m. Robert R. Corson, son of Dr. Richard Corson, of New Hope.

183. Hannah, b. 9th mo. 18, 1831, m. Francis Bacon, son of John.
184. Emily, b. 12th mo. 2, 1834, m. Chas. L. Bacon, son of Chas. W.
185. Owen, b. 1838, d. in infancy.

V. (139.) EDWARD FOULKE, of Richland, son of Edward and Elizabeth b. 5th mo. 26, 1792, d. 2d mo. 16, 1859, m. MATILDA GREEN, dau. of William and Mary. (MATILDA, b. 1st mo. 20, 1809.)

VI. Children of Edward and Matilda:
186. Elizabeth, b. 1st mo. 31, 1833, m. Jacob B. Edmunds.
187. Joseph W., b. 10th mo. 31, 1834, d., m. Mary Ann Strawn.
188. William G., of Philadelphia, member of the bar, b. 1st mo. 5, 1837, m. Anna C. Jeanes, dau. of Isaac and Caroline, and has issue: Edward, b. 1874, Anna L., b. 1880, Walter L., b. 1882.
189. Martha R., b. 7th mo. 4, 1839, d. unm.
190. Evan, b. 6th mo. 18, 1842, d. unm.
191. Mary G., b. 9th mo. 6, 1844, d. unm.
192. James, b. 9th mo. 3, 1847 (druggist, Jersey City).
193. Agnes, b. 3d mo. 29, 1855, d. unm.

V. (146.) CALEB FOULKE, of Richland, son of Everard and Ann, b. 8th mo. 29, 1783, d. 2d mo. 22, 1852, m. JANE GREEN (b. 2d mo. 8, 1785, d. 3d mo. 3, 1835), dau. of Benjamin and Jane.

VI. Children of Caleb and Jane:
194. Caroline, b. 1808, d. in infancy.
195. Caroline, b. 2d. mo. 25, 1810, d. 12th mo. 17, 1838.
196. Maryetta, b. 7th mo. 30, 1811, d. 4th mo. 26, 1851, m. Aaron Penrose, and had issue: Benj. F., m. Alice Thompson; Caroline, m. David J. Ambler; Rebecca, m. Lewis J. Ambler.
197. Benjamin G., b. 1813, m. Jane Mather.
198. Eleanor, b. 3d mo. 12, 1816, d. 8th mo. 13, 1842, m. Samuel J. Levick, and had issue: Jane, m. Edwin A. Jackson.

V. (153.) ANTRIM FOULKE, physician, of Gwynedd, son of Theophilus and Hannah, b. at Richland, 3d mo. 21, 1793, d. in Philadelphia, 9th mo. 6, 1861, m. LETITIA LANCASTER, dau. of Thomas and Ann, of Whitemarsh. A sketch of him will be separately given. (LETITIA b. 12th mo. 8, 1799, d. 1st mo. 6, 1877).

244 HISTORICAL COLLECTIONS OF GWYNEDD.

VI. Children of Antrim and Letitia:

199. John L., b. 2d mo. 14, 1822, d. in Philadelphia, 10th mo. 30, 1870. He was educated at Joseph Foulke's, and at Benj. Hallowell's, Alexandria, studied medicine with his father, and graduated with distinction from the Univ. of Penna., in the Class of 1841. He pursued his profession at Gwynedd with great success, his pleasing manners and professional skill securing him a large practice. In 1859 he removed to Philadelphia, and practiced there. In 1863, he made a voyage to Havana, and in 1864 to Liverpool, as surgeon of the packet *Saranak;* returning, he entered the U. S. service, and continued as a hospital surgeon to the end of the war. He m. Jan. 1, 1857, Anzonette Poulson (d. 1863), dau. of Charles A. and Sarah (Wood) Poulson, of Philadelphia; and had one child, Charles Antrim, b. 1st mo. 1, 1863, d. 12th mo. 29, 1865.
200. Ann L., b. 4th mo. 26, 1824, d. 2d mo. 17, 1845, unm.
201. Henry, b. 10th mo. 23, 1825, d. 2d mo. 13, 1864, m., 1852, Maria L. Banks, and had issue: (1) William W., b. 1853, m. 1884, Elizabeth C. Kent, dau. of Rodolphus (dec'd) and Sarah (Clark) Kent; (2) Letitia L., b. 12th mo., 1854, m. 1880, Ellis Clark Kent, son of Rodolphus and Sarah, and has issue, surname *Kent:* Ellis C., jr., b. 1881, and Henry Antrim Foulke, b. 1884; (3) May, b. 6th mo. 16, 1856; (4) Hannah, b. 8th mo. 12th, 1860, d. 3d mo. 29, 1876.
202. Jane, b. 8th mo. 16, 1827, d. 2d mo. 13, 1833.
203. Hannah, b. 6th mo. 11, 1829, m. 9th mo. 17, 1851, Thomas W. Baily, of Philadelphia, son of William and Catharine.
204. William, b. 6th mo. 9, 1831, d. 10th mo. 28, 1855. He studied medicine, and had graduated at the University of Pennsylvania, in the Class of 1854.

VI. (160.) DANIEL FOULKE, of Gwynedd, son of Joseph and Elizabeth, b. 2d mo. 21, 1814, m. 1st, 1847, ELIZABETH C. FOULKE (b. 1827, d. 1849), dau. of William [1] and Susanna, of Gwynedd; and, 2d, LYDIA WALTON (d. 3d mo. 23, 1884), dau. of Joseph, of Chester County.

VII. Children of Daniel and Elizabeth:

205. Anna, b. 11th mo. 5, 1848, m. Henry S. Colladay; and has issue: Elizabeth F., b. 1871, William F., b. 1873, Henry D. J., b. 1878.

---

[1] See No. 172, this Genealogy.

Children of Daniel and Lydia W.:
206. Edwin M., b. 10th mo. 10, 1854, m. Elva Jones, dau. of Mark, of Plymouth, and has issue: Esther B., b. 1878, Helen E., b. 1880, Lydia W., b. 1884.
207. Abigail W., b. 1856.
208. Joseph T., b. 1863. (Graduate of Friends' Central School, Philad'a, and, 1884, student-at-law.)

VI. (161.) THOMAS FOULKE, of New York, son of Joseph and Elizabeth, of Gwynedd, b. 5th mo. 28, 1817, m. 1840, HANNAH SHOEMAKER (b. 2d mo. 25, 1804; d. 10th mo. 6, 1876), dau. of Abraham and Margaret. (Abraham Shoemaker was originally of Montgomery County, the elder brother of Thomas, of Gwynedd. He became a successful and wealthy merchant of New York city.) Soon after his marriage, THOMAS removed to New York, and was there engaged, for nearly twenty years, in the public schools, having charge, as superintendent, during much of the time, of two of the largest grammar schools. (One of these contained 40 teachers, and 2000 pupils.) In 1861, he resigned to take charge of the Friends' Institute, in Rutherford Place, and having organized it, conducted this for three years, leaving it then to the charge of his nephew, Hugh Foulke, jr. About 1857 he appeared in the ministry of the Friends, and was subsequently acknowledged as a minister. He has since traveled extensively in the exercise of his gift.

VII. Children of Thomas and Hannah:
209. William Dudley, b. 1848, m. Mary T. Reeves.
210. Edwin M., d. in childhood.
[A dau. d. in infancy.]

VI. (173.) WILLIAM FOULKE, of Gwynedd, son of William and Margaret, b. 2d mo. 24, 1802, d. 7th mo. 12, 1882, m. SUSANNA CONARD (b. 7th mo. 7, 1803, d. 6th mo. 19, 1871), dau. of Jonathan and Hannah.

VII. Children of William and Susanna:
211. Hannah C., b. 3d mo, 12, 1826, d. 7th mo. 16, 1876, m. 1850,

George A. Newbold, son of Samuel and Abigail, and had issue: Clara, William F.

212. Elizabeth C., b. 6th mo. 10, 1827, d. 6th mo. 17, 1849, m. Daniel Foulke (No. 160.)
213. Margaretta, b. 9th mo. 11, 1830, d. 12th mo. 18, 1865, m. 1864, James Q. Atkinson, of Upper Dublin.
214. Lewis Morris, of San Francisco, Cal., b. 8th mo. 6, 1832, m. Elizabeth Edson, whose family were from Mass. He went to California, 1853, and was several years U. S. Supervisor of Internal Revenue. His children are: Elizabeth, Edson, Susanna Marguerite.
215. Anna M., b. 6th mo. 5, 1834, m. 1855, Charles B. Shoemaker, of Cheltenham, son of Richard M. and Amelia B.; and has issue: Charles Francis, b. 1856, d. 1876; William F., b. 1859; Amelia B., b. 1862, d. 1863; Benjamin H., b. 1864; Lewis F., b. 1867; Ella, F., b. 1873.
216. Ellen, b. 7th mo. 7, 1838, d. 12th mo. 29, 1863, m. Joseph K. Matlack, and had issue: Marian, who m. Sumner G. Brosius, and has issue: Charles S.
217. William Henry, b. 4th mo. 26, 1840, m. Priscilla Frick.
[Jonathan C., b. 1828, Lydia C., b. 1836, d. in infancy].

VI. (176.) DR. CHARLES FOULKE, of New Hope, Bucks co., son of Edward and Tacy, b. at Gwynedd, Dec. 14, 1815, d. Dec. 30, 1871, m. HARRIET M. CORSON, dau. of Dr. Richard Corson, of New Hope. DR. CHARLES practiced his profession some time at Gwynedd, and then removed to New Hope, where he remained.

VII. Children of Charles and Harriet M.:
218. Richard, of New Hope, physician, graduate Univ. of Pennsylvania, m. Louisa Vansant, and has issue: Charles, Clarabel, Rebecca, d. in childhood.
219. Edward, of Washington, D. C., m. Eliza Vanhorn, dau. of —— Vanhorn, of Yardleyville, Bucks Co.
220. Thomas, of Yonkers, N. Y., d. 1883, at New Hope, unm.

VI. (197.) BENJAMIN G. FOULKE, of Richland, son of Caleb and Jane, b. 7th mo. 28, 1813, m. 1837, JANE MATHER (b. 3d mo. 24, 1817), dau. of Charles and Jane, of Whitpain. BENJA-

FOULKE FAMILY GENEALOGY. 247

MIN has been for several years clerk of Philadelphia Yearly Meeting, and is a conveyancer and farmer.

VII. Children of Benjamiu and Jane:

221. Caleb, b. 12th mo. 3, 1839, d. 10th mo. 20, 1865.
222. Charles M., b. 7th mo. 25, 1841, was educated at Foulke's school, at Gwynedd, and the Friends' Central School, Philad'a, entered upon mercantile business in Philad'a, 1861, and retired, 1872. He m. Dec. 10, 1872, at Paris, France, in the presence of the American minister, Hon. E. B. Washburne, Sarah A. Cushing, dau. of Horace C. and Harriet C., of New York City; and has issue: Horace C., b. July 6, 1876; Helen S., b. July 12, 1878; Gladys, b. April 29, 1881; Gwendolyn, b. Dec. 31, 1883.
224. Job Roberts, b. 2d mo. 23, 1843, trust officer of Provident Life and Trust Co., of Philadelphia, m. 5th mo. 25, 1869, Emma Bullock, dau. of Samuel and Jemima R., of Mt. Holly, N. J., and has issue: Roland R., b. 5th mo. 10, 1874; Rebecca Mulford, b. 7th mo. 18, 1875.
224. Anna, b. 1846.
225. Jane, b. 1848, d. 1853.
226. Ellen, b. 1850.

VII. (209.) WILLIAM DUDLEY FOULKE, of Richmond, Ind., son of Thomas and Hannah S., b. New York, 11th mo. 20, 1848, m. October, 1872, MARY T. REEVES, dau. of Mark E. and Caroline M., of Richmond, Ind. (previously Cincinnati, O.) WILLIAM graduated A. B., 1869, at Columbia College, New York city, with the honors of his class for general average and Greek; received degree of A. M., in 1872; in 1871, after study of law, LL. B.; was admitted to the bar in New York city in May, 1870, and in Indiana in 1876. In November, 1882, he was elected to the Senate of Indiana for a term of four years, and has taken a prominent position in that body.

VIII. Children of William D. and Mary T.:

227. Caroline R., b. July 28, 1873.
228. Lydia H., b. September 8, 1875.
229. Mary T. R., b. November 14, 1879.
230. Arthur Dudley, b. May 17, 1882.
231. Lucy Dudley, b. Jan. 25, 1884.

XVI.

The Early Roads.

NATURALLY, roads to meeting, to mill, and to market required immediate attention. For thirty years after the first arrival they formed one of the most important objects of the settlers' concern. Their desire for a road to Philadelphia was first shown. To the Court of Quarter Sessions of Philadelphia county, June, 1704, there was presented "the petition of the inhabitants of North Wales," who recite "that there are in the said Township above thirty families already settled, and probably many more to settle in and about the same, especially to the northward thereof, and as yet there is no road laid out to accommodate your petitioners, but what Roads or Paths have formerly been marked are removed by some and stopped by others:" they therefore ask an order from the court for "a Road or Cartway from Philadelphia through Germantown to the utmost of their above-mentioned Township of North Wales."

Upon this, the court "ordered that the said road [be laid out] from Philadelphia through Germantown, and so to the house of Edward Morgan, in North Wales, and that Edmund Orpwood, Robert Adams, William Howell, John Humphrey, Toby Leech, John Cook, Robert Jones, Owen Roberts, or any six of them, do lay out said road, and make return at the next sessions."

This road appears to have been laid out at this date — say 1704–5. It began at Whitemarsh,[1] went past where Spring-

---

[1] From Whitemarsh up, this was called "the North Wales road." In 1713, the "inhabitants of Bebber township,"— now Perkiomen,— asking for a road from Skippack downward, desired it should go "unto the North Wales, or Gwynedd road, at Edward Farmer's mill."

THE EARLY ROADS. 249

House now is, and then up through the township, substantially on the bed of the present turnpike. That it extended as far as what is now Towamencin, is fairly certain, because Edward Morgan had his lands there, above the Gwynedd line. "The house of Edward Morgan," mentioned in the order of court, was most probably "in North Wales."

Even earlier than this, however, the "Welsh road" originated. The mills on Pennypack creek, about Huntington valley and below, were the first to which the settlers turned their attention, and their road from Gwynedd down was begun as early as 1702. At the March sessions of court, 1711, a petition was presented, reciting as follows:

> That whereas for about nine years past a road was laid out from a bridge in the line between the lands of John Humphrey and Edward Foulk in Gwynedd to the mills on Pemapeck, which said road having been and is likely to be of a general service to several of the adjacent townships as well as the undersigned, and not being yet confirmed by authority and recorded, [they ask it may be laid out, etc. The signers are as follows:]

William Jones,	Edman Maguah,	Ellis Davis,
Thomas Evan,	Hugh Evan,	Rowland Hughs,
Jno. Hugh,	Evan Griffith,	George Lewis,
Robert Jones,	Hugh Griffith,	Edward Roberts,
Edward Ffoulk,	Evan Jones,	Rowland Robert,
Robert Evan,	Evan Griffith,	Evan Evans,
Owen Evan,	Hugh Robert,	Jno. Evans,
Jno. Humphrey,	Ellis Lewis,	Hugh Foulke,
Cadwalader Evan,	Evan Pugh,	Evan Evans,
Thomas Foulke,	Robert Humphrey,	Morris Robert,
Cadwalader Jones,	John Robert,	John William,
Nichlas Robert,	Ellis Roberts,	David Jones,
Ellis Hugh,	John Roberts,	Richard Pugh,
Edward Morgan,	Robert Thomas,	Humphrey Ellis,
Richard Lewis,	Samuel Thomas,	John Barnes,
Morris Edward,	Alexander Edward,	Jo. Iredell,
Richard Whitton,	Hugh Griffith,	Peter Davis,
John Morgan,	Robert Ffletcher,	Uimas Luckens,
Wm. Roberts,	Thomas Canby,	Thomas Palmer,
John Cadwalader,	Thomas Roberts,	Robert Whitton.

The court appointed as viewers John Cadwalader, Thomas Kinderdine, Robert Jones, Rowland Hugh, Owen Evan, and Thomas Canby, who at the June session (1712), reported the road, which they had laid out on March 28th. Their report, however, is endorsed: "There being a question against this return, the court ordered a review, and appointed Toby Leech, Thomas Rutter, Benjamin Duffield, Peter Taylor, and Robert Jones, of Merion," to make it. The remonstrance, as found in the file of court records, was as follows:

The Petition of Robert Evans, of the Township of Gwynedd, in the said county, Thomas Siddon and Ephraim Heaton, both of the said county, humbly sheweth: [That the road as laid out from Gwynedd to Pemapeck Mills will incommode and injure the signers. They assign the following specifications]:

1. For that it cuts the sd Robert Evan's land, being but 150 acres, so that 40 acres of it is separated from the water.

2. For that this road very much incommodes your petitioner Thomas Siddon's lands, and cuts your petitioner Ephraim Heaton's land cross from one corner to another, and is laid out through his corn-field.

3. For that the greater part, if not all those that laid out this Road were either Petitioners or Contenders for it.

4. For that when Joseph Fisher's land comes to be settled the lands of several inhabitants of Gwynedd and others must be cut in pieces to branch into the road as now laid out, whereas if it had gone up that division line between the sd Fisher and Gwynedd, it would be a more general accommodation and bring the Road along your petitioners Heaton's and Siddon's lines upon a more direct course and better answers the Inhabitants on both sides the last mentioned line, there being two Townships already settled with many families, joyning upon Gwynedd township above the said Fisher's tract.

[They therefore ask a hearing, with the opportunity to prove their case. The signers are as follows]:

Joseph Ffishore,
David Marple,
Peter Lester,
Thomas How,
James Haines,
Nath. Page,
Patrick Holly,
benjamin Charlesworth,
Evan Morgan,
John Nash,
William Rundols,
Thomas Fitzwater,
John Bradfield,
Joseph Hall,
Fd. Barch,
Mikel trump,
Nicholas Hicket,
Richard Carver,
George Burson,
John Trout,
Thomas Siddon,

Samuel Hallowell,	Thomas Hallowell,	Rouberd Evan,
David James,	Joshua Holt,	Ephraim Heatton,
Methusaleh Griffith,	James McVeagh,	William Story,
Bartholomew Longstreth,	Abra'm Griffith,	Abraham hill,
John Hurford,	George Phillips,	John Evans,
Mathis Tyssen,	Allen Foster,	Morris Davies,
Willem Hendricks,	Nicholas Scull,	Henry Jones,
John Cunnard,	John ffisher,	William Roberts,
John Huntsman,	Richard Rogan,	Thomas David.
Joseph Charlesworth,	Alexander Guah,	

The second jury made their report to the court at the March sessions, 1712. They located the road[1] somewhat differently from the previous jury, though not with any important variation. Their last course and distance was precisely the same: "north 59 degrees west, 166 perches to the above said bridge" [at John Humphrey's].

At the June sessions, 1714, the following petition was presented:

The humble petition of several of the inhabitants of Montgomery, Gwinedth, and Richlands, within the said county, showeth:

That your petitioners many of them being newly settled in these parts, having want of roads to meetings, mills, and market, do therefore pray this Worshipful Court that you will be pleased to order a Convenient road to be laid out from Joseph Growden's plantation in Richlands aforesaid to John Humphrey's at North Wales.

The court thereupon appointed Edward Farmer, Thomas Rutter, Thomas Siddon, Robert Jones, of Merion, Thomas Jones, and Robert Evan, or any four of them, a jury of view.

At the March sessions, 1715, the following petition was presented:

The petition of the subscribers, inhabitants of Gwynedd, Montgomery, Skippack, and other of the adjacent townships, humbly sheweth:

---

[1] This road was the present "Welsh road," up as far as the point on the Horsham and Upper Dublin line, near Pennville, and above that point the road by Three Tuns up to the Spring-House. The Welsh road, up the township line above Pennville, was opened several years later.

That inasmuch as the mill late of David Williams in plymouth[1] is built on a spring which neither the Drought of Sumer nor winter's ffrost hinders from supplying the neighbourhood with grinding when all or most of the other mills are dormant . . . . . . our and others being so supply'd in times of such necessity lays [us] under great obligations to frequent the said mill [they therefore ask convenient roads to it] several of which said roads have been made use for these tenn or twelve years past, but obstructed at the pleasure of ill minded and contentious persons. [They then suggest the roads as named in the record of the court, adding] and your petitioners bringing their corn to mill in order to bring the meal to markett another road wants a confirmation leading from the said mill to the Great Road from Parkysomeny to Philadelphia, without which your petitioners must labor under great hardships and difficulties, for what is more necessary than a Convenient road to places of worship and to mills and marketts" [etc. The petition is signed by thirty persons, most of them Gwynedd people].

The jury on this were William Harman, Matthew Holgate, Rowland Ellis, jr., Richard Jones, John Rhodes, and Thomas Stroud, who laid out the road from the meeting-house, at Gwynedd, to the mill on the Schuylkill — now Spring Mill — owned then by Anthony Morris and Robert Jones; and from the mill eastward to the Perkiomen road, at a point just below where the village of Barren Hill now is. They made their return to June sessions, 1716, giving the courses and distances, "beginning at a corner tree of Robert Evans's land, about 15 perches north-east from the said Gwynedd meeting-house." The first half dozen of courses and distances are as follows: "South 12° w., 440 p.; s. 45° w., 30 p.; s. 12° w., 500 p.; s. 28° w., 130 p.; s. 45° w., 138 p.; s. 13° e., 80 p.; s. 4° e., 52 p.;" etc., etc.

The location of this road did not, it appears, give universal satisfaction. At the same sessions, — June, 1716, — a remonstrance was presented from a resident of Gwynedd, as follows:

---

[1] This was a geographical error. The mill was situated at Spring Mill (as now known) in Whitemarsh.

THE EARLY ROADS.

The petition of David Jones, of Gwynedd,[1] in the county of Philadelphia, humbly sheweth: That inasmuch as by force and virtue of a late order of court for a road to be laid out for the use and service of Robert Jones and Anthony Morris in Whitemarsh, your petitioner, upon the laying out of the same is much damnified and discommoded by so dividing and parceling one hundred acres of land, the tract of your petitioner, that he, your said petitioner must unavoidably leave his settlement except relieved by this honorable court, which it's presumed may be easily done by carrying the said road to the line a few perches off, which when done the same may be as commodious without either damnifying your petitioner or any other to his knowledge. There is another road laid out by Thomas Fairman about 10 or 12 years ago, that goes through part of my land without so much damnifying me, which said road is now turned, to my considerable damage, to save discommoding the large tracts of others, but I am ready and willing the old road should be continued, and to allow more land to enlarge it, if required.

At the same time a remonstrance was presented from Whitemarsh township concerning the location of roads "to and from Robert Jones's mill to divers points in this county," and especially representing that one "from his mill up to the great road that goes to Whitemarsh mill and so thence to town" was solely for Robert Jones's private benefit, and would be very expensive to the township. Upon this Abraham Dawes, Isaac Dilbeck, John Ball, Thomas Strod, John Hank, and John Nicholls were appointed. The court, however, received at the same sessions the report of the original jury, and approved it, as appears by the following records:

Pursuant to an order of Court held for this City and County last March, wherein it was ordered that we should view and lay out certain roads leading from North Wales and adjacent settlements to Plymouth, thence to Robert Jones's mill, and so to the road leading from Perkioming to Philadelphia; which said roads, after View and Consideration thereof [we] think convenient to make return of the same according to the several courses and

---

[1] David Jones owned the farm, now Eliza S. Davis's, on the Plymouth road, by the Wissahickon. A draft of the road, among the files of the Court, shows his house located on the east or lower side of the road, and it is probable that it crossed the Wissahickon above the present place, and nearer to the State road.

distances and a draft of the whole hereunto annexed. (Signed by William Harman, Matthew Holgate, Rowland Ellis, jun., Richard Jones, John Rhodes, Thomas Stroud.)

Which is confirmed by the court. The mill is to be at the charge of cutting the Road from the mill to the great road, and after cut to be maintained as other roads are.

But it seems that general acquiescence was not given to the location of the road, even after it had been formally located by the court, and the following report was filed at the December sessions, 1716:

Thomas Ellis, Constable of Whitpain Township, presents John Huntsman and Edward Endehaven for stopping up the great road laid out from Gwynedd meeting-house to Plymouth meeting-house, and to Anthoney Morris and Robert Jones his mill, which said road was laid out and allowed by all the Inhabitants of the Township the same runns thro' ye said Huntsman and Endehaven [and they] have this fall plowed and sowed their land and fenced in the said road and still refuse to open the same tho' often thereunto required.

At the December sessions, 1717, the following petition was presented:

To the Honorable the Justices at the County Court of Quarterly Sessions, held at Philadelphia the 2d day of December, 1717. The petition of the subscribers, Inhabitants of the Township of Montgomery and the parts adjacent humbly sheweth: That your petitioners and others the neighboring inhabitants are very much incommoded for want of a road from Montgomery aforesaid to the great road from the Township of Gwynedd to Philadelphia, wherefore [they suggest that a convenient one to meeting and market would be] beginning at the plantation of Theophilus Williams and now thence as near as may be on a direct course to John Humphrey's Bridge on the great road aforesaid. [The signers of this petition are as follows:]

John Williams,	John Roberts,	Joseph Bate,
Evan Griffith,	George Lewis,	Theophilus Williams,
Griffith Hugh,	William Williams,	Morris Davis,
Rowland Roberts,	William Story,	Jenkin Evans,
John David,	Richard Lewis,	Cadwallader Morris,
David Hugh,	Francis Dawes,	William Morgan,
John Johnson,	Garatt Petterson,	John Bartholomew.

THE EARLY ROADS.

The court thereupon appointed as a jury of view: David Potts, William Harmer, Isaac Knight, Morris Morris, Toby Leech, jun., and Humphrey Bates, who at the March sessions, 1717, made the following return:

And now here at this day, viz., at the Sessions of the Peace of our Lord the King held at Philadelphia, came the aforesaid [jury just named] and return that pursuant to an order of Court bearing date the second day of December, anno 1717, for the laying out a road from Theophilus Williams's plantation thro' the township of Montgomery to the great road from Gwynedth to Philadelphia, they had laid out the said road: Beginning at a hickory tree standing on the bank of Neshaminy creek, in Theophilus Williams's land, thence s. 19° e., 20 p.; s. 30° e., 120 p.; s. 12° e., 70 p.; s. 5° w., 46 p.; s. 3° w., 124 p.; s. 40° e., 72 p.; s. 190 p.; s. 24° e., 100 p.; s. 11° e., 110 p.; s. 24° e., 360 p.; s. 4° w., 486 p.; s. 16° w., 90 p.; s. 56° w., 48 p., to the Gwynedth road about 8 perches to the southward of a bridge on the Gwynedth road commonly called John Humphrey's bridge. Which said road is by this Court confirmed.

A draft of the road thus laid out is among the court files. It shows the beginning squarely from the bank of the creek, the course generally southward, until in the last course it bears sharply westward, and comes into the Gwynedd road nearly at a right angle. It is, obviously, the old road, which the present Spring-House and Hilltown turnpike substantially follows.

At the December sessions, 1721, there is the following record:

Upon the petition of Rowland Hughes and Robert Humphreys of the township of Gwynedth, setting forth the necessity of a road to be laid out from their plantations to the great road leading to Philadelphia by a school-house lately erected[1] by their neighbourhood, which said road might be laid out thro' the partition lines without detriment to any person. [The court appointed as a jury:] Edward Farmer, Rowland Ellis, Everard Bolton, Toby Leech, jr., Humphrey Ball [Bate?], and John Jones, carpenter, or some four of them. [The petition of Hugh and Humphrey, on the files of the court, recites that they "being of late debarr'd of a direct road from their habitations to the great road from Philadelphia to and through Gwynedd aforesaid"—"inasmuch as several of the neighbourhood in conjunc-

---

[1] This is the first evidence I have of a school in the township.

tion with your petitioners have erected a school-house upon the great road aforesaid,"—they desire a road from Robert Humphrey's "by the said school-house."

At the September sessions, 1723, "divers of the inhabitants of the Townships of North Wales and Horsham" asked a road "from the corner of Ephraim Heaton's field to Horsham meeting-house," whereupon the court appointed John Cadwalader, John Evans, John Humphrey, Rowland Hugh, Thomas Iredell, Sampson Davis, or any four of them, a jury. December, 1723, they reported that on November 27th, "with the assistance of a surveyor" (Peter Taylor), they laid it out, "Beginning at or in the North Wales road, near the corner of the said Ephraim Heaton's field, thence e. 14½° n., 440 p.; e. 14° n., 144 p.; thence s. e. along Fisher's line, 208 p.; thence e. 5° s., 92 p., to Horsham meeting-house." Which report the court confirmed, *nisi*.

At the March sessions, 1727:

Upon the petition of several of the inhabitants of the county of Philadelphia [representing their want of roads] to places of Worship, Mills, and Market, [and asking] a road to be laid out, beginning at or near a creek by John Jones' house, in the upper part of Gwynedth township and turn off at the Great Road through some part of the said John Jones' land to the Susquehannah Road or Line, six or seven miles along the same and running partly by the meeting-house and Garret Clement's mill to a branch of Perkyoming Creek; [the Court ordered that] Henry Penebecker, John Jones, of North Wales, John Newberry, William Harmar, Peter Wence, and William Roberts, or any four of them, do view and judge if there be occasion for the road petitioned for, and if one road can be laid out to accommodate the said petitioners and those of Skippack who now petition for a road from a branch of the Perkyoming to the said Skippack Road, and if they judge that there is necessity for a road " [then to lay it out, etc.]

The original petition referred to in this record remains on file. It is signed mainly by residents in Towamencin, thirty names altogether. Nearly half sign in German, and some of these are undecipherable. As far as can be made out they are as follows:

THE EARLY ROADS. 257

Jacob Gaedtschalck,	Joseph Lucken,	Christian Kuntzig,
Gaetschalck Gaetschalck,	John Edwards,	Carl Ludwig Raeber,
hendry hendricks,	Jacob Hill,	Andreas Schwartz,
William Nash,	Christopher Buhler,	Nicholas Enser,
Herman Gaedschalck,	Hans Lebo,	Chr. Meyer,
Abraham Lucken,	Gabriel Beyer,	Christian Breneman.
Hugh Evan,	John Lucken,	

The jury made their return to the June court [1728], that they had laid out a road, "Beginning at the Beech Tree near the North Branch of Parkyoming; thence n. 76° e. 48 perches, thence s. e. 262 p., thence s. 22° e. 52 p., thence s. 25° e. 90 p., thence [by eleven courses] to Skippack creek, thence s. 67° e. 26 p., thence s. e. 424 p., to Hugh Evan's fence; thence e. 16 p., thence s. 12° e. 18 p., thence s. e. 219 p., thence s. 40° e. 146 p., thence s. 62° e. 150 p. to the great road going along by John John's at North Wales to Philadelphia." Which report the court confirmed, *nisi*.

At the June Sessions, 1728, there was presented the following:

The petition of the subscribers Inhabitants of Montgomery and the adjacent parts, on behalf of themselves and others, humbly sheweth: That your petitioners and others having long labored under divers difficulties and inconveniences occasioned by the want of a legally established road leading to public places of Worship, Markett & Mill are by necessity constrained to make application [for roads] leading from and beginning at the Bucks County line in the Line dividing the Lands now or late of Andrew Hamilton and Thomas Shute and running along the said Division Line and then taking and running along the line dividing the lands of John Roberts, [black]-smith, and Garrett Peters, to Gwynedd meeting-house and answering (in a straight line) the road leading thence directly to Robert Jones and Anthony Morris his mill. [Signed by]:

Joseph Naylor,	Samuel Thomas	Jno. Bartholomew,
Thomas Reess,	Theophilus Williams,	Griffe Hugh,
Griffith Evans,	John David,	James Davies,
George Shoumaker,	John Williams,	David Evans,
daniel Kirk [?]	William Morgan,	David Johns,
John Richard,	Evan Steven,	Joseph Eaton,
Thomas Edward,	Garet Peters,	Rowland Roberts,
Daniel Williams,	John Jones,	Th. Bartholomew,
Richard Williams,	John Robert,	Joseph Ambler.

17

Upon this petition the Court appointed Rowland Hugh, Robert Humphrey, Humphrey Jones, George Lewis, Evan Griffith, and Rees Harry a jury. They made their report (signed by all but Harry) to the September Court, stating that they had surveyed a road on the 19th of 6th month (August), and located it as follows:

From Bucks County line, beginning at a black oak in the said line, thence s. 44° w. along a straight line 316 p., dividing the lands of Andrew Hamilton and Thomas Shute, thence s. 63° w. 18 p. to a black oak; thence upon a straight line s. 44° w. 140 p., thence s. 67° w. 72 p; thence s. 44° w. along a straight line 360 p., dividing the lands of John Bartholomew and Rowland Roberts, John Roberts, [black]-smith, and Garrett Peterson; thence s. 3° e. 196 p; thence s. 44° w. 174 p.: thence s. 15° w. 55 p.; thence s. 45° w. 10 p.; thence s. 3° w. 80 p.; thence s. 25° w. 30 p., falling into the great road by Gwynedd meeting-house, answering the end of the road that leads to Robert Jones's and Anthony Morris's mill.

This return the Court confirmed, *nisi*. A draft submitted with the report shows that Andrew Hamilton's land in Montgomery (he owned also on the Bucks side of the county line), lay along the lower side of the new road, with Shute's land on the upper side. The end of the road at Gwynedd meeting-house met directly the road to Plymouth, and so formed a cross-roads with the "great road" running upward through Gwynedd.

At the September Court, 1731, was presented the following:

We ye inhabitants of the Township of Montgomery and others near joyning, Humbly petition: Whereas there is a road Lately laid out and confirmed at the last court of Quarter Sessions held at Newtown for ye County of Bucks, beginning at James David's corner on ye county Line and thence Leading to pine Run mills and to Buckingham meeting-house, which road will be very usefull to us and those near us in the County of Bucks in order to pass & Repass to ye said pine run mills and also to markett and to have intercourse between several places of worship. [They therefore ask] an order to extend ye said road into this township from ye county line as far as ye great road and to fall into the same by or near Isaac James's corner, and to branch out somewhere near Isaac James, as may be thought most convenient to lead to ye Baptist meeting-house in this township. [Signed by]

THE EARLY ROADS. 259

Thomas James,	Jno: Davis,	Thomas Rees,
Evan Steven,	Thomas Lewis,	Thomas John,
David Stevens,	David James,	Joseph Naylor,
William George,	Griffith Hugh,	John Roberts,
Simon Mathews,	Joseph Eaton,	George Lewis,
William Morgan,	Thos. Bartholomew,	Richard Lewis,
Benj. Griffith,	James David,	William Williams,
Griffith Owen,	Simon Butler,	Samuel Thomas,
Isaac Evan,	William Thomas,	Joseph Ambler.

Upon this petition the Court appointed John Jones, carpenter, John David, of Plymouth, Theophilus Williams, Joseph Bates, David Evans, and Jenkin Evans a jury, who reported at December Court, and presented a good draft of their road, showing not only its courses and distances, but the land-holders on each side, and even the topographical features. The road ended by "coming into the great road at Isaac James's corner," but a branch from a point east of this ran up to the Baptist meeting-house.

Up to 1734, the road to Plymouth supplied the only public way to the Schuylkill. In June, 1734, a petition was presented to the Court for a road from the Swedes' Ford to North Wales meeting-house, and a jury, consisting of Reese Williams, Rowland Hugh, Robert Rogers, Richard Thomas, Hugh Jones, and Job Pugh, reported a road at the September session; but Isaac Norris, who owned a large part of the present township of Norriton, and borough of Norristown, strenuously objected that it would damage his property, "cutting asunder the best part of his tract," and a review was ordered, which seems to have had the effect of postponing any definite action. In September, 1737, however, a new petition was presented, which said that several roads from Bucks county now led to North Wales meeting-house, but that to get from there to the Swedes' Ford, the way was very roundabout, making it inconvenient for travelers, as well as residents. John Bartholomew, George Lewis, David Evans, Jonathan Potts, Jonathan Robeson, and Abraham Dawes were appointed a jury, and reported at the March term, 1738, their road being thus described:

Beginning at a hickory tree standing near the landing of the Swedes Ford, on the south west side of the river Schuylkill, thence n. 31° e. 33 p. to a stump, standing at the landing on the n. e. side of Schuylkill, thence the same course, n. 31° e., on Norris's land, 59 p. to a road leading to Norris's Mills, thence n. 59° w., along the aforesaid road 160 p. to a stake, thence n. 19° e., along Norris's land, 280 p. to a line of Samuel Evan's land, thence n. e. along a line between the said Evans, Edward Farmer, and Aaron Roberts, 136 p. to a corner of said Evans's land, thence n. 24° e., 71 p., to a corner of Roger Pugh's land, thence n. e. along the line dividing the lands of Roger Pugh, Norris, and Robert Rogers, 196 p. to a stake, thence n. 61° e. along Robert Rogers's and Norris's land, 138 p. to Manatawny road, thence n. e. by a line of Cadwallader Evan's land, 44 p. to said Evan's corner, thence n. 65° e. along land leased of Ellis Ellis, and part of Whitpaine's tract, 222 p. to a small sapling in a line of George Fitzwater's land, thence n. e. along line dividing the said George Fitzwater's, Thomas Fitzwater's and Whitpaine's tract, 406 p. to a white oak standing near Skippack road, thence the same course along the line of Peter Indehaven, Henry Levering, Daniel Levering, Samuel Linderman, and Jacob Levering, 404 p. to a stake; thence n. 14° w. through Jacob Levering's and Ellis Pugh's lands 106 p. to a stake in the line dividing Evan Evans and the aforesaid Pugh's land, thence n. e. along the line of the said Evan Evans, Ellis Pugh, Thomas Evans, William Roberts, Owen Evans, and Margaret Evans, 464 p. to North Wales road, thence s. 52° e. along the said road 84 p. to North Wales meeting-house, being in all 8 miles, 243 p.

Which said road is by this court confirmed, and the Overseers of the High Ways are Ordered by this Court to open the same, according to law, for a public use.

In 1737 the Court granted a private road, to be laid out 20 feet wide, to enable the settlers about Penllyn to reach "the great road," on their way to Philadelphia. It was laid out, "beginning at a stone in the line of Edward Foulke, jun., thence n. e. between his lands and Lewis Williams's, 74 perches, then on L. W.'s land s. e., joining the land of Thomas David, 96 perches to a black oak near the line, then same course on Thomas David's land, to the far corner of the grave-yard, then on the line between Thomas David and Lewis Williams, and between Thomas David and Evan Roberts, s. e. 126 perches to the great road near the school-house."

What "the grave-yard" was I do not know,—probably a family burial-place. The school-house is no doubt the same referred to previously in the petition of Rowland Hugh, and it must have stood on "the great road,"—the present turnpike,—well down toward the Upper Dublin line.

The Plymouth road was reviewed, in 1751, by a jury consisting of William Dewees, Archibald McClean, Peter Robison, Joseph Waln, Rees Harry, and Wickard Miller, the line varying considerably in the upper courses from the road laid out in 1716. Their road began "at Spring Mill door," and ran by 30 courses and distances, by Plymouth meeting-house, the Dutch church land (Boehm's), to Wissahickon creek, and "North Wales road near the meeting-house." The whole length of the road was 9 miles, 7 perches; from Plymouth m. h. to North Wales m. h., 7 miles, 24 perches.

The road from Spring-House to Boehm's Church (intersecting the Plymouth road at the latter point) was laid out in the spring of 1760 by John Trump, Benjamin Davids, John Potts, Peter Cleaver, and Charles Jolly, and the same jury at the same time laid out the township-line road between Gwynedd and Whitpain, from the present State road down to the Upper Dublin line. The road to Boehm's is thus described:

Beginning near a stone spring-house[1] in Gwynedd road; thence extending south-west 331 perches on a line between Evan Evans, Elizabeth Davis, and Hannah [Hannaniah?] Pugh on the one side, [and] John Evans and Edward Foulke on the other side; thence, South 75° West, 60 perches to the end of William Foulke's lane; thence, South 69° West, 32 perches along said Foulke's lane; thence, South 58° West, 25 perches, to William Foulke's house; thence, South 48° West, 50 perches to said Foulke's Mill; thence, South 84° West, 68 perches through the land of William Foulke, and the land of John Roberts, to a stake; thence, South-west, 148 perches on a line between John Roberts' and Richard Thomas's land; thence,

---

[1] Here, doubtless, is the origin of the name of the present village, "the Spring-House." There was no tavern at this time, probably, or it would have been mentioned.

South 15° West, 55 Perches through the lands of John Roberts and John Lewis; thence, South-west, 140 perches on a line between John Lewis, James Brown, Charles Cress, and Philip Duder, into a road leading from Gwynedd to Plymouth, near a Dutch meeting-house.

[So much of interest as to ownership of land, location of places, etc., etc., is disclosed by a study of the road records, that I regret that I am unable to devote more space to this chapter. The most important roads in the township have now mostly been accounted for.]

XVII.

Early Settlers in Montgomery.

THE first settlers in Montgomery were, like those in Gwynedd, immigrants from Wales, and their arrival followed hard upon that of the company who bought Turner's tract. The Montgomery lands had been held by a number of speculative purchasers, none of whom had made a settlement. Among these were William Stanley, an Englishman, who had a warrant from Penn, so early as 1683, for 5000 acres; Richard Pierce, whose warrant was for 500 acres; and Thomas Fairman, the Philadelphia surveyor, who had title for a large tract. In March, 1699, Alexander Edwards purchased of Fairman 1100 acres,[1] and probably moved to it soon after. He was a Welshman, and had lived in Radnor, Chester (now Delaware) county, where in 1692 his daughters Bridget and Jane had respectively married, under the oversight of Haverford monthly meeting, Griffith Miles and James James, both "of Radnor."

Alexander Edwards was certainly one of the first settlers, and probably the very earliest, in Montgomery. He died in 1712, and described himself in his will as "of Montgomery," showing that the township had been created before that time. It was his son Alexander Edwards, jun., who married Gwen Foulke, dau. of Edward. He (A. E. jr.), in 1707, bought 200 acres of his father, and at once sold half of this to David Hugh Griffith. This tract included the Gordon or Rynear property, on the Horsham road.

---

[1] When the tract was re-surveyed, in 1702, it was found to contain,— differing from the usual result,— only 996 acres, and for this quantity the Commissioners gave him a patent.

Theophilus Williams, who married Grace Foulke, Edward's daughter, was also an early settler, and the place where he lived, at the upper end of the township, adjoining the Hatfield line, is shown[1] by the description of the road laid out from there, downward, through the township.

James Shattuck, who may or may not have been an actual resident, received in 1708 a patent for 250 acres, it being surveyed to him in right of Richard Pierce. This he sold in 1711 to William Morgan, who in 1723 sold part of it to Joseph Ambler. The latter was the first of the name in Montgomery, and the ancestor of a large family. His tract included the farm, recently the estate of Edward Ambler, fronting on the Horsham road, above the State road.

John Bartholomew, whose name frequently appears in the road records (chap. XVI.), bought, in 1716, 150 acres of Margaret Pugh, situated where the hamlet of Montgomery Square now is. John is said to have been a weaver, as well as a farmer, and he established, it is believed, the first hotel at that place,— probably near the close of his life. He was the son of George Bartholomew, who at one time owned the famous Blue Anchor tavern in Philadelphia, and who is said to have been a descendant of the Barthelémi family, of France. From a deed recorded in Philadelphia it appears that John moved to Montgomery from Bucks county. He owned two farms, a house and lot in the city, and a number of slaves. Among his grandchildren were Col. Edward Bartholomew of Philadelphia county, and Capt. Benjamin Bartholomew of Chester county, both of whom were members of the Constitutional Convention of 1776, and bore a distinguished part in the Revolutionary War. He died October 30, 1756, at an advanced age (71), leaving a widow, Mary, and eleven children. Seward, in his Journal, mentions that the celebrated preacher George Whitefield spent one night at the house

---

[1] See preceding chapter, p. 255.

of John Bartholomew, of Montgomery, after preaching in the neighborhood, and was kindly entertained by his family.

Jenkin Evans, an early settler in Montgomery, who came from Wales, purchased 108 acres of Thomas Shute, in December, 1717. This tract lay in the north corner of the township, adjoining the Hatfield line, and between the road to Perkasie (now the Bethlehem turnpike), and the county line. He may have been a brother to David Evans, who bought a large tract of land in Hatfield about the same time, and who was (through his daughter, Rachel, his only child, who married Peter Evans), the ancestor of a numerous family in Hatfield and Montgomery. Jenkin Evans appears to have been twice married. His first wife was Alice Morgan, daughter of Edward, whom he married in 1718; when he died, in 1770, he left a widow, Jane, with two sons, Jenkin, jun., and Walter, the latter a minor,—and five daughters, Elizabeth, Rachel, Sarah, Mary, and Ellinor, as well as several grandchildren. He was buried in the Baptist burying-ground, and was probably an active member of the Baptist congregation. Mr. Mathews says he gave an acre of land from the corner of his farm, on which the first permanent church edifice was built.[1] His son, Jenkin Evans, jun., removed into New Britain, bought the Butler grist mill on Neshaminy (where the village of Chalfont now is), and was some time a member of the Legislature from Bucks county.

Among the very earliest settlers in Montgomery was Thomas Lewis, a native of Wales, who in 1701 bought 484 acres in the south corner of the township from Thomas Fairman. He was, no doubt, a Friend. He died in the summer of 1723, leaving 280 acres of his farm to his son George, 150 acres to his son Richard, and 50 to a grandson, Thomas. George Lewis married,

---

[1] This gift has been ascribed to a John Evans. But Mr. Mathews thinks Jenkin and John were probably the same person. This seems doubtful, because John and *Sarah* Evans his wife were two of the constituent members, in 1719, whereas Jenkin had married, in the Friends' meeting, in 1718, his wife's name being *Alice*.

in 1708, Jane Roberts, and was a prominent member of Gwynedd meeting. The memorial of him by the monthly meeting says "he was a native of Wales, of a peaceable and inoffensive life and conversation. He was an elder thirty years, even to his death, which was on the 9th of 12th month, 1752, in the 72d year of his age." He left but one child, Elizabeth, who married, in 1728, Isaac Jones, of whom some details will be given below.

Richard Lewis appears to have had, besides his son Thomas who got the 50 acres of land, other children, including Edward and Mary. Thomas married, in 1734, Hannah Morgan, daughter of Edward, jun.

Isaac Jones came to Montgomery while quite a young man. He was the son of David and Katherine Jones, who came from Wales in 1699, and settled at Merion. Isaac was born 7th mo. 5, 1708, and married, 1728, Elizabeth Lewis, daughter of George, she being eighteen and he twenty. Notwithstanding this early marriage, they "lived happily together" for seventy years. Old George Lewis, it is said, made an agreement with them a few years before his death, by which he gave them a life right in his real estate, in return for food and clothes, a room in his house, the use of a riding-horse, and two barrels of cider a year. He reserved the right to cook for himself, if he preferred, in which case they were to pay him £12 a year, in lieu of the "diet."

Isaac Jones had purchased, in 1746, some land of Thomas Lewis, jr. On this he built, in 1765, a large brick house, which stood for more than a century. In it, in 1798, he died, past the age of ninety, and his wife, surviving two years, attained an equal age. Their son Isaac married Gainor Ambler,[1] and this couple also died in the old house, after a married life of nearly seventy years,— Isaac, in 1840, aged 93, and Gainor, June 20, 1847, in her 92d year. Isaac's sister, Ruth, who had lived there all her life, died in the same house, at the age of 88 ; and Mary

---

[1] Gainor was the daughter of John and Ann (Foulke) Ambler. See Foulke Genealogy.

EARLY SETTLERS IN MONTGOMERY.

Roberts, daughter of Eldad, who made her home with the Joneses, died there also, in 1859, aged nearly 93. This house, which was pulled down some years ago, stood in the extreme south corner of the township, on a cross road from the turnpike to the Horsham road.

Of John Jones, carpenter, who settled in Montgomery about 1710, taking up about 300 acres, part of which must have been Alexander Edwards's purchase, adjoining Gwynedd, some special genealogical details will be given later. He was an active and useful citizen, prominent for many years in the business affairs of the township.

A return was made, in 1734, to Governor Thomas Penn, of the names of the freeholders in the several townships of Philadelphia, " with the quantity of land they respectively hold therein, according to the uncertain returns of the constables." This list for Montgomery township shows twenty-nine names, as follows:

	Acres.		Acres.
Joseph Naylor,	189	Garret Peters,	150
Robert Thomas,	200	Moses Peters,	150
John Starky,	200	Rowland Roberts,	100
Joseph Ambler,	90	Francis Dawes,	100
John Bartholomew,	300	Thomas Williams,	100
Joseph Eaton,	150	William Storey,	100
William Williams,	200	Richard Lewis,	150
William Morgan,	100	Isaac Jones,	100
Samuel Thomas,	100	John Robert,	200
John Williams,	100	James David,	100
Joseph Bate,	200	David Evans,	100
Thos. Bartholomew,	30	Isaac James,	200
Griffith Hugh,	100	Jenkin Evans,	50
John Jones, carp'r,	300	Jenkin Jones,	—
John Roberts,	90		

Isaac James, who is named as holding 200 acres of land, was one of an important and numerous family, who settled early in Montgomery and New Britain. John James, his father, came from Pembrokeshire, Wales, in 1711, and bought land in Montgomery. When the Baptist congregation was organized, in 1719, he, his wife, Sarah, and their three sons, William, Thomas, and Josiah, were five of the eleven constituent members. John and his two elder sons bought 1000 acres of "the Hudson tract," in New Britain, in 1720, and probably removed there at that time.

XVIII.

Affairs Before the Revolution.

FEW other than Welsh settlers made their appearance in either Gwynedd or Montgomery, before 1734; a small number from England were the only exceptions. The greater part of them were, or soon became, Friends; a minority, chiefly settlers in Montgomery, were Baptists. But as they were all originally members of the Established Church of England, they were the objects of concern from Rev. Evan Evans, the Welsh missionary preacher sent out by the Bishop of London, in 1700. He wrote to the bishop, in 1707, describing the Welsh settlers at Radnor and Merion, and added:

> There is another Welsh settlement called Montgomery, in the county of Philadelphia, twenty miles distant from the city, where there are considerable numbers of Welsh people, formerly in their native country of the communion of the Church of England; but about the year 1698, two years before my arrival in that country, most of them joined with the Quakers, but by God's blessing some of them were induced to return, and I have baptised their children and preached often to them. I visited them since, and prevailed upon them to meet every Lord's-day, about forty in number, where one that can understand the language well, and is a sober discreet man, reads the prayers of the church, the proper psalms and lessons, omitting the absolution, etc., what properly belongs to the priest's office, and then reads some portion in a book of devotion to the people.

By "Montgomery" he evidently means the whole settlement, including Gwynedd. But it is difficult to see where a congregation of forty could have been collected from among the settlers, between 1700 and 1707, for the Established Church. Such a gathering certainly was not long maintained. Some members of St. Thomas's church, at Whitemarsh, may, at so early a day, have belonged in Gwynedd or Montgomery, but they must have been very few, and there was no other Episcopal church within their reach for many years.

The Baptist meeting in Montgomery, the oldest of the denomination in Montgomery county, and the fourth oldest in Pennsylvania,[1] owed its humble beginning to the zeal of a handful of the Welsh settlers. June 20, 1719, eleven persons formed the society,— John Evans, and Sarah, his wife; John James, Sarah, his wife, and their three sons, William, Thomas, and Josiah; James Lewis, David Williams, and —— Lably.[2] Whether any house was built before 1731 appears a matter of doubt, but in that year a substantial structure of stone, with an interior gallery, was built upon an acre of ground given for the purpose by John (or Jenkin?) Evans. The present house was built in 1816. Since 1720 ten preachers have served the church: (1) Benjamin Griffith, the zealous though uneducated pastor of the first flock, who served from 1720 to 1767, when he died, aged 84; (2) John Thomas, who had been assistant minister for many years, and who had sole charge from 1767 until his death, about 1780; (3) David Loofborough, under whose pastorate, in 1783, the church was regularly chartered by the Legislature, but who remained only a few years; (4) Joshua Jones, who was pastor from 1794 to 1802, when he died on the day after Christmas, aged 82; (5) Silas Hough, M. D., who preached and practiced his profession of medicine for eighteen years, until his death, May 14, 1823; (6) Samuel Smith, who was pastor four years; (7) Thomas Robinson, who closed his service of six years by his death, May 27, 1838; (8) William Matthews, who continued nine years; (9) George Higgins, who took charge

---

[1] Its predecessors were Cold Spring (Bucks Co.), 1684; Pennepack, 1687; Philadelphia, 1695.

[2] Most accounts say there were ten constituent members: the list here given was furnished the author by Rev. George Higgins, in 1859.

AFFAIRS BEFORE THE REVOLUTION.

May 1, 1850, and continued until his death in 1869; and since that time to the present (10) N. B. Baldwin.

Towamencin township, which had been unorganized, and regarded as a part "adjacent Gwynedd," was created in 1728. At the March session of the Court, in Philadelphia, a petition was presented, which is thus minuted on the record:

> Upon the petition of divers Inhabitants between the townships of Gwyneth and Skippack Creek, on the north-easterly side of Providence, setting forth that a great many families are settled upon a large tract of land containing about 5500 acres, whereof a Draught is to the said petition annexed, praying this Court would erect the same into a Township, the Court taking the said Petition into consideration do erect the said Portion of land into a Township as the same is laid out and described in the Draught . . . . and that the same be called by the name of Towamensing.

The petition above mentioned bears this memorandum: "The desire of the subscribers is that the township may be called Towamensen [that] being the Indian name of the creek y^t springs and runs through the same." The signers to the petition are twenty-eight in number. Several of their signatures are undecipherable, the remainder being as follows:

Jacob Hill,	Joseph Lucken,	Gaetschalck Gaetschalck,
Cadwalader Evans,	Abraham Lucken,	William Evan,
Daniel Morgan,	Lorenz Hendrich,	John Edwards,
Daniel Williams,	John Morgan,	Lennert Hendrich,
P. Wench,	Edward Morgan,	Hugh Evan,
henry Frey,	Jan Gaetschalcks,	Peter Tagen,
henry hendrich,	herman Gaetschalck,	Christian Wever.

The Schwenckfeldters, forming a large and compact body of German settlers, came into Pennsylvania, in 1734, and while most of them secured lands in the adjoining townships on the north-west, some came into Gwynedd, either in 1734, or within a few years afterward. Their settlement in the western corner of the township, adjoining their meeting-house in Towamencin, has since grown to cover a dozen or more farms, and to include about that number of families. Their religious views, especially their opposition to war, made them, like the Mennonites and Dunkers, congenial settlers in Penn's province, and friendly neighbors with the Quakers in Gwynedd. I have not made careful studies as to the precise time when each of them came into the township, but the Heebners, Kriebles, and others doubtless came early.[1] Christopher Neuman, or Neiman, a Schwenckfeldter, who came to Philadelphia in the immigration of 1734, was in Gwynedd before 1751, for in that year he bought 225 acres in the western corner of the township (afterward, in 1768, purchased by Philip Hoot, ancestor of the family of that name), from the executors of Edward Williams, and he is described in the deed as "of Gwynedth." Neuman's wife was Susanna Muehmer; their daughter Rosina married Heinrich Schneider,—changed, later, to Henry Snyder,—and had a large family: Rosina, George, Christopher, Henry, Christian, Abraham, Isaac, Susanna, John, and Regina. The father was a Lutheran, when he courted Rosina (and ran away with her, at night, after she descended from her window upon a ladder, Mr. Mathews says), but he and his family became Schwenckfeldters subsequently.

Up to 1734, however, there were substantially no German settlers in Gwynedd. The list of freeholders furnished in that year to Governor Thomas Penn, "according to the uncertain returns of the constables," shows forty-nine names of Gwynedd landholders, and of these only one, Leonard Hartling, is apparently a German. Five others, John Wood, Peter Wells, John Harris, John Parker, and Thomas Wyat, were probably English. The whole list is as follows:

Evan Griffith,	William Roberts,	Robert Parry,
John Griffith,	Evan Roberts,	Jenkin Morris,
Hugh Griffith,	Edward Roberts,	John Chilcott,
John Jones, penman,	Robert Roberts,	Leonard Hartling,
John Jones, weaver,	Edward Foulke,	Peter Wells,
John Jones, son of Robert,	Evan Foulke,	John Harris,
Cadwallader Jones,	Thomas Foulke,	Elizabeth Roberts,
Hugh Jones, tanner,	John David,	John Parker,

---

[1] Mr. Mathews says Melchoir Krieble settled in Gwynedd in 1735.

AFFAIRS BEFORE THE REVOLUTION. 273

Robert Hugh,	Thomas David,	Catherine Williams,
Rowland Hugh,	Lewis Williams,	Thomas Evans, jun.,
Owen Evans,	William Williams,	Cadwallader Evans,
Evan Evans,	Robert Humphrey,	Robert Evan, ap Rhiderth,
Thomas Evans,	John Humphrey,	Gaynor Jones,
Hugh Evans,	John Wood,	Rees Nanny,
Robert Evans,	Theodore Ellis,	Hugh Jones,
Morris Roberts,	Rees Harry,	Thomas Wyat.

Appended to this list, in the original document, is the following memorandum, explaining why the numbers of their respective acres did not accompany their names:

The Townsp: of Gwinedeth have hitherto refused to give the Constables an Account of their land, for which reason it is not known what they hold.

Others of the early German settlers will be here named. John Frey, son of Henry Frey, of Towamencin, whose name is on the petition for the erection of that township, bought a hundred acres from Jane Jones, William John's widow, in 1735, its location being about a mile southeast of Lansdale. (Most of the tract, in recent time, in the ownership of Abraham Krieble.) Frey sold the place in 1742 to Paul Brunner, another German, from Salford, whose widow subsequently married (about 1757) George Gossinger, a German "redemptioner," who had learned the trade of a tanner, and so passed the place into his control.

Philip Hoot, who had been living in New Hanover, came into Gwynedd in 1768, and bought the Neuman farm, 225 acres, alluded to above, of David Neuman. (Philip died 1798, aged 68 years and 4 months, and was buried at Wentz's church, in Worcester. He left his homestead to his son Peter, who married, 1792, Barbara Kriger.)

Abraham Danehower, ancestor of the family of that name, bought 136 acres, in 1762, of David and Sarah Cumming. This was the present homestead of George W. Danehower, occupied by Frank Myers, and the original residence of William John.[1]

---

[1] See p. 65, including the foot-note.

Abraham was born in Germany, September 27, 1722, came to Pennsylvania between 1740 and 1755, and died May 9, 1789, and was buried at St. John's, Whitpain. Beside him rests his wife, named Catherine (b. 1724, d. 1798). Their children included George, who died in 1793, in his 45th year; Abraham, jr., who bought a farm on the Bethlehem road, just above the Spring-House, of Samuel Evans; Henry, John, Catherine, who married Jacob Snyder; Elizabeth, who married Philip Hurst; and Sarah, who married Philip Fetterman.

In the summer of 1745 a fatal disease, the exact nature of which we can now only conjecture, visited Gwynedd. The meeting records show that from the 4th to the 31st of July, 24 members died, and from the 4th to the 24th of August, 15 died. On one day, the 4th of August, three deaths are recorded.[1] This, in a population of at most but a few hundreds, was a heavy death-rate. Most of the victims were children, but a number were from among the elders of the community, and few families escaped. Among those who died at this time were Evan Foulke, the immigrant (son of Edward), and three of his children; the father, first, on July 25th, one child on the 29th, and two others on August 4th and 5th.

---

[1] Mr. Buck, in his Gwynedd historical sketch, in *Scott's Atlas*, says 63 belonging to the meeting died from July 1 to August 24. This exceeds the number which I was able to find on the records.

XIX.

Gwynedd in the Midst of the Revolution: Sally Wister's Journal.

DANIEL WISTER, who married Lowry Jones, daughter of Owen Jones, sen., of Wynnewood, Lower Merion, and who was therefore connected with Caleb and Amos Foulke, (whose wives, Jane and Hannah, were also daughters of Owen Jones), was a merchant in Philadelphia, and, a fortnight after the battle of Brandywine, removed his family to Gwynedd, in anticipation of the British occupancy of the city. On the 25th of September, 1777, the day on which Howe and Cornwallis reached Germantown, Miss Sally Wister, the eldest daughter of Daniel, a bright girl of fifteen years, began to keep a journal of her observations and experiences in the retreat at Gwynedd, which she continued, with some interruptions, until, in the following June, the British army left Philadelphia, and her family returned to their city home.

This journal was addressed by its author to her friend Deborah Norris, but it is remarkable that the apprehension intimated in its opening lest it should never reach the eye for which it was intended, came near to being realized: it was not until years after Miss Wister's death that it was given by Mr. Charles J. Wister, her brother, to her old friend, who had then become Mrs. Logan, of Stenton.

Some extracts from the journal, but a small part only of its piquant and graphic details, are given by Watson in his *Annals;* it has been once published in full, in the rare edition of *American Historical and Literary Curiosities*, compiled by the late venerable

John Jay Smith. Its descriptions, however, of persons and events, and especially the view it gives us of social conditions in the very midst of some of the most important military operations of the revolutionary struggle, make it an extremely interesting historical document, aside from its charms as a *naive* and perfectly frank narrative of personal experiences.

In the nine months which the journal covers occurred the battle of Germantown, the siege and reduction of the forts below Philadelphia, the surrender of Burgoyne, the manœuvres at Whitemarsh, the march to Valley Forge, the winter encampment there, the operations of the "Cabal" against Washington, the conclusion of the treaty with France, the gaieties of the British occupation of Philadelphia, and Lafayette's "affair" at Barren Hill. But a little distance away from the hills of Gwynedd, the greatest of the actors in the Revolutionary drama were playing their parts,— Washington, Greene, Lafayette, Wayne, Steuben, Kalb, and all the distinguished list.

The Wisters were quartered in the old house at Penllyn,— the Foulke mansion, where William Foulke had died two years before, and which was at this time the home of his widow, Hannah, and her unmarried children. The different members of the family are alluded to in various places in the journal, and the allusions explained by foot-notes.

Journal.

TO DEBORAH NORRIS:—

Though I have not the least shadow of an opportunity to send a letter, if I do write, I will keep a sort of journal of the time that may expire before I see thee : the perusal of it may some time hence give pleasure in a solitary hour to thee and our S. J.

Yesterday, which was the 24th of September, two Virginia officers called at our house, and informed us that the British army had crossed the Schuylkill. Presently after, another person stopped, and confirmed what they had said, and that General Washington and army were near Pottsgrove.[1] Well, thee may be sure we were sufficiently scared; however, the road was very still till evening. About seven o'clock we heard a great noise. To the door we all went. A large number of waggons, with about three hundred of the Philadelphia militia. They begged for drink, and several pushed into the house. One of those that entered was a little tipsy, and had a mind to be saucy. I then thought it time for me to retreat; so figure me (mightily scared, as not having presence of mind enough to face so many of the military), running in at one door, and out at another, all in a shake with fear; but after a little, seeing the officers appear gentlemanly, and the soldiers civil, I called reason to my aid. My fears were in some measure dispelled, tho' my teeth rattled, and my hand shook like an aspen leaf. They did not offer to take their quarters with us; so, with many blessings, and as many adieus, they marched off.

I have given the most material occurrences of yesterday faithfully.

FOURTH DAY, September 25th.[2]

This day, till twelve o'clock, the road was mighty quiet, when Hobson Jones came riding along. About that time he made a stop at our door, and said the British were at Skippack road; that we should soon see their light horse, and [that] a party of Hessians had actually turned into our lane. My dadda and mamma gave it the credit it deserved, for he does not keep strictly to the truth in all respects; but the delicate, chicken-hearted Liddy[3] and I were wretchedly scared. We could say nothing but "Oh! what shall we do? What will become of us?" These questions only augmented the terror we were in. Well, the fright went off. We seen no light horse or Hessians. O. Foulke[4] came here in the evening, and told us that General Washington had come down as far as the Trap, and that General McDougle's brigade was stationed at Montgomery, consisting

---

[1] The battle of Brandywine had occurred on October 11th, and the surprise and massacre at Paoli on the night of the 20th. Howe crossed at Gordon's Ford (now Phœnixville), and Fatland Ford, on the 23d, to the east side of Schuylkill, and moved down to Philadelphia. Washington was at Pottsgrove for several days, and then moved over to the Perkiomen.

[2] This date, presuming the day of the week to be accurately given, should be the 24th, and it may be here observed that the dates of the month are not for some time correctly given in the journal, being a while one day ahead, and then two days, until December 5th, when they become correct.

[3] Lydia Foulke, who afterward married John Spencer. She was some six years the elder of Miss Sally.

[4] Owen Foulke, son of Caleb. He was Miss Sally's first cousin, their mothers being sisters.

of about 16 hundred men. This he had from Dr. Edwards, Lord Stirling's aid-de-camp; so we expected to be in the midst of one army or t'other.

FIFTH DAY, September 26th.

We were unusually silent all the morning; no passengers came by the house, except to the mill, and we don't place much dependance on mill news. About 12 o'clock, cousin Jesse[1] heard that General Howe's army had moved down towards Philadelphia. Then my dear, our hopes and fears were engaged for you. However, my advice is, summon up all your resolution, call Fortitude to your aid, don't suffer your spirits to sink, my dear; there's nothing like courage; 'tis what I stand in need of myself, but unfortunately have but little of it in my composition. I was standing in the kitchen about 12, when somebody came to me in a hurry, screaming, "Sally, Sally, here are the light horse!" This was by far the greatest fright I had endured; fear tack'd wings to my feet; I was at the house in a moment; at the porch I stopt, and it really was the light horse. I ran immediately to the western door, where the family were assembled, anxiously waiting for the event. They rode up to the door and halted, and enquired if we had horses to sell; he answered negatively. "Have not you, sir," to my father, "two black horses?"—"Yes, but have no mind to dispose of them." My terror had by this time nearly subsided. The officer and men behaved perfectly civil; the first drank two glasses of wine, rode away, bidding his men to follow, which after adieus in number, they did. The officer was Lieutenant Lindsay, of Bland's regiment, Lee's troop. The men, to our great joy, were Americans, and but 4 in all. What made us imagine them British, they wore blue and red, which with us is not common. It has rained all this afternoon, and to present appearances, will all night. In all probability the English will take possession of the city to-morrow or next day. What a change it will be! May the Almighty take you under His protection, for without His divine aid all human assistance is vain.

"May heaven's guardian arm protect my absent friends,
From danger guard them, and from want defend."

Forgive, my dear, the repetition of those lines, but they just darted into my mind.

Nothing worth relating has occurred this afternoon. Now for trifles. I have set a stocking on the needles, and intend to be mighty industrious. This evening our folks heard a very heavy cannon. We suppose it to be fired by the English. The report seem'd to come from Philadelphia. We

---

[1] Jesse Foulke, brother to Caleb and Amos, and therefore a "connection by marriage," but not of kin, at all; the term "cousin" is purely complimentary.

hear the American army will be within five miles of us to-night. The uncertainty of our position engrosses me quite. Perhaps to be in the midst of war, and ruin, and the clang of arms. But we must hope the best. * * *

Here, my dear, passes an interval of several weeks, in which nothing happen'd worth the time and paper it would take to write it.[1] The English, however, in the interim, had taken possession of the city.[2]

SECOND DAY, October 19th.

Now for new and uncommon scenes. As I was lying in bed, and ruminating on past and present events, and thinking how happy I should be if I could see you, Liddy came running into the room, and said there was the greatest drumming, fifing, and rattling of waggons that ever she had heard. What to make of this we were at a loss. We dress'd and down stairs in a hurry. Our wonder ceased. The British had left Germantown, and our army were marching to take possession. It was the general opinion they would evacuate the capital.[3] Sister B.[4] and myself, and G. E.[5] went about half a mile from home, where we cou'd see the army pass. Thee will stare at my going, but no impropriety, in my opine, or I should not have gone. We made no great stay, but return'd with excellent appetites for our breakfast. Several officers call'd to get some refreshments, but none of consequence till the afternoon. Cousin P.[6] and myself were sitting at the door; I in a green skirt, dark short gown, etc. Two genteel men of the military order rode up to the door: " Your servant,

---

[1] We are unfortunately given nothing in relation to the battle of Germantown, which occurred October 4th, in this interval. The omission is difficult to understand, because she alludes, later, to "the battle of Germantown, and the horrors of that day."

[2] They had occupied the city September 26th, two days after the first date in the journal.

[3] On this date the British withdrew from Germantown into Philadelphia, and the Americans moved down the Skippack road, and the roads adjacent, to take a nearer position. Washington's headquarters, for some days, were at "James Morris's, on the Skippack road," and on the 2d of November, at Whitemarsh, at the residence of George Emlen, here mentioned. It was the movement of troops down the Morris road, no doubt,—"half a mile away,"—that Miss Sally and her friends went to see.

[4] Miss "Betsy,"—Elizabeth—the writer's sister.

[5] George Emlen.

[6] Priscilla Foulke, sister of Caleb, Amos, and Jesse; "Cousin" simply by courtesy, as she was not of kin to Miss Sally.

ladies," etc.; ask'd if they could have quarters for General Smallwood. Aunt F.[1] thought she could accommodate them as well as most of her neighbors,— said they could. One of the officers dismounted, and wrote "Smallwood's Quarters" over the door, which secured us from straggling soldiers. After this he mounted his steed and rode away. When we were alone, our dress and lips were put in order for conquest, and the hopes of adventures gave brightness to each before passive countenance. Thee must be told of a Dr. Gould, who, by accident, had made acquaintance with my father,— a sensible, conversible man, a Carolinian,— and had come to bid us adieu. Daddy had prevailed on him to stay a day or two with us. In the evening his Generalship came, with six attendants, which compos'd his family. A large guard of soldiers, a number of horses and baggage-waggons, the yard and house in confusion, and glitter'd with military equipments. Gould was intimate with Smallwood, and had gone into Jesse's to see him. While he was there, there was great running up and down stairs, so I had an opportunity of seeing and being seen, the former the most agreeable, to be sure. One person, in particular, attracted my notice. He appear'd cross and reserv'd; but thee shall see how agreeably disappointed I was. Dr. Gould usher'd the gentlemen into our parlour, and introduc'd them, — "General Smallwood, Captain Furnival, Major Stodard,[2] Mr. Prig, Captain Finley, and Mr. Clagan, Colonel Wood, and Colonel Line." These last two did not come with the General. They are Virginians, and both indispos'd. The General and suite are Marylanders. Be assur'd I did not stay long with so many men, but secur'd a good retreat, heart-safe so far. Some sup'd with us, others at Jesse's. They retir'd about ten, in good order. How new is our situation! I feel in good spirits, though surrounded by an army, the house full of officers, the yard alive with soldiers,—very peaceable sort of people, tho'. They eat like other folks, talk like them, and behave themselves with elegance; so I will not be afraid of them, that I won't. Adieu. I am going to my chamber to dream, I suppose, of bayonets and swords, sashes, guns, and epaulets.

THIRD DAY, MORN., October 20th.

I dare say thee is impatient to know my sentiments of the officers; so, while Somnus embraces them, and the house is still, take their characters according to their rank. The Gen'l is tall, portly, well made: a truly martial air, the behaviour and manners of a gentleman, a good understanding,

---

[1] Aunt F., wife of Amos Foulke, and sister to Miss Sally's mother.

[2] This gentleman, frequently and fully spoken of in the journal, is presumed to be Major Benjamin Stoddert, of Maryland, who was Secretary of the Navy from 1798 to 1801, under Adams and Jefferson.

SALLY WISTER'S JOURNAL.

and great humanity of disposition, constitute the character of Smallwood.[1] Col. Wood, from what we hear of him, and what we see, is one of the most amiable of men; tall and genteel, an agreeable countenance and deportment. The following lines will more fully characterize him:—

> "How skill'd he is in each obliging art,
> The mildest manners and the bravest heart."

The cause he is fighting for alone tears him from the society of an amiable wife and engaging daughter; with tears in his eyes he often mentions the sweets of domestic life. Col. Line is not married: so let me not be too warm in his praise, lest you suspect. He is monstrous tall and brown, but has a certain something in his face and conversation very agreeable; he entertains the highest notions of honour, is sensible and humane, and a brave officer; he is only seven and twenty years old, but, by a long indisposition and constant fatigue, looks vastly older, and almost worn to a skeleton, but very lively and talkative. Capt. Furnival — I need not say more of him than that he has, excepting one or two, the handsomest face I ever saw, a very fine person; fine light hair, and a great deal of it, adds to the beauty of his face. Well, here comes the glory, the Major, so bashful, so famous, etc., he should come before the Captain, but never mind. I at first thought the Major cross and proud, but I was mistaken; he is about nineteen, nephew to the Gen'l, and acts as Major of brigade to him; he cannot be extoll'd for the graces of person, but for those of the mind he may justly be celebrated; he is large in his person, manly, and an engaging countenance and address. Finley is wretched ugly, but he went away last night, so I shall not particularize him. Nothing of any moment to-day; no acquaintance with the officers. Cols. Wood and Line, and Gould, dined with us. I was dress'd in my chintz, and looked smarter than night before.

FOURTH DAY, Oct. 21st.

I just now met the Major, very reserv'd: nothing but "Good morning," or "Your servant, madam;" but Furnival is most agreeable; he chats every opportunity; but luckily has a wife! I have heard strange things of the Major. With a fortune of thirty thousand pounds, independent of any body, the Major is vastly bashful; so much so he can hardly look at the ladies. (Excuse me, good sir; I really thought you were not clever; if 'tis bashfulness only, will drive that away.)

Fifth day, Sixth day, and Seventh day pass'd. The General still here; the Major still bashful.

---

[1] He commanded Maryland troops in the Revolutionary army, from 1776 to 1780, and served with credit. He was Governor of Maryland from 1785 to 1788.

First Day Evening.

Prepare to hear amazing things. The General was invited to dine, was engag'd; but Colonel Wood, Major Stodard, and Dr. Edwards[1] din'd with us. In the afternoon, Stodard, addressing himself to mamma, "Pray, ma'am, do you know Miss Nancy Bond?" I told him of the amiable girl's death. This major had been at Philadelphia College. In the evening, I was diverting Johnny at the table, when he drew his chair to it, and began to play with the child. I ask'd him if he knew N. Bond. "No, ma'am, but I have seen her very often." One word brought on another one. We chatted a great part of the evening. He said he knew me directly as he seen me. Told me exactly where we liv'd. It rains, so adieu.

Second Day, 26th October.

A rainy morning, so like to prove. The officers in the house all day.

Second Day, Afternoon.

The General and officers drank tea with us, and stay'd part of the evening. After supper I went with aunt, where sat the General, Colonel Line, and Major Stodard. So Liddy and I seated ourselves at the table in order to read a verse-book. The Major was holding a candle for the General, who was reading a newspaper.[2] He look'd at us, turn'd away his eyes, look'd again, put the candlestick down, up he jumps, out of the door he went. "Well," said I to Liddy, "he will join us when he comes in." Presently he return'd, and seated himself on the table. "Pray, ladies, is there any songs in that book?" "Yes, many." "Can't you favor me with a sight of it?" "No, Major; 'tis a borrow'd book." "Miss Sally, can't you sing?" "No." Thee may be sure I told the truth there. Liddy, saucy girl, told him I could. He beg'd, and I deny'd; for my voice is not much better than the voice of a raven. We talk'd and laugh'd for an hour. He is clever, amiable, and polite. He has the softest voice, never pronounces the *r* at all.

I must tell thee, to-day arriv'd Colonel Guest[3] and Major Leatherberry; the former a smart widower, the latter a lawyer, a sensible young fellow,

---

[1] Dr. Enoch Edwards, brother of Major Evan Edwards, and after the Revolution a prominent citizen and judge of the Philadelphia courts. He lived in Byberry, on a farm left him by his father, and died there in April, 1802. He served on the staff of Lord Stirling.

[2] Such was "the light of other days!"

[3] This is doubtless Colonel Nicholas Gist, of Maryland, who was first a captain, under Smallwood, and then rose to the command of the regiment. He was in the fight near Mooretown, in December, when Howe made the demonstration on Washington's lines at Whitemarsh.

and will never swing for want of tongue. Dr. Diggs came Second day; a mighty disagreeable man. We were oblig'd to ask him to tea. He must needs pop himself between the Major and me, for which I did not thank him. After I had drank tea, I jump'd from the table, and seated myself at the fire. The Major follow'd my example, drew his chair close to mine, and entertain'd me very agreeably. Oh, Debby; I have a thousand things to tell thee. I shall give thee so droll an account of my adventures, that thee will smile. "No occasion of that, Sally," methinks I hear thee say, "for thee tells me every trifle." But, child, thee is mistaken, for I have not told thee half the civil things that are said of us *sweet* creatures at "General Smallwood's Quarters." I think I might have sent the gentlemen to their chambers. I made my adieus, and home I went.

THIRD DAY, MORN.

A polite "good morning" from the Major, more sociable than ever. No wonder; a stoic cou'd not resist such affable damsels as we are.

THIRD DAY, EVE., October 27th.

We had again the pleasure of the General and suite at afternoon tea. He (the General, I mean) is most agreeable; so lively, so free, and chats so gaily, that I had quite an esteem for him. I must steel my heart! Captain Furnival is gone to Baltimore, the residence of his belov'd wife. The major and I had a little chat to ourselves this eve. No harm, I assure thee: he and I are friends.

This eve came a parson belonging to the army. He is (how shall I describe him?) near seven foot high, thin, and meagre, not a single personal charm, and very few mental ones. He fell violently in love with Liddy at first sight; the first discover'd conquest that has been made since the arrival of the General. Come, shall we chat about Col. Guest? He's very pretty; a charming person; his eyes are exceptional; very stern; and he so rolls them about that mine always fall under them. He bears the character of a brave officer: another admirer of Liddy's, and she of him. When will Sally's admirers appear? Ah! that indeed. Why, Sally has not charms sufficient to pierce the heart of a soldier. But still I won't despair. Who knows what mischief I yet may do?

Well, Debby, here's Doctor Edwards come again. Now we shall not want clack; for he has a perpetual motion in his head, and if he were not so clever as he is, we should get tired.

FOURTH DAY, October 28th.

Nothing material engaged us to day.

FIFTH DAY, October 29th.

I walked into aunt's this evening. I met the Major. Well, thee will think I am writing his history; but not so. Pleased with the rencounter. Betsy, Stodard, and myself, seated by the fire, chatted away an hour in lively and agreeable conversation. I can't pretend to write all he said; but he shone in every subject that was talk'd of.

Nothing of consequence on the 30th.

SEVENTH DAY, October 31st.

A most charming day. I walked to the door and received the salutation of the morn from Stodard and other officers. As often as I go to the door, so often have I seen the Major. We chat passingly, as, "A fine day, Miss Sally." "Yes, very fine, Major."

SEVENTH DAY, NIGHT.

Another very charming conversation with the young Marylander. He seems possessed of very amiable manners; sensible and agreeable. He has by his unexceptional deportment engaged my esteem.

FIRST DAY, MORN.

Liddy, Betsy, and a T—y prisoner of state went to the mill. We made very free with some Continental flour. We powder'd mighty white, to be sure. Home we came. Col. Wood was standing at a window with a young officer. He gave him a push forward, as much as to say, "Observe what fine girls we have here." For all I do not mention Wood as often as he deserves, it is not because we are not sociable: we are very much so, and he is often at our house. Liddy and I had a kind of adventure with him this morn. We were in his chamber chatting about our little affairs, and no idea of being interrupted: we were standing up, each an arm on a chest of drawers; the door bang'd open!—Col. Wood was in the room; we started, the colour flew into our faces and crimson'd us over; the tears flew into my eyes. It was very silly; but his coming was so abrupt. He was between us and the door. "Ladies, do not be scar'd, I only want something from my portmanteau; I beg you not to be disturbed." We ran by him, like two partridges, into mamma's room, threw ourselves into chairs, and reproach'd each other for being so foolish as to blush and look so silly. I was very much vex'd at myself, so was Liddy. The Colonel laugh'd at us, and it blew over.

The army had orders to march to-day; the regulars accordingly did.[1] General Smallwood had the command of militia at that time, and they being in the rear, were not to leave their encampment until Second day. Observe how militaryish I talk. No wonder, when I am surrounded by people of that order. The General, Colonels Wood, Guest, Crawford, and

---

[1] This was the movement to Whitemarsh.

Line, Majors Stodard and Leatherberry, din'd with us to-day. After dinner, Liddy, Betsy, and thy smart journalizer, put on their bonnets to take a walk. We left the house. I naturally look'd back; when, behold, the two majors seem'd debating whether to follow us or not. Liddy said, "We shall have their attendance;" but I did not think so. They open'd the gate, and came fast after us. They overtook us about ten poles from home, and beg'd leave to attend us. No fear of a refusal. They inquir'd when we were going to neighbor Roberts's.[1] "We will introduce you to his daughters; you us to General Stevens." The affair was concluded, and we shorten'd the way with lively conversation. Our intention of going to Roberts's was frustrated; the rain that had fallen lately had raised the Wissahickon too high to attempt crossing it on foot. We alter'd the plan of our ramble, left the road, and walk'd near two miles thro' the woods. Mr. Leatherberry, observing my locket, repeated the lines:

> "On her white breast a sparkling cross she wore,
> That Jews might kiss, and infidels adore."

I repli'd my trinket bore no resemblance to a cross. "'Tis something better, madam." 'Tis nonsense to repeat all that was said; my memory is not so obliging; but it is sufficient that nothing happen'd during our little excursion but what was very agreeable and entirely consistent with the strictest rules of politeness and decorum. I was vex'd a little at tearing my muslin petticoat. I had on my white dress, quite as nice as a First-day in town. We returned home safe. Smallwood, Wood, and Stodard drank tea with us, and spent the greater part of the evening. I declare this gentleman is very, very entertaining, so good natur'd, so good humor'd,—yes, so sensible; I wonder he is not married. Are there no ladies form'd to his taste? Some people, my dear, think that there's no difference between good nature and good humour; but, according to my opinion, they differ widely. Good nature consists in a naturally amiable and even disposition, free from all peevishness and fretting. It is accompanied by a natural gracefulness,—a manner of saying every thing agreeably; in short, it steals the senses, and captivates the heart. Good humour is a very agreeable companion for an afternoon; but give me good nature for life. Adieu.

SECOND DAY, MORN, November 1st.[2]

To-day the militia marches, and the General and officers leave us.

---

[1] Squire Job Roberts's, in Whitpain, a short distance away.

[2] Second day,—Monday,—was November 3d. The dates are here two days wrong, and as the reader may perceive for himself, are inconsistent with those heretofore given, which were one day wrong.

Heigh ho! I am very sorry; for when you have been with agreeable people, 'tis impossible not to feel regret when they bid you adieu, perhaps for ever. When they leave us we shall be immur'd in solitude. The Major looks dull.

SECOND DAY, NOON.

About two o'clock the General and Major came to bid us adieu. With daddy and mammy they shook hands very friendly; to us they bow'd politely. Our hearts were full. I thought the Major was affected. "Goodbye, Miss Sally," spoken very low. We stood at the door to take a last look, all of us very sober. The Major turn'd his horse's head, and rode back, dismounted. "I have forgot my pistols," pass'd us, and ran upstairs. He came swiftly back to us, as if wishing, through inclination, to stay; by duty compell'd to go. He remounted his horse. "Farewell, ladies, till I see you again," and canter'd away. We look'd at him till the turn in the road hid him from our sight. "Amiable major," "Clever fellow," "Good young man," was echoed from one to the other. I wonder if we shall ever see him again. He has our wishes for his safety.

Well, here's Uncle Miles.[1] Heartily glad of that am I. His family are well, and at Reading.

SECOND DAY, EVEN.

Jesse, who went with the General, return'd. We had a compliment from the General and Major. They are very well disposed of at Evan Meredith's, six miles from here. I wrote to P. F.,[2] by Uncle Miles, who waited on General Washington next morn.

THIRD DAY, MORN.

It seems strange not to see our house as it used to be. We are very still. No rattling of waggons, glittering of musquets. The beating of the distant drum is all we hear. Colonels Wood, Line, Guest, and Major Leatherberry are still here; the two last leave to-day. Wood and Line will soon bid us adieu. Amiable Wood; he is esteem'd by all that know him! Everybody has a good word for him.

Here I skip a week or two, nothing of consequence occurring. (Wood and Line are gone.) Some time since arriv'd two officers, Lieutenants Lee and Warring, Virginians. I had only the salutations of the morn from them. Lee is not remarkable one way or the other; Warring an insignificant piece enough. Lee sings prettily, and talks a great deal; how good

---

[1] Colonel Samuel Miles, of the Pennsylvania troops in the Revolutionary army. His wife was Catharine Wister, sister of Miss Sally's father.

[2] Polly Fishbourn, a young lady representative of a well-known Philadelphia family, and an intimate friend of Miss Sally. She was at Whitemarsh.

turkey hash and fried hominy is (a pretty discourse to entertain the ladies), extols Virginia, and execrates Maryland, which, by-the-by, I provok'd them to; for though I admire both Virginia and Maryland, I laugh'd at the former, and prais'd the latter. Ridiculed their manner of speaking. I took a great delight in teazing them. I believe I did it sometimes illnatur'dly; but I don't care. They were not, I am certain almost, first-rate gentlemen. (How different from our other officers.) But they are gone to Virginia, where they may sing, dance, and eat fry'd hominy and turkey hash all day long, if they choose. Nothing scarcely lowers a man, in my opinion, more than talking of eating, what they love, and what they hate. Lee and Warring were proficients in this science. Enough of them!

December 5th, SIXTH DAY.[1]

Oh, gracious! Debby, I am all alive with fear. The English have come out to attack (as we imagine) our army, three miles this side.[2] What will become of us, only six miles distant? We are in hourly expectation of an engagement. I fear we shall be in the midst of it. Heaven defend us from so dreadful a sight. The battle of Germantown, and the horrors of that day, are recent in my mind. It will be sufficiently dreadful, if we are only in hearing of the firing, to think how many of our fellow creatures are plung'd into the boundless ocean of eternity, few of them prepar'd to meet their fate. But they are summon'd before an all-merciful judge, from whom they have a great deal to hope.

SEVENTH DAY, December 6th.

No firing this morn. I hope for one more quiet day.

SEVENTH DAY, NOON, 4 o'clock.

I was much alarm'd just now, sitting in the parlour, indulging melancholy reflections, when somebody burst open the door. "Sally, here's Major Stodard!" I jumped. Our conjectures were various concerning his coming. The poor fellow, from great fatigue and want of rest, together with being expos'd to the night air, had caught cold, which brought on a fever. He cou'd scarcely walk, and I went into aunt's to see him. I was surpris'd. Instead of the lively, alert, blooming Stodard, who was on his feet the instant we enter'd, he look'd pale, thin, and dejected, too weak to rise, and "How are you, Miss Sally?" "How does thee do, Major?" I seated myself near him, inquir'd the cause of his indisposition, ask'd for the General, receiv'd his compliments. Not willing to fatigue him with too

---

[1] The dates are now accurate; December 5th fell on Sixth day,—Friday.

[2] This was Howe's famous demonstration against Washington's position at Whitemarsh, which was fully expected to be a general battle. The British left the city on the afternoon of December 4th.

much chat, I bid him adieu. To-night Aunt H—— F——, Sen'r,[1] administer'd something. Jesse assisted him to his chamber. He had not lain down five minutes before he was fast asleep. Adieu. I hope we shall enjoy a good night's rest.

FIRST DAY, MORN, December 7th.

I trip'd into aunt's. There sat the Major, rather more like himself. How natural it was to see him. "Good morning, Miss Sally." "Good morrow, Major, how does thee do to-day?" "I feel quite recover'd, Sally." "Well, I fancy this indisposition has sav'd thy head this time." Major: "No, ma'am; for if I hear a firing,[2] I shall soon be with them." That was heroic. About eleven I dress'd myself, silk and cotton gown. It is made without an apron. I feel quite awkwardish, and prefer the girlish dress.

FIRST DAY, AFTERNOON.

A Mr. Seaton and Stodard drank tea with us. He and I had a little private chat after tea. In the even, Seaton went into aunt's; mamma went to see Prissa, who is poorly; papa withdrew to talk with some strangers. Liddy just then came in, so we engag'd in an agreeable conversation. I beg'd him to come and give us a circumstantial account of the battle, if there should be one. "I certainly will, ma'am, if I am favor'd with my life." Liddy, unluckily, took it into her head to blunder out something about a person being in the kitchen who had come from the army. Stodard, ever anxious to hear, jump'd up. "Good night to you, ladies," was the word, and he disappeared, but not forever. "Liddy, thee hussy; what business had thee to mention a word of the army? Thee sees it sent him off. Thy evil genius prevail'd, and we all feel the effects of it." "Lord bless me," said Liddy, "I had not a thought of his going, or for ten thousand worlds I would not have spoke." But we cannot recall the past. Well, we laugh'd and chatted at a noisy rate, till a summons for Liddy parted us. I sat negligently on my chair, and thought brought thought, and I got so low spirited that I cou'd hardly speak. The dread of an engagement, the dreadful situation (if a battle should ensue) we should be in, join'd to my anxiety for P. F.[3] and family, who would be in the midst of the scene, was the occasion. And yet I did not feel half so frighten'd as I expected to be. 'Tis amazing how we get reconciled to such things.

---

[1] Hannah Foulke, widow of William.

[2] Though no firing seems to have been heard, it was on this day that two severe skirmishes occurred between the armies,—one on Edge Hill, near Mooretown, and the other in Cheltenham, probably near Shoemakertown. There were a number killed, and many wounded.

[3] Polly Fishbourn.

Six months ago the bare idea of being within ten, aye, twenty miles, of a battle, wou'd almost have distracted me. And now, tho' two such large armies are within six miles of us, we can converse calmly of it. It verifies the old proverb, "Use is second nature."

I forgot one little piece of intelligence, in which the girls say I discover'd a particular partialty for our Marylanders, but I disclaim anything of the kind. These saucy creatures are forever finding out wonders, and forever metamorphosing mole-hills into mountains.

> "Friendship I offer, pure and free;
> And who, with such a friend as me,
> Could ask or wish for more?"

"If they charg'd thee with vanity, Sally, it wou'd not be very unjust." Debby Norris! be quiet; no reflections, or I have done. "But the piece of intelligence, Sally!" [It] is just coming, Debby.

In the afternoon we heard platoon firing. Everybody was at the door; I in the horrors. The armies, as we judg'd, were engag'd. Very compos'dly says the Major to our servant, "Will you be kind enough to saddle my horse? I shall go!" Accordingly the horse was taken from the quiet, hospitable barn to plunge into the thickest ranks of war. Cruel change! Seaton insisted to the Major that the armies were still; "nothing but skirmishing with the flanking parties; do not go." We happen'd (we girls I mean) to be standing in the kitchen, the Major passing thro' in a hurry, and I, forsooth, discover'd a strong partiality by saying, "Oh! Major, thee is not going!" He turn'd round, "Yes, I am, Miss Sally," bow'd, and went into the road; we all pitied him; the firing rather decreas'd; and, after persuasions innumerable from my father and Seaton, and the firing over, he reluctantly agreed to stay. Ill as he was, he would have gone. It show'd his bravery, of which we all believe him possess'd of a large share.

SECOND DAY, December 8th.

Rejoice with us, my dear. The British have return'd to the city.[1] Charming this! May we ever be thankful to the Almighty Disposer of events for his care and protection of us while surrounded with dangers. Major went to the army. Nothing for him to do; so returned.

Third or Fourth day, I forget which, he was very ill; kept his chamber most of the day. In the evening I saw him. I pity him mightily, but pity is a poor remedy.

---

[1] They reached Philadelphia on the evening of this day, plundering the farms between Edge Hill and the city, as they marched in.

FIFTH DAY, December 11th.

Our army mov'd, as we thought, to go into winter quarters,[1] but we hear there is a party of the enemy gone over Schuylkill ; so our army went to look at them.[2] I observ'd to Stodard, "So you are going to leave us to the English." "Yes, ha! ha! ha! leave you for the English." He has a certain indifference about him that, to strangers, is not very pleasing. He sometimes is silent for minutes. One of these silent fits was interrupted the other day by his clasping his hands and exclaiming aloud, "Oh, my God, I wish this war was at an end!"

NOON.

The Major gone to camp. I don't think we shall see him again. Well, strange creature that I am ; here have I been going on without giving thee an account of two officers,— one who will be a principal character ; their names are Capt. Lipscomb and a Mr. Tilly ; the former a tall, genteel man, very delicate from indisposition, and has a softness in his countenance that is very pleasing, and has the finest head of hair that I ever saw ; 'tis a light shining auburn. The fashion of his hair was this — negligently ty'd and waving down his back. Well may it be said,

"Loose flow'd the soft redundance of his hair."

He has not hitherto shown himself a lady's man, tho' he is perfectly polite.

Now let me attempt a character of Tilly. He seems a wild, noisy mortal, tho' I am not much acquainted with him. He appears bashful when with girls. We dissipated the Major's bashfulness ; but I doubt we have not so good a subject now. He is above the common size, rather genteel, an extreme pretty, ruddy face, hair brown, and a sufficiency of it, a very great laugher, and talks so excessively fast that he often begins a sentence without finishing the last, which confuses him very much, and then he blushes and laughs ; and in short, he keeps me in perpetual good humour ; but the

---

[1] Early in the morning of this day, 11th December, the camp at Whitemarsh was broken up, and the Americans marched (doubtless up the Skippack road to Broadaxe, and thence westward) to the ferry at Matson's Ford—now Conshohocken. The weather was cold, no snow had fallen, the roads were frozen, and those of the men who were barefoot left such crimson marks on the ground, that afterward Washington made the statement which has passed into history : "You might have tracked the army from Whitemarsh to Valley Forge by the blood of their feet."

[2] This was a force under Cornwallis, 3000 strong, that had gone out to collect food and forage in the Merions, and which, as unexpectedly to themselves as to the Americans, encountered Sullivan, at the head of the latter column, at the ford. There was no battle, however.

creature has not address'd one civil thing to me since he came. But I have not done with his accomplishments yet, for he is a musician,— that is, he plays on the German flute, and has it here.

FIFTH DAY, NIGHT.

The family retir'd; take the adventures of the afternoon as they occur'd. Seaton and Captain Lipscomb drank tea with us. While we sat at tea, the parlour door was open'd; in came Tilly; his appearance was elegant; he had been riding; the wind had given the most beautiful glow to his cheeks, and blow'd his hair carelessly round his cheeks. Oh, my heart, thought I, be secure! The caution was needless, I found it without a wish to stray.

When the tea equipage was remov'd, the conversation turn'd on politicks, a subject I avoid. I gave Betsy a hint. I rose, she followed, and we went to seek Lyddy. We chatted a few moments at the door. The moon shone with uncommon splendour. Our spirits were high. I proposed a walk; the girls agreed. When we reach'd the poplar tree, we stopp'd. Our ears were assail'd by a number of voices. "A party of light horse," said one. "The English, perhaps; let's run home." "No, no," said I, "be heroines." At last two or three men on horseback came in sight. We walked on. The well-known voice of the Major saluted our hearing with, "How do you do, ladies." We turn'd ourselves about with one accord. He, not relishing the idea of sleeping on the banks of the Schuylkill, had return'd to the mill. We chatted along the road till we reach'd our hospitable mansion. Stodard dismounted, and went into Jesse's parlour. I sat there a half hour. He is very amiable. Lipscomb, Seaton, Tilly, and my father, hearing of his return, and impatient for the news, came in at one door, while I made my exit at the other.

I am vex'd at Tilly, who has his flute, and does nothing but play the fool. He begins a tune, plays a note or so, then stops. Well, after a while, he begins again; stops again. "Will that do, Seaton? Hah! hah! hah!" He has given us but two regular tunes since he arriv'd. I am passionately fond of music. How boyish he behaves.

SIXTH DAY, December 12th, 1777.

I ran into aunt's this morning to chat with the girls. Major Stodard join'd us in a few minutes. I verily believe the man is fond of the ladies, and, what to me is astonishing, he has not display'd the smallest degree of pride. Whether he is artful enough to conceal it under the veil of humility, or whether he has none, is a question; but I am inclined to think it the latter. I really am of opinion that there is few of the young fellows of the modern age exempt from vanity, more especially those who are bless'd with exterior graces. If they have a fine pair of eyes, they are forever rolling them about; a fine set of teeth, mind, they are great laughers; a genteel person, forever changing their attitudes to show them to advantage. Oh, vanity, vanity; how boundless is thy sway!

But to resume this interview with Major Stodard. We were very witty and sprightly. I was darning an apron, upon which he was pleas'd to compliment me. " Well, Miss Sally, what would you do if the British were to come here?" " Do," exclaimed I ; " be frighten'd just to death." He laugh'd, and said he would escape their rage by getting behind the representation of a British grenadier that you have upstairs. "Of all things, I should like to frighten Tilly with it. Pray, ladies, let's fix it in his chamber to-night." " If thee will take all the blame, we will assist thee." "That I will," he replied, and this was the plan. We had brought some weeks ago a British grenadier from Uncle Miles's on purpose to divert us. It is remarkably well executed, six feet high, and makes a martial appearance.[1] This we agreed to stand at the door that opens into the road (the house has four rooms on a floor, with a wide entry running through), with another figure, that would add to the deceit. One of our servants was to stand behind them; others were to serve as occasion offer'd. After half an hour's converse, in which we raised our expectations to the highest pitch, we parted. If our scheme answers, I shall communicate it in the eve. Till then, adieu.

SIXTH DAY, NIGHT.

Never did I more sincerely wish to possess a descriptive genius than I do now. All that I can write will fall infinitely short of the truly diverting scene that I have been witness of to-night. But, as I mean to attempt an account, I had as well shorten the preface, and begin the story.

In the beginning of the evening I went to Liddy and beg'd her to secure the swords and pistols which were in their parlour. The Marylander, hearing our voices, joined us. I told him of our proposal. Whether he thought it a good one or not I can't say, but he approv'd of it, and Liddy went in and brought her apron full of swords and pistols. When this was done, Stodard join'd the officers. We girls went and stood at the first landing of the stairs. The gentlemen were very merry, and chatting on public affairs, when Seaton's negro (observe that Seaton, being indisposed, was appriz'd of the scheme) open'd the door, candle in hand, and said, "There's somebody at the door that wishes to see you." " Who ? All of us ?" said Tilly. " Yes, sir," said the boy. They all rose (the Major, as he said

---

[1] This figure is still preserved, and stands (1884) in the hall of Mr. Charles J. Wister's residence at Germantown.

afterwards, almost dying with laughter), and walked into the entry, Tilly first, in full expectation of news. The first object that struck his view was a British soldier. In a moment his ears were saluted, "Is there any rebel officers here?" in a thundering voice. Not waiting for a second word, he darted like lightning out of the front door, through the yard, bolted o'er the fence. Swamps, fences, thorn-hedges,[1] and plough'd fields no way impeded his retreat. He was soon out of hearing. The woods echoed with, "Which way did he go? Stop him! Surround the house!" The amiable Lipscomb had his hand on the latch of the door, intending to make his escape; Stodard, considering his indisposition, acquainted him with the deceit. We females ran down stairs to join in the general laugh. I walked into Jesse's parlour. There sat poor Stodard (whose sore lips must have receiv'd no advantage from this), almost convuls'd with laughing, rolling in an arm-chair. He said nothing; I believe he could not have spoke. "Major Stodard," said I, "go to call Tilly back. He will lose himself,—indeed he will;" every word interrupted with a "Ha! ha!" At last he rose, and went to the door; and what a loud voice could avail in bringing him back, he tried. Figure to thyself this Tilly, of a snowy evening, no hat, shoes down at the heel, hair unty'd, flying across meadows, creeks, and mud-holes. Flying from what? Why, a bit of painted wood. But he was ignorant of what it was. The idea of being made a prisoner wholly engrossed his mind, and his last resource was to run.

After a while, we being in more composure, and our bursts of laughter less frequent, yet by no means subsided,—in full assembly of girls and officers,—Tilly enter'd. The greatest part of my risibility turn'd to pity. Inexpressible confusion had taken entire possession of his countenance, his fine hair hanging dishevell'd down his shoulders, all splashed with mud; yet his bright confusion and race had not divested him of his beauty. He smil'd as he trip'd up the steps; but 'twas vexation plac'd it on his features. Joy at that moment was banished from his heart. He briskly walked five or six steps, then stop'd, and took a general survey of us all. "Where *have* you been, Mr. Tilly?" ask'd one officer. (We girls were silent). "I really imagin'd," said Major Stodard, "that you were gone for your pistols. I follow'd you to prevent danger,"— an excessive laugh at each question, which it was impossible to restrain. "Pray, where were your pistols, Tilly?" He broke his silence by the following expression: "You may all go to the D——l." I never heard him utter an indecent expression before.

At last his good nature gain'd a compleat ascendence over his anger,

---

[1] This fixes the fact that the thorn-hedges which for many years divided a number of fields and farms, about Penllyn, had been planted before the Revolution.

and he join'd heartily in the laugh. I will do him the justice to say that he bore it charmingly. No cowardly threats, no vengeance denounced. Stodard caught hold of his coat. "Come, look at what you ran away from," and drag'd him to the door. He gave it a look, said it was very natural, and, by the singularity of his expressions, gave fresh cause for diversion. We all retir'd to our different parlours, for the rest of our faces, if I may say so.

Well, certainly, these military folks will laugh all night. Such screaming I never did hear. Adieu to-night.

December 13th.

I am fearful they will yet carry the joke too far. Tilly certainly possesses an uncommon share of good nature, or he could not tolerate these frequent teazings. Ah, Deborah, the Major is going to leave us entirely—just going. I will see him first.

SEVENTH DAY, NOON.

He has gone. I saw him pass the bridge. The woods which you enter immediately after crossing it, hinder'd us from following him further. I seem to fancy he will return in the evening.

SEVENTH DAY, NIGHT.

Stodard not come back. We shall not, I fancy, see him again for months, perhaps for years, unless he should visit Philadelphia. We shall miss his agreeable company. But what shall we make of Tilly? No civil things yet from him. Adieu to-night, my dear.

December 14th.

The officers yet here. No talk of their departure. They are very lively. Tilly's retreat the occasion; the principal one, at least.

FIRST DAY, NIGHT.

Captain Lipscomb, Seaton, and Tilly, with cousin H. M.,[1] dined with us to-day. Such an everlasting bore as Tilly I never knew. He caused us a good deal of diversion while we sat at table. Has not said a syllable to one of us young ladies since Sixth day eve. He tells Lipscomb that the Major had the assistance of the ladies in the execution of the scheme. He tells a truth.

About four o'clock I was standing at the door, leaning my head on my hand, when a genteel officer rode up to the gate and dismounted. "Your servant, ma'am," and gave me the compliment of his hat. Went into aunt's. I went into our parlour. Soon Seaton was call'd. Many minutes had not elapsed before he enter'd with the young fellow whom I had just seen. He introduced him by the name of Captain Smallwood. We seated

---

[1] Cousin Hannah Miles, daughter of Colonel Miles.

ourselves. I then had an opportunity of seeing him. He is a brother to General Smallwood. A very genteel, pretty little fellow, very modest, and seems agreeable, but no personal resemblance between him and the Major. After tea, turning turning to Tilly, he said, "So, sir, I have heard you had like to have been taken prisoner last Friday night." "Pray, sir, who informed you?" "Major Stodard was my author." "I fancy he made a fine tale of it. How far did he say I ran?" "Two miles; and that you fell into the mill-pond." He rais'd his eyes and hands, and exclaimed, "What a confounded falsehood." The whole affair was again reviv'd. Our Tillian here gave a mighty droll account of his "retreat," as they call it. He told us that, after he had got behind our kitchen, he stop'd for company, as he expected the others would immediately follow. "But I heard them scream, 'Which way did he go? Where is he?' 'Aye,' said I, to myself, 'he is gone where you shan't catch him,' and off I set again." "Pray," ask'd mamma, "did thee keep that lane between the meadows?" "Oh, no, ma'am; that was a large road, and I might happen to meet some of them. When I got to your thorn hedge, I again stop'd. As it was a cold night, I thought I would pull up my shoe-heels, and tie my handkerchief round my head. I began to have a suspicion of a trick, and, hearing the Major hollow, I came back."

I think I did not laugh more at the very time than to-night at the rehearsal of it. He is so good-natured, and takes all their jokes with so good a grace, that I am quite charm'd with him. He laughingly denounces vengeance against Stodard. He will be even with him. He is in the Major's debt, but he will pay him, etc.

December 15th.

Smallwood has taken up his quarters with us. Nothing worth relating occur'd to-day.

3d, 4th, and 5th day.

We chatted a little with the officers. Smallwood not so chatty as his brother or nephew. Lipscomb is very agreeable; a delightful musical voice.

SIXTH DAY, NOON, December 19th.

The officers, after the politest adieus, have left us. Smallwood and Tilly are going to Maryland,[1] where they live; Seaton to Virginia; and Lipscomb to camp, to join his regiment. I feel sorry at this departure, yet 'tis a different kind from what I felt some time since. We had not contracted so great an intimacy with those last.

---

[1] General Smallwood's brigade went to Wilmington, where they passed the winter.

SEVENTH DAY, December 20th.

General Washington's army have gone into winter quarters at the Valley Forge.[1] We shall not see many of the military now. We shall be very intimate with solitude. I am afraid stupidity will be a frequent guest. After so much company, I can't relish the idea of sequestration.

FIRST DAY, NIGHT.

A dull round of the same thing over again. I shall hang up my pen until something offers worth relating.

February 3d and 4th.

I thought I never should have anything to say again. Nothing happen'd all January that was uncommon. Capt. Lipscomb and Mas[2] stay'd one night at Jesse's, and sup'd with us. How elegant the former was dres'd. And indeed I have forgot to keep an exact account of the day of the month in which I went down to G. E.'s, with P. F.;[3] but it was the 23d or 24th of February. After enjoying a week of her agreeable company at the mill, I returned[4] with her to Whitemarsh. We went on horseback,—the roads bad. We however surmounted this difficulty, and arrived there safe.

SECOND DAY, EVE.

G. E. brought us a charming collection of books,—"Joe Andrews," "Juliet Grenville," and some *Lady's Magazines*. P. F. sent us "Caroline Melmoth."[5]

FOURTH DAY, 26th.

I thought our scheme of going to Fr'd F.'s was entirely frustrated, as S. E. was much indispos'd. About twelve she got better. We made some alteration in our dress, step'd into the carriage, and rode off. Spent a most delightful day. As we approach'd the house, on our return, we perceiv'd several strangers in the parlour. Polly's face and mine brighten'd up at the discovery. We alighted. Polly swung open the door, and introduc'd

---

[1] The army had been at Gulf Creek (near Conshohocken, but west of the Schuylkill), for a few days, but left there on the 19th, and marched to Valley Creek, to begin the winter encampment.

[2] So in copy. Not intelligible.

[3] To George Emlen's (at Whitemarsh, close by the present station of Sandy Run), with Polly Fishbourn.

[4] The language here, not entirely clear, means that Polly Fishbourn had been "at the mill,"—at Penllyn,—when Miss Sally "went down" with her.

[5] We get some clue, here, as to the attractive literature of the times. "Joseph Andrews" was Fielding's famous novel, published in 1742. The *Lady's Magazine* was a London monthly, whose issue was begun October, 1759, "by John Wilkie, book-seller, Fleet Street."

us to Major Jameson and Captain Howard, both of the dragoons, the former from Virginia, the latter a Marylander. We all seem'd in penseroso style till after supper. We then began to be rather more sociable. About ten they bid us adieu. I dare say thee is impatient to know my sentiments of the swains. Howard has very few external charms; indeed, I cannot name one. As to his internal ones, I am not a judge. Jameson is tall and manly, a comely face, dark eyes and hair. Seems to be much of a gentleman. No ways deficient in point of sense, or, at least, in the course of the evening, I discover'd none.

Fifth and Sixth day, and Seventh day, pass'd away very agreeably. No strangers.

FIRST DAY, EVE.

This day my charming friend and myself ascended the barren hills of Whitemarsh, from the tops of which we had an extensive prospect of the country round. The traces of the army which encamp'd on these hills are very visible. Rugged huts, imitations of chimneys, and many other ruinous objects, which plainly show'd they had been there. D. J. S. dined with us.

SECOND DAY.

Very cold and windy. I wonder I am not sent for. Read and work'd by turns.

THIRD DAY.

A raw, snowy day. I am sent for, nevertheless. Adieu.

[NORTH WALES, at my habitation at the mill.]

March 1st, 1778, THIRD DAY, EVE.

Such a ride as I have had, O dear Debby. About two o'clock the sleigh came for me. Snowing excessively fast, though not sufficiently deep to make it tolerable sleighing; but go I must. I bid adieu to my agreeable friends, and with a heavy heart and flowing eyes, I seated myself in the unsociable vehicle. There might as well have been no snow on the ground. I was jolted just to pieces. But, notwithstanding these vexations, I got safe to my home, when I had the great pleasure of finding my dear parents, sisters, and brothers well, a blessing which I hope ever to remember with thankfulness.

Well, will our nunnery be more bearable now than before I left it? No beaus since I left here, so I have the advantage of the girls. They are wild to see Major Jameson.

MAY 11th, 1778.

The scarcity of paper, which is very great in this part of the country, and the three last months not producing anything material, have prevented me from keeping a regular account of things; but to-day the scene begins to brighten, and I will continue my nonsense. In the afternoon, we were just seated at tea,— Dr. Moore[1] with us. Nelly (our girl) brought us the wonderful intelligence that there were light horse in the road. The tea-table was almost deserted. About fifteen light horse were the vanguard of 16 hundred men under the command of General Maxwell. I imagin'd that they would pass immediately by, but was agreeably disappointed. My father came in with the General, Colonel Brodhead, Major Ogden, and Captain Jones.

The General is a Scotsman,— nothing prepossessing in his appearance; the Colonel, very martial and fierce; Ogden, a genteel young fellow, with an aquiline nose. Captain Cadwallader Jones — if I was not invincible, I must have fallen a victim to this man's elegancies (but, thank my good fortune, I am not made of susceptibilities),—tall, elegant, and handsome,— white fac'd with blue regimentals, and a mighty airish cap and white crest; his behaviour is refin'd,— a Virginian. They sat a few minutes after tea, then bid us adieu.

This brigade is encamp'd about three miles from us.

FIRST DAY, EVENING.

This afternoon has been productive of adventures in the true sense of the word. Jenny R., Betsy, Liddy, and I, very genteelly dress'd, determined to take a stroll. Neighbor Morgan's was proposed. Away we rambled, heedless girls. Pass'd two picket guards. Meeting with no interruptions encouraged us. After paying our visit, we walked towards home, when, to my utter astonishment, the sentry desir'd us to stop; that he had orders not to suffer any persons to pass but those who had leave from the officer, who was at the guard house, surrounded by a number of men. To go to him would be inconsistent with propriety; to stay there, and night advancing, was not clever. I was much terrified. I tried to persuade the soldier to let us pass. "No; he dared not." Betsy attempted to go. He presented his gun with the bayonet fix'd. This was an additional fright. Back we turn'd; and, very fortunately, the officer (Captain Emeson), seeing our distress, came to us. I ask'd him if he had any objection to passing the sentry. "None at all, ma'am." He waited upon us, and reprimanded the man, and we, without any farther difficulty, came home.

THIRD DAY, June 2d.

I was standing at the back window. An officer and private of dra-

---

[1] Dr. Charles Moore, of Montgomery, no doubt.

goons rode by. I tore to the door to have a better view of them. They stop'd. The officer rode up, and ask'd for Jesse, who was call'd.

AFTERNOON, 4 o'clock.

Oh, Deborah; what capital adventures. Jesse came. The idea of having light horse quarter'd at the farm was disagreeable; the meadows just fit to mow, and we had heard what destruction had awaited their footsteps. This was the dialogue between Jesse and the officer: " Pray, sir, can I have quarters for a few horsemen?" "How many?" "Five and twenty, sir. I do not mean to turn them into your meadows. If you have any place you can spare, anything will do." And he dismounted, and walk'd into aunt's parlour. I, determin'd to find out his character, follow'd. "I have," replied Jesse, "a tolerable field, that may perhaps suit." "That will do, sir. But if you have any objection to putting them in a field, my men shall cut the grass, and bring it in the road. I am under the necessity of quartering them here, but I was order'd. I am only an inferior officer." Some elegant corporal, thought I, and went to the door. He soon join'd me, speaking to his man, "Ride off, and tell Mr. Watts we rendezvous here."

He inquir'd the name of the farmer, and went into aunt's; I into the back room. The troop rode up. "New scenes," said I, and moved upstairs, where I saw them perform their different manœuvres. This Mr. Watts is remarkably tall, and a good countenance. I adjourn'd to the parlor. The first officer march'd up and down the entry. Prissa came in. "Good, now, Prissa. What's the name of this man?" "Dyer, I believe." Captain Dyer. Oh, the name! "What does he say?" "Why, that he will kiss me when he has din'd." "Singular," I observ'd, "on so short an acquaintance." "But," resum'd Prissa, "he came and fix'd his arm on the chair I sat in: 'Pray, ma'am, is there not a family from town with you?' 'Yes.' 'What's their name?' 'Wister.' 'There's two fine girls there. I will go chat with them. Pray, did they leave their effects in Philadelphia?' 'Yes, everything, almost.' 'They shall have them again, that they shall.'" There ended the conversation. But this ugly name teas'd me. "Oh, Sally, he is a Virginian; that's in his favour greatly." "I'm not sure that's his name, but I understood so." Prissa left us. I step'd into aunt's for Johnny and desir'd him to come home. Up started the Captain: "Pray, let me introduce you, ma'am." "I am perfectly acquainted with him," said I, and turned to the door. "Tell your sister I believe she is not fond of strangers." I smil'd, and returned to our parlour.

THIRD DAY NIGHT, nine o'clock, aye, ten, I fancy.

Take a circumstantial account of this afternoon, and the person of this extraordinary man. His exterior first. His name is not Dyer, but Alexander Spotswood Dandridge, which certainly gives a genteel idea of the man. I will be particular. His person is more elegantly form'd than any I ever saw; tall and commanding. His forehead is very white, though the lower part of his face is much sunburn'd; his features are extremely pleasing; an even, white set of teeth, dark hair and eyes. I can't better describe him than by saying he is the handsomest man I ever beheld. Betsy and Liddy coincide in this opinion.

After I had sat a while at home, in came Dandridge. He enter'd into chat immediately. Ask'd if we knew Tacy Vanderen. Said he courted her, and that they were to be married soon. Observ'd my sampler, which was in full view. Wish'd I would teach the Virginians some of my needle wisdom; they were the laziest girls in the world. Told his name. Laugh'd and talk'd incessantly. At last, "May I" (to mamma) "introduce my brother officer?" We assented; so he call'd him. "Mr. Watts, Mrs. Wister, young Miss Wister. Mr. Watts, ladies, is one of our Virginia children." He sat down. Tea was order'd. Dandridge never drank tea; Watts had done; so we sat to the table alone. "Let's walk in the garden," said the Captain; so we call'd Liddy, and went (not Watts). We sat down in a sort of a summer-house. "Miss Sally, are you a Quaker?" "Yes." "Now, *are* you a Quaker?" "Yes, I am." "Then you are a Tory." "I am not, indeed." "Oh, dear," replied he, "I am a poor creature. I can hardly live." Then, flying away from that subject, " Will you marry me, Miss Sally?" "No, really; a gentleman after he has said he has not sufficient to maintain himself, to ask me to marry him." "Never mind what I say, I have enough to make the pot boil."

Had we been acquainted seven years, we could not have been more sociable. The moon gave a sadly pleasing light. We sat at the door till nine. Dandridge is sensible, and (divested of some freedoms, which might be call'd gallant in the fashionable world) he is polite and agreeable. His greatest fault is a propensity to swearing, which throws a shade over his accomplishments. I ask'd him why he did so. "It is a favorite vice, Miss Sally." At nine he went to his chamber. Sets off at sunrise.

FOURTH DAY, MORN, 12 o'clock.

I was awaken'd this morn with a great racket of the Captain's servant calling him; but the lazy fellow never rose till about half an hour past eight. This his daylight ride. I imagin'd they would be gone before now, so I dressed in a green skirt and dark short gown. Provoking. So down I came, this Captain (wild wretch) standing at the back door. He bow'd and call'd me. I only look'd, and went to breakfast. About nine I took my work and seated myself in the parlour. Not long had I sat, when in came Dandridge,—the handsomest man in existence, at least that I had ever seen. But stop here, while I just say, the night before, chatting upon dress, he said he had no patience with those officers who, every morn, before they went on detachments, would wait to be dress'd and powder'd. "I am," said I, "excessively fond of powder, and think it very becoming." "Are you?" he reply'd. "I am very careless, as often wearing my cap thus" (turning the back part before) "as any way." I left off where he came in. He was powder'd very white, a (pretty colored) brown coat, lapell'd with green, and white waistcoat, etc., and his

"Sword beside him negligently hung."

He made a truly elegant figure. "Good morning, Miss Sally. You are very well, I hope." "Very well. Pray sit down," which he did, close by me. "Oh, dear," said I, "I see thee is powder'd." "Yes, ma'am. I have dress'd myself off for you." Will I be excused, Debby, if I look upon his being powder'd in the light of a compliment to me? "Yes, Sally, as thee is a country maid, and don't often meet with compliments." Saucy Debby Norris!

'Tis impossible to write a regular account of our conversation. Be it sufficient to say that we had a multiplicity of chat.

About an hour since, sister H. came to me and said Captain Dandridge was in the parlour, and had ask'd for me. I went in. He met me, caught my hands. "Oh, Miss Sally, I have a beautiful sweetheart for you." "Poh! ridiculous! Loose my hands." "Well, but don't be so cross." "Who is he?" "Major Clough. I have seen him. Ain't he pretty, to be sure? I am going to headquarters. Have you any commands there?" "None at all; but" (recollecting), "yes, I have. Pray, who is your commanding officer?" "Colonel Bland, ma'am." "Please give my compliments to him, and I shou'd be glad if he would send thee back with a little more manners." He reply'd wickedly, and told me I had a little spiteful heart. But he was intolerably saucy; said he never met with such ladies. "Not to let me kiss you. You're very ill-natur'd, Sally." And, putting on the sauciest face, "Sally, if Tacy V*nd*r*n won't have me, will you?" "No, really; none of her discarded lovers." "But, provided I prefer you to her, will you consent?" "No, I won't." "Very well, madam." And after saying he would return to-morrow, among a hundred other things, he elegantly walk'd out of the room. Soon he came back, took up a volume of Homer's Iliad, and read to us. He reads very well, and with judgment. One remark he made, that I will relate, on these lines,—

"While Greece a heavy, thick retreat maintains,
Wedg'd in one body, like a flight of cranes."

"G—d knows our army don't do so. I wish they did." He laugh'd, and went away.

FOUR O'CLOCK, AFTERNOON.

Major Clough, Captain Swan, and Mr. Moore, a Lieutenant of horse, din'd with Dandridge. The latter, after dinner, came in to bid us adieu. He sat down, and was rather saucy. I look'd very grave. "Miss Betsy, you have a very ill-natured sister. Observe how cross she looks." He pray'd we might part friends, and offer'd his hand. I gave him mine, which he kiss'd in a very gallant manner; and so, with truly affectionate leave, he walked to the parlour door, "God Almighty bless you, ladies;" bow'd, went into the road, mounted a very fine horse, and rode away; leaving Watts and the troop here, to take care of us, as he said. "Mr. Watts, Miss Sally, is a very worthy man; but, poor soul, he is so captivated with you,—the pain in his breast all owing to you,—he was caught by this beauty-spot," tapping my cheek. He could not have thought it was meant for an addition, as the size of it shew'd the contrary. But he is gone; and I think, as I have escap'd thus far safe, I am quite a heroine, and need not be fearful of any of the lords of the creation for the future.

SIX O'CLOCK, EVENING.

Watts drank tea with us. A conversable man. Says that the Dandridges are one of the genteelest families in Virginia,—relations of General Washington's wife. He appear'd very fond of the Captain, who has had a liberal education. Very sensible and brave. I sat in the entry all last evening, as did Betsy. But first, let me say, Fifth day morn we chatted on a variety of subjects; and amongst others, he mentioned the cruelty of the Britons, which I agreed, was very great. He said he would retaliate whenever he had an opportunity. I strenuously opposed such a procedure, observing that it would be erring in the same way, and tho' they might deserve it, yet it would be much nobler to treat them with lenity. Remember the lines of Pope,—

"That mercy I to others show,
That mercy show to me."

"I perfectly remember them. Your sentiments are noble; but we must retaliate sometimes."

A horseman deliver'd this message: "Let the troop lie on their arms, and be ready to march at a moment's warning." He immediately gave these orders to the sergeant. Every soldier was in motion. I was a good deal frighten'd, and ask'd Watts the reason. He fancy'd the British were in motion, tho' he had not receiv'd such intelligence. "What will thee do if they come here?" "Defend the house as long as I can, ma'am." I was shock'd. "Bless my heart; what *will* become of us?" "You may be very safe. The house in an excellent house to defend; only do you be still. If the British vanquish us, down on your knees, and cry, 'Bless the king.' If we conquer them, why you know you are safe." This added to my fright. I called my dear mamma, who was much indispos'd. Dadda was gone to Lancaster. Mamma ask'd him the same questions, and he gave her the same answers. I was in a fearful taking, and said if I thought such a thing would happen, I would set off, though nine o'clock, and walk to Uncle Foulke's. "No, don't go to-night, Miss Sally. I will take you there to-morrow. Don't be uneasy. This is nothing. I often go to bed with my boots on upon some alarms." "But thee will take off thy boots to-night?" "Yes, I will, indeed." "Is thee really in earnest about defending the house?" "No, madam; for believe me, if I hear the enemy is in motion, I will immediately depart, bag and baggage."

This dispell'd my fears, and after wishing me a good night, he retir'd to his chamber. Imagine my consternation when our girl came running in, and said the lane was fill'd with light horse. I flew to the side door. It was true. My joy was great when I heard Major Clough ask if this was Captain Dandridge's quarters. I answer'd in the affirmative. He rode round to the other door. Watts, though gone to bed, was call'd. He chatted apart to the Major a while, then went off towards Skippack road, follow'd by a large party of horse and waggons. My fears were all renew'd; and, as if we were to be in perpetual alarms, by came another party, much larger, in dark clothes. These we all thought *were* British. They halted. All as still as death. The officer rode up to the door. "Does Mr. Foulke live here?" "Yes," said somebody. "Is there not a family from town here,— Mr. Wister's?" I recollected the voice, and said, "Captain Stodard, I presume?" "Yes, madam. Are you Mr. Wister's wife?" "No, his daughter." "Is your papa at home?" "No," I reply'd, but invited him in to see mamma. He agreed; dismounted, as did many other officers; but he alone came into our parlour. Watts follow'd to bid us adieu. They sat a few minutes; told us that two of their men had deserted, and when that was the case, they generally moved their quarters. Watts told him how I was frighten'd. He said I paid but a poor compliment to their chivalry. I only smil'd. The alarm had partly depriv'd me of the power of speech.

They sat about fifteen minutes, then rose, and after the politest adieus, departed. All the horse follow'd — about one hundred and fifty. I never saw more regularity observ'd, or so undisturb'd a silence kept up when so large a number of people were together. Not a voice was heard, except that of the officer who gave the word of command. The moon at intervals broke thro' the heavy black clouds. No noise was perceiv'd, save that which the horses made as they trotted o'er the wooden bridge across the race. Echo a while gave us back the sound. At last nothing was left but remembrance of them. The family all retir'd to their respective chambers, and enjoyed a calm repose.

This Captain Stodard is from New England, and belongs to Colonel Sheldon's regiment of dragoons. He made an acquaintance with my father at Germantown, whilst our army was at that place, and had been here once before. He is clever and gentlemanly.

FIFTH DAY, June 4th, 2 o'clock.

Oh, gracious! how warm is this day. But, warm as it is, I must make a small alteration in my dress. I do not make an elegant figure, tho' I do not expect to see a stranger to-day.

SIXTH DAY, June 5th, MORN, 11 o'clock.

Last night we were a little alarm'd. I was awaken'd about 12, with somebody's opening the chamber door. I observ'd cousin Prissa talking to mamma. I asked what was the matter. "Only a party of light horse." "Are they Americans?" I quickly said. She answer'd in the affirmative, (which dispell'd my fears), and told me Major Jameson commanded, and that Captains Call and Nixon were with him. With that intelligence she left us. I resolved in my mind whether or not Jameson would renew his acquaintance; but Morpheus buried all my ideas, and this morning I rose by, or near seven, dress'd in my light chintz, which is made gown-fashion, kenton handkerchief, and linen apron. "Sufficiently smart for a country girl, Sally." Don't call me a country girl, Debby Norris. Please to observe that I pride myself on being a Philadelphian, and that a residence of 10 months has not at all diminished the love I have for that place; and as soon as one capital alteration takes place (which is very much talk'd of at present), I expect to return to it with a double pleasure.

Dress'd as above, down I came, and went down to our kitchen, which is a small distance from the house. As I came back, I saw Jameson at the window. He met me in the entry, bow'd:—"How do you do, Miss Sally?" After the compliments usual on such occasions had pass'd, I invited him him into our parlour. He followed me in. We chatted very sociably. I inquir'd for P. F. He said he had seen her last First-day; that she was well. Her mamma had gone to Lancaster, to visit her daughter Wharton,[1] who, as I suppose you have heard, has lost her husband.

I ask'd him whether Dandridge was on this side the Delaware. He said, "Yes." I wanted sadly to hear his opinion, but he said not a word. The conversation turn'd upon the British leaving Philadelphia. He firmly believ'd they were going. I sincerely wish'd it might be true, but was afraid to flatter myself. I had heard it so often that I was quite faithless, and express'd my approbation of Pope's 12th beatitude, " Blessed are they that expect nothing, for they shall not be disappointed." He smil'd, and assur'd me they *were* going away.

He was summon'd to breakfast. I ask'd him to stay with us. He declin'd the invitation with politeness, adding that he was in a hurry,—oblig'd to go to camp as soon as he could. He bow'd, " Your servant, ladies," and withdrew immediately. After breakfast they set off for Valley Forge, where Gen'l Washington's army still are.

I am more pleas'd with Major Jameson than I was at first. He is sensible and agreeable,—a manly person, and a very good countenance. We girls differ about him. Prissa and I admire him, whilst Liddy and Betsy will not allow him a spark of beauty. Aunt's family are charm'd with his behavior,— so polite, so unassuming. When he disturb'd them last night, he made a hundred apologies,— was so sorry to call them up,—'twas real necessity oblig'd him. I can't help remarking the contrast between him and Dandridge. The former appears to be rather grave than gay, — no vain assuming airs. The latter calls for the genius of a Hogarth to characterize him. He is possess'd of a good understanding, a very liberal education, gay and volatile to excess. He is an Indian, a gentleman, grave and sad, in the same hour. But what signifies? I can't give thee a true idea of him; but he assumes at pleasure a behavior the most courtly, the most elegant of anything I ever saw. He is very entertaining company, and very vain of his personal beauties; yet nevertheless his character is exceptional.

SIXTH DAY, NOON AND EVENING.

Nothing material occurr'd.

SEVENTH DAY, NIGHT.

A dull morn. In the afternoon, Liddy, Betsy, R. H., and self went to one of our neighbors to eat strawberries. Got a few. Return'd home; drank tea. No beaus. Adieu.

---

[1] The "mamma" was Mrs. William Fishbourn. Her daughter Elizabeth was the second wife of Thomas Wharton, jr., President of the Supreme Executive Council (acting Governor). He d. at Lancaster (the seat of the Pennsylvania government at this time), on May 22, 1778.

20

First Day, Evening.

Heigh-ho! Debby, there's a little meaning in that exclamation, ain't there? To me it conveys much. I have been looking what the dictionary says. It denotes uneasiness of mind. I don't know that my mind is particularly uneasy just now.

The occurrences of the day come now. I left my chamber between eight and nine, breakfasted, went up to dress, put on a new purple and white striped Persian, white petticoat, muslin apron, gauze cap, and handkerchief. Thus array'd, Miss Norris, I ask your opinion. Thy partiality for thy friend will bid thee say I made a tolerable appearance. Not so, my dear. I was this identical Sally Wister, with all her whims and follies; and they have gain'd so great an ascendency over my prudence, that I fear it will be a hard matter to divest myself of them. But I will hope for a reformation.

Cousin H. M. came about nine, and spent the day with us. After we had din'd, two dragoons rode up to the door; one a waiting-man of Dandridge's, the faithful Jonathan. They are quarter'd a few miles from us. The junior sisters, Liddy and Betsy, join'd by me, ventur'd to send our compliments to the Captain and Watts. Prissa insists that it is vastly indelicate, and that she has done with us. Hey day! What prudish notions are those, Priscilla? I banish prudery. Suppose we had sent our *love* to him, where had been the impropriety? for really he had a person that was love-inspiring, tho' I escap'd, and may say, *Io triumphe*. I answer not for the other girls, but am apt to conclude that Cupid shot his arrows, and that maybe they had effect. A fine evening this. If wishes could avail, I would be in your garden with S. J., R. F., and thyself. Thee has no objection to some of our North Wales swains,—not the beau inhabitants, but some of the transitory ones. But cruel reverse. Instead of having my wishes accomplish'd, I must confine myself to the narrow limit of this farm.

Liddy calls: "Sally, will thee walk?" "Yes." Perhaps a walk will give a new turn to my ideas, and present something new to my vacant imagination.

Second Day, Third Day, Fourth Day.

No new occurrences to relate. Almost adventureless, except General Lacy's riding by, and his fierce horse disdaining to go without showing his airs, in expectation of drawing the attention of the mill girls, in order to glad his master's eyes. Ha! ha! ha! One would have imagin'd that vanity had been buried within the shades of N. Wales. Lacy is tolerable; but as ill luck would order it, I had been busy, and my *auburn ringlets* were much dishevell'd: therefore I did not *glad his eyes*, and cannot set down on the list of honours receiv'd that of a bow from Brigadier-General Lacy.

FIFTH DAY, NIGHT, June 18th.

Rose at half-past four this morning. Iron'd industriously till one o'clock, din'd, went up stairs, threw myself on the bed, and fell asleep. About four, sister H. wak'd me, and said uncle and J. F. were down stairs; so I decorated myself, and went down. Felt quite lackadaisical. However, I jump'd about a little, and the stupid fit went off. We have had strange reports about the British being about leaving Philadelphia. I can't believe it. Adieu.

SIXTH DAY, MORN, June 19th.

We have heard an astonishing piece of news! The English have entirely left the city! It is almost impossible! Stay, I shall hear further.

SIXTH DAY, EVE.

A light horseman has just confirm'd the above intelligence! This is *charmante!* They decamp'd yesterday. He (the horseman) was in Philadelphia. It is true. They have gone. Past a doubt. I can't help exclaiming to the girls,—

"Now are you sure the news is true? Now are you sure they have gone?" "Yes, yes, yes!" they all cry, "and may they never, never return."

Dr. Gould came here to-night. Our army are about six miles off, on their march to the Jerseys.

SEVENTH DAY, MORN.

O. F.[1] arrived just now, and related as *followeth:*— The army began their march at six this morning by their house. Our worthy General Smallwood breakfasted at uncle Caleb's.[2] He ask'd how Mr. and Mrs. Wister and the young ladies were, and sent his respects to us. Our brave, our heroic *General Washington* was escorted by fifty of the Life Guard, with drawn swords. Each day he acquires an addition to his goodness. We have been very anxious to know how the inhabitants of Philadelphia have far'd. I understand that General Arnold, who bears a good character, has the command of the city, and that the soldiers conducted with great decorum. Smallwood says they had the strictest orders to behave well; and I dare say they obey'd the order. I now think of *nothing* but returning to Philadelphia.

---

[1] Owen Foulke, son of Caleb.

[2] The Meredith house, on the Swedes' Ford road.

So I shall now conclude this journal, with humbly hoping that the Great Disposer of events, who has graciously vouchsaf'd to protect us to this day through many dangers, will still be pleas'd to continue his protection.

SALLY WISTER.

North Wales, June 20th, 1778.

XX.

Revolutionary Details.

THERE is no record or tradition of any bloodshed in Gwynedd during the war of the Revolution, though the place was so near to many important military operations. But detachments of the American army moved through it many times, and from September, 1777, to June, 1778, the people must have been almost daily reminded by the visits of soldiers of the conflict that was raging about them.

When Washington was on the Perkiomen, previous to his attack at Germantown, General McDougall's brigade, consisting of about sixteen hundred men, was posted "at Montgomery," and from there it marched down to the battle, moving, no doubt, by the Bethlehem road to the Spring-House, and then down to Whitemarsh. After the battle, the current of the retreat swept upward through Gwynedd. General Francis Nash, of North Carolina, who was mortally wounded early in the action, and whose remains lie with those of Colonel Boyd, Major White, and Lieutenant Smith, in the Mennonite graveyard above Kulpsville, is said to have died at Heist's tavern, having been brought that far in a wagon. The Friends' meeting-house, according to tradition, was used as a hospital, and a number of soldiers who died in it are believed to have been buried in the south corner of the graveyard, where there is now a considerable space with no stones or other marks.

During the winter of 1777-78, while the Americans were at Valley Forge, and the British in Philadelphia, scouting and foraging parties were continually moving through the township.

General Lacey, with his militia, was occasionally here, and some of his official reports are dated at North Wales. It is a tradition that a party of his men had been posted at the tavern (now William H. Jenkins's store, then belonging to Jacob Wentz, of Worcester), on the turnpike above the meeting-house, and that as they were carelessly marching away, with their muskets laid in their baggage wagon, for greater ease of movement, a detachment of British surprised and captured them. This incident is so fairly characteristic of the militia-men whom Lacey was trying to make serviceable to the American cause, that it may be regarded as true. As an offset, however, there is the further tradition that John Fries, of Hatfield, afterward the famous auctioneer who raised the "Rebellion" of 1798 against the window tax, "on one occasion, while the British held Philadelphia, headed a party of his neighbors, gave pursuit to the light horse that were driving stolen cattle to the city, and rescued them about the Spring-House tavern."

Another affair at the Spring-House is described in the *New Jersey Gazette*, the patriot sheet published at Burlington, while the British held Philadelphia,— of the date of February 18, 1778, as follows:

ON SATURDAY LAST (FEBRUARY 15, 1778), A CONsiderable body of British Light Infantry, accompanied by a party of light horse, made an excursion into the country as high as a place called the Spring-House Tavern (Gwynedd Township, Philadelphia County), about sixteen miles from Philadelphia, where they made prisoners a Major Wright of the Pennsylvania Militia, and a number of persons in the Civil Department, such as Magistrates, Assessors, Constables, etc., who were pointed out by the Tories inhabiting that neighborhood. The Enemy went in three divisions, part of them through Germantown, where they broke many windows, seized all the leather, stockings, etc., and returned to Philadelphia on the evening of the same day, after having committed many other acts of licentiousness and cruelty on the persons of those they term Rebels.

REVOLUTIONARY DETAILS. 311

This incursion was certainly one of the boldest and most serious which the royal troops attempted. It is barely possible that it and the traditional surprise at Wentz's tavern, mentioned above, may have been the same affair. The allusion to "the Tories inhabiting that neighborhood" must be taken with many grains of allowance: how thorough the sympathy even of the non-fighting Friends was for the American cause, and how much they dreaded the royal troops, is fully disclosed in the pages of the Sally Wister Journal, in the preceding chapter.

The Friends, as a body, took no part in the war, on either side. Their peace principles were fairly preserved. A few entered the revolutionary service, but none in Gwynedd, so far as there is evidence, took the king's side. Mordecai Roberts, Eldad's son, is said to have served in the Continental army and fought at Germantown. The meeting records show that he was disciplined for "joining the military men in their exercises," and finally disowned, in June, 1777. In September, 1779, the minutes mention another case where "—— —— consented to the payment of a Fine in Lieu of Personal Military Service; which in writing he acknowledged sorrow for, but afterwards appealed to have the like fine remitted, and also was present at a muster, from which it appears that his sorrow was not such as worketh true repentance," etc., etc. In December, 1779, Joseph Ambler, son of John, makes acknowledgment for paying a fine in lieu of personal military service, and taking the oath of allegiance.[1]

Under the militia law of that time, all the men within the military age were enrolled by companies, and regarded as members of these, whether they mustered or not. If they did not attend muster, or respond when called into service, they incurred a fine. In Gwynedd township there were two such com-

---

[1] These are, however, a very small part of the similar instances. My friend Charles Roberts, of Philadelphia, who has more carefully inspected the meeting records, says there were many disownments for taking part in the war,—as many as a dozen on one meeting day.

panies, and in Montgomery one. The officer for the lower division of Gwynedd, was at first Captain Dull (Christian, the tavern keeper at Spring-House, no doubt), and subsequently Captain Troxel; in the upper division, Captain Bloom; and in Montgomery, Captain Hines. The companies belonged to "the Fourth Battalion of Philadelphia County Militia, commanded by Colonel William Dean." Printed accounts, showing the fines collected between 1777 and 1780 from those persons who did not muster or march when called on, are in existence, and one list of collections for Gwynedd is as follows:

Captain Dull's Company, in Gwynedd, Lower Division.

Name.	Fines. £ s. d.	Name.	Fines. £ s. d.
Christian Wolfinger,	15 0 0	Brought forward,	463 15 0
Enoch Morgan,	20 0 0	Ezekiel Cleaver, jun.,	37 10 0
George Selsor,	20 0 0	Daniel Morgan,	37 10 0
Conrad Gearhart,	22 10 0	William Stemple,	37 10 0
Joseph Leblon,	22 10 0	David Roberts,	37 10 0
John Smyth,	22 10 0	John Evans,	37 10 0
Geo. A. Snyder,	22 10 0	Garret Clemens,	37 10 0
William Moore,	15 0 0	John Everhart,	37 10 0
Adam Fleck,	22 10 0	William Roberts,	22 10 0
John Getter,	22 10 0	William Johnstone,	37 10 0
Ezekiel Cleaver,	37 10 0	Owen Evans,	37 10 0
Hugh Foulk,	37 10 0	John Sidons,	15 0 0
Joshua Foulk,	37 10 0	Nicholas Rial,	37 10 0
Levi Foulk,	37 10 0	Conrad Clime,	6 0 0
Jesse Foulk,	37 10 0	John Singer,	37 10 0
Griffith Edwards,	37 10 0	John Selsor,	20 0 0
Samuel Sidons,	22 10 0	Jacob Preston,	11 5 0
David Morris,	11 5 0	Thomas Evans,	37 10 0
Carried forward,	463 15 0	Total,	988 10 0

REVOLUTIONARY DETAILS. 313

Captain Bloom's Company, Upper Division of Gwynedd.

Name.	Fines. £ s. d.	Name.	Fines. £ s. d.
Jacob Wisner,	20 0 0	Brought forward,	380 4 0
Benjamin Harry,	20 0 0	John Luken,	37 10 0
Rees Roberts,	20 0 0	Daniel Hoffman,	37 10 0
Samuel Wheeler,	20 0 0	Thomas Shoemaker,	37 10 0
Melchoir Crible,	20 0 0	William Hoffman,	37 10 0
Caleb Foulk,	22 10 0	John Thomson,	30 0 0
Levi Jenkins,	22 10 0	George Roberts,	37 10 0
John Erwin,	22 10 0	Jacob Young,	37 10 0
Jacob Smith,	22 10 0	Isaac Kulp,	30 0 0
Job Luken,	22 10 0	Joseph Long,	37 10 0
John Dilcart,	9 0 0	Jacob Albright,	22 10 0
Jacob Wiont,	7 10 0	Isaac Lewis,	28 2 6
Samuel Casner,	28 2 0	Amos Roberts,	20 0 0
William Springer,	28 2 0	Joseph Lewis,	37 10 0
John Evans,	20 0 0	David Harry,	20 0 0
William Williams,	37 10 0	George Maris,	37 10 0
Jacob Hisler,	37 10 0	Rees Harry,	15 0 0
Carried forward,	380 4 0	Total,	935 17 6

These fines, in the case of strict Friends, must have been obtained by seizure and sale of some of their property, as they could not, under their Discipline, pay them voluntarily. Another list of collections, later than that given above, shows much heavier fines, several running up to £200, and Garret Clemens,[1] in the lower division, paying £300. These were sums in Continental currency, however, and therefore not so extremely serious as they appear.

When the American army moved from Valley Forge to New Jersey, in June, 1778, the whole of it doubtless marched through Gwynedd, and at least a part of it encamped there over night, June 19–20. We may repeat here the lines from Miss Wister's journal, which fix these facts:

---
[1] He was not a Friend, but a Mennonite, or a Dunker.

June 19. Dr. Gould came here to-night. Our army are about six miles off on their march to the Jerseys.

June 20. Owen Foulke arrived just now. The army began their march at six this morning, by their house. Our worthy General Smallwood breakfasted at Uncle Caleb's. Our brave, our heroic General Washington was escorted by fifty of the Life-Guard with drawn swords.

The march from Valley Forge was down the main roads, including the Perkiomen and Skippack, to the Swedes' Ford road, and then across on it by Doylestown to Wells's Ferry (New Hope), where the army crossed the river into New Jersey. That Washington himself encamped in Gwynedd on the night of the 19th is most likely: Owen Foulke's explanations to the family at Penllyn show that he rode by Caleb's house[1] next morning, and it is known that he reached Doylestown that night.

---

[1] The old Meredith house, now J. Lukens's, repeatedly mentioned in this volume.

XXI.

Taxables in Gwynedd in 1776.

THE following is the assessor's list[1] of taxables in Gwynedd in the year 1776. It shows the names of all who were holders of land, those who had horses and cows, and the number of such animals, and the names of those "single men" who were liable only to a poll-tax. The records show that John Jenkins was the assessor, and Henry Bergey the collector.

Name.	Land, acres.	Horses.	Cows.	Name.	Land, acres.	Horses.	Cows.
Jesse Foulke,	210	6	6	Peter Buck,	50	1	2
Thomas Evans,	230	2	6	George Shelmire,	96	1	1
George Snider,	150	3	6	George Shelmire, jr.,		3	2
Michael Hawke,	150	2	4	William Ervin,	100	2	2
Jephthah Lewis,	200	2	6	Alexander Major,	150	2	6
Eneas Lewis,	160	2	3	Joshua Foulk,	200	3	6
Isaac Lewis,		2	3	John Sparry,	100	2	5
Reese Harry,	200	2	6	George Fleck,		2	3
Humphrey Jones,	180	3	5	Ann Week,	100		
Geo. Gossinger,	100	2	5	George Week,	7	1	1
Melchior Crible,	119	3	5	Samuel Castner,	50	2	4
Philip Hood,	300	4	6	John Everhart,	150	2	4
Isaac Kolb,	143	3	6	Nicholas Rile,	50	2	6
Isaac Kolb, jr.,	143	2	5	Adam Fleck,	140	3	6
Philip Heist,	120	2	4	John Davis, jun.,	75	1	1
John Thomson,	123	3	4	David Davis,	75	3	3
Thomas Shoemaker,	110	2	3	Robert Davis,	75		
Margaret Johnson,	100	2	4	Samuel Kastner,	80		2

[1] For the copy of the records here used I am indebted to the kindness of Mr. William J. Buck.

Name		
Stephen Bloom,	35	2 . 2
Daniel Williams,	130	3 . 4
Amos Roberts,	189	3 . 8
John Davis,	170	3 . 6
Enoch Morgan,	100	2 . 5
Nicholas Selser,	100	2 . 4
Morris Morris,	30	1 . 2
Henry Rapp,		1 . 1
George Miller,		
Jacob Albrough,		2 . 2
Samuel Gamble,	29	1 . 1
Martin Swink,	160	2 . 4
Abram Donnenhauer,	135	2 . 6
Jacob Heistler,	147	4 . 4
Henry Snider,	175	3 . 6
Peter Troxall,	170	3 . 6
John Troxall,	170	3 . 6
Thomas Evans, jr.,	140	2 . 4
Baltzer Spitznagel,		. 1
William Williams,	120	3 . 5
George Maris,	450	4 . 6
Conrad Dimond,	40	1 . 2
Walter Howell,	100	2 . 2
Thomas Layman,		. 1
Michael Hoffman,	200	. 2
Jacob Sigfried,		1 . 2
Barnaby Beaver,	50	
Mathew Lukens,	130	2 . 6
Martin Hoffman,		. 1
John Jenkins,	252	3 . 5
Sarah Griffith,	300	2 . 3
Joseph Griffith,	100	2 . 2
Benjamin Rosenboyer,	50	1 . 2
John Knipe,	150	1 . 3
William Dixey,	10	1 . 1
Garret Clemens,	136	3 . 6
John Conrad,	60	2 . 3
Christian Dull,	8	1 . 1
John Shelmire,	14	1 . 1
Daniel Leblance,	75	2 . 2
William Roberts,	100	2 . 4
Ezekiel Cleaver,	140	4 . 8
John Evans,	250	3 . 8
Michael Cousler,	40	2 . 2
Peter Young,	50	1 . 4
Jacob Smith,	100	1 . 2
Jacob Smith, Jr.,		1 . 2
Jacob Wiant,	130	3 . 4
Peter Hoffman,		1 . 2
Levi Foulke,	100	3 . 6
Martin Raker,	57	2 . 2
Wm. Johnson,	123	2 . 2
Hugh Foulke,		3 . 2
Conrad Gerhart,	120	2 . 5
John Siddons,		1 . 1
Conrad Smith,		2 . 2
William Moore,		2 . 2
Job Lukens,	20	1 . 1
Henry Bergey,	50	2 . 3
Adam Smith,		1 . 1
Matthias Booz,		. 1
Wendle Fetter,	15	. 1
William Springer,		2 . 4
John Singer,	50	1 . 2
Philip Hurst,	80	2 . 5
John Troxall,	25	2 . 1
Wm. Hoffman,		2 . 4
Evan Davis,	15	. 1
Nicholas Shubert,	7	. 1
Christian Delacourt,		
Michael Itzell,	1	. 1
Jacob Brown,		. 2
Jacob Walton,		1 . 1
Jacob Preston,		
John Delacourt,		. 2
Benjamin Williams,		
Philip Berkheimer,		

TAXABLES IN GWYNEDD IN 1776.

Single Men.

Hugh Evans,	Joseph Long,	John Selser,
John Jenkins, jr.,	John Williams,	Christian Knipe,
John Kidney,	Evan Roberts,	George Sperry,
John Evans,	Eleazar Williams,	Wm. Oman,
Robert Roberts,	Tillman Kolb,	Samuel Singer,
David Harry, jr.,	Griffith Edwards,	Conrad Booz,
Reese Harry,	Jacob Booz,	George Ganger,
Benj. Harry,	Wm. Smith,	Joseph Yost,
Joseph Lewis,	Reese Roberts,	Benj. Gregory,
John Johnson,	Robert Roberts,	Ab'm Donnenhauer.
Enoch Morgan,	Henry Selser,	

The list gives some miscellaneous information. It states that Jesse Foulke had a "grist and saw mill," Thomas Evans and George Snider had each "1 servant," Amos Roberts had "9 children," so likewise had Henry Snider; Thomas Evans, jun., "supports his mother," Barnaby Beaver had a "grist mill," and Matthew Lukens a "saw mill;" William Dixey is marked "cripple," William Ervin "aged," Christian Dull "tavern," and Alexander Major "8 children."

Besides those in the list who have already been particularly alluded to in the genealogical or other preceding chapters, some details may be conveniently added here concerning a few others.

Jephthah and Enos Lewis were brothers, the sons of William Lewis.[1] Their land was on the Wissahickon, between the present stations of Acorn and Lukens, on the Stony Creek railroad. (It forms, now, at least four farms: those of George S. Thomas, the heirs of Zebedee Comly, John Nicom, and Job Supplee.) Jephthah Lewis died in December, 1786. His wife's name was Ann, and he left a daughter Mary, and a son Joseph. The last named lived a bachelor, very saving and rather eccentric, and died in February, 1828, aged 83. He was a justice of the peace for many years, well known in his time, and after his death long remembered, as "'Squire Josey" Lewis. His house

---

[1] See details concerning him, pp. 67-68.

was on the Thomas farm, south-west of the creek. Among his peculiarities was his great care of his timber land, as he was anxious lest he should not have enough fire-wood to last him his life-time. Much of his farm was covered with woods, making a favorite resort for the "gunners" of the country about, though the 'Squire was chary of his permission to come upon his premises, especially after finding that somebody had "holed" a 'possum, or perhaps a 'coon, and had cut down the tree to make sure of their prize.[2] After his death, the woodland was laid off in lots by a survey made by Cadwallader Foulke, and the timber sold at public sale. The homestead farm, 108 acres, was bought by Joseph Williams, who sold it in 1856 to Edward Barber, and the portion east of the creek, 101 acres, was bought by Jacob Schwenk, who sold in 1846 to Zebedee Comly.

Enos Lewis (called Eneas, in the assessor's list) owned the land now Job Supplee's and John Nicom's. His house is presumed to have been Job Supplee's present house. His wife, married 1736, was Jane, daughter of Ellis Lewis, the elder, of Upper Dublin, and their children included a son Isaac, and a daughter Ellen. These two children inherited Enos's estate. Ellen having married Edward Roberts (son of Robert, of Gwy-

---

[2] The author's great uncle, Jesse Jenkins, an enthusiastic hunter and fisher, was one who enjoyed the shooting in 'Squire Josey's woods, and was rather a favorite in getting his permission for it. Mr. Mathews says that on the day of the 'Squire's funeral "a terrible storm of snow and wind prevailed, rendering the roads almost impassable. A few friends and neighbors gathered early in the morning, and with great difficulty conveyed his body to its last resting place at Gwynedd. When they returned, a much larger number had collected, and the funeral rites were celebrated in old-fashioned style." When his personal property was sold, "an immense number of articles and utensils were found about the premises, and the sale never had a parallel in the township. Levi Jenkins, of Montgomery, was the auctioneer, and it required five days to dispose of the goods." His estate was valued at $60,000, and over $1,000 in money was found secreted about the premises His property went to collateral heirs.

nedd), her son Enos got the present Nicom place,[1] by his grandfather's will; and the homestead was received by Isaac. Jephthah died August 20, 1778. Isaac married Sarah Jenkins,[2] daughter of John, the elder of that name (the one named above as assessor, 1776), but died a comparatively young man (his will dated December 30, 1792), leaving three children, Enos, Ann, and Mary. Of these, Enos married Margaret Dewees, of Trappe (who survives, 1884, aged about 84), but left no issue; Ann married Joseph Reiff, of Upper Dublin, and left five children: Enos L., Jacob, Isaac, Sarah, and Mary; and Mary married Israel Bringhurst, of Trappe, and had a large family.[3]

Rees Harry's land included the present (or recent) farms of Hunter E. Van Leer, Thomas Layman, and T. Peterson, on the Wissahickon, between Mumbower's mill and North Wales. Rees Harry, here named, was the son of the Rees Harry who is named in the freeholders' list of 1734. The latter was the son of David

---

[1] This property Enos held to his death, July 23, 1820, when it passed to his children, Nathan, John, Edward, and Ann. Ann d. 1849; her brothers were quiet bachelors, but Nathan, late in life, married Barbara Root, and d. 1860, leaving three children.

[2] Sarah, after her husband's death, kept store at Montgomery Square. Among the 'Squire John Roberts papers is her bill for sundry supplies furnished him, in 1802-3—candles, 1 s. 4½ d. per ℔.; sugar, 11¼ d.; coffee, 1 s. 10½ d.; tea, 1 s. 10½ d. per quarter lb.; molasses, 2 s. 9½ d. per half gallon; brimstone, 8 d. per ℔.; whiskey (2 items in a pretty long bill), 1 s. 10½ d. per quart; and a spelling book, a cyphering book, an "assistant" (arithmetic), and other articles.

[3] Mary Lewis b. July 4, 1771, m. September 27, 1792, d. August 11, 1846. Their children were seven: (1) William M., d. 1857, unm.; (2) Enos L., physician, graduate Univ. of Penna., successful practitioner at Lawrenceville, Chester Co., d. 1863, unm.; (3) Wright A. Bringhurst, of Trappe, member Legislature of Penna., 1835-36, d. 1876, unm., leaving estate of $160,000, of which he left about $110,000 to Upper Providence township and Norristown and Pottstown boroughs, to be invested in dwelling houses, and the rents used for the benefit of the poor; (4) Israel, jr., b. 1804, accidentally killed, 1816; (5) Anne, m. Wm. B. Hahn, M. D., d. 1880, without issue; (6) Lewis B., M. D., graduate Univ. of Penna., d. unm., 1832, at Louisville, Ky., while on a Southern tour; (7) Mary Matilda, m. Francis Hobson, of Limerick, and had issue Frank M., Sarah A. (F. M. Hobson m. Lizzie Gotwalts, and had issue: Mary M., and Freeland G. Hobson, Esq., of the Montgomery Co. bar.)

Harry, of Plymouth, and married, 1727, Mary Price, of Haverford. He (Rees, the elder) died about 1739; his son Rees died 1788. In the latter's will six children are mentioned: Benjamin, John, David, Jane, Ann, Lydia. Benjamin Harry d. about 1810, unmarried, leaving a large estate, in which his sister Ann had a life right. After her death, in 1822, 228 acres of it, were sold to Samuel Maulsby, who in 1833 sold to Thomas Smith. (This included the present Van Leer farm, and the Frank Johnson farm, and was in part the same as Rees Harry's land of 1776.)

Isaac Kolb (now Kulp) was from Germany, and acquired (between 1759 and 1769) the land now, or recently, Julius Schlemme's and Simon Kulp's farms, east of North Wales. He was, it is believed, a Mennonite. His son Isaac, jr., born December, 1750, married, 1778, Rachel Johnson, and died 1828. He had seven children: Benjamin, Elizabeth, Catharine, Mary, Jacob, Sophia, and John. Benjamin, born August 20, 1779, died May 16, 1862, married Ellen Hoxworth, daughter of Edward and Mary, of Hatfield, and had eight children, including Isaac, Enos, Simon and Oliver, and Ann, who married Asa Thomas.

Philip Heist's land lay on the hill, below North Wales, and included the farms of J. S. Zebley and Henry Ray. Heist died between 1776, in which year he made his will, and 1780, when his executors conveyed half an acre of land to trustees for the erection of St. Peter's church.

Thomas Shoemaker was the son of George, of Warrington, Bucks county, and married Mary Ambler, daughter of Joseph, of Montgomery. He owned the farm north-east of North Wales, which remained many years in his family, and is now or recently was, the property of ——— McKee.

Wendel Fetter was a German, and bought, in 1773, the fifteen acre lot back of North Wales (adjoining Thomas Shoemaker), which Robert Roberts had left by his will, in 1760, to his daughter Ellen.[1] The lot belonged from 1827 to 1852 to

---

[1] See p. 193.

Christian Godfrey Speelman, a devout German Methodist, who sometimes held meetings in his own house, and afterward to Abel Stockdale, and later to Frank Jones.

Amos Roberts' farm included the Silas White and adjoining properties (the old home of Robert Evans, the first settler, was upon it).

Martin Swink's land was on the turnpike, below North Wales, including the present farm of Fritz Hartman (the home of Thomas Evans, the first settler). Swink sold it to George Heist, in 1784, and he set up a tavern there.

Abram Danenhower's land was the George W. Danenhower place near Kneedler's, now occupied by Frank Myers (the home of William John,[1] the first settler).

Jacob Heisler owned the farm on the Allentown road, afterward the Kneedlers', where he established the tavern.

The Troxalls owned the property at Mumbower's mill. They sold it in 1777 to Samuel Wheeler.

Barnaby Beaver, who had the grist-mill, owned back of North Wales, and his mill was that which still exists there, on the Wissahickon.

John Jenkins' land in Gwynedd was at Lansdale, and below the township line.

Garret Clemens lived in the east corner of the township. The old abandoned stone house on the Welsh road (township line) was his place of residence. He was a religious man, a Dunker probably, and was heavily fined, as the preceding chapter shows, for not bearing arms. His wife was Keturah; their daughter Mary married Charles Hubbs, one of the sons of John Hubbs and Jane Evans.[2]

---

[1] See p. 65.

[2] See Evans Genealogy, p. 161. Charles Hubbs was some time a resident at Germantown; he studied medicine (in a power of attorney to Amos Lewis, about 1806, he calls himself "apothecary"), afterward lived in Worcester township, removed to Pipe Creek, in Western Maryland (where he was in 1807), and later

Christian Dull, described as having a "tavern," set up the hotel at Spring-House, a few years before the Revolution, and he continued there for many years. He was a hard, and perhaps a grasping man; at any rate, traditions were long maintained of some of his sharp dealings.[1] Even more severe things were said about him, as appears by some advertisements in the Philadelphia newspapers. Here is one from the Philadelphia *Gazette* of February 17, 1783:

NORTH WALES, February 11, 1783.

WHEREAS, SOME EVIL PERSON HAS PROPAGATED a report very injurious and hurtful to my character, I hereby challenge such to appear in an open, bold manner, and meet me on the ground of Justice, and dare them to impeach me with any act unbecoming a gentleman and an honest man, which character I have ever held dear; and I further offer a reward of ONE HUNDRED GUINEAS to any person or persons who will prove the author of a report that I was privy to robbing a Collector — a circumstance I totally deny, either with respect to collectors, or any person or persons; and now charge the author, or authors, of such scandalous reports to be lying calumniators, and am determined to prosecute any person who may in future endeavor to circulate such report to my disadvantage.

CHRISTIAN DULL.

---

to Mt. Pleasant, Ohio. He has numerous descendants in the West. He joined the Dunkers, and became a preacher; and was a man of marked character. His son, John Evans Hubbs, m. Louisa Stitcher, and had one daughter, Virginia, now of Philadelphia. After his death Louisa m. Samuel Gillingham, of Philadelphia.

[1] One story, whose date, I think, must have been toward the close of Dull's life, was to this effect: He had for an occasional customer at his bar, the village blacksmith, and the latter had indiscreetly allowed some of his drams to be "chalked down." In time, the landlord produced a bill, with such length of items that the smith was astonished. It read: "To one glass of whisky. To ditto. To ditto. To ditto. To ditto." on down the sheet, and the total was of alarming figures. The blacksmith protested, especially complaining of the "ditto," alleging that he had had but a few drinks, but in vain; Dull was inexorable, and the bill had to stand. The blacksmith, however, waited his chance to get even, and in time found it. The hostler's bucket had to be re-hooped, and as the work was left to be charged against Dull, the bill was delayed for some time, and thus brought in: "To hooping the hostler's bucket. To ditto. To ditto. To ditto." and so on, at much length, equaling the account for drinks. The landlord now objected, but the smith was inexorable in his turn, and, as the story goes, got his account allowed as an offset to the other.

Six years later Christian was still under the necessity of advertising rewards for the discovery of his defamers. The *Gazette* of April 1, 1789, contains the following:

MONTGOMERY COUNTY, March 28, 1789.

ONE HUNDRED GUINEAS REWARD.— WHEREAS, a false and wicked report has been contrived, and for some weeks past spread through the City of Philadelphia and several of the Counties, charging the subscriber and his wife, who keep the Spring-House Tavern, in Montgomery County, with the MURDER, etc., of one or more travellers, in order to get their property, conceiving it to be my duty, which I owe to the community of which I am a member, to my relations, and friends, and neighbors, and particularly to a tender wife and seven children (several of them young and helpless), whose welfare or misery in life greatly depend upon the character which I have, and shall leave after me, to endeavor to bring to light such dark and horrible Assassins of Character, I do hereby offer a reward of ONE HUNDRED GUINEAS to any person who shall discover to me any legal evidence of the contriver of said charge, or of the author, or authors, of the report, and of ONE HALF JOHANNES for any certain information whereby such discovery may be made.

CHRISTIAN DULL.

Dull lived on into the present century (his death occurred about 1821), and Esquire John Roberts was one of the executors of his estate. He left a son, Christian Dull, jr., who was a person of education, at least, and was some time a school teacher. From papers left by 'Squire John, however, it appears that he (the son) was in debt, and harassed by his creditors. A letter from him, in 1822, is written from the jail at Norristown, where he was confined for debt. It shows good penmanship, and is clearly expressed, as will appear:

July 28th, 1822.

Friend Roberts:—I was advised to serve my creditor with a bread notice, but he has not come forward to pay my weekly allowance. I shall be removed next Thursday before Judge McNeill for a clearance, which will cost $1 to the Gaoler, one dollar for serving the notices, 35 cents turnkey fees, and $2 for my board two weeks at 14 cents per day, making the amount of $4.35, which I hope you will send me, or else I must let him (the Gaoler) have my coat, which is worth $10. I cannot get away without, and the longer I stay the more expense on me. Altho' you say it is the most proper place for me to be at, [yet] if I leave my coat, which is a good one, I will have to have a new one this winter. I will not be allowed more than $4.35 for the coat. I have sent a receipt, which I hope will answer; you have not any money of mine in your hands, but will have, and then can pay yourself. I should suppose there was no risk on your part. I am your friend as usual, C. DULL.

P. S. If I do not get money at this time from you I will have to have new bread notices served and [words illegible] and a dollar a week board. I have no one to assist me unless you do.[1]

Martin Raker, who is named as having fifty-seven acres, lived near where Lansdale now is, and his property is now in the possession of Charles S. Jenkins. He was a Lutheran, and one of the four first trustees of St. Peter's church, below North Wales.

George Snyder (properly George Adam Snyder) was a German, who owned the Isaac Ellis farm (now James Gillen's), on the Upper Dublin line, with other property. He got it in 1762, of Francis Titus, and died 1792, leaving three sons: Adam, Jacob, and John.

John Everhart owned the farm now Charles Lower's (formerly John Devereux's), in the lower end of the township. He bought in 1762, of George Klippinger, of Upper Dublin (he having bought of Rowland Hugh, son of John, the first settler), and sold it in 1793 to David Lukens.

---

[1] As a specimen of the experience of the occupant of a debtor's prison, so late as 1822, this letter seems worth printing in full, aside from any personal interest it may have. Dull was no doubt enlarged at this time; there are other papers relating to him in the John Roberts collection, of dates 1821 and 1823.

XXII.

The Boones, Lincolns, and Hanks.

THE Boones, Lincolns, and Hanks all appear on the Gwynedd meeting records, though none of either name probably resided in the township in early times. George Boone, the elder, the first of his family known to us, was from Bradwinch, near Exeter, in Devonshire, and seems to have come over in 1717. At any rate, the Gwynedd meeting records show this minute, dated 31st of 10th month (December), in that year:

George Boone, senior, produced a certificate of his Good Life and Conversation from the Monthly [Meeting] att Callumpton, in Great Britain, w^h was read & well rec'd.

This George, the elder, died in Berks county (the Oley or Exeter Friends' settlement), February 2, 1740, aged 78 years. He left, it is said, "eight children, fifty-two grandchildren, ten great-grandchildren,—in all seventy, the number that Jacob took down to Egypt." His wife was Mary, who was born in the same place as her husband, and died aged 72. They were both buried in the Friends' ground at Oley.

In 1721, John Rumford, who had been a member with Friends, at Haverford, and George Boone, who had been a member at Abington, being now settled at Oley, applied at the same time to Gwynedd meeting, for membership. This George was the son of the other; he had been several years at Abington (and I think, therefore, came over before his father), where he was clerk of the monthly meeting, and a prominent and useful man. He had married, in 1713, Deborah Howell (b. 8th mo. 28, 1691, d. 1st mo. 26, 1759, at Oley), daughter of William and

Mary. Deborah was a preacher, and Exeter (Oley) monthly meeting left a memorial of her. She and George had ten children: George, Mary, Hannah, Deborah, Dinah, William, Josiah, Jeremiah, Abigail, and Hezekiah, their births ranging from 1714 to 1734. (The first five are recorded at Gwynedd, before the establishment of the Oley monthly meeting.) William married Sarah Lincoln, 1748.

Besides this son George, the elder George Boone had, as stated above, seven other children: including Squire, who m. Sarah Morgan, Mary, who m. John Webb, James, who m. Mary Foulke,[1] Joseph Benjamin, and two others. Squire and Sarah Boone had nine children (perhaps more), recorded at Oley from 1724 to 1740. Of these Daniel, the Kentucky pioneer, was the fourth son and sixth child, and the meeting records give his birth, 8th mo. (October) 22, 1734. I have no doubt that Squire Boone was in Berks county with the other members of his family, in 1820, or thereabout; and as he bought 250 acres of land in what is now Exeter township, in 1730, it is beyond reasonable question that his son Daniel was born there in 1744. The various speculations as to the place of his birth, by which it is assigned to Bristol, Bucks county, and other locations, seem to have no good foundation whatever.

Squire Boone was one of the trustees of the property of Oley meeting, in 1736, showing both his substantial character and Quaker affiliations, at that date. But he is said to have been disowned in 1748 for countenancing the "disorderly" marriage of his son Israel, the previous year. A little later it was[2] that he removed with his family to North Carolina, settling at Holomant ford, on the river Yadkin. From there, after he grew to manhood, Daniel went over into Kentucky, and

---

[1] For the first two of these marriages, both at Gwynedd meeting, see list, p. 114. For the last see Foulke Genealogy, p. 213.

[2] James Boone's family Bible says: "They left Exeter on the 1st day of May, 1750."

entered upon his famous career as the explorer and pioneer settler of that State.[1]

The Lincolns were an Oley family, some of them Friends. They intermarried repeatedly with the Boones, and were connected also with the Foulkes. But they had only a slight, if any, connection with Gwynedd, as the monthly meeting at Oley was established soon after Mordecai Lincoln, the first of the name in that neighborhood, arrived there. He, it is said, was born in Massachusetts, removed to New Jersey, bought lands there in 1720, and again removed, before 1735, to the Oley settlement. (His home was in Amity township.) He was probably twice married. He died between February 23, 1735, and June 7, 1736 (these being the dates of making and proving his will), leaving lands in New Jersey to his son John, and to his daughters Hannah, Mary, Ann, and Sarah; and the home-

---

[1] Among the papers of my grandfather, Chas. F. Jenkins, I find this letter:

WASHINGTON TOWN, MASON COUNTY, KEN.

Respected Friend:—I expect thee art ready to conclude that I have forgot thee being so far off, but thee may rest ashured that I have not. I often think of the many agreeable hours we have spent in conversation and sociability, which distance now deprives us of. But no more Introduction—I proceed to give thee a little sketch of the times. After my being disappointed in getting my land from Col. Boon, as probably thee may have heard before now, which lay'd me under the necessaty of following my trade. Since I came to this place and after three months paying for my board and washing, I made an acquaintance with a young woman which after a while I married, and now I live in as much harmony with her I flatter myself as ever man and wife did and find the matrimonial life far more agreeable than I ever Expected to do. I have told thee what I have done, I will inform thee what I am doing. I have taken a five acre Lot to put corn in to the shares, my share will be two-thirds of the crop, which if the season proves favorable I expect an Hundred and Seventy Bushels of Corn. Here is great encouragement for farmers, much more than for mechanicks. I must stop wrighting for I have no more room and paper is scarce in this town.

May 10th, 1790.   ABSALOM THOMAS.

A memorandum on the letter says A. T. was the first cousin of Margaret Foulke (dau. of Theophilus, afterward wife of Cadwallader, the surveyor), to whom the letter was addressed. "He was one of the pioneers of Kentucky, and left Richland to seek his future under the celebrated Col. Daniel Boone."

stead lands in Amity to his sons Mordecai and Thomas. He also made provision for an expected child, and this, without doubt, was Abraham Lincoln (who d. 1806, aged 70), who married Ann Boone.[1] John, the eldest son,—a half brother only of Abraham, who was by the second wife,—was the direct ancestor of Abraham Lincoln, President of the United States. He, John, sold his Jersey land in 1748, and about 1750 removed southward, going ultimately to Rockingham county, Virginia, where he settled. His son Abraham went over into Kentucky in 1782, but was killed there two years later, by the Indians. He and Daniel Boone were no doubt well acquainted. Daniel at least twice (October, 1781, and February, 1788) returned to visit his relations in Berks county, and he would naturally enough have passed through Virginia, and tarried with his neighbors and kinsfolk, the Lincolns of Rockingham county.

Abraham Lincoln, who was killed in 1784, in an Indian fight (in which his son Mordecai, a boy of 14, killed one of the Indians), had three sons: Mordecai, Josiah, and Thomas. The President was the son of the last named,—his only child.

It will be observed that the removal of Squire Boone and his family to North Carolina, and of the Lincolns to Virginia, was at about the same period — 1750. There was, at that time, an extensive emigration to the Southern States from the settlements in Eastern Pennsylvania. It was a very interesting movement, and the history of it would be well worth following in detail. With it, besides the Boones and Lincolns, went another family, the Hanks, and these were more closely connected with Gwynedd than either of the others.[2] The precise name of the head of the Hank family who thus removed, is uncertain, but

---

[1] Ann was the daughter of Mary Foulke; see page 213.

[2] John Hanke, of Whitemarsh, m. Sarah Evans, of Gwynedd, dau. of Cadwallader, the immigrant. See pp. 110-149. (She, after his death, m. Thomas Williams; see p. 116.) It was the daughter of John and Sarah, Jane Hank, who was the wife of John Roberts, of Whitpain, and the mother of 'Squire Job Roberts.

Mr. David J. Lincoln, of Birdsboro', Berks county, in a letter to me, September, 1883, thinks it was John, and says: "He lived on the Perkiomen turnpike, six miles east of Reading, in Exeter township, and within half a mile of Mordecai Lincoln, great-great-grandfather of the President. This John Hank, with John and Benjamin Lincoln, moved to Fayette county, and from there Mr. Hank went southward."

As to a removal, first, to Fayette county, I do not know; but, as has already been noted (p. 196), John Hank was in Rockingham county, Va., at least as early as 1787, when his daughter Hannah married Asa Lupton. That this John was the one described by Mr. Lincoln is probable, or he may have been a son of the Berks county man, for the latter was in all probability the same John Hank who was born 1712, the son of the Whitemarsh yeoman and Sarah Evans, of Gwynedd.[1]

Good-natured, easy-going Thomas Lincoln, of Kentucky, married, for his first wife, Nancy Hank. The tradition was that her family were from Virginia. She was a tall woman, above middle height, with black hair, uneducated, but of marked character, and a mind naturally vigorous. Her experience in the rude frontier life, with a husband who did not "get along," was hard. The glimpses we get of her in the biographies of her great son are sombre, and probably to her the President owed that underlying element of sad thoughtfulness in his nature, always so apparent, and so in contrast with the humorous surface traits that came from his father. Nancy Hank, I have no doubt, was the daughter, or granddaughter, of that John who was in Rockingham county, Virginia, in 1787. Her family name was English, but her black hair we may believe she had from the Welsh blood of her ancestress Sarah Evans, of Gwynedd.

---

[1] See p. 149.

XXIII.

St. Peter's Church.

NO other settled place of worship than the Friends' meeting existed in Gwynedd until the Revolution. Those who were Baptists had their membership at Montgomery; any Episcopalians there might have been went to St. Thomas's, at Whitemarsh; and the Schwenkfeldters had their meeting in Towamencin. But the body of the German residents of the township, by the time of the Revolution, were of the Palatinate immigration from the upper Rhine, and were either Lutherans or German Reformed. They had within their reach the churches in Whitpain and Worcester. The German Reformed members went to Boehm's Church, which was founded at least as early as 1740, or to Wentz's Church, in Worcester; while the Lutheran Church of St. John's, in Whitpain, above Centre Square, dates back of 1770. In all of these the Gwynedd people were interested: Michael Henkey (Hænge?), George Gossinger, Adam Fleck, and Peter Young, of Gwynedd, were of the building committee of St. John's, in 1773, and Abram Danehower was one of the trustees to whom the committee conveyed the property.

About 1772, however, a movement had begun to build a church in Gwynedd, for the joint use of the Lutheran and German Reformed members. In that year, Philip Heist bought of Abraham Lukens, sen., 51 acres of land, on the northeasterly side of the turnpike, below North Wales, where the old burying-ground now is. Half an acre of his land he gave for the site of a church, and although he omitted, for some reason, to make a deed, a building was erected on it before 1780. In

ST. PETER'S CHURCH. 331

that year his executors made a deed, dated June 10th, for the ground, reciting that "the same is intended, and is hereby granted to remain for religious purposes: that is to say, for a church of worship already erected thereon for the use of the High Dutch Lutheran, and the High Dutch Reformed, or Presbyterian congregations," etc. It is said that this first building was a small frame edifice. It stood, no doubt, on the same spot where subsequently the large stone church of 1817 (torn down a few years ago, when both congregations had secured new buildings at North Wales), was erected.

To provide even the small house of frame doubtless taxed the resources of both congregations. It is the tradition that the first preachers held services in the open air, on the hillside where Heist's farm lay. This, however, could have been but temporary, for the reasons already stated, that Boehm's and Wentz's, at no great distance, supplied sanctuaries for the Reformed, and St. John's for the Lutherans.

The records of both congregations at St. Peter's are very limited. No early minute books are now discoverable, and it is even impracticable to give the names of the pastors of the Reformed congregation. For a list of the Lutheran pastors, notes concerning them, and other data, I am indebted to Rev. George Diehl Foust, who is now, 1884, in charge. The first pastor of whom we have knowledge (there must have been others earlier) was Rev. Anthony Hecht. He officiated from 1787 until 1792. In a record of the holy communion, administered July 13, 1788, that day is called "the day of consecration," which suggests that for some reason the church must have been used some time before it was consecrated. In a marriage record, made October 15, 1788, the church is spoken of as the "North Wales Congregation."

The next pastor was Rev. Jacob Van Buskirk, who began about 1793. He was born at Hackensack, N. J., February 11, 1739. It is said that he came to his death suddenly, August 5,

1800. He was about to start for his church, and was in the act of mounting his horse, when the Master whom he served called him. He lies buried near where stood the altar of the church in which he officiated.[1]

Next was Rev. Henry Geisenhainer. The length of his pastorate cannot be determined; but there is a record showing that while here he was married to Ann Maria Sherer by Rev. F. W. Geisenhainer, pastor of New Goshenhoppen church.

Next in the list is Rev. S. P. F. Kramer, and following him is Rev. "Whalebone," which must be Rev. C. F. Wildbahn, D. D., who is buried at Centre Square. After him was Rev. J. H. Rebenach, from 1805 to 1811. (During his pastorate occurred the murder of Henry Weaver,[2] at whose burial he officiated, and of which he made a brief record.)

Next appear the names of Revs. David and Solomon Schaeffer. They lived at Germantown, and must have held service here, though it must have been only temporarily.

The next pastor was Rev. John K. Weiand, from 1812 to 1826. He was the last pastor to officiate in the old frame structure. During his time the need of a new church was felt, for the winds and storms of nearly forty years had seriously affected the frail temple of worship. Rev. Mr. Foust has the original subscription book for the building of the second church. It is a large volume of sixty pages, and is kept very systematically. The first page, after expressing the object of the subscription,

---

[1] Mr. Van Buskirk owned the farm at Gwynedd station, recently the estate of Rodolphus Kent. At his death, he left a wife and ten children. His widow subsequently married Philip Hahn.

[2] This was a famous event in the local annals. As he passed along the road, H. W. was shot by some person concealed behind a corn shock in a field beside it. The time was the dusk of evening, October 5, 1805, the place on the State road, just at the turn near the Gwynedd-Montgomery line. The victim was the son of George Weaver, the Montgomery Square hotel-keeper. A man who was believed to have to have done the deed lived near by, and soon after killed himself. Both Henry Weaver and he were buried in the old St. Peter's churchyard.

ST. PETER'S CHURCH. 333

states that the managers will build the new church "as soon as $3,000 are subscribed." It is dated November 8, 1815. The collectors were George Neavil, who collected $1,967; Jacob Kneedler, who collected $745.50; Conrad Shimmel, who collected $298.50; Joseph Knipe, and Philip Lewis. Among the subscribers were Jacob Schwenk, Philip Hurst, Joseph Knipe, John Martin, Adam Fleck, Abraham Dannehower, Jacob, George, Joseph, Adam, Samuel, and Daniel Kneedler, Christian Rex, Henry Hallman, and many others. When they began to build is not recorded, but on the last page of the subscription book is the following receipt: "Rec'd, May 27th, 1817, of the church wardens the sum of seventy-three dollars, being collected on the day the corner stone was laid. John Hurst." Nor is it known when the work was finished. The church was built of stone, much larger than the first one. It was plastered over, and it is said, was painted yellow; hence it was soon called the "yellow church," and in later day, "the Old Yellow Church." The interior was high, and had a high "goblet" pulpit, of old-fashioned style, in which the preacher perched himself far above the heads of his hearers. It also had galleries on three sides of the building.

The next pastor was Rev. George Heilig. He began October 22, 1826, and continued until 1843, the longest pastorate in the history of the church. During his time an organ was introduced into the church service; Samuel Kneedler was organist, and Abraham Dannehower was leader of the choir. Hitherto the service had been all in the German language, but the necessity of English service was now recognized, and the pastor introduced it. For a time he officiated alternately in each language. During this pastorate the Sunday-school was organized, of which some notes are given below. Mr. Heilig went from here to Hamilton, Monroe County, Pa., and died at Catasauqua, in September, 1869.

The next pastor was Rev. Jacob Medtart, from 1843 to 1855.

He was unable to preach in German, and during his time the sermon in that language was discontinued. The service has been entirely in the English language since that time. Following Mr. Medtart was Rev. John W. Hassler, who had charge from 1856 to 1862, when he resigned to become chaplain in the army. (He was, in 1884, pastor at New Holland, Pa.) From 1863 to 1867, during the trying times of the war, when political feeling ran high, Rev. P. M. Rightmyer officiated. (He now, 1884, lives in Brooklyn, N. Y.) In 1868, Rev. Ezra L. Reed, now at Lancaster, Pa., succeeded. Mr. Reed was the last preacher in the second church. Half a century had passed since it had been built, and it needed repairs. The Reformed congregation had decided to leave it, and to build a church of their own in the town of North Wales, near by. The Lutheran congregation, after due discussion, resolved upon the same course. March 1, 1867, subscription books were opened, and a site having been obtained in the borough, the corner stone of the present church was laid June 6, 1868. The work of erection was completed the following year, and on January 1, 1870, the service of dedication was performed, Rev. J. W. Hassler preaching from Psalms cxxvi., 4.

From the beginning, up to this time, St. Peter's Lutheran congregation had been connected with St. John's, at Centre Square, one pastor serving both, but in 1870 this arrangement was dissolved, and each church has now its own pastor. Since 1870, the pastors at St. Peter's have been: Rev. Lewis G. M. Miller, 1874–75; Rev. Wm. H. Myers, 1876–78; Rev. Theophilus Hcilig, 1878–80; and Rev. George Diehl Foust, the present incumbent, who entered upon his pastorate July 1, 1880.

The records, as already mentioned, are imperfect. They show, however, lists of nearly 1,000 infant baptisms, over 100 adult baptisms, and nearly 600 confirmations. The Sunday-school was organized early in the pastorate of Rev. Geo. Heilig, — probably about 1831 or '32. The first superintendent was

ST. PETER'S CHURCH. 335

Noah Snyder; after him his brother Oliver Snyder. A record book that has been preserved shows the existence of a library for the use of the school, in 1837, and also shows that in July of that year there were 10 teachers and 60 scholars in attendance. In June, 1840, John B. Johnson became a member of the church, and shortly after was made superintendent of the Sunday-school. He served in that capacity nearly thirty years, Charles Hallman being his assistant during the last six years. The sessions were held in the afternoon. The first open-air celebration ever held in this neighborhood was given by the Sunday-schools of St. Peter's and St. John's. It took place in a woods which then stood above where the Franklinville school-house now stands, in July, 1841. Many people attended, and there were speeches and singing. The celebrations occurred frequently after that. For eight years preceding the preparation of these pages Abel K. Shearer has been superintendent of the school, and its present membership is about 150.

Only a few details can be furnished concerning the Reformed congregation that used the two old churches jointly with the Lutherans. As has been stated, the arrangement subsisted from the beginning until the new churches were built, about 1869–70, in North Wales borough, and during the hundred years it appears to have been satisfactory to both congregations. Each occupied the church in turn, and neither disturbed the other.

One of the pastors of the reformed congregation was Rev. John George Wack, who is still well remembered by the older people. He was a picturesque figure, a man of marked character, and a practical Christian. For many years he was pastor of Boehm's and Wentz's churches, and from 1834 to 1845 he preached regularly at St. Peter's. He had a farm and mill in Whitpain, and labored diligently with his own hands for the support of his family, besides preaching for at least three different congregations during most of his life. He was a classical scholar, wrote easily in Latin, was familiar, of course, with German, as well as English, was very fond of music, and built an organ with his own hands. "In personal appearance he was of medium size, and erect; in habits orderly, frugal, and laborious. His character for childlike simplicity and unsuspecting confidence was remarkable." In 1802 he took charge of both Wentz's and Boehm's; in 1806 he extended his care also to the distant church at Hilltown, Bucks county. These charges he retained until 1828, when he surrendered Hilltown; in 1834 he gave up Boehm's, and began to minister at St. Peter's, as already mentioned; in 1845, after forty-three years' ministry at Wentz's, he closed his active service, though he preached occasionally to the Gwynedd congregation, later.[1]

Mr. Wack was the son of Rev. Casper and Barbara Wack, of Bucks county. He died in 1856, aged eighty, and is buried at Boehm's. During his long pastorate he is said to have married seven hundred and twenty-four couples, preached five thou-

---

[1] This incident, related to me on the best authority, concerns good Parson Wack, and another most excellent and courageous man,—Dr. Antrim Foulke. Late in the summer—about August and September—of 1829, a bad fever prevailed through Gwynedd and adjoining townships. It was perhaps typhoid, was very fatal, worst along the streams, marked by ague, etc. Near Wack's mill was a family, "very bad off," and all down with it. The dread of fever was great, and nurses could not be had. Mr. Wack, however, helped them devotedly, and Dr. Foulke gave them his constant medical care. One day the two men stood beside the bed of a girl, one of the family, who was desperately ill. She had no nurse, and needed instant attention, if her life was to be saved. "Well, George," said Dr. Foulke, "if thee will help me, we will move her, and change her bed clothing, and her own clothing. It is simply a question of life or death." Father Wack did not hesitate; he was too simple and brave a Christian for that; the two men, alone, performed the unpleasant duty, and the sick girl, thus helped, afterward recovered. But Dr. Foulke went home with "the fever on him," and said at once that he was marked for sickness. He lay for six weeks, much of the time critically ill. His arm began to mortify, but before it had progressed, he noted the symptom himself, and saw that his case was at a desperate turn. Sending Tom Wolf, his faithful black man, to the woods for sassafras roots, he had them made into an enormous poultice, and instantly applied. The flesh of the arm sloughed off, but, thanks to a very strong constitution and the care of his wife,—a skillful nurse, and one of the most devoted of wives,—he regained his health.

sand times, baptised a thousand infants, and confirmed an equal number of catechumens. His son, Rev. Charles P. Wack, is a distinguished minister of the Reformed church; his daughter Abigail married Philip S. Gerhard; his daughter Amanda married Rev. Alfred B. Shenkle.

XXIV.

Social Conditions Among the Early Settlers.

OF the social conditions existing amongst the Welsh settlers some idea will have been formed by the reader from the chapters already given. Rev. Joseph Mathias, for many years the Baptist pastor at Hilltown, in a large manuscript volume which he left behind him, has some details on this subject.[1] The drink of the settlers, he says, was at first principally water. After a while, New England rum was used, and after the orchards grew to perfection and bore fruit, cider and whiskey[2] became plenty. Their bread was made of wheat or rye meal, ground and bolted. Besides bread, the wheat flour was cooked in various ways. Some made "dumplings" in pots with meat and vegetables, and often apples were used in this way,—*i. e.* "in dumplings." Flour was made into puddings, mixed with eggs and milk, etc., "and boiled in bags, sometimes in the same pot with meat, and sometimes alone." Beef suet was used to enrich the puddings, and they were eaten with "plenty of dip." Batter cakes were made of flour, eggs, and milk, baked in a frying pan with lard, and skillfully turned by tossing. Sometimes these were used for dessert, with sugar sprinkled on them. Usually the settlers had plenty of meat,—beef, pork, and poultry, chiefly,—sometimes mutton.

---

[1] Rev. Joseph Mathias was himself of Welsh descent, and very familiar with all the traditions respecting the early settlers. He was born at Hilltown, 1778, and died 1851, at his home near where Chalfont now is. He was called to the ministry in 1804, and preached till his death.

[2] He means, no doubt, spirits distilled from apple juice,—*i. e.* apple brandy, though this was very commonly called apple whiskey.

EARLY SOCIAL CONDITIONS.

"But few depended on wild meat or fowls, though occasionally they took time to hunt and procure some."

In clearing new land, further says Mr. Mathias, the small trees were grubbed up by a party of neighbors who joined and made a "frolic." The large trees were girdled, and when they fell, the logs were divided in convenient lengths by fires kindled along them at proper distances. They had small horses, who wore collars of straw. The harness was principally of tow cloth, ropes, and raw hide. "There were no wagons, carts, or wheeled carriages." "No people have ever been more united in interest, the labor on the land being mostly performed by companies, by way of exchange, many hands making light work of heavy jobs." Much labor was done by the women: picking, carding, and spinning of wool, swingling, hatcheling, and spinning of flax. There were "frolics" to pull flax, gather grain, etc. In the harvest field sometimes the workers were bitten by rattlesnakes. "I recollect hearing that my grandmother was bitten while in the field. There being no remedy at hand, one of her companions sucked out the poison with his mouth, throwing off the saliva; and she speedily recovered."

We may study with interest, in this connection, the inventory of the household goods of William John, of Gwynedd, who died in 1712, in the earliest years of the settlement. He was, judging by the large tract which he bought,—nearly three times the size of any other,—a rich man according to the circumstances of the times. The inventory in the house includes the following articles:

1 Rugg, 4 new blanketts, 7 new blanketts and one old Double coverlid, 2 ditto, 1 ditto, 2 single ditto, 3 ditto, one double ditto, 3 tow double coverlids, 7 cushin cases, 1 side of curtains, 7 pairs sheets, 5 table-cloths, 10 napkins, 4 bolster cases and 2 pillow cases, 8 chairs, 2 tables, 2 Dutch wheels, and 2 other spinning wheels, 6 lbs. of hatcheled flax, 6 of flaxen yarn, 37 of course tow yarn, 4 of woolen yarn, 28 of wool, 40 yards of linen, 2 buck-skins (appraised at 7s. 6d.); 55 lbs. of hemp, chafing dish, brass pans, wooden ware, pewter, 3 meal sives, earthen ware.

Alexander Edwards, sen., who died in Montgomery, in the same year (1712), left in his will "one half of my pewter," to be equally between his daughter Martha and the children of the daughter Margaret, and in another clause he provided:

I give my bigest Iron pot to my daughter Martha's eldest daughter, and I give my least Iron pot to my daughter Bridget's eldest daughter.

Robert John, who died in Gwynedd, in 1732, from the inventory of his personal estate was probably the wealthiest citizen of the township. The list shows several articles indicating refinement and even some degree of luxury.

Included in it are the following, valued as stated:

	£	s.	d.		£	s.	d.
6 Cane chairs,	4	0	0	2 Little wheels,	0	15	0
2 Small walnut tables,	2	10	0	14 Flag bottom chairs,	1	1	0
Window curtains,	0	3	0	6 Candlesticks, 2 flesh forks,	0	15	0
5 doz. glass bottles,[1]	0	15	0				
Chyney ware, and glasses on mantel piece	0	16	0	Smoothing-box and heater,	0	5	0
				Pewters,	3	16	0
3 Brass candlesticks,	0	9	0	4 Brass pans,	4	7	0
1 Desk on a frame,	3	0	0	2 pairs scales and weights,	0	12	0
6 Leather Chairs,	1	16	0	5 Iron potts and pott hooks,	3	0	0
4 Arm chairs,	1	6	0	1 Gridiron, brander, and frying pans,	1	5	0
1 Warming pan and 1 looking glass	1	10	0				
				1 Long frame table,			
Money scales and weights and little box	0	6	0	5 Oak chairs,	1	5	0
				2 Lignum vitæ morters,	1	5	0
2 Great spinning wheels,	0	12	0	25 yards of lincy woolcy	2	15	0

The quantity of furniture shown above was unusually large. No other Gwynedd inventory of that time, that I have examined, shows so much.

The inventory of Jenkin Jenkin's personal estate, in Hatfield, in 1745, shows much the same list as Robert John, but there were a few different or otherwise notable articles, as follows:

---

[1] They seem to have been all empty!

EARLY SOCIAL CONDITIONS. 341

	£	s.	d.
4 Brass pans,	11	0	0
All the pewters,	3	0	0
1 Rug,	1	10	0
Earthenware,	0	10	0
Tin ware,	0	4	0
Iron pots, a kettle, and hangers,	2	0	0
8 chairs,	0	16	0
A table and dough trough,	1	0	0
A coutch,	0	7	0

	£	s.	d.
A chest with drawers,	1	0	0
2 Buckskins,	1	16	0
5 Coarse sheets,	1	0	0
2 Sheets,	1	0	0
1 Diaper table-cloth, and 3 napcins,	0	10	0
Brand irons, frying pan and bakeston,	2	10	0
Wooling yarn,	6	0	0
Lining yarn,	1	12	0

The inventory of Robert Evans, of Gwynedd, 1746, included:

1 feather bed and furniture, 2 chaff beds and furniture, 1 chaff bed and 2 pillows, 6 lbs. worsted yarn, 5 lbs. of combed worsted, 4 yards of lincy, 3½ yards of cloth, 26 lbs. of wool, 1 great and 3 little wheels, a dough trough.

Evan Evans (the preacher, who lived at Mumbower's mill), who died in 1747, had a large number of items in his inventory such as these:

Sundry remnants of linnen (£5 10s.); table linnen, a piece of new linnen, flax and tow yarn, 6½ lbs. of worsted, linnen yarn, 20 lbs. of wool, etc., etc.

The character and number of these items indicate that they may have been on hand as part of the product of the fulling-mill which there is some evidence Evan Evans or his son Abraham had established before 1747. Other items in the same inventory were these:

21 chairs, a settle, a long table, 3 "ovil" tables, sundry earthenware, a brass kettle and other brass things, sundry pewters, sundry wooden vessels, funnel, grater, bellows, tongs and fire shovel, a baking plate, 3 iron potts, 2 pairs of pott hangers, cheese press, dough trough, a looking-glass.

These inventories show clearly enough the character and extent of the household belongings. There were few dishes of any finer ware than earthen; brass and pewter ones were the most esteemed. Jenkin Jenkins had some tin-ware. The iron pots were valued enough to be made heirlooms. The "dough-trough" was in nearly every house. No clocks are named in any of these inventories. The best beds were filled with feathers, but many plain people contented themselves with a tick filled with chaff. For cooking, the frying-pan, the chafing-dish, the grid-iron, and the kettle were used. The "smoothing-box and heater" mentioned in Robert John's inventory were no doubt a smoothing-iron, with a cell in the heel for the insertion of a heated piece of metal,—such as hatters and others still use. The "settle" appears in Evan Evans's house, and he, like Robert John, had a looking-glass. For making the bed comfortable on a cold night, the warming-pan was already in use. Robert John's "Chyney-ware" appears to have been unknown in other houses.

Of the simplicity of manners amongst the Friends we get a glimpse in this letter, sent by Benjamin and Ann Mendenhall, of Chester county, to Owen and Mary Roberts, of Gwynedd, soliciting the latter's daughter Mary for their son Benjamin:

CONCORD, ye 20 of ye 6 Mo., 1716.

Beloved Friends,
Owen Roberts and Mary his wife.

Our Love is unto you, and to your son and daughter. Now this is to let you understand that our son Benjamin had made us acquainted that he has a kindness for your daughter Lydia, and desired our consent thereon, and we having well considered of it and knowing nothing in our minds against his proceeding therein, have given our consent that he may proceed orderly, that is to have your consent, and not to proceed without it. And it is our desire that you will give your consent. Also now, as touching his place that we have given him for to settle on, we shall say but little at present.

Ellis Lewis knows as well of our minds and can give you as full account of it, as we can if we were with you, but if you will be pleased to come down, we shall be very glad to see you, or either of you, and then you might satisfy yourselves.

Now we desire you when satisfied, to return us an answer, in the same way as we have given you our minds.

No more, but our kind love to you and shall remain your Loving friends, BENJAMIN AND ANN MENDENHALL.

That the business thus delicately introduced, and promoted perhaps by the settlements which Benjamin and Ann had made for their son (which Ellis Lewis could tell all about), prospered, we know by the records. Benjamin Mendenhall, jr., married Lydia Roberts, at Gwynedd meeting-house, 3d mo. 9th, 1717.

Conduct was not always so circumspect, however, with young people about marrying. The monthly meeting records, 1723, show a minute like this:

H—— J—— and wife produced a paper condemning their letting loose their affections to one another before a timely permission from Parents and Relations,—which was read & ordered to lye by ye clerk for further Tryal.[1]

Some other extracts from the disciplinary proceedings of the monthly meeting may be here made:

1718. This meeting being given to understand that J—— W—— at a certain time hath been too much overtaken with the Excess of Strong Liquor, he being present att this meeting Confessed the same and Condemned himself and the Spirit that led him thereunto, with a firm resolution to take better care for the future.

1718. Reported by Gwynedd Overseers that D—— H—— lately was too apparently seen in the Excess of Drink. [Not being present, he was notified to appear, which subsequently he did, "confest his failures," and promised reform.]

1725. E—— F—— brought in a paper condemning his immoderate use of strong drink.

The following extracts from the minutes, of a much later date, relate to the same subject:

3d mo. 29, 1763. —— —— has contracted considerable debts at Taverns, more than he is able to pay.

11th mo. 26, 1765. —— —— retails liquors without license, etc., very contrary to the advice of Friends.

7th mo. 26, 1796. [Answer to query :] Several members decline the use of liquor in time of harvest.

7th mo. 25, 1797. Some members retail liquors.

---

[1] I do not think this means anything more than is expressed,—that the young people engaged to marry, without getting permission.

7th mo. 31, 1798. None retailing or distilling except four women, whose husbands are not in membership.

8th mo. 26, 1800. In relation to —— —— we are of the mind that part of the charge of assaulting his neighbors had better be expunged, and say that he threw a glass of wine at a certain person in an angry manner, & at the same time used unbecoming language.

In relation to marriages and burials, a tendency to what the meeting regarded as excess was early observed.

8th mo. 26, 1725. This meeting hath had in consideration ye large provisions in marriage and burials, wch after some discourse was referred to next meeting.

A memorandum amongst the papers of Ellis Lewis, the elder, of Upper Dublin, shows the following items of expense, at the time of his funeral, in 1753:

	£	s.	d.
To a Windin sheete, ...		15	9
To Wine, Rum, Sider and other small things in cash,	2	16	11
To Digin the Greave, ...	0	10	0

The drinkables, it seems, were much the heaviest items of expense!

The records of the Friends' meeting show that "differences" would sometimes arise among members, but there is pleasing evidence that the efforts to speedily end them were successful. Here is a case in point:

1718. Being informed of some Difference Depending between Richard Morris and John Rees, viz: the s$_d$ John Rees has lost or mislaid his deed w^h he had of Richd Morris, on a tract of land he purchased of the said Richard; Now the advice of this meeting is that they, in a friendly manner, Refer the matter Depending to two able judicious men. Both being present [they] agreed to refer the same to David Lloyd and Robert Jones of Meirion, & to stand to their Determination and final judgment.

This was a satisfactory procedure, for a few months later

Account was given that ye differences depending between Richard Morris and John Rees was fully ended.

There was, it seems, some "difference" between Rowland Ellis and Owen Owen. This is mentioned in the minutes several times, and the case probably never came to a definite conclusion. But at one meeting, in the 9th month, 1724, a committee was appointed to "advise 'em to stand to the judgment of ye Friends," and the papers relating to the controversy were directed to be placed in the custody of John Humphrey, who was not to allow them " to be shown or read to any one, or to be transcribed." Two months later the papers were brought to the meeting, "folded, sealed, and delivered to John Humphrey, to be safely kept by him, and not unsealed without this meeting consent." The whole affair then rested. Afterward, Rowland Ellis died, and in 1741, John Humphrey being dead also, the meeting ordered the papers to be destroyed.

Some further interesting glimpses of the manners of the time may be obtained from other minutes of disciplinary action by the monthly meeting:

1730. S. E. appeared at this meetting and confess'd he had unadvisedly gone into bad Company at a Certain Time, and also had actual engag'd in the wicked practice of playing Cards, with other Indecent things, all which he frankly Confessed & openly Condemn'd and express'd Sorrow on the occasion, [etc.]

1730. E. M. appeared at this meeting, Confessing his faults for Indulging some of his neighbours to fiddle and keep undue liberty in his house, [etc., etc.] This meeting being sorrowfully affected with the prevalence of undue Liberties, such as shooting matches, Singing & Dancing, and the like disorders, wch too many of our youths fall into, we can do no less than recommend it to all parents, masters, mistresses, overseers, and other faithfull friends, to Discourage and Crush the growth of such Disorders as much as in 'em lies.

1742. The meeting adjudges that a man that does not pay his debts Deprives himself of being in fellowship with us unless he surrenders his all.

1750. [The minutes state at some length that] —— —— joined the Society by convincement, declaring he had no bye ends. He soon married a Friend, and declared he never owned our principles.

1756. [This appears to be the first answering of the Queries. To the 1st:] Meetings are attended, and the hour observed, and as for sleeping, chewing tobacco, and taking snuff, we fear some are not so clear as might be wished for, notwithstanding the repeated advices, [etc.]

1760. ———, daughter of ——— ———, says she was married by a Swede minister in Philad'a, but this meeting being doubtful of the varacity do appoint William Foulke and John Evans to use their endeavors to find the certainty by enquiring of said Minister.

1761. ——— ——— went out in marriage pretty soon after the decease of her former husband, and it appearing to be her third offense of that kind, the Meeting, [etc.]

1766. R. R., tanner, is disowned for not binding his children out, when unable to make a living.

XXV.

Agriculture, Slaves, Schools, Hotels, Stores, etc.

SOME idea of the agricultural methods of the early settlers may be gathered from the inventories of personal property attached to their wills. In 1712, William John's inventory showed his grain crops to be wheat, rye, and oats; he had also hay; and these were "in the barn," showing that he, at least, had by that time built a barn. He had 21 cattle of all sorts, 5 of the horse kind, in addition to "1 old mare with her breed in the woods." He had "7 stock of bees," showing attention already given to them, and Jenkin Jenkin's inventory, 1745, includes 18 hives of bees. Owen Evans, 1723, also had bees, and his inventory includes "6 acres of new land fallow for barley."

Cider was made quite early. Robert John, 1732, had "an apple mill and press." Jenkin Jenkin's inventory includes "7 hogseds and 3 barrels of sider."

As to implements and tools, there were none up to 1750 but of the simplest sort. Robert John had 3 plows, 1 harrow, 3 hoes, an iron bar, mauls, wedges, axes, spades, shovels, dungforks, pitch forks, a broadaxe, 2 cross-cut saws, "sithes," sickles, 2 grindstones. The sickle, of course, was the implement for reaping grain, but Jenkin Jenkin's inventory (1743) mentions "a cradle," in connection with "a sythe and 4 siccles," showing the use of the cradle as early as that. He had also "a cuting box."

Sheep were raised by Robert Evans, whose inventory, 1746, showed 22 head of them, as well as 20 hogs, and Evan Evans, the preacher, 1747, had 30 head of sheep. Robert Evans's crops were partly in "yᵉ barn," and he had a lot of "flax unrotted." Jenkin Jenkin's crop items include flaxseed and buckwheat.

Of vehicles of any sort there is no mention in any of these early inventories, except a cart. Robert John had one, and Evan Evans had "a cart and thiller's gears;" he had also a sled. Those who travelled went on horseback, and in the inventories the "riding-horse" is usually mentioned separately and appraised at a considerably higher price than the horses used for farm work. It was common, also, to appraise the saddle with the horse. That the sale of a horse was attended with some formality at times is shown by a bill of sale among the papers of Ellis Lewis, of Upper Dublin, given to him, in 1728, by John Clark, "of Elizabethtown, in East New Jersey," for "a black horse, branded I F on the near buttock, with a few white hairs in yᵉ forehead, and a few white on his hind off leg." (The price was £3 5s.)

Some memoranda in the little book of Samuel and Cadwallader Foulke give clues to the time of agricultural operations.[1] Thus:

On the 5th day of May, 1773, fell a snow of several Inches deep, & was succeeded by the greatest crops of wheat that was known for more than 30 years.

9th of July, 1801, Began Reaping. 15th do., Finished Reaping and all our grain in the Barn.

12th of July, 1802, began Reaping. 17th, finished reaping and all our grain in the barn.

1803, May 8th, a snow of 4 or 5 inches.

On the last day of March, 1807, was the greatest snow ever known at that season.

On the first day of Nov'r, 1810, it began snowing, which continued 32 hours, and drifted for two days, & was attended with unusual freezing. After one moderate day it began Raining on the 8th. The 10th in the even-

---

[1] The first of these items refers to Richland; the others mostly, if not all, to Gwynedd. It is notable that the time given for the beginning of harvest is later than now.

ing was the greatest fresh in Wissahickon that had happened for 16 years. The sun has not shone from the 8th until the [date omitted].

March 30, 1823, there was a snow near a foot deep, attended with the hardest gale for 12 hours, ever known, by which thousands of cords of wood were blown down.

1834, May 14th, 15th, and 16th, the ground was froze each morning.

Concerning the slaves in Gwynedd, the meeting records furnish some clues. Here are a few extracts from the monthly meeting minutes:

4th mo. 27, 1756. [Answer of Monthly Meeting to 10th Query :] We have but very few negroes amongst us, and they we believe are tolerably well used.

7th mo. 25, 1758. A Friend among us has sold a negro slave to another since our last Quarter. Querie: is that an offence?

1st mo. 29, 1760. [Answer to Query:] Some slaves are brought to meetings at times.

2d mo. 26, 1760. Thomas Jones has purchased a slave, and he appearing in this meeting in a plyable frame of mind, expressed disposition of using him well if he should live; this meeting desires him to adhere to the Principle of doing unto others as he would be done unto, which will teach him how to use him in time to come.

3d mo. 30, 1761. Richard Thomas has purchased a slave, and he being in this meeting, Friends had a good opportunity to lay the inconsistency of the practice before him, [etc.]

10th mo. 27, 1761. Mordecai Moore sold a slave for a term of years, but says that he has such a regard for the unity of Friends that if it was to do again he would not do it.

1st mo., 1780. Miles Evans agrees to manumit his negro man. A committee of the meeting is appointed to advise the negro with respect to his conduct when free.

7th mo. 27, 1784. [Women's branch of the Monthly Meeting answering the query, said:] No slaves amongst us. Those set free are under the care of the committee.

10th mo., 1770. Jonathan Robeson acknowledges selling a negro woman, who was very troublesome in his family for several years. He never intends to do the like again.

Jenkin Jenkin's inventory, 1745, shows "a servant man" appraised at £8, and "a negro woman," £40. The former was probably an indentured servant, and the latter a slave. Items of the "time" of indentured servants occur in many of the inventories. In Evan Evan's inventory, 1728: "a servant lad, £15, and a servant maid, 1 yr to serve, £4." In Robert John's, 1732: "The time of 5 bound servants, £50." In Evan Evan's, 1747: "A servant man's time, 2 yrs, £10."

In 1757, as appears from an old memorandum of account, the pay of a farm laborer, David Evans, in the employ of Ellis Lewis, of Upper Dublin, for reaping and mowing, was 2 shillings 6 pence per day—about 33 cents. For threshing less than that was paid. Some items in the account run thus:

			s.	d.
1757.	2 days	Reepin,	5	0
"	4 "	mowin second grass,	10	0
"	6 "	thrashin wheat,	12	0
1759.	5 "	mowing grass,	12	6
"	3 "	thrashin buckwheat,	4	0

As to schools and education, the first school-house in the township undoubtedly was that in the lower end, mentioned by Rowland Hugh and Robert Humphrey, 1721, in their petition for a road. In 1729, it appears that "Marmaduke Pardo, of Gwynedd, schoolmaster," was married at Merion, so that Gwynedd had a teacher at least that early, if not—as is reasonable—in 1721, when the school-house was provided.[1]

Of the teachers following Marmaduke Pardo I have no

---

[1] Marmaduke came from Pembrokeshire, Wales, with the following quaint certificate, dated April 18, 1727: "We whose names are hereunto subscrib'd, being the Curate and others of the inhabitants of the parish of St. David's, do hereby certify whom it may concern that ye bearer hereof, Marmaduke Pardo, of the City of St. David's, and county of Pembrock, hath to ye utmost of our knowledge & all appearance liv'd a very sober and pious life, demeaning himself according to ye Strictest Rules of his profession, viz., wt what we call Quakerism, & yt he hath for these several years past took upon himself ye keeping of a private school in this city, in which Station he acquitted himself with ye common applause, and to ye general satisfaction of all of us who have committed our children to his care and tuition," etc. [Signed by Richard Roberts, curate, and about 25 others.]

account. Samuel Evans (son of Owen and Ruth) was a teacher "at North Wales," toward the close of the last century. A school was kept under the oversight of the Friends at the meeting-house, at least as early as 1793. Joseph Foulke, in a manuscript furnished the writer, in 1859, recalled the following facts:

My earliest recollection of schools which I attended was at Gwynedd meeting. There was no house for the purpose, but what was called "the little meeting-house" was used. An old tottering man by the name of Samuel Evans was teacher. The reading books were the Bible and Testament; we had Dilworth's Spelling-Book, and Dilworth's Assistant (or Arithmetic). Grammar was a thing hardly thought of; there was however a small part of the spelling-book called "A New Guide to the English Tongue," and a few of the older pupils learned portions of this, by rote, and would occasionally recite to the master, but the substance appeared to be equally obscure both to master and scholar.

My next schooling was in 1795, in the house late the property of William Buzby, on the Bethlehem road, above the Spring-House. It was a kind of family school, taught by Hannah Lukens. (Here Dr. Walton, of Stroudsburg, laid the foundation of his education.) I next went to Joshua Foulke, my father's elder brother, and an old man. He taught in a log school-house, near the 18-mile stone on the Bethlehem road. My father, with the help of his neighbors, built this house [about 1798], on a lot set apart for the purpose at the southern extremity of his premises. This log school-house stood about thirty years, and besides Joshua Foulke, we had for teachers William Coggins, Hannah Foulke, Benjamin Albertson, Hugh Foulke (my brother), John Chamberlain, Christian Dull, Daniel Price, and Samuel Jones. (I have probably not named all, or given them in the order in which they came.)

The free school of Montgomery, however, was more popular. The salary paid there, $160 a year, secured more competent teachers than other schools in the neighborhood. I can remember when the teacher's pay was from a dollar to ten shillings per quarter for each scholar, and he obtained his board by going about from house to house among his employers, and it was a remark that people would trust a teacher to instruct their children to whom they would not lend a horse!

Many interesting data ought to be available concerning this "free school at Montgomery." It was maintained for many years, and the old house yet stands. Here William Collom, an accomplished teacher, taught about 1820. Benjamin F. Hancock was teacher there, when his son, the General, was born. Among the scholars at one time, were Samuel Aaron, Samuel Medary, and Lewis Jones, and a flourishing debating society was maintained about William Collom's time.

George I. Evans of Emerson, Ohio, says of his father, Jonathan Evans: "He taught school for two years, perhaps, near Everard Foulke's, about half a mile east of Bunker's Hill, and 1½ miles from Quakertown; after that he moved to Gwynedd and taught school there. I think he moved to Sandy Hill [Whitpain] in 1816 or '17, and remained there until after 1824. He also taught in Worcester, and in 1826 and 1827 he taught at the end of uncle John Ambler's lane, in an old log house on Captain Baker's place. I think he got as low as $6 a month for teaching."

The public schools of Gwynedd township date their history from the year 1840. In 1834, during the administration of Governor Wolf, the first common school law passed the Legislature. It left the school districts the option of acceptance or rejection by a vote of the school directors, who were elected by the people. This law was objected to as needlessly elaborate, and in various respects unsuitable for the circumstances of the people. However fair or otherwise this charge may have been, comparatively few schools were organized under it, in any part of the State. In 1835 its repeal was nearly carried through the Legislature. The Senate passed the repealing act by a decisive vote, but in the House, Thaddeus Stevens led the opposition, and by his passionate eloquence and persistent earnestness, secured a majority in the negative.[1] The next year, in Governor Ritner's administration, the law was amended, and with this change the friends of public schools began their work in earnest.

---

[1] This was the time of Stevens' greatest service in behalf of public education. See, for some account of the scene in the House, Armor's *Lives* of the Governors of Penna.

SCHOOLS AND EDUCATION. 353

In 1834, the Gwynedd Board of Directors were Peter Hoot, Thomas Shoemaker, Solomon Kriebel, Jesse Spencer, William Buzby, and Charles F. Jenkins. On the vote for accepting or rejecting the State system, the members were unanimous in the negative.

In 1835 and 1836 the votes of the directors were to the same effect. But in 1837, under the provisions of the amended law of '36, the people voted on the question of adoption, at the township election, in March. For three years the opposition was successful, the votes being as follows:

1837, March —, for Adoption, 23; for Rejection, 100.
1838,   "   16, "   "   73; "   "   128.
1839,   "   15, "   "   46; "   "   125.

The contest of 1838 was a warm one, and while the friends of the schools showed a great increase of strength, their decisive defeat evidently discouraged them for the next year. But a very persuasive element had now entered into the case. The State appropriations to the school district were piling up. They had begun in 1835, under the Act of '34. By special acts and resolutions passed from year to year by the Legislature, it had been provided that such appropriations should still be open to the acceptance of the districts, up to a date in the future,—this date being in each act moved a year ahead. And in 1837 there had come from the national treasury to that of the State that large sum (nearly three millions of dollars) which was Pennsylvania's share of the Surplus distributed under the Act of Congress of 1836. This money was largely applied to the public schools,[1] and the effect it had on the Gwynedd appropriation will be seen by the following statement:

---

[1] The enormous influence exercised by this large expenditure, under the practical and effective amendments of 1836, can hardly be overestimated. The school system of Pennsylvania sprang at once into vigorous life. Within three years, the permanent State appropriation rose from $75,000 to $400,000; and whereas there were but 762 public schools open at the end of 1835, there were, only three years later, no less than 5,000.

State Appropriations to Gwynedd School District :

For year beginning June, 1835		$83.37
" " " " 1836		228.27
" " " " 1837		799.80
" " " " 1838		353.00
" " " " 1839		326.00

When the vote came to be taken, once more, at the township election in March, 1840, there was, therefore, nearly eighteen hundred dollars to the credit of the school district, and open to its use in the event of a vote for accepting the system, but to be covered into the general fund of the State, in the event of a fresh rejection. With this aid, the friends of the schools triumphed. On March 20th of that year, the vote stood :

For Acceptance, 86 ; for Rejection, 80.

The Directors in 1840 were Charles Greger, John Boileau, John Jenkins, Samuel Linton, Samuel B. Davis, Charles F. Jenkins. The adoption of the system made necessary the laying of a tax, and this was fixed at $228.26. The following statement shows the district's share of the State appropriation, and its amount of tax, from 1840 to 1845 inclusive :

Year	State Appropriation		Tax	
1840.	$326;		$228.26	
1841.	"	326;	"	225.42
1842.	"	410;	"	320.65
1843.	"	410;	"	266.83
1844.	"	245;	"	296.87
1845.	"	192;	"	301.80

The report of the State Superintendent for 1844 showed the progress which Gwynedd had by that time made. There were 4 schools, 4 teachers (all males); 255 male and 197 female pupils. The average compensation of teachers per month was $20. The schools were open 9 months in the year. 13 pupils were instructed in the German language. It is interesting to note that in that year, 19 townships of the county, a majority of the whole number, still rejected the State system. Gwynedd and Montgomery were the only two in this section accepting; Hatfield,

Horsham, Towamencin, Worcester, Whitpain, and Upper Dublin having so far refused.

The four schools open, in 1844, were the "upper eight-square," on the Allentown road; one on the Sumneytown road opposite Frederick Beaver's; one at Gwynedd meeting-house, partly supported by the meeting fund; one at the "lower eight-square," on the turnpike below Spring-House. The two "eight-square" were actually octagonal in shape, a plan then thought to be a very good one.

The first hotel in the township was no doubt that of Thomas Evans, on what is now the turnpike, a mile below Acuff's. On which side of the road it stood may be somewhat uncertain, but probably on the south-west side, where there used to be traces of an old building, a well, etc. Rowland Roberts' hotel, in Montgomery, must have been on the Bethlehem road, below Montgomery Square. It existed in 1749, as we know by his will. Christian Dull established his hotel at the Spring-House, before the Revolution—probably about 1765-70, and continued to keep it for many years. He was the landlord when Alexander Wilson, afterward the famous ornithologist, stayed over night there in his pedestrian tour to Niagara Falls, in October, 1804, and "wrote up" the place in a not particularly complimentary manner.[1]

---

[1] Wilson's poem, "The Foresters," describing his trip, says:
  Mile after mile passed unperceived away,
  Till in the west the day began to close,
  And Spring-House tavern furnished us repose.
  Here two long rows of market folks were seen,
  Ranged front to front, the table placed between,
  Where bags of meat, and bones, and crusts of bread,
  And hunks of bacon all around were spread;
  One pint of beer from lip to lip went 'round,
  And scarce a bone the hungry house-dog found;
  Torrents of Dutch from every quarter came,
  Pigs, calves, and sour-kraut the important theme;
  While we, on future plans revolving deep,
  Discharged our bill, and straight retired to sleep.

Another hotel was established at Spring-House by Thomas Scarlett; this was in the building now occupied as a store by Isaac Hallowell. For many years there were two, until the railroad cut off the stream of the market-folks whom Wilson encountered, and one became quite sufficient for public accommodation.

Before buying the Maris property, by the meeting-house, and establishing his hotel there, David Acuff kept tavern at Spring-House for a number of years. I have seen his licenses for years from 1811 to 1816. He bought the Maris property of Jesse J. Maris, in 1818, and at the August Term, 1819, petitioned the court for a license. This, however, was not granted him until 1827. The petition of 1819 recites that his place is "where the great road leading from Doylestown to Plymouth Meeting crosses the great road leading from Philadelphia to Kutztown," and that there are no hotels between Spring-House and George Heist's, on the latter road, or "between Montgomery Square and Pigeontown" on the other.

The tavern at Kneedler's was long known as Heisler's. (Reading Howell's map, 1792, shows it by that name,—though mis-spelled Heister's.) When it was established is not certain. In 1776, Jacob Heisler had 147 acres of land, according to the assessor's list, but he is not marked as having a tavern. Henry Kneedler, who had married his granddaughter, Margaret Heisler (daughter of Jacob, jun.), acquired the property in 1840, and the hotel is now kept by Jacob Heisler Kneedler.

George Heist's tavern, on the turnpike, below the old St. Peter's churchyard, was a famous place in its time. The large buildings, now used for a dwelling, were put up to accommodate the public. Heist bought the property of Martin Swink, in 1784, and established the tavern then.

As has been already stated, the central part of the present store building and residence of William H. Jenkins was a hotel during the Revolution. Jesse Evans, the tailor, when he sold most of his property to George Maris,[1] in 1755, retained this, (now W. H. J.'s). but as he became insolvent, the sheriff sold it for him, in November, 1764, to Jacob Wentz, of Worcester. He, in 1769, built the middle part of the house, and rented it out for a tavern. Who was the landlord is not known. Owen Ferris, " of Towamencin, gentleman," bought the property of Wentz, in 1778, and in 1782 sold it to John Martin, who in 1794 sold to Edward Jenkins. The last named built the present store end of the building, and kept store there until his death in 1829, when the property descended to his son, Charles F. Jenkins.

Earlier than Edward Jenkins's store at this place was that of Owen Evans, in the Meredith house. (He calls himself "storekeeper" in a deed to his son Samuel.) This store Samuel Evans probably continued; in his deed for the sale of 88½ acres[2] to Amos Roberts, in 1765, he calls himself "store-keeper," also.[3]

'Squire John Roberts was doubtless the most important merchant in Gwynedd, for many years. His store was at the Spring-House, a particularly good place for business in the old times. He began there soon after the close of the Revolution, some of his accounts that I have seen being of so early a date as 1786. His papers show that he dealt largely in flaxseed and linen, buying the former of the farmers and exporting it, from Philadelphia, to the Irish ports,—Belfast, Dublin, Newry, and Cork. In return he received the linens. His operations were sometimes directly with the Irish commission houses, but more frequently he conducted them through Caleb and Owen Foulke, of Philadelphia. The shipments each way were quite large:

---

[1] See Jesse Evans, p. 166. It is there stated that when he sold to Geo. Maris, the W. H. Jenkins lot was included, but this is an error. In the garden behind the wagon-house there is an old well, and beside it, in Jesse Evans' time, stood a log house.

[2] The Meredith place; now Est. of J. Lukens.

[3] He is the same mentioned previously in this chapter as a school teacher, in 1793.

whether they were ultimately at a profit to John may be doubted. Months were required for returns, each way, and the various charges for insurance, freight, storage, commissions, etc., were about 30 per cent. of the prices realized on the flaxseed.[1] John closed his business at the Spring-House, in 1794, by selling out to John Hubbs, for whom his brother-in-law, Amos Lewis, of Upper Dublin, became security. (John Hubbs did not prove to be a successful store-keeper, and did not long continue.)

The first grist-mill in the township was doubtless that on the Wissahickon, at Penllyn, built by William Foulke. Its date of erection is uncertain, but it was some years before the Revolution. Pretty nearly contemporary with it, but rather later, was the mill north of North Wales, formerly John L. Heist's. In the 1776 list it is entered as Barnaby Beaver's.

At Mumbower's, there was a saw and fulling-mill in Evan Evans's time, as appears by his will, 1747, but if there was a grist-mill before the Revolution it does not seem to have been then kept up, as the tax-list of 1776 does not mention it.

According to Gordon's *Gazetteer*, there were in Gwynedd, in 1832, two grist-mills and three saw-mills. (There were returned to the assessor 307 houses, and 776 cattle.)

The construction of the turnpike from Spring-House upward by Montgomery Square was set on foot in 1813, a charter having been granted by the Legislature, and approved by the Governor, on January 16 of that year. The name of the corporation, "The Spring-House, Northampton Town and Bethlehem Turnpike Company," showed the ambitious design which was entertained, and which, compared with the actual progress of the work, was altogether too large for the means at command. The commissioners named in the charter were William Tilghman and Peter

---

[1] An "account sales" of William and Samuel Hanna, of Newry, 30th July, 1787, shows the sales "in course of the season," of 107 hogsheads of flaxseed, for £310 7s. 2½d.; on which the various charges, under ten different headings, were £84 4s. 1d.

Kneplay, of Philadelphia; John Roberts, Evan Jones, Silas Hough, and John Weaver, of Montgomery township; Samuel Sellers, Andrew Schlicher, and William Green, of Bucks county; James Greenleaf, Abraham Rinker, Jacob Hartzel, and Peter Wint, of Lehigh county; and George Huber and Owen Rice, of Northampton county.

The road was to begin at Spring-House, and go by Montgomery Square, Trewig's tavern, Sellers' tavern, Swamp Meeting-House [Quakertown], to Fry's tavern, and from there to the borough of Northampton,[1] in Lehigh county, "with a convenient section to the town of Bethlehem." The roadway was not to be less than 50 nor more than 60 feet wide, of which at least 21 feet was to be made an artificial road, "bedded with wood, stone, gravel, or any other hard substance, well compacted together, and of sufficient depth to secure a solid foundation to the same; and the said road shall be faced with gravel or stone pounded, or other small hard substance, in such manner as to secure a firm, and as near as the materials will admit, an even surface," etc., etc.

The stockholders organized by a meeting "at the public-house of Philip Shellenberger," May 24, 1813, electing Evan Jones President, George Weaver Treasurer, and Owen Rice, Hugh Foulke, Edward Ambler, John Roberts, Benjamin Rosenberger, Thomas Lester, James Wilson, John Gordon, Henry Leidy, John Todd, Benjamin Foulke, and Isaac Morris managers.

The managers met first, August 23, 1813, at John Weaver's hotel, and elected Cadwallader Foulke and John Houston surveyors. Next day they met at David Acuff's hotel, Spring-House, and remained for further meetings on the two following days. There was some controversy over the route. One proposition, negatived by a vote of 6 to 3, was to run "in a straight line from Spring-House to George Weaver's;" another (yeas 4, nays 8), that it "be carried along the North Wales road

---

[1] The present borough of Allentown.

until where the [Treweryn] creek intersects the same, from thence through the lands of Messers. Foulke, Sheive, and Evans, in an oblique direction to the Swedes' Ford road, thence along it to George Weaver's." Some other propositions were made, and finally, 9 to 3, the road as now located was fixed on.

The subsequent construction of the road was very slow. It never got to "Northampton Town," or even to Quakertown, but stopped at Hilltown, and the corporate title was changed finally to the Spring-House and Hilltown Turnpike Company. The State granted aid to a considerable amount: by an act in 1816, the Governor was authorized to subscribe to 200 shares of stock ($10,000); by another, in 1821, he was required to subscribe for 300 shares more; in 1824, he was directed to pay Patrick Logan, a contractor who had been at work on the road, $1593, a balance due him, and the balance due under the Act of 1816 (and a supplement, 1817), stated to be $7157, when the road was completed to Trewig's tavern. In 1833, an act of the Legislature recited that "owing to the embarrassed situation of their funds," the Company had no prospect of complying with the conditions of the Act of 1821, and the Governor was ordered to pay the whole $15,000 State aid, as soon as they should complete not less than 2½ miles more road.

The turnpike from Spring-House to Sumneytown,[1] 17 miles, was made in 1847-48. A general meeting to organize the com-

---

[1] Sumneytown is a village directly "up country" (n. w.) in Marlborough township. This road was the route of travel for the people of a large section of country to the markets in Philadelphia, and until the construction of the railroad, hundreds of wagons,—two, four, and six-horse teams,—passed each week through Gwynedd on their way to and from the city. Flour from the mills on Perkiomen, farm produce of all kinds, linseed oil, and blasting powder, formed their main freightage. It was usual for many of these to go down on Monday and Thursday afternoons, reaching the city in time for the Tuesday and Friday markets, completing their sales, and returning on Wednesday and Saturday. It formed an extensive traffic, and the hotels along the road were busy places on the days when the "hucksters," mill-teams, hay-teams, and market farmers passed up or down. But after 1856, the railroad having been completed, this was broken up.

pany was held at Jonas Boorse's hotel, in Lower Salford, May 20, 1847, and Charles F. Jenkins was elected president, Isaac W. Wampole treasurer, and Ellis Cleaver, Henry Kneedler, Seth Lukens, Jonas Boorse, Jonas C. Godshalk, Solomon Artman, Nathaniel Jacoby, and George Snyder managers. The President and committees of the managers, with Jacob Pruner, jr., as surveyor, located the route (varying very little from the bed of the old road), starting from the Spring-House on May 27th, and reaching "the upper end of Summeytown on the morning of June 3d." This work fixed the width of the road (50 feet), and its angles; subsequently Lawrence E. Corson, of Norristown, fixed the grades. The road was divided into half-mile sections, for construction. All bridges with a span of over six feet were to be separately contracted for. The first nine sections, from Spring-House upward, were contracted for by Robert Scarlett and David Acuff, at $2700 each; two more, above, were taken by John Boileau, at $2600 each,--this covering all of the road in Gwynedd.[1] The bridge over the run at Spring-House, and that over Evans run (between Gwynedd m. h. and North Wales), were built by Robert Scarlett, and he also raised the walls of the bridge over Treweryn. The work of construction was so far advanced that the lower nine miles were inspected by the Governor's committee in June, 1848, and the remainder in September,[2] and upon favorable report, the Governor issued his certificate, September 8, 1848, authorizing the erecting of toll-gates and the collection of tolls.

Charles F. Jenkins, to whose energy the rapid construction of this important work was largely due, continued to be the president of the company until January, 1849, when he resigned, and Algernon S. Jenkins was elected, continuing to the present time, 1884.

---

[1] In consideration of the relief of the township in its road supervision, Gwynedd subscribed $3000 to the capital stock of the company.

[2] John E. Gross, John Shearer, and John S. Missimer were the Governor's committee.

Besides the details given in Chapter XVI. about the early roads, some other facts concerning the highways may be noted. In 1722, the monthly meeting records that several Friends were "under streight for want of a convenient road to ye meeting-house." In 1749, the meeting paid Richard Jacobs £1 16s. "for laying out a road from New Providence meeting-house to Gwynedd meeting-house "—a curious sharing of the functions of the Court!

There was formerly an old road up by Jacob B. Bowman's house, leaving the Swedes' Ford road by the corner of the woods recently cleared off, and entering the Lansdale road up by J. Schlemme's. This was a "private road," 24 feet wide, laid out by order of the Court, in 1758. It started from the township line, about where Lansdale is, and came by lands (among others) of George Howell, Thomas Shoemaker, Robert Roberts, John Thompson, Hugh Evans, and Jesse Evans, " into Montgomery road." Its length was 3½ miles, 33 perches.

"John Humphrey's bridge," mentioned in the Welsh road proceedings of 1709, was unquestionably the first bridge in the township, and it seems to have been a well-known landmark. The bridge over Treweryn, on the turnpike, was built in ——. Before that the stream was forded, and Henry Jones says his mother told him she got through with difficulty when it was swollen by a freshet. The bridge over Wissahickon, near Kneedler's was built in 1819. That on the State Road, over the Wissahickon, was built by the county, in 1833. William Hamill, S. E. Leach, and Benjamin B. Yost were the county commissioners. Samuel Houpt was the contractor for building, and was paid $2,557.30. This probably included the materials, except sand, for which $189 was paid, as appears by the county account, published in January, 1834.

The bridge over the Wissahickon, on the Plymouth road, at the mouth of Treweryn, was built in 1839, by the county, John Schaffer, Abel Thomas, and Silas Yerkes being in that year the county commissioners. I have seen among Franklin Foulke's papers duplicates of three of the contracts made for its erection. In one, Henry H. Rile contracted "to find the stone for bridge or quarry leave, for which said quarry leave the commissioners doth agree to pay to the said Rile the sum of $12\frac{1}{2}$ cents per perch, to be measured in the wall, after the completion of said bridge, the rim stone excepted." In another, Rile contracted "to furnish sufficient boarding and lodging for all the labourers that is employed to work at said bridge, except those that wish to board themselves, for the sum of 15 cents per meal; the commissioners is not to pay the board for any of the labourers when they are not at work at said bridge." In the third, Collom Clime and Charles Cox contracted "to furnish lime of the best quality sufficient to build said bridge, for which said lime said commissioners doth agree to pay $13\frac{1}{2}$ cents per bushel," measured at the bridge, if required.

The "State Road" was laid out by commissioners, under an Act of General Assembly of 1830. It was, however, only a fragmentary construction, so far as the route through Gwynedd was concerned. The old road-beds were in part used, and new pieces were made, of which the most important was that from the intersection of the Plymouth road, below Acuff's, down to the Wissahickon and up the hill to the township line, at or near which the bed of the old Swedes' Ford road was reached.

XXVI.

Genealogical Details Concerning Early Families.

MORGAN.

The first settler in Gwynedd or its vicinity, named Morgan, was Edward. He seems to have been here as early as 1704, as the road upward through Gwynedd, made in that year, was to go as far as his place. He was a tailor by trade, a Welshman by birth, no doubt, and was probably advanced in years when he came. He had lived, previously, near Philadelphia. In February, 1708, he bought 300 acres of land in what is now Towamencin, of Griffith Jones, merchant, Philadelphia. The tract lay along William John's land, and was therefore on the township line. In 1714 he bought 500 acres more, near by, of George Claypoole, of Philadelphia, who, like Griffith Jones, was a speculative holder of the Towamencin lands. By 1713 he had apparently moved to Montgomery; in the deed from Claypoole he is described as "yeoman, of Montgomery."

Edward Morgan no doubt had several children. His sons probably received and held his Towamencin lands. In the list of 1734, for that township, there appear: Joseph Morgan, 200 acres; Daniel Morgan, 200; John Morgan, 100. In 1727, Morgan Morgan, of Towamencin, died, leaving a will, in which he mentions his wife Dorothy, his brothers Joseph, John, and William, his two sons Edward and Jesse (both minors), and his niece Elizabeth, John's daughter.

In the marriage lists previously given will be found the following marriages of probable sons and daughters of Edward Morgan:

EARLY FAMILIES. 365

1710. Elizabeth Morgan m. Cadwallader Morris.
1713. Margaret Morgan m. Samuel Thomas.
1713. William Morgan m. Elizabeth Roberts.
1721. John Morgan m. Sarah Lloyd.
1718. Daniel Morgan m. Elizabeth Roberts.
1720. Sarah Morgan m. Squire Boone.
1728. Joseph Morgan m. Elizabeth Lloyd.
1731. William Morgan, widower, m. Cath. Robeson.

That all these were children of the first Edward Morgan is not certain but probable. (Several of them are designated as son, or daughter, " of Edward," as will be seen by reference to the list).

Daniel Morgan, named above, who m. Elizabeth Roberts, was a minister among the Friends. He d. 7th mo. 6, 1773, having had a stroke of paralysis, some time before. A memorial concerning him says he was born in the district of Moyamensing (Philadelphia) in 1691, but that "while still young his parents removed to Gwynedd, then just being settled." His wife was also a preacher; her memorial says she was born in Wales, came over while young, appeared in the ministry after her marriage, went to England, in 1743, on a religious visit, in company with Susanna Morris, and remained two years, visiting most of the meetings in Great Britain. In her old age she was injured by a fall from her horse. She d. 11th mo. 14th, 1777, in her 88th year. (Her children, Benjamin and Ruth, are named in the Roberts Genealogy.)

CLEAVER.

The Cleaver Family of Gwynedd and Montgomery are the descendants of Peter Klever, one of the early German settlers at Germantown. He was, no doubt, one of the company that included the Shoemakers, the Lukenses, the Conrads, and others of the Quaker immigrants, who came from the lower Rhine, after the arrival of Pastorius and the earliest of the settlers. He is on the record as having been naturalized, as of Germantown, in 1691, and he died in Bristol (adjoining Germantown) in 1727, leaving children: Isaac, John, Peter, jr., Derrick, and Agnes, besides two married daughters, Christiana Melchior and Eve Adams. Isaac, the eldest son, had land in Cheltenham, and probably removed there; John received his father's place in Bristol township, and had a family, including Elizabeth, Peter, William, Sarah, John, and Hannah; while Peter Cleaver, jr., removed to Upper Dublin, and was there before 1734, as he is returned in the list of that year as the owner of 100 acres of land.

This Peter Cleaver, jun., of Upper Dublin, is frequently mentioned as a road juror, etc. His wife's name was Elizabeth. He died in 1776, and mentions in his will his sons John, Isaac, Ezekiel, Peter, and Nathan, and his daughter Elizabeth. The last married John Roberts, son of John, of Whitpain; while her brother Nathan married Ruth Roberts, a daughter of John, and removed to Montgomery, where he bought 137 acres which had been part of the Isaac Jones property, in the extreme lower end of the township. His children were: Phœbe, who m. Amos Griffith; David, Jonathan, who m. Ann Jones; Nathan, jr., who m. Martha Shoemaker; Salathiel, who m. Mary Shoemaker. (Of these sons, Jonathan had one son, Elias, who m. Anne Acuff; Nathan had three children: David, Jesse, Rebecca; and Salathiel had six children: Lydia, Nathan, Josiah, Daniel, Silas, John).

Ezekiel Cleaver, named above (son of Peter, of Upper Dublin), m. Mary Lewis, dau. of Ellis Lewis, 2d, and his wife Mary. From this couple are descended another branch of the family, including Ezekiel, Solomon, and Ellis, all well-known residents of Gwynedd a few years ago.

JONES—LEWIS.

John Jones, carpenter, of Montgomery, came into the township from Merion, about 1710. He married at Gwynedd meeting-house, 4th mo. 9, 1713, Jane Edward, daughter of Edward Griffith. Both were valued members of the Society of Friends, and there are memorials of them by Gwynedd monthly meeting, — that of Jane Jones in the printed collection of 1787, and that of her husband unpublished. John Jones was a prominent, active, and valuable citizen, in his day. He owned a large property, including what in modern times has been two farms, lying in Montgomery, above the State road, along the Gwynedd line. His home was on the upper farm (lately belonging to Edwin Moore), and part of the house is said to have been built by him with bricks which he made on the premises.

This John Jones was the son of Rees John William, repeatedly mentioned in this volume, and particularly described in the foot note, p. 95. The record of Rees John's children, from Haverford m. m., shows that his son John was born 4th mo. 6, 1688. He was therefore 22 when he came to Montgomery, and 25 when he was married. His children were: Hannah, who m. William Foulke; Catharine, d. in infancy; Margaret, b. 1717, d. 1745; Priscilla, b. 1719, d. 1742, m. Evan Jones, of Merion; *Evan* (see below); *Jesse* (see below); Katharine, b. 1726, d. 1741; Jane, b. 1728, d. 1806; Benjamin, d. in childhood; Ruth, d. in infancy. John Jones, carpenter, the father, d. 12th mo. 30, 1774; his wife, Jane, had d. 5th mo. 14, 1757.

Jesse, the son named above, probably removed to Buckingham. His wife's name was Mary. Their son Josiah m., 1798, Elizabeth Watson, dau. of Thomas and Sarah, by whom he had three children: Ezra, Sarah, and Elizabeth; and he appears to have married a second time, his wife being Elizabeth, daughter of Thomas Wilson, by whom he had one son, Wilson. There are probably no male descendants of Jesse Jones now living.

Evan Jones, of Montgomery, inherited his father's estate,

He was b. 12th mo. 26, 1720, and d. 8th mo. 31, 1801. He m., 1766, Hannah Lawrence, dau. of Henry, of Haverford, dec'd. Their children included: John, d. unm.; *Henry* (see below); Hannah, d. unm.; *Evan* (see below). Hannah, widow of Evan, sr., d. 1825.

Henry Jones, named above, m., Jane Lewis, 1805, dau. of Amos and Eleanor, of Upper Dublin. He d. comparatively a young man, — 10th mo. 19, 1813. He left four children: Lewis, Clement, John L., and Henry. (The last two are now living, and they are, I believe, the only male representatives of the family of John Jones, carpenter.) Henry Jones's house was the lower part of the Montgomery estate,— now the Armstrong farm, on the State road. He died there, having built the buildings that now stand, — the house, barn, and wagon-house. The place was tenanted, after his death, by Jacob Zorns and Mathias Young, and in the spring of 1821, his widow removed to her father's place at Three Tuns, in Upper Dublin. (Her father died in the autumn following.)

Evan Jones, jr., son of Evan, and brother of Henry just mentioned, was a conspicuous citizen. (See biographical sketch.) He was four times married: to Sarah Ely, dau. of William and Cynthia, of Buckingham; to Lowry Miles (née Foulke), dau. of Caleb and Jane, of Gwynedd; to Hannah Paul; and to Mary Lukens. By his first wife he had two daughters who grew up: Jane, who m. Jonathan Maulsby, and Cynthia E., who m., 1st, Dr. Evan Lester, of Richland, and 2d, Evan Green, of Columbia, Pa. By his second wife Evan Jones, jr., had one son, Owen, who d. 3 years old; but of his children there was no issue except Evan Jones Lester, son of Cynthia, by her first husband.

Of Henry Jones's sons, Lewis m. Mary Livezey, who survives him, living on their homestead in Gwynedd, on the Upper Dublin line. They had no children. Clement m. late in life, but left no children. Henry m. Mary Y. Shoemaker; they have no issue. John L. m. Margaret, dau. of Benjamin and Anne

EARLY FAMILIES. 369

Garrigues, and had several children, of whom but one now survives: Jane, m. to Dr. Franklin T. Haines, of Rancocas, N. J.

Henry Jones's wife, as already mentioned, was Jane, daughter of Amos Lewis. The first of the Lewis Family, in Upper Dublin, was Ellis, 1st, who came from Merion. (He may very well have been of the same family as the Lewises of Montgomery township,—see p. 265.) His wife's name was Anne. He purchased the property which is now John L. Jones's farm (in the occupancy of Amos Ely), and David L. Lukens's farm. He d. 1753, his wife surviving until 1756. Their children included *Ellis* (see below); Lewis, m. Anne Lord; Jane, m. Enos Lewis, of Gwynedd; Elizabeth, m. William Spencer.

Ellis Lewis, 2d, m. 10th mo. 18, 1729, at Abington meetinghouse, Mary Tyson, dau. of Matthias and Mary, of Abington. Mary Lewis, the wife, d. 1st mo. 17, 1763, and Ellis m., 2d, Ellen Evans, dau. of John and Eleanor, of Gwynedd. (See p. 161.) Ellis d. 1783, and his wife survived him. His children, all by his first wife, were 11 in number, of whom six died young. The others were: Ellis, jr., b. 1730, d. unm. 1759; Mary, m. Ezekiel Cleaver; Ann, m. John Saunders; John; and *Amos* (see below).

Amos Lewis was twice married. His wives were sisters, Eleanor and Rachel Hubbs, of Gwynedd, daughters of John and Jane (and nieces of Ellis Lewis, 2d's, second wife. See p. 161). Amos had by each wife one daughter: by his first wife he had Jane, who m. Henry Jones, of Montgomery, named above; and by his second, Eleanor, who m. Jesse Lukens. From the latter marriage there is a large family: the Jones branch has been given above.

SPENCER.

The first of the Spencer family, in Pennsylvania, was Samuel, of Upper Dublin. The tradition has always been that he was a sea captain, and that after bringing his family here, about 1700, he returned for one more voyage and was lost (or died) at sea. How

24

this tradition grew up it is hard to say, but documentary evidence shows its incorrectness. Samuel Spencer's will is on record in Philadelphia. It describes him as "late of Barbadoes, but now of the county of Philadelphia, merchant, being sick of body, but of good and perfect memory," [etc.] This shows him to have been on land, and ill, at the date of the will, which was November 20, 1705, and as its probate was made a month later, December 20, 1705, it is evident that his decease immediately followed, so that no voyage and death at sea could have occurred.

Samuel Spencer, as is known in various ways, left two sons, Samuel and William. These the will names : " I give and bequeath unto my eldest son, Samuel Spencer, £20, to be paid unto him when he shall come to the age of 21 years, without any interest, [he] to be fitted with a good suit of cloaths fitt for such a lad, and to be forthwith sent to Barbadoes to his relacions there. I give and bequeath unto my son William Spencer, £20," etc., etc.

Of Samuel Spencer's "relacions," in Barbadoes, we get some clue from old English documents. Peter Spencer, aged 15, and John Spencer, aged 19, went from Gravesend to Barbadoes in the ship *Expedition*, Peter Blackler master, November 20, 1635, and James Spencer, aged 25, went in the *Falcon*, Tho: Irish master, December 19, 1635. In 1679, a list of the inhabitants of the parish of Christ Church, Barbadoes, showed John Spencer, owning 23 acres of land and 7 negroes. In 1680, a "list of the inhabitants in and about the Town of St. Michaels," Barbadoes, showed John Spencer and wife, with 2 children, 3 hired servants, and 3 negroes. In the 30th of Charles II. that monarch appointed Robert Spencer (with three others) collector of the royal revenue in Barbadoes and other West India Islands, for seven years.

Samuel Spencer's two sons were, as the will shows, minors when their father died.[1] Their mother, in all probability, was

---

[1] They were in fact young children. Samuel was b. 8th mo. 22, 1699. William was b. 11th mo. 1, 1701. (William m. Elizabeth Lewis, dau. of Ellis, 1st, of Upper Dublin, and removed to Bucks county, where he has numerous descendants.)

previously deceased. It is well established that her name was Elizabeth, and that she was a Whitton; it is also said that her two brothers brought up the Spencer lads,—Samuel not having been sent back to Barbadoes, at all. In 1742, Richard Whitton, of Upper Dublin, yeoman, made his will, and after some bequests left to his "two cousins, Samuel Spencer and William Spencer," all his "lands, houses, tenements, and plantations," etc.,—this being a large property in Upper Dublin.

Samuel Spencer, 2d, m. 1723, Mary Dawes, dau. of Abraham and Edith, and their children were 13 in number, including Jacob, who m. Hannah Jarrett, whose sons John and Jarrett married respectively Lydia Foulke, of Gwynedd (see p. 227), and Hannah Evans, of Gwynedd (see p. 163). Jesse Spencer, of Penllyn, was John's son.[1]

Two other sons of Samuel, 2d, and Mary, were the following:

1. Joseph, b. 2d mo. 21, 1726, m. Hannah Lukens, dau. of John, of Bristol [adj. Germantown]. This couple had one son, Samuel, who d. young. Joseph then m. Abigail West (subsequently Abigail Conrad), and had one son, Nathan. This Nathan m. Rachel Pim, dau. of Thomas, of Chester county, and had children: Thomas P., Joseph, Sarah, *Hephziba*, Maria.

2. John, b. 9th mo. 1, 1731, m. Elizabeth Kirk, dau. of John and Sarah, and had 8 children. One these was Sarah, who m. Jonathan Thomas, of Moreland, son of Mordecai and Elizabeth. Jonathan and Sarah had children: *Spencer*, Mordecai, and Elizabeth. *Spencer Thomas* m. *Hephziba Spencer*, named above,—his second cousin. Their eldest daughter,[2] Anna Maria, m. 1841, Algernon S. Jenkins,[3] of Gwynedd.

JENKINS.

The Jenkins family of Gwynedd and neighboring townships

---

[1] See Foulke Genealogy, p. 227, for details concerning Jesse Spencer.

[2] Their other children were Sarah, Mordecai, Caroline, Lemuel, Elizabeth, Lydia, Jonathan, Mary, Hannah. Spencer Thomas was a prominent and esteemed citizen of Upper Dublin.

[3] Algernon S. Jenkins had issue by his 1st wife one son: Howard M.; by his 2d wife, Alice A. Davis, one son: George Herbert.

are descended from Jenkin Jenkin, a Welshman, who came to this place in or about 1729. The family record in an old Welsh Bible which was formerly in possession of John Jenkins, of North Wales, shows the following:

>Jenkin Jenkins died September 15, 1745, aged 86 years.
>Mary Jenkins died November 27, 1764, aged 74.
>John Jenkins born February 15, 1719.

This, therefore, fixes the birth of Jenkin Jenkin in 1659, and of his wife in 1690. November 17, 1730, Jenkin Jenkin bought of Joseph Tucker land in Hatfield, 350 acres, " reaching from the Gwynedd line nearly or quite to the Cowpath road, and from the Montgomery line about to the road running from Lansdale to Colmar." On this he settled, and he was " of Hatfield," when he made his will in 1745. He had bought, in 1738, of the proprietaries, 357 acres of land on the Conestoga, in Earl township, Lancaster county, closely adjoining the Welsh settlers of Carnarvon and Brecknock, and as there were some named Jenkins among them, it is not unlikely they may have been kinsmen, and that he may have come over from Wales with some of that company,—their arrival being about 1729, also. Jenkin Jenkin, at his death, left 4 children, as follows:

1. *John*, who rec'd 150 acres of the Hatfield property, and half the Conestoga property. He was b. (as above), Feb. 15, 1719, in Wales, and m. Sarah Hawkesworth, dau. of Peter and Mary. (She was b. in 1720, in England, and d. Jan. 16, 1794.) They had eight children. (See below.)

2. Mary, d. unm.

3. Jenkin, jr., m. —— Thomas. He rec'd, by his father's will, 200 acres in Hatfield, and a share in the Conestoga tract. He had four children: David, d. unm.; Elizabeth, m. John Banes; Hannah, d. unm.; Eleanor, m. —— McPherson.

4. Elizabeth, m. John Hawkesworth, son of Peter and Mary ; and had seven children.

John Jenkins, named above, was the progenitor of all of this family who now bear the name, his brother Jenkin having no sons. John was a prominent and useful citizen. (He was the assessor of Gwynedd township, as mentioned in the 1776 tax-

list.) He bought land in Gwynedd, in 1746, adjoining Lansdale. He died in 1803 (or 1804). His eight children were as follows:
 1. John, 2d, b. 1742, d. 1805, an officer in the Revolutionary army. He m. Elizabeth Lukens, wid. of Abraham, and had six children : Owen, m. Mary Tennis; Sarah, m. Peter Hoxworth; Jesse, m. Mary Aaron ; John, m. Ann Todd[1]; Edward, m. Margaret Server[2]; Elizabeth, m. Issacher Rhoads.
 2. Levi, m. Susan Sheive, and had 9 children, including Rev. John S. Jenkins, a prominent minister of the Baptist denomination ; and Levi, jr., who m. Sarah Smith and had 6 children, including Joseph S., Eder, John S., and Anne.
 3. Ann, m. Hugh Kousty.
 4. Edward, b. July 12, 1758, d. 1829, m. Sarah Foulke, dau. of Theophilus (see Foulke Genealogy), and had 6 children : Charles F., m. Mary Lancaster[3]; Ann, d. unm.; Jesse,[4] m. Mary R. Ambler; Margaret, m. Peter C. Evans ; Rachel, m. Meredith Conard; Caleb, died a lad.
 5. Jesse, born 1760, d. 1794, unm.
 6. Elizabeth, m. Owen Hughes, and had 8 children.
 7. Mary, m. Peter Wentz, and had 7 children.
 8. Sarah, m. Isaac Lewis, and had 3 children. (See details about Isaac Lewis, p. 319.)

HOXWORTH.

Peter Hawksworth[5] and his wife Mary came from England about 1730, and settled in Hatfield. Peter died between Febru-

---

[1] John, who m. Ann Todd, lived to extreme old age, dying at North Wales (at the house of his son-in-law, Abel Lukens), Oct. 5, 1880, in his 97th year. His children were Naomi, who m. Abel Lukens; Charles T., m. Sarah Lukens; Jane, m. Samuel J. Rhoads; Ann T., m. Jacob B. Rhoads; Silas T., m. Eliza Morgan; John S., m. Eliza Stover; Milton, m. Sarah Ellis.

[2] Edward, b. May 9, 1786, d. Jan. 29, 1872; and had issue: Philip S., m. Hannah Zieber; Mary Ann, m. Chas. D. Matthews; Charles S., m. Tacy Styer.

[3] Chas. F. and Mary had 7 children, of whom 5 d. young. The others were Algernon S., who m. Anna Maria Thomas, and Alice A. Davis; and William H., who m. Catharine Hallowell.

[4] Jesse removed to Peoria county, Ill., in 1840, and survives, 1884. Of his children, Albanus is married and has children.

[5] The spelling of the name in England was probably Hawkesworth. It became changed, here, first to Hawksworth, and then to Hoxworth.

ary 26, 1767, and March 22, 1769,—these being the dates of making and proving his will. His wife died soon after. They are said to have been buried at St. Thomas's churchyard, Whitemarsh. Their children were 6 in number, including Edward, Ann, and Rachel, of whom nothing further is known, and the following:

1. Sarah, m. John Jenkins, the elder. (See preceding section.)
2. John, m. Elizabeth Jenkins (sister of John, just named), dau. of Jenkin and Mary, and had 7 children: Mary, m. Zachariah Clawson; Edward, m. Mary Hoxworth (see below); John, d. unm.; Elizabeth, m. Henry Newberry; Ann, m. C. Wells; Sarah, m. Kenneth Makenzie; and "Colonel" Peter, who m. Sarah Jenkins. (See below.) *John* bought land, in 1761, located in Hatfield, from his father, and d. aged 44, early in the Revolution. He had been a soldier in the French and Indian War, and had served in the Revolutionary army, but was taken sick and died, while so engaged.
3. Peter, who was twice married. By his first wife he had 7 children. His second wife was Ann Wentz, dau. of Philip and Mary (Jenkins) Wentz, by whom he had 4 children.

Edward Hoxworth, above (son of John and Elizabeth), lived in Hatfield. He was b. Sept. 22, 1760, and d. Jan. 11, 1847. He entered the Revolutionary army when only 15 years old, and served throughout the war. He received a pension to the end of his life. He was a member of the company of which John Jenkins, 2d, was a lieutenant. "He was a small-built man, but exceedingly lithe and active. In his younger days he would leap over an ordinary-sized horse without touching." His wife, Mary (b. 1760, d. 1823), was the dau. of Peter (No. 3 above), and therefore first cousin to her husband. They had 9 children, as follows:

1. Ann, m. Benjamin Krupp; 2 children.
2. Ellen, m. Benjamin Kulp; 8 children.
3. John, m. ——— Smith.
4. Israel, m. Mary Slough; 7 children.
5. Mary, m. Robert Gordon; 7 children.
6. Margaret, d. unmarried.
7. Edward, m. C. Nonnemacher; 3 children.

EARLY FAMILIES.

8. Elizabeth, m. B. F. Hancock (see below).
9. Sarah, m. Jesse Godshalk ; 9 children.

"Col." Peter Hoxworth, of Hatfield, b. Jan. 16, 1776, d. Nov. 11, 1850, m. Sarah Jenkins, dau. of John, 2d, and Elizabeth. He was an officer in the war of 1812, and subsequently a colonel of Pennsylvania militia. For many years he was a justice of the peace, and he was also director of the poor, of Montgomery county. He had eight children: Elizabeth, m. Henry Lukens; Ann, m. John S. Cliffton; John J., m. D. Swartz; Owen, d. unm; Enos L., m. Ann Mattis ; Matilda, m. B. A. Morris ; Mary, m. J. Santman; William J.,[1] m. Catherine A. Biery.

Elizabeth Hoxworth (No. 8, above), dau. of Edward and Mary, b. December 8, 1801, d. January 25, 1879, m. Benjamin F. Hancock. Their children were Winfield Scott and Hilary Baker (twins), b. Feb. 14, 1824, and John, b. March 23, 1830, m. Augusta Camp, and has issue 11 children. (Biographical notices of Gen. Hancock and his father will be found in the next chapter.)

CASTNER.

The Castner Family are descended from Paul Kastner, who was one of the early German, or Hollandish, settlers at Germantown. He is named with Peter Klever in the naturalization list of 1691, and was a Friend, as in 1692 he was one of those who signed the testification of the Yearly Meeting against George Keith. He d. in 1717, and his will is on record in Philadelphia, witnessed by Francis Daniel Pastorius.

Jacob Castner, who may have been a son, or grandson, of Paul, was a resident of Upper Dublin, in 1754. He d. between December, 1763, and February 26, 1767, and in his will men-

---

[1] To William J. Hoxworth, now of Macungie, Lehigh county, I am indebted for all the details concerning this family, and also for many of those relating to the Jenkins Family. (William J., b. Oct. 6, 1821, m. Catharine A. Biery, and has issue: Mary Ella, Emilie A., Lewis C. (d.), Charles H., William A. (d.), Sarah G., John S. (d.)

tions his wife Ann, daughters Sarah and Elizabeth, and sons Samuel, Andrew, and George. The will shows that he had one tract of 81 acres of land, in Gwynedd, which he had bought of Robert Combs, and another of 21, in Gwynedd, bought of Catharine Jones, while he lived on a tract of 299 acres in Upper Dublin, adjoining Ellis Lewis, and he had also 100 acres in East Nottingham, Chester county, purchased of George Churchman. The main tract of the Gwynedd land, which he left to Sarah and Samuel, lay below the Spring-House, on the road to the Three Tons, including what was recently the Wm. Smith farm. The Upper Dublin tract he left chiefly to Andrew, and this included the old Siddons place, now or recently Malachi Stout's. The Chester county property he left to "Daniel and Susanna, the children of my son Jacob, deceased."

Samuel Castner lived on the Gwynedd place,[1] and d. there Feb. 22, 1806. His estate was settled by David Lukens and Amos Lewis, executors. He left a legacy of £8 in Pennsylvania money to Gwynedd meeting. His brother Andrew had died a few years earlier,—about 1796 or '97. His estate was settled by Cadwalader Evans, jr., and Amos Lewis, ex'rs.

George Kastner (who may have been the son named in Jacob's will) was in Whitpain, in 1734, and had 200 acres of land. His will was made April 27, 1776, and proved Oct. 19 of the same year. His wife was Elizabeth; he mentions his sons Thomas, dec'd, and his (Thomas's) widow, and daughter Margaret. He also mentions his grandchildren named Conrad, and other grandchildren named Ottinger, his sons-in-law Thomas Mee, Lewis Jones, Philip Richardson, and William Streeper,— the last deceased. He leaves his six daughters, Mary, Magdalene, Elizabeth, Hannah, Lydia, and Margaret, residuary legatees.

---

[1] Henry Jones says it was the tradition that he gave his property away (perhaps to his family), on condition that they should build him "a little house by the big spring," near the main dwelling, and in this little house he ended his life. Traces of it, near the spring, were visible fifty years ago.

Samuel Castner, of Gwynedd (grandfather of Jesse, recently deceased), lived on the Swedes' Ford road, where George W. Castner (his great-grandson), now lives. He was b. June 4, 1737, and d. November 5, 1833. His dau. Elizabeth, m. Nathan Chapin, who was a teacher in Philadelphia. Their son, William Chapin, has been for many years principal of the Institution for the Blind, in Philadelphia.[1]

Jesse Castner, the elder, a son of Samuel, m. Margaret Rhodes, dau. of Ezekiel, of Norriton. (The ceremony, January 1795, before Esq. Frederick Conrad.) The Gwynedd monthly meeting records show the birth of their children : Melinda, b. 5th mo. 8, 1796; Charles, b. 10th mo. 25, 1798; Mary, b. 12th mo. 5, 1800; Rachel, b. 11th mo. 7, 1803; Margaret, b. 5th mo. 19, 1805; Anne, b. 10th mo. 19, 1806. The records also show the death of Margaret, wife of Jesse, in 1809 (two dates given: 8th mo. 30, and 10th mo. 31). Jesse m. a second time, and had one son, Jesse, jr., lately deceased.

ROBERTS.

Besides the members of the Roberts Family of whom details have been given in Chapter XIV., there were several others living in Gwynedd, named Roberts, but of a different family. Ellis Roberts, tailor, whose daughter Lydia m. Benjamin Mendenhall, lived below Penllyn, having bought in 1714 the lower William John tract, of his (W. J.'s) daughters, Gaynor, Ellen, and Catharine. Besides his daughter Lydia, he had a son,— and possibly other children.

Ellis had also two brothers, John and William. William m. Mary Pugh, widow of Ellis Pugh, jr., and daughter of Owen Evans. She d. 1748, and he before her. Her will mentions two daughters of her son Ellis Roberts.

---

[1] His son Dr. John B. Chapin, for many years physician in charge of the great Willard Insane Hospital in New York State, is now in charge of the Penna. Hospital for the Insane, in Philadelphia.

John Roberts, the other brother of Ellis, d. in 1725, leaving his wife Ellinor and brother Ellis his executors. His will mentions no children. His widow, Ellinor, d. the same year. They probably had no children, as none are mentioned in either's will.

There was still another Roberts family in Gwynedd, making a third. Edward Roberts was the first of this line who appears here. He d. 1748–49, "being old and far advanced in years." His son Robert m. Jane Evans, dau. of Robert Evans, of Merion, and their son was Amos Roberts, who was the father of George Roberts, who owned the old Robert Evans place (now Silas White's). Edward Roberts' wife was Ann, and she was living when he made his will, October 3, 1748. His daughter Margaret m. Hugh Evans, and afterward Robert Jones, of Merion. His daughter Gainor was the first wife of Edward Foulke.

JONES.

The name Robert John, or Robert Jones, was the possession of several different persons within the scope of this history. One of these was "of Merion," and d. 1746. (He was the son of John ap Thomas, and the father of Robert Jones, 2d, who m. Catharine Evans, Hugh's widow.)

Robert John, repeatedly alluded to in this volume, owned the land where North Wales now is, and d. 1732.

Another Robert Jones, of Gwynedd, m., 1717, Ann Coulston, dau. of William, of Plymouth. He afterward became of Worcester, and d. there, 6th mo. 24, 1773.[1] He was born in Denbighshire, Wales, 10th mo. 9, 1690, and his wife, Ann, was b. in Yorkshire, England, "near Moor Land," 8th mo. 18, 1695.[2]

---

[1] His family Bible came into the possession of Watson Ambler, of East Bradford, Chester Co., in 1869. This Bible (printed in Dublin, 1714), an entry in it says, R. J. "bought of Cadwallader Foulke, in Philadelphia, the 4th day of the 12th mo., 1732, and paid two pounds, being the price thereof. Also paid 20 shillings more for binding and brassing of clasps since I bought it. 1762."

[2] As she was the daughter of William Coulston, of Plymouth, this fixes the place whence he came.

Their children were William, Margaret, Ann, m. Jacob Bell; Elizabeth, Robert, Josiah, Grace, m. ——— Jones, and Owen Thomas; Hannah, m. ——— Prichard; Enos. Ann, the mother, d. 4th mo. 21, 1772.

Still another Robert Jones, "of Gwynedd, cordwainer," d. 1745, probably unmarried. He left bequests to his cousin John Evans, to his cousin Elizabeth Evans, wife of Thomas, his cousin Owen Evans, son of Thomas; to Edward, Thomas, Griffith, and John Evans, sons of Thomas; to Cousin Peter Evans, to cousin Thomas Griffith, to his cousins, the children of Joseph Williams, etc.

XXVII.

Biographical Notices.

Doctor Cadwalader Evans.

HE was born at Gwynedd, in 1716, the son of the first John Evans and his wife, Eleanor. I am inclined to regard him as perhaps the most distinguished member of this branch of the Evans family; he was certainly one of the most eminent professional men of his day. He studied medicine under the direction of the famous Dr. Thomas Bond, of Philadelphia, and afterward at the University of Edinburgh, and in London, when, returning to Philadelphia, he settled there, and soon enjoyed a large practice. He became a friend and correspondent of Franklin, and was deeply interested in scientific and philanthropic work. (He was elected a member of the American Philosophical Society, in 1767. In 1770-71, he appears among the managers of the "society for the cultivation of silk.") He married, January 22, 1760, Jane Owen, daughter of Owen Owen, of Philadelphia, but had no children. His wife died 1768. A paragraph in the *Pennsylvania Gazette*, of March 17th, in that year, says:

Yesterday se'ennight died Mrs. Jane Evans, the wife of Dr. Cadwalader Evans, of this city, much respected and lamented by all who knew her. [The funeral was large; her remains interred at the Friends' burial ground in this city.]

And the same journal, July 7, 1773, has the following obituary paragraph:

On the 30th of last month died, beloved and lamented, in the 57th year of his age, Dr. Cadwalader Evans, one of the Physicians of the Philadelphia Hospital, after a lingering Illness, which he sustained with that Composure and Resignation of Mind which are a certain Evidence and a happy Consequence of having filled the Sphere of Life allotted to him with Rectitude and Integrity. * * * * * He was justly esteemed an eminent, candid, and successful Physician; his knowledge was deep and liberal, his Principles rational, improved by an extensive Practice, a diligent Observation, and a penetrating Judgment. * * * * * In his Sentiments he was liberal, in Argument solid, acute, and facetious, but above all in his Friendships he was ardent, steady, and sincere.

His Remains were interred in Friends' Burying Ground at North Wales, amongst many others of his ancient and worthy Family, attended by a large Number of respectable People, both from the City and Country.

In his will, dated January 24, 1773, and probated July 17, he appoints Abel James and Owen Biddle, merchants, of Philadelphia, and his brothers Rowland and John Evans, executors; who are to sell all his property, real and personal, not specially devised. "I give all my plate, which belonged to my late dear wife Jane, unto her beloved niece, Ann Biddle, the wife of John Biddle. I give the China Jarrs, which was my said dear wife's, to the daughters of the said John Biddle, and Ann Morris, the daughter of Tacy Forbes. * * * * I direct my said Executors to have made two silver pint canns and a silver Cream Jugg, one of the said Canns and cream jugg I give to my sister Margaret Williams, and the other of them I give to my sister Eleanor Lewis." The residue of his property he divides into four parts, one for his brother Rowland, one for his brother John, one for his sister Elizabeth, and the fourth in trust for his sister, Jane Hubbs, and after her death, for her three daughters, Rachel, Ellinor, and Mary.

John Evans (Second).

The second John Evans, of Gwynedd, called John "the elder," is thus described by the late Joseph Foulke:

"Among the remarkable persons that I recollect in those early days [about 1800] was John Evans, the elder. He was a tall, spare person, with a long visage, and very wrinkled face. He carried a smooth cane, with a carved head and natural curve. He wore loops in his hat, with the rim slightly turned up behind and at the two sides. He and two or three others of Gwynedd were among the first who took a firm stand against the use of ardent spirits. They banished it from their houses and harvest fields, though in the face of great difficulties. One of the last meetings that John Evans attended, he spoke on this subject, saying that 'where he had endeavored most he had effected least,' but urging his hearers to persevere."

Rowland Evans.

Rowland Evans (b. 1718, d. 1789), son of John and Eleanor, of Gwynedd, and brother to Dr. Cadwalader, was prominent in public affairs for many years. He was appointed a justice of the peace in 1749, 1752, 1757, and 1761. He was a member of the Provincial Assembly for Philadelphia County in 1761, and from that year on to 1771, inclusive (except 1764). His residence was first in Gwynedd, and in 1760 he owned part of his father's tract. At a later date (as early as 1766) he removed to Providence, and he was in business there for a number of years. The Philadelphia *Gazette*, June 30, 1784, contains his card, announcing that he "has lately removed from his former Residence in Providence Township, Philadelphia County," and that he is prepared to draw "Deeds, mortgages, articles of agreement, and other instruments of writing, at his house on the east side of Fourth street, a few doors below Race street." September 14, 1785, he was appointed one of the Commissioners of the General Loan Office of Pennsylvania, and he held this place until his death, August 8, 1789. Like his brother Cadwalader, he took an interest in scientific study, and he was elected a member of the "American Society for the Promotion of Useful Knowledge," which was united with the American Philosophical Society, in 1769. The Pennsylvania *Gazette* of Wednesday, August 19, 1789, contained the following notice:

On Saturday se'ennight died Rowland Evans, Esquire, of this city, in the seventy-second year of his age. Previous to the revolution this gentleman was for many years a member of the Legislature and a Justice of the

Peace, both of which he filled with great ability, dignity, and applause. And since the conclusion of the war, he was appointed one of the Trustees of the general loan office of this commonwealth, which he held to the time of his death, and on Sunday following a great assemblage of people attended at the deposit of his remains in the Quakers' burial ground in this place [Philadelphia].

Cadwalader Evans, junior.

Cadwalader Evans, jr., was the son of John and Margaret. He was born at Gwynedd, December 25, 1762, resided there until 1812, when he removed to Philadelphia, and died in the city, in 1841. He received a good education, and with unusual energy and mental vigor, made his mark early. He was trained as a surveyor, and for many years, in his own neighborhood and elsewhere, followed his profession with success. In the mature and later years of his life he performed important work in surveying in distant parts of the State, especially the western counties. In 1790 he was first elected to the Legislature, and he then entered upon a lengthened career as a member of the House. He was chosen continuously from Montgomery county for nine years,—1790 to 1798 inclusive,—his colleagues including James Vaux, Jonathan Roberts, Nathaniel B. Boileau, Frederick Conrad, and other prominent and able men. Among these, though he was under thirty when first elected, he at once took a prominent part, being placed on important committees in his first year; his name appears in many places in the House journal coupled with that of Albert Gallatin, and others of the most distinguished members in that period. In 1798, the last year the Legislature met in Philadelphia, he was unanimonsly chosen Speaker of the House. Again in 1802, and in 1805, he was elected from Montgomery county, and in 1814, after his removal to Philadelphia, he was elected one of the city members.

In 1816 he sold the old family homestead in Gwynedd to Charles Willing Hare, Esq., of Philadelphia. He was one of the local directors of the Bank of the United States, after its recharter in 1816. In 1813 he had been among the first to actively urge the construction of a canal along the Schuylkill, from Philadelphia to the coal regions, and he was elected the first president of the company, and served in that capacity for many years. In 1830, when, on account of advancing age, he resigned the presidency, the stockholders, at their annual meeting, voted that he should be presented a silver vase as a testimonial of their high appreciation of his services. Joseph Foulke, in his manuscript Reminiscences, furnished the author, says of C. E.:

He began his distinguished career about the 18th or 19th year of his age. One of his first engagements was surveying for the road jury, and laying out what is now called the "lower State road," at least the western section of it terminating in what is now the Bethlehem turnpike. This was in 1786. He was a man of quick and clear perception, of ready utterance, and a powerful disputant; he was eminently gifted in conveyancing, and in drawing instruments of writing. * * * The last office he filled, I think, was one of the Electors that made Gen. Harrison President, in 1840. As a surveyor in old time, though a young man, he stood high, and great confidence was reposed in him. He, Robert Loller, and Archibald McClean did most of the surveying in our parts until about 1807, when Cadwalader Foulke came to Gwynedd and took a large portion of the business.

Samuel Medary.

The prominence of Mr. Medary, for many years, in the political affairs of the State of Ohio, and the several important public places which he held, entitle him, no doubt, to be regarded one of the most distinguished men born in Gwynedd or Montgomery. He was born near Montgomery Square, in 1801. His father, Jacob Medary, was a farmer, in very moderate circumstances, who lived in Montgomery township for a number of years.[1]

---

[1] In April, 1820, as appears by an old document among the Cadwallader Foulke papers, he was in Gwynedd, a tenant on George Ingels' farm (now Mumbower's mill and W. M. Singerly's), and his goods were levied on by Constable George Neavel upon a landlord's warrant issued by Esq. Giffin, to satisfy Ingels' claim for a year's rent, $275, and also another execution for debt. The sale was stayed, upon an arrangement by which an assignment was made to Cadwallader Foulke and others.

The son's education, such as it was, was obtained at the free school at Montgomery Square. About 1819–20, says his old friend, William Chapin, " when I first made his acquaintance, he was teaching the school at Gwynedd meeting. He was fond of reading, and eagerly went through the newspapers at Edward Jenkins's store. The identity of the different writers awakened his curiosity, and aroused his desire to write, too. I encouraged him to try, and he did so, sending his first article to David Sower, at Norristown, for insertion in the *Herald*, over the signature 'Sylvanus.' Much to his gratification, and somewhat to his surprise, it was promptly printed, and he then wrote frequently, sometimes contributing poetry over the signature of 'Arion.' "

About 1822, he left Gwynedd for the South, going to Montgomery county, Va. There he married, and later determined to try his fortunes in the West. On his way down the Ohio river, by advice of a fellow passenger on the steamboat, he determined to settle in Ohio. (" He came to Clermont county," says his daughter, Mrs. Nevins, " in 1826.") He soon became conspicuous by his writing, and speaking at political meetings, strongly maintaining the Democratic cause, as represented by General Jackson. He presently established a small newspaper called the *Ohio Sun* ; in 1831 he was elected to the Legislature, serving for two terms as Senator. He was now one of the most prominent among the younger Democratic leaders of the State. " Mr. Tilden said to me not long ago," says Mrs. Nevins, in a letter, 1883, " that though my father was several years his senior, they were both very young men during the administration of President Jackson, and that they met at his table at the White House, both being enthusiastic admirers, and in a manner *protégés*, of that remarkable man."

In 1837 he removed to Columbus, the capital of the State, and purchased (or established?) the *Statesman*, which under his direction became the leading party newspaper, through which he exercised for years a commanding influence. As part of his reward, his party made him State Printer, and in 1853 President Pierce offered him the post of minister to Chili, but this he declined. Later, President Buchanan appointed him Governor of the Territory of Minnesota, and he served as such a brief term. When Minnesota became a State, and was admitted to the Union, 1858, the President transferred him to Kansas, as Governor of that then distracted Territory. He there remained until 1860, and then returned to Columbus, where he established *The Crisis*, and conducted it until his death, November 2, 1864. The cause of his death (says his daughter) was obscure. He had been one of those who appeared to be poisoned at the National Hotel, in Washington, at the time of Mr. Buchanan's inauguration, and he never appeared entirely well after that mysterious occurrence.

Mr. Medary had twelve children, most of whom survived him. These were: Virginia (Mrs. Wilson); Sara (Mrs. Massey); Kate (Mrs. Blair); Louise (Mrs. Smith, who died in 1861); Missouri, who died in infancy; Samuel Adams; Flora (Mrs. Nevins); Charles Stewart, William Allen, Frederick Henry, who died in July, 1883; Laura Willey, and Jacob.

"When General Hancock was appointed a cadet at West Point, in 1840," says Mrs. Nevins, "my father was one of the Board of Visitors, and the General has told me that when he arrived there with his father, the latter took him to see his old friend, *my* father, before presenting him to the officers of the Academy."

'Squire John Roberts.

'Squire John Roberts, born in 1750, was for many years one of the most conspicuous figures in Montgomery and Gwynedd. I have already mentioned his store-keeping at Spring-House. After selling out there he removed to his Montgomery farm, where he permanently remained. He had been appointed a justice of the peace, in 1791, by Governor Mifflin, his commission authorizing him to act for the townships of Hatfield, Montgomery, and Gwynedd, and he continued to act in that capacity until his death, which occurred June 17, 1823. He was a man of very considerable force and energy, a marked character in whatever he undertook. Samuel Aaron, afterwards the distinguished preacher and teacher, was "brought up" by him, and so was Benjamin F. Hancock. "Tom Wolf," afterward Dr. Antrim Foulke's faithful servitor, lived with him. He is remembered by one of the older Friends, now surviving, as coming to Gwynedd meeting occasionally, in winter time, in his sleigh, a tall man, dressed in gray. He transacted a large amount of business, including the settlement of estates, etc. His executors were Cadwallader Foulke and William Foulke, and a very serious part of their duty was the settlement of his ownership of a tract of 751 acres on Bentley's creek, Bradford county, near Towanda. 'Squire John had bought it, in 1808, of Jas. Chapman, who held under a Pennsylvania patent, but the lands were occupied by settlers under the Connecticut claim, and the 'Squire was obliged in 1815 to establish his rights by suits of ejectment. It was not until 1830, seven years after his death, that the business was concluded. He was never married; his estate, after some bequests, went to collateral heirs.

'Squire Job Roberts.

Job Roberts, who was seven years younger than 'Squire John, but who survived to a much greater age, was also a man of marked character. He was born, lived, and died in Whitpain, but close to the Gwynedd line, and for many years he was one of the most conspicuous figures in the business and social circles of Gwynedd. Born March 23, 1757, he d. August 20, 1851, having passed nearly half of his 95th year. Early in life he showed both mechanical and agricultural enterprise. He did much to improve the methods of farming, planted hedges, introduced the feeding of green fodder to cattle, instead of grazing, built a barn which was enormously large, according to the usual standard, but which he soon had full of crops, and introduced, almost if not quite as early as Judge Peters, the use of gypsum, or land plaster. In a volume which he published in 1804, called "The Pennsylvania Farmer," he said he had raised from 10 acres of land 565 bushels of wheat; and afterward, about 1820, as he stated to the late Hon. Job R. Tyson, he secured 360 bushels from a lot of 6 acres. He was one of the first in Pennsylvania to introduce and breed Merino sheep, and during the movement to establish the manufacture of silk he was one of its most zealous promoters. "Various articles of his silk manufacture, such as cloth, stockings, and other parts of dress," were still in existence, in 1856, of a date as far back as the Revolution. In 1780 he drove to Gwynedd meeting in a carriage of his own manufacture, and this, it is said, was the only carriage then, and for 25 years after, seen at that meeting.

In 1791, Gov. Mifflin appointed him a justice of the peace, and he continued as such until 1820, when he resigned. He displayed in that office a judgment and discretion so remarkable that he was widely known, much consulted, and generally esteemed. Altogether, his learning, his enterprise, his abilities, and his fine character made him a notable figure of his time.[1]

Cadwallader Foulke.

Though born at Richland, Cadwallader Foulke spent twenty-five years of his mature life in Gwynedd, and died there. He was, besides his primary occupation of farmer, a surveyor and conveyancer, and in the pursuance of these occupations he went in all directions into the neighboring, and even distant, townships of the county for many years. Few men of business were

---

[1] In 1856, Hon. Job R. Tyson read before the Montgomery Co. Agricultural Society an elaborate biography of Job Roberts, which was printed, nearly in full, in the *Germantown Telegraph*, of December 17th, in that year. Mr. Tyson's address has furnished the material for most if not all of the published sketches of 'Squire Job's life.

better known in this section, and few had so high a reputation for exactness, intelligence, and good judgment within the line of his undertakings. His surveys were carefully made; and his drafts, many of which are still in existence, are found to be valuable whenever consulted.[1] He was the son of Samuel and Ann Foulke, and was born 7th mo. 14, 1765. He died 3d mo. 22, 1830. He was apprenticed in his youth to Edward Ambler, of Montgomery, to learn weaving, and in 1792 he married his first cousin, Margaret Foulke, daughter of Theophilus. As such a marriage was against the rule of Friends, it was not accomplished "according to the order of the Society," but in the presence of his cousin Theophilus Foulke, a justice of the peace, and subsequently Richland meeting had the case up as a matter of discipline for some time. Cadwallader, however, continued a Friend, and he was a valuable member at Gwynedd. At his death he left to his son Franklin Foulke's charge a large collection of business papers, including his own accumulations, and many from the estate of 'Squire John Roberts and others, and these, which ultimately came into the hands of Algernon S. Jenkins (one of the executors of Franklin Foulke), have been of much use in compiling the facts stated in this volume.

Charles Roberts.

He was the son of Joseph, of Montgomery, and was born at the old homestead ("White Cottage Farm") July 26, 1784. The death of his father threw him at an early age upon his own resources, and he turned his attention to the occupation of teaching. After having charge of schools in Whitemarsh (1799), at Buckingham (1800-02), at Springfield, N. J. (1803), and attending Westtown school for six months (1802-03), he went to

---

[1] Esq. John C. Boorse, of Towamencin, in a communication to the North Wales *Record*, April, 1884, said he had followed in his surveys many drafts made by Cadw. Foulke, and had always found them unusually satisfactory and accurate. "It appears that he always must have had his chain correct, and his compass in proper adjustment, and noting all the variations."

Philadelphia, where, in 1805, he took charge of the Pine street Friends' school. This he conducted with much success until 1818, meantime applying himself with diligence to the improvement of his own education. In 1822 he was elected a member of the Legislature from Philadelphia, and served one term. He became identified with many benevolent and business undertakings. He was one of the original directors of the Franklin Fire Insurance Co., a director of the Ridge Turnpike Co., a director of the House of Refuge, a member and treasurer of the Board of Guardians of the Poor, for many years a manager of the Pennsylvania Hospital, a manager of the Pennsylvania Co. for Insurances on Lives, etc., etc. Having married, in 1810, Hannah, the daughter of Solomon White, a successful merchant, he was much engaged in the oversight of property, the adjustment of business, etc., in addition to the engagements already noted. In person he was a tall and robust man, "fully six feet high, and of very strong bodily frame." He had his stature at sixteen, and from that age, he said in after life, he supported himself. Among his strong characteristics, says a memoir by a member of his family, were his particular and methodical habits, his excellent health, his regular and temperate order of life, his integrity and uprightness, his rule "not a dollar for extravagance or dissipation," and his method, "without haste, without rest." He died in Philadelphia, July 9, 1845.

Joseph Roberts.

Joseph Roberts, brother of Charles above, was born at Montgomery, March 22, 1793, and went some years after his brother, to Philadelphia, where he engaged in teaching in the Friends' schools. In 1822-3-4 he had charge of the William Penn Charter School. A reference to the lists of those who sent their sons to him shows many of the most prominent citizens of that time —Wm. Rawle, Chas. J. Ingersoll, Francis Gurney Smith, Thomas P. Cope, Horace Binney, and others, his students including

Horace Binney, Jr., Alfred Cope, Henry Reed, John A. Dahlgren, and others who became distinguished men. He was deeply interested in scientific matters, and corresponded with Bowditch, and others of kindred tastes. He was a member of the American Philosophical Society, and he received in 1829 the honorary degree of A. M. from the University of Pennsylvania. He died August 25, 1835, unmarried.

Benjamin F. Hancock.

He was born in Philadelphia, the son of Richard and Anna Maria, October 19, 1800. Richard Hancock, the father, a seafaring man, was one of those seized by the British upon the pretext that he was an English subject, and he was for some time confined in Dartmoor prison; later, having returned home, he went on another voyage, and died of ship fever at sea. Meanwhile, his wife, left in low circumstances, placed her son Benjamin with 'Squire John Roberts, at Montgomery, and he was brought up there. He married Elizabeth Hoxworth, daughter of Edward and Mary, and while he was teaching "the free school" at Montgomery Square, in 1824, his twin sons, Winfield S. and Hilary B., were born. He had been occupying his leisure time with the reading of law, and having completed his studies under the direction of Hon. John Freedley, and removed to Norristown, he was admitted to the bar of Montgomery county, in 1828. He there continued to reside until his death, February 1, 1867. He was prominent in his profession, but not aspiring, and he held no public position of distinction. For twenty or more years he was one of the directors of the public schools of Norristown, and from 1866 to his death, he served as U. S. Collector of Internal Revenue. Early in the term of his residence at Norristown he was for some time district attorney of Montgomery county, by the Governor's appointment. His remains are interred in the Montgomery Cemetery at Norristown, with those of his wife.

Joseph Foulke.

Amongst the community of the Friends, at Gwynedd, the most conspicuous figure, for many years, was Joseph Foulke. He was born there, May 22, 1786. In 1817, he appeared as a minister, and was admitted a member of the meeting of ministers and elders in 1821, after which he continued in the ministry to the end of his life, more than forty years. He made numerous visits to distant meetings, including those in New Jersey, New York, Canada, Maryland, Ohio, and Indiana. He had learned the trade of a wheelwright (which was also originally the trade of his father), and had expected to pursue it as an occupation, but his inclinations turned to teaching, and in 1811 he took charge of the Friends' School at Plymouth, where he continued for six years; and then, after teaching one year at Upper Dublin, he established in the autumn of 1818, a boarding school for young men and boys, at Gwynedd, on part of his father's estate. This school he conducted for many years with marked success, and it was continued later, until about 1860, in the charge of his sons Daniel and Joseph, and his nephew, Hugh Foulke, Jr. Joseph published (Philadelphia: 1844) a memoir of Jacob Ritter (a preacher among Friends, who had been a Revolutionary soldier: see in Watson's *Annals* details of his confinement in the British prison in Philadelphia). He also conducted for many years the publication of the "Friends' Almanac," furnishing for it the astronomical calculations. In 1836 he visited Washington as one of a committee of Philadelphia Yearly Meeting to influence Congress against the admission of Arkansas as a slave State. (See Curtis's Life of Jas. Buchanan, Vol. I., p. 337: Vol. II., p. 181.) His MS. journal, giving many interesting details of his life, has been repeatedly drawn upon for this work.

Evan Jones.

Evan Jones was born in Montgomery on the old homestead of his grandfather, John Jones, carpenter. He was the son of

Evan and Hannah Jones. He learned the trade of tanning with
his cousin Isaiah Jones, of Buckingham, and, returning to Montgomery, established a tannery at Montgomery Square, where he
was in business for several years. In 1815, he, with Thomas
Shoemaker, Cadwallader Foulke, and Cadwallader Roberts, purchased the Evans estate (now partly Bellows's), of Chas. Willing
Hare, and about two years later (the purchase meantime proving to be a bad speculation), Evan took the homestead, himself,
with a large part of the land, and removed to it, making it his
home for the remainder of his life. He there dispensed a liberal
hospitality; his house was the place of entertainment for many
visiting Friends and others. His means, measured by the local
standard, were ample, and his social disposition made his fireside attractive and pleasant. He was an active member of the
Friends, was clerk of meetings for business,[1] and generally a pillar of the Society, locally. He filled many important business
positions, being amongst other things the first President of the
Bethlehem Turnpike Co. In 1840, he was the Whig candidate
for County Commissioner,[2] and received the highest vote of any
on the ticket. His four marriages have already been mentioned,
(p. 368).

Dr. Antrim Foulke.

Dr. Antrim Foulke, the son of Theophilus, the younger, was
born at Richland, March 23, 1793. The accidental death of his
father, when he was but three years old, left him to the sole care
of his mother. At her desire he learned the trade of a coach-

---

[1] Geo. I. Evans, of Emerson, O., says: I was at meeting at Gwynedd, the day of the "Separation," [1827 or '28] and Isaiah Bell and Ezra Comfort demanded the use of the meeting house "to hold Gwynedd monthly meeting in." Evan Jones said that the business of Gwynedd monthly meeting had been transacted, and for his part he was not willing they should have the house, but if they would go home with him he would give them their dinners, and they might have a private room to transact any business they wanted. [Isaiah and Ezra were "Orthodox" Friends. Gwynedd meeting adhered, by a large majority, to the other body.]

[2] His opponent was Mehelm McGlathery.

maker, but having completed it, at the age of twenty-one, he turned his attention to the profession of medicine, and studied with Dr. Joseph Meredith, at Gwynedd, whom he joined, after completing his studies, as a partner, and so continued until Dr. Meredith's death. He then remained in practice at Gwynedd, with remarkable success, until 1848, when he removed to Philadelphia, and there practiced until his death, in 1861. He was by many elements of character admirably fitted for his profession, and his wide range of visits to the country around his residence testified to the confidence reposed in him.

Rev. Samuel Helffenstein.

Among the notable figures in Gwynedd, for many years, was Rev. Samuél Helffenstein. He was born in Philadelphia (at Germantown), April 17, 1775, his father being Rev. John C. A. Helffenstein, the pastor of the German Reformed Church at Germantown. The latter died in 1790, and the widow took her son before the Synod, assembled at Philadelphia, and at her desire they assumed his care and education for the ministry. He was licensed and ordained in 1796 or 1797, and received about this time a call to the pastorate of Boehm's and Wentz's churches, which he accepted, but in 1798 returned to Philadelphia to the pulpit of the Race Street Church, made vacant by the death of Rev. Dr. Hendel. Here, for thirty-two years, he labored with zeal and fidelity, but in 1832, having resigned, he retired to his farm in Gwynedd, where he remained until his death, October 17, 1866. In 1846, he published a system of Didactic Theology, embodying the substance of the lectures which during his Philadelphia work he had delivered to the numerous theological students who prepared for the ministry under his direction. (The list of these includes many prominent names in the Reformed church.) In 1824 the Synod invited him to become Professor of Theology in a theological seminary intended to be established at Carlisle,

in connection with Dickinson College, but he saw fit to decline this. His wife was Anna Christina Steitle, daughter of Emanuel of Gwynedd, to whom he was married in 1797, and of their children, twelve in number, three (Rev. Samuel, Jr.; Rev. Albert, and Rev. Jacob), became eminent ministers; two (Dr. Abraham and Dr. Benjamin) became physicians; one, Emanuel, a lawyer and conveyancer; one, Jonathan, a farmer; one, Isaac, a merchant; and one daughter, Catharine, married Augustus Miller. Rev. Samuel Helffenstein was buried in the family vault in the cemetery grounds of the old St. Peter's church.

Charles F. Jenkins.

He was the son of Edward, and the great-grandson of Jenkin Jenkin, the immigrant. He was born at Gwynedd, March 18, 1793, and died there February 5, 1867. He received instruction at the academy of Enoch Lewis, the eminent teacher and mathematician, at New Garden, Chester county; but he added to his opportunities of education a studious and intellectual habit, reading throughout his life, with intelligence and zest, upon an extensive range of subjects. Having been brought up in his father's store in Gwynedd, he engaged in mercantile business in Philadelphia (on Second street, nearly opposite Christ church), for twelve or more years, with good success; but in 1830, upon the decease of his father, he returned to Gwynedd, and took the store, which he conducted nearly to the close of his life. He took a very active interest in public affairs, was for many years a director of the public schools, and was repeatedly the candidate of his party (it being, however, in the minority for a long period), for the Legislature. His promotion of the construction of the turnpike has already been mentioned. He was, besides, secretary for many years of the Bethlehem turnpike, a director of the Bank of Montgomery County, and of the Montgomery County Mutual Fire Insurance Company, etc., etc.

Winfield Scott Hancock.

His distinguished career in the Army of the United States, especially during the great war for the suppression of the Rebellion, and his candidacy for President of the United States, supported by nearly one-half of the American people, must be taken to designate General Hancock as the most eminent native of the two townships to which this volume relates. He was born February 14, 1824, near Montgomery Square, at the old mansion-house of 'Squire John Roberts. Through his mother, Elizabeth Hoxworth, he has a strain of Welsh blood, from Jenkin Jenkin, who was his mother's great-grandfather.

It would be impracticable, here, to present a complete biography of General Hancock, or even a fairly full abstract of the events in his military career. I shall only mention a few local, family, and personal details. His father having removed to Norristown, when he was about four years old, he was educated there, in the "Old Academy," his teachers being Eliphalet Roberts, Rev. A. G. Harned, Jr., and Stapleton Bonsall. He was a manly, vigorous boy, full of spirit, and inclined to military ideas. In 1840, Hon. John B. Sterigere, M. C., appointed him a cadet at West Point, and he entered the Academy, July 1st, of that year. He graduated June 30, 1844, and being brevetted second lieutenant, was assigned to the Sixth Regiment of Infantry. From that time his service has been a part of the public record of the country. He married, January 24, 1850, Almira D. Russell, daughter of Samuel Russell, a merchant of St. Louis, Mo., by whom he has had two children: Russell, now a planter in Mississippi, and Ada Elizabeth, who died of typhoid fever, in New York, at the age of eighteen. He has now (1884) been for some years stationed at Governor's Island, New York, but he regards Pennsylvania as the State to which he belongs, and he has taken much interest, within the past ten years, in tracing his family relationship, and fixing in a permanent form facts relating to his parents, and more distant ancestry.

INDEX.

⁂ No attempt has been made to index the several genealogical chapters; and, except in a few instances, names occurring only in them will not be found in the index.

Abington Quarterly Meeting established, 80.
Acuff, David, 356, 361.
Agriculture, early methods and implements of, 347, 348, wages, 350.
Baptist Church in Montgomery, establishment of, 270; pastors of, 270.
Bartholomew, John, 264.
Bate, Humphrey, 67.
Beaver, Barnaby, 316, 321.
Bees, 347.
Boileau, John, 361.
Book of Memorials of 1787, 83.
Boone family, 4, 325, 327.
BOONE, GEORGE, 80, 325, 326; Geo., jr., 325; Squire, 114, 326; Daniel, 326, 327, 328.
Bricks, 14.
Bridges, 362, 363.
Brunner, Paul, 273.
Carpenter, Sam'l, 49.
Castner family, genealogy of, 375-377.
Chapin, William, 377.
Churches, 269, 270, 320, 321.
Cider, 347.
Cleaver family, genealogy of, 365, 366.
Clemens, Garret, 313, 316, 321.
Coed-y-foel, farm in Wales, 35.
Corson, Lawrence E., 361.
Danenhower, Abraham, 272, 321.
Deaths, lists of, 136, 142.
Dillwyn, George, 87.
Disease, fatal, 1745, 274.
Disputes, settled by monthly meeting, 344, 345, 346.
Dull, Christian, 316, 322, 323, 355.
Dull, Christian, jr., 323, 324.
Dysentery, on the *Robert and Elizabeth*, 30.

Early families, details concerning, 364-379.
Edwards, Alexander, jr., 263.
Edwards, Alexander, Sen., 263, 340.
Ellis, Rowland, 24, 74, 83, 345.
Evans, Cadwalader, immigrant, his family, 50; purchase of land, 54; place of residence, 59; reads church service for the settlers, 75; preacher, 82; memorial, 84.
Evans, Cadwalader, jr., biographical sketch of, 383.
Evans, Dr. Cadwalader, biographical sketch of, 380, 381.
Evans, Ellen, 16.
Evans, Evan, preacher, 84, 341, 347, 348, 350.
EVANS FAMILY, descended from Evan ap Evan, 65; gen'gy of, 143-185.
Evans, Hugh, reminiscence of Penn's visit, 60.
Evans, Jenkin, of Montgomery, 265.
Evans, John, son of Cadw., preacher, 85; memorial of, 86.
Evans, John, "the elder," biographical sketch of, 381.
Evans, Jonathan, teacher, 352.
Evans, Mary, wife of Owen, 91.
Evans, Owen, immigrant, 50, 51; purchase of land, 54, 57.
Evans, Rev. Evan, 269.
Evans, Robert, immigrant, 50; purchase of land, 54, 57; place of residence, 57; preacher, 82; Thos. Chalkley's allusion to him, 83.
Evans, Robert (son of Owen), household articles, 341, 347.
Evans, Rowland, biographical sketch of, 382.

Evans, Thomas, patent to, 25; original tract of, 54, 57; his place of residence, 59, 69; four sons, 69; second marriage, 70, removal to Goshen, 71.
Everhart, John, 324.
Exeter (Oley) monthly meeting, 80.
Fetter, Wendel, 320.
First settlers, number of, 50; families of, 51; arrival of, 21; homes, 54; size and location of their tracts, 57.
Fothergill, John, visits Gwynedd, 87.
Foulke, Cadwallader, biographical sketch of, 388.
Foulke, Dr. Antrim, 336; biographical sketch of, 393.
Foulke, Edward, immigrant, 29; narrative of his removal, 32; ancestry of, 32; circumstances of, in Wales, 36; his family, 50, 51; his original tract, 54, 57; home of, in Gwynedd, 61.
FOULKE FAMILY, Gen'gy of, 210-247.
Foulke, Hugh (3d), Indian garden, 19.
Foulke, Joseph, 351; biographical sketch of, 392.
Foulke, Thomas (son of Edward, the immigrant), 61.
Foust, Rev. George D., 331, 334.
Freeholders, list of Montgomery, 267; Gwynedd, 272.
Frey, John, early German settler, 273.
Friends, early, in township, details concerning, 82-92; meeting, establishment of, 72-81; preachers, 82-92; action in the revolution, 311; militia fines, 312.
Fries, John, of "Rebellion," 310.
Funeral expenses, 344.
Geisenhainer, Rev. Henry, 332.
GENEALOGICAL DETAILS CONCERNING EARLY FAMILIES, 364-379.
Geology of Gwynedd, 11-14; mezozoic belt, 11-12; trap dyke in tunnel hill, 12; plant bed in tunnel, 13; triassic deposit, 13; clay, sand, building-stone, 15; Prof. Lesley's statement, 12-13; theory of Prof. Lewis, 13.
Gerhart, Nicholas, 105 years old, 138.
Gossinger, George, 273.
German settlers in Gwynedd, early, 272-274.
Griffith, Alice, preacher, 89.
Griffith, Hugh, first settler, 50; tract of land, 54, 57.
GWYNEDD.—Topographical features, 1; scope of its history, 2; analysis of its history, 3; more extended of do., 3-9; chronological sketch of do., 9; geology of, 11-14; Indian traces in, 15-20; arrival of Welsh settlers in, 21-31; origin of name, 39-48; population of, 49-53; William Penn's visit to, 60; arrival of Schwenckfeldters in, 271; freeholders in 1734, 272; fatal disease in, 274; revolutionary operations in, 274-308; revolutionary details concerning, 309-314; taxables in, in 1776, 315-324; social conditions among the early settlers of, 338-346; public school system established in, 352-355.
Hancock, B. F., biographical sketch of, 391.
Hancock, W. S., biographical sketch of, 396.
Hank Family, 328, 329.
Hank, John, 329; Nancy, mother of President Lincoln, 329.
Hassler, Rev. John W., 334.
Harry, Rees, 319.
Hecht, Rev. Anthony, 331.
Heilig, Rev. George, 333.
Heilig, Rev. Theophilus, 334.
Heisler, Jacob, 321, 356.
Heist, Philip, 320.
Heist's tavern, 309, 321, 356.
Helffenstein, Samuel, biographical sketch of, 394.
Hoot, Peter, 273.
Hoot, Philip, 273.
Horses, use of, etc., 348.
Hoskens, Jane, reference to Gwynedd Friends, 85.
Hotels, 355, 356.
Household articles of early settlers, 339, 340, 341.
Howell, Deborah, 325, 326.
Hoxworth family, genealogy of, 373, 375.
Hubbs, Charles, 321, 322.
Hugh, Evan ap, first settler, purchase of land, 54, 57; residence of, 67; his sons David and Hugh Pugh,67.
Hugh, John, original settler, his family, 50; his land, 54, 57.
Humphrey, John, of Gwynedd, 50, 51, 59, 61, 64.
Humphrey, John, of Merion, narrative of his experience in Wales, 93-106; his will, 94.
Humphrey, Samuel, mentioned in John Humphrey's narrative, 96; his descendants, 96, 97.
Indentured servants, 350.
Indians, traces of them in Gwynedd, 15-20; Ellen Evans, discourse with, 16; traditions of at Mum-

bower's mill, 16; supposed battles of, 16, 17; stone implements of, 17, 18, 19; traditional "garden" of, 19; Prof. D. B. Brunner's work on, 19.
Intemperance, condemned by monthly meeting, 343.
James, Isaac, 267.
Jenkins, Algernon S., 361.
Jenkins Charles F., 361,373; biographical sketch of, 395.
Jenkins, Charles F. (2d), 18.
Jenkins, Edward, 357.
Jenkins family genealogy of, 371-373.
Jenkin, Jenkin, household articles, 341, 347; agricultural do., 349.
Jenkins, John, 315, 321.
Johnson, John B., 335.
John, Rees ("Rees John William"), 95.
John, Robert, 30; his will and children, 68; other references, 340, 347, 348, 350.
John, William, his family, 50; tract of land, 54, 57; place of residence, 65; his children, 66; inventory, 339, 347.
John, William, and Thomas ap Evan, their purchase of the township, etc., 21-27, 29; deeds to other settlers, 54; Robert Turner's deed to, 56.
Jones, Evan, biog. sketch of, 392.
Jones family (descendants of Robert John), 378.
Jones family (descendants of John Jones, carpenter), genealogy of, 367-369.
Jones, Isaac, 266.
Jones, Margaret, preacher, 91.
Kolb, Isaac, 320.
Kramer, Rev. S. P. F., 332.
Lacey, Gen. John, militia, 310.
Land, David C., Indian relics, 18.
Lesley, Prof. J. P., 12-13.
Levick, Dr. J. J., 75.
Lewis, Amos, 369.
Lewis, Ellis, 344, 348, 350.
Lewis, H. Carvill, 13.
Lewis, Isaac, 319.
Lewis, Jephthah and Enos, 317: "Squire" Joseph, 318.
Lewis, Thomas, 265.
Lewis William, 67.
Lincoln Family, 327-328.
Lincoln, Mordecai, 327; Mordecai, 2d, 328; Thomas, 328; Abraham, 328; John, 328; Abraham, 2d, 328; Mordecai, 3d, 328; Thomas, father of the President, 328, 329; Abraham, President U. S., 328.

Liquor, use and sale of, 343, 344; John Evans's efforts against, 382.
Lloyd-Price, Richard J., Esq., 35.
Longevity, instance of, 138; in Jones family of Montgomery, 266.
Marriages, lists of, from Haverford records, 107-113; from Gwynedd records, 113-131; from Samuel and Cadw. Foulke's memorandum books, 132-136.
Marriages, two, in Aug., 1714, 78.
Marriage, with undue haste, condemned by monthly meeting, 343.
Mathias, Rev. Joseph, 338.
Medary, Samuel, biographical sketch of, 384.
Medtart, Rev. Jacob, 333.
Meeting, Friends', establishment of, 72-81; first house, of logs, 77; second house, 77; monthly meeting established, 78; house enlarged, 79; present house, 81.
Mendenhall, Benjamin, marriage to Lydia Roberts, quaint letter, 342.
Militia, in Revolution, 312-313; fines paid, 312-313.
Miller, Rev. Lewis G. M., 334.
Mills, 317, 358.
MONTGOMERY, early settlers in, 263-268; list of freeholders in 1734, 267; establishment of Baptist church, 270; allusion to by Rev. Evan Evans, 269.
Morgan, Edward, 248, 249.
Morgan family, genealogy of, 364, 365.
Murder of Henry Weaver, 332.
Myers, Rev. Wm. H., 334.
Nancarro, Susan, 60.
Neuman, Christopher, 272.
Norris, Deborah (afterwards Mrs. Logan), 275.
OWEN FAMILY, descended from Owen ap Evan, 65.
Owen, Owen, difference with Rowland Ellis, 345.
Pardo, Marmaduke, early immigrant, first school teacher, 350.
Patents to original settlers, 54.
Patent to Thomas Evans, 25.
Penn, Letitia, 60.
Penn, William, visit to Gwynedd, 60.
Population, statistics of, 51.
Powell, David, 21, 55.
Preston, Charles L., Indian relics, 18.
Price, Roger, of Rhiwlas, Wales, 35.
Public school system, 352-355.
Raker, Martin, 324.
Rebenach, Rev. J. H., 332.
Reid, Rev. Ezra L., 334.
Resurvey of the township, 55, 56, 57.

Revolutionary operations in Gwynedd, 274-308, 309-314; militia, 311-313.
Rhirid Flaidd, 32-35.
Richland monthly meeting established, 80.
Rightmyer, Rev. P. M., 334.
Roads, early, 248-262, 362, 363.
Roberts, Amos, 321.
Robert and Elizabeth, The, 30.
Roberts, Ann, preacher, 90.
Roberts, Charles, biographical sketch of, 389.
Roberts, Ellwood, Indian relics, 17.
ROBERTS FAMILY, genealogy of, 186-209.
Roberts families (other than descendants of Robert Cadwalader), 377, 378.
Roberts, Hugh, early preacher, 22, 30.
Roberts, 'Squire Job, biographical sketch of, 387.
Roberts, 'Squire John, 323, 357; biographical sketch of, 386.
Roberts, Joseph, biographical sketch of, 390.
Rumford, John, 325.
Scarlett, Robert, 14, 361; Thos., jr., 17.
Schaeffer, Rev. David, Solomon, 332.
Schools and education, 350, 355; first school house, 255, 350.
School system of Pennsylvania, 352.
Schwenckfeldters, arrival of, 271; details relating to, 272.
Shearer, Abel K., 335.
Sheep, 347.
Shoemaker, Thomas, 320.
Slaves, 349.
Snyder, George, 324.
Snyder, Henry, 272.
Snyder, Noah, Oliver, 335.
SOCIAL CONDITIONS AMONGST EARLY SETTLERS, 338-346.
Spencer family, genealogy of, 369-371.
Spring-House, origin of name, 261; Revolutionary incident at, 311.
Stevens, Thaddeus, 352.
State Road, 363.

St. John's Lutheran Church, 330.
St. Thomas's Episcopal Ch., 269, 330.
Stores, 357.
Storms, unusual weather, etc., 348.
St. Peter's Church, 330-337; movement to establish, 330; first building erected, 330; pastors of, 331-334; second building erected, 333; separation of the congregations, 334; new buildings erected by each, 334; Sunday-school of, 334, 335; reformed congregation of, 335.
Surname, changes of, by Welsh, 64.
Swink, Martin, 321.
Taxables, 1741, 51; in 1776, 315-324.
Teachers, early, 350, 351.
Thomas, Absalom, 327.
Towamencin towns'p, erection of, 271.
Treweryn, river in Wales, 36.
Trotter, William, preacher, 90.
Troxel [Troxall], 312, 316, 321.
Turner, Robert, 24, 28, 54; deed to Wm. John and Thos. Evans, 56.
Turnpike, Bethlehem, construction of, 358, 359, 360; Spring-House and Sumneytown, construction of, 360.
Van Buskirk, Rev. Jacob, 331.
Vehicles, of early settlers, 348.
Wack, Rev. John George, 335; Rev. Charles P., 337.
Weaver, Henry, murder of, 332.
Weiand, Rev. John K., 332.
Welsh Bible of 1678, 75.
Welsh history, in connection with name Gwynedd, 39-48.
Welsh language, used by first settlers, 74; sermons in, 83.
Welsh tract, 21.
Wentz's church, 330.
Wildbahn, Rev. C. F., 332.
Williams, Theophilus, 264.
Wilson, Alexander, the ornithologist, reference to Spring-House, 355.
Wister, Daniel, 275.
Wister, Sally's, Journal, 274-308.
Wolf, Governor, 352.